THE
AMERICAN ALPINE
JOURNAL

1993

COLOR PLATE 1

Photo by Tommy Bonapace

Pendulum on the Ridge Betwe
Cuatro Dedos and Bifida, Cei
Torre Region, Patagonia.

THE
AMERICAN ALPINE
JOURNAL

1993

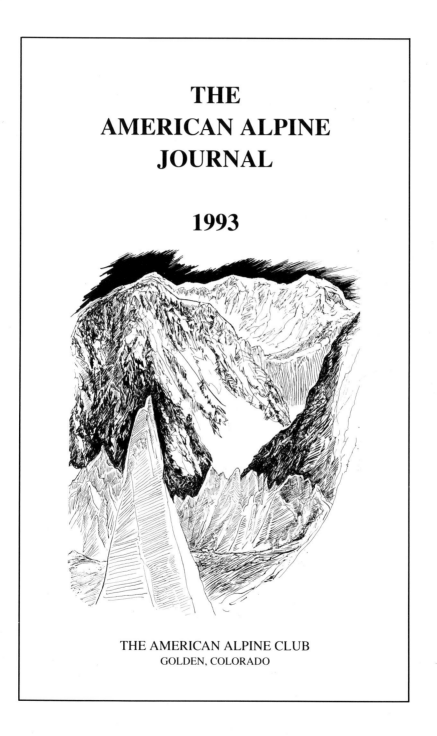

THE AMERICAN ALPINE CLUB
GOLDEN, COLORADO

COVER PHOTO: Mount Everest from the West. North Col on the left and South Col on the right. *Watercolor painting by Dee Molenaar.*

ISSN 0065-6925
ISBN 0-930410-55-6

Manufactured in the United States of America

*Articles and notes submitted for publication
and other communications relating to*

THE AMERICAN ALPINE JOURNAL

should be sent to

THE AMERICAN ALPINE CLUB
710 TENTH STREET
GOLDEN, COLORADO 80401 USA

FRIENDS OF

THE AMERICAN ALPINE JOURNAL

THE FOLLOWING PERSONS HAVE MADE CONTRIBUTIONS
IN 1992 IN SUPPORT OF THE CONTINUED PUBLICATION OF
THE AMERICAN ALPINE JOURNAL

JOHN M. BOYLE

YVON CHOUINARD

PETER RITTENHOUSE KELLOGG

NEW YORK SECTION OF THE A.A.C.

WILLIAM LOWELL PUTNAM

MARION & VERNE READ

VINCENT & MILDRED STARZINGER

and with special thanks to

THE HENRY AND LYDIA HALL AAJ ENDOWMENT FUND

THE AMERICAN ALPINE CLUB

OFFICIALS FOR THE YEAR 1993

THE AMERICAN ALPINE JOURNAL

VOLUME 35　　●　　ISSUE 67　　●　　1993

CONTENTS

PLATE 1

Photo by Graham Little

PANCH CHULI II. West Ridge in center and Southwest Ridge on right.

Panch Chuli

CHRISTIAN BONINGTON

HE BLOB OF LIGHT was a reassuring gleam, the head torch of one of the team, slowly descending the dark and craggy buttress to the tent where I had elected to stay that morning. I had been tired, worried about the distance we still had to go to reach the summit and anyway a team of five would have been cumbersome and slow. It had been a long wait from 3:30 A.M. the previous morning, through the day, till eleven o'clock that night, when at last I caught a glimpse of a light far above at the top of the buttress.

It was now three o'clock. They had been on the go for 24 hours and were very nearly down. I had lit the gas stove to heat some water for tea. I could actually hear them, though I couldn't make out the words. I had the tent door open to watch their progress more easily, when a flicker of light caught my attention. The blob of light was tumbling crazily down the buttress and then went out. I think I heard the scraping of crampons on rock. It could only be a fall and whoever had fallen surely was dead. I couldn't stop myself from crying, the climax to 24 hours of growing anxiety.

Everything had gone so well—up to that point. Six of us had left Britain early in May to join six Indian climbers for climbing in the Panch Chuli range in the Indian Himalaya. A two-day bus journey from Delhi across the plains and up into the foothills had taken us to the small town of Munsiary, nestling on a hill slope immediately opposite the Panch Chuli Peaks. Panch Chuli II, a stately cone of snow and ice towering above the other four peaks, at 6904 meters (22,650 feet) is the highest in the range. (The peaks are numbered from northwest to southeast and not by their height.)

Panch Chuli has always been worshipped and admired by local people, pilgrims and traders on their way to Tibet. Its name signifies the five hearths of the legendary Pandavas who, according to the Hindu epic *Mahabharata,* are supposed to have cooked their last meal on the five peaks on their way to Nirvana. The first mountaineer to reconnoiter the approaches to the range from the east was Hugh Ruttledge in 1929. W.H. Murray's Scottish expedition and K.E. Snelson and J. de V. Graaf attempted the mountain from the east by the Sona and Meola Glaciers respectively in 1950, but they made little progress. In 1951, Heinrich Harrer and F. Thomas made an attempt from the west up the Uttari Balati Glacier, reaching the foot of the west ridge at 6000 meters, a very impressive achievement by a two-man team. In 1952, P.N. Nikore of India

1

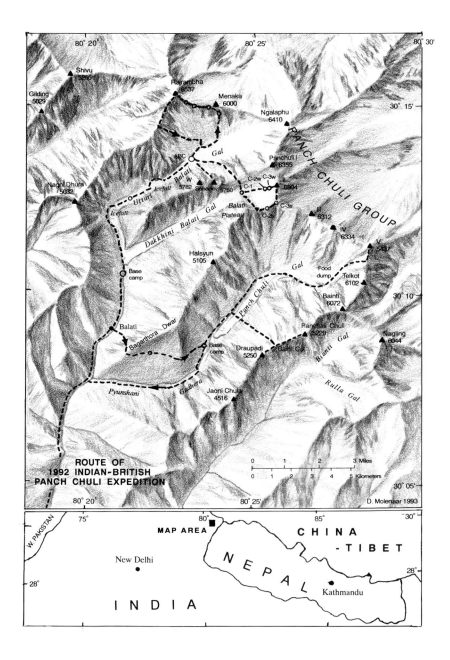

ROUTE OF
1992 INDIAN-BRITISH
PANCH CHULI EXPEDITION

D. Molenaar 1993

claimed the solo ascent of Panch Chuli II, but this has been discounted. Another attempt was made in 1964 by an expedition led by Squadron Leader A.K. Chaudhury. They failed on Panch Chuli II, but they claimed ascents of Panch Chuli III, IV and V, the latter two on the same day. There is little doubt that they mistook the three small peaks running down from the southwest ridge of Panch Chuli II for these three difficult peaks. It is obvious that Panch Chuli III (6312 meters, 20,708 feet), Panch Chuli IV (6334 meters, 20,780 feet) and Panch Chuli V (6437 meters, 21,120 feet) were unclimbed.

Panch Chuli I (6355 meters, 20,850 feet) was the first peak of the range to be climbed when it was ascended by an Indo-Tibetan Border Police expedition led by Hukam Singh in 1972. The southwest ridge of Panch Chuli II was climbed the following year by another large ITBP expedition led by Mahendra Singh when 18 climbers reached the top after almost the entire route had been fixed with rope. (*AAJ, 1974,* pages 210-211.) In 1991, two Indian Army expeditions climbed the northwest ridge and the east ridge. (*AAJ, 1992,* page 229.) Another peak in the area, Rajrambha (6537 meters, 21,447 feet), was first climbed from the north by another ITBP team in 1976.

The approach was short but dramatic, up the steep, heavily forested Balati valley to the foot of the Uttari Balati Glacier. It was refreshing to walk up such an unspoilt valley. Dense fir forests gave way to rhododendron, birch and bamboo. There were hot springs halfway and everywhere, a profusion of wild flowers. There was no sign of our predecessors. It was so very different from the popular areas in the Himalaya, which are strewn with rubbish and where trekkers and climbers outnumber the local people.

Base Camp was below the snout of the glacier at the extraordinarily low altitude of 3270 meters. We reached it on May 18 and immediately started finding a route to Advance Base within striking distance of the peaks around the glacier. At this stage, the entire team worked together, making a route past three precipitous and very dangerous icefalls. We placed Advance Base below a little rock buttress on the north side of the glacier at 4840 meters on May 26 and were at last ready to go climbing.

We were more a climbing meet than an expedition in the traditional sense. I had invited my five partners from Britain as three climbing pairs who could tackle freely any of the many peaks as the whim took them. We would climb alpine-style, carrying tents and food to try to reach objectives in a single push. The Indians, led by Harish Kapadia, had Panch Chuli II as their goal and planned to climb it in traditional style with a small team of high-altitude porters and a limited amount of fixed rope.

Graham Little from Scotland and I were the first to move up to Advance Base and were immediately attracted to the peak that soared up on the southeast side of the valley. We later named the double-summited mountain Sahadev for the second-youngest brother of the Pandavas. Sahadev West is marked on the map as P 5782. We set out at 1:45 A.M. on May 28, reaching the foot of the steep northwest snow arête at dawn. We pulled over a terrifying bergschrund and reached the 5750-meter summit of Sahadev East by eight in the morning to be rewarded with magnificent views of Panch Chuli II in the immediate foreground and Nanda Devi, one of the most beautiful mountains in the world, in the background.

The other four members of the British team, Stephen Venables, Dick Renshaw, Victor Saunders and American transplant Stephen Sustad decided to traverse Rajrambha, the second highest peak in the area. They spent five days climbing its long east ridge, taking in an unclimbed 6000-meter peak on the way. Venables and Saunders managed to fall though cornices, Saunders also became a mobile lightning conductor when they were hit by a violent thunder storm, but they succeeded in crossing the peak and getting back down the south face to return to Advance Base.

Meanwhile, the Indian team had found a route up a shelf leading from the upper Uttari Balati Glacier to the Balati Plateau and established Camp I on a shoulder at the start of the plateau at 5760 meters. On June 5, Muslim Contractor, Monesh Devjani and sirdar Pasang Bodh moved up to Camp II SW at 6120 meters on the southwest col, supported by Harish Kapadia, Bhupesh Ashar and porter Yograj. The summit team fixed 100 meters of rope on the lower rock step that day. On June 6, they established Camp III SW on the southwest ridge at 6400 meters. June 7 dawned cloudy and windy, but they set out at 4:45 A.M. and in two hours reached the foot of the upper rock band at 6600 meters. Above the band, they climbed steep ice to the junction of the southwest and west ridges at 6800 meters. The route to the summit from there had stretches of hard ice and huge cornices overhanging the Meola Glacier to the east. Using protection, they climbed slowly, reaching the summit at 10:15 A.M. in heavy cloud. On the descent they had difficulty locating their tent in a white-out with strong winds. Because of the unsettled weather, no second summit bid was made.

Little and I accompanied the Indian team to Camp I to try a new route on the only unclimbed ridge on Panch Chuli II. On June 5, we branched left onto the upper Balati Plateau through a complex crevasse system to establish Camp II W at 6120 meters at the foot of the west ridge. On the 6th, we pressed on up unrelenting hard ice in an exhausting 14-hour day, trying to find somewhere flat enough to pitch our tent. We had to belay the whole arête and at 6400 meters were forced onto the west face to avoid a sérac barrier. Progress was often slow on unstable snow. It wasn't until 3:30 P.M that we found a possible tent site below a sérac wall. On June 7, we worked our way below a series of sérac walls and crevasses on the upper west ridge to camp early in the afternoon at the bergschrund below the summit cone at 6730 meters. It had been a short day, but we wanted to be in position to reach the summit early with a good chance of a view and to be able to leave our sacks behind. It snowed heavily all night but dawned fine, cold and windy. We set out at six A.M., joined the southwest ridge 150 meters below the top and reached the summit at seven A.M. on June 8 to enjoy a magnificent view of Gurla Mandhata in Tibet and Api and Nampa in Nepal to the east. We returned to the tent and crossed to the southwest ridge to descend to the southwest col, where we received a wonderful reception from the

PLATE 2

Photo by Graham Little

View from Summit of Panch Chuli II. Rajrambha is in the right middle and Nanda Devi in the background.

Indian team. We descended to Base Camp in deteriorating weather. This marked the end of the Uttari Balati Glacier phase of the expedition.

* * * * *

After only three days' rest, we set out for the Pyunshani valley, crossing the shoulder of the lower part of the southwest ridge of Panch Chuli II, through dense pathless forest, to drop down into a hidden valley. The weather, by this time, seemed to be breaking down into a monsoon pattern, with wet, cloudy days and warm nights. We were very nearly out of food. We had already experienced one accident when Vijay Kothari, one of the Indian members, had slipped on his way up to Advance Base and had broken his ankle. He had to be evacuated by helicopter. Two others, Graham Little and Bhupesh Ashar, had to return home because of work commitments.

We reached the foot of the Panch Chuli Glacier and camped beside a stream in a birch forest at 3320 meters on June 16. We had just six days before we had to be back down at the camp to be met by three porters promised by Harish Kapadia. He and the three remaining Indians were to explore the Panchali Glacier and climb some minor peaks before going back to pay of the porters and finish up the expedition in Munsiary. The timing was tight but we had just enough time to tackle one of the unclimbed Panch Chuli peaks. We set out up the Panch Chuli Glacier on the 17th, carrying four days' food. We camped near the head of the lower part of the glacier, immediately below Panch Chuli IV, and picked out a line up its south ridge. We couldn't see Panch Chuli V, which was hidden around the corner, and so, late in the afternoon, we walked up the glacier to where it came into sight. The second highest of the Panch Chuli peaks looked challenging and alluring. Its south ridge seemed to offer a feasible route to the summit, though there was some dead ground between the top of the icefall immediately in front of us and the ridge itself. There was little discussion. It was a unanimous decision. We planned to set out at two A.M. the next morning, but as we melted snow for breakfast tea, distant thunder heralded a storm, which reached us a few minutes later. Rain pattered on the roofs of our two tents and we went back to sleep, to be woken by Renshaw three hours later with the news that the weather had cleared.

By 4:30, in the early light of dawn, we set out for the first icefall. Bypassing it on its left bank, we plodded up a long snow corridor to its top. Climbing unroped, the others quickly pulled ahead of me. They were younger than I. I had had a shorter period of rest after my ascent of Panch Chuli II. At the top of this first icefall, the glacier opened out and easy slopes led to the next barrier, a tumbling icefall fed by glaciers coming down from the south of Panch Chuli V. We were beginning to realize that the dead ground, which we had dismissed so lightly the previous afternoon, was both more extensive and more difficult than we had expected.

A snow gully leading up to the south retaining wall of the icefall gave the possibility of bypassing the icefall itself. The start was guarded by a waterfall pouring over rock. Saunders, reknowned for his ability in wet and horrid places, was volunteered to try it. Plunging into the waterfall, he swam up over the initial overhang and then teetered across water-swept rocks to reach the snow. The rest of us followed up the rope he fixed, able to stay comparatively dry. Another snow slope seemed endless but we reached the top of the gully on a little shoulder at 5000 meters. The view was not encouraging. We had to cross a heavily crevassed glacier, bristling with sérac walls, to reach another fearsome icefall, which in turn led up to the high basin below Panch Chuli V. It was becoming a complex and potentially dangerous approach.

We used another gully to bypass the third icefall, but it was four P.M. before we reached the upper basin and camped by a huge crevasse at 5400 meters. We had been on the go for twelve hours and were tired. It snowed that night and we had another delayed start. We discussed whether to go on or not. I was in favor of retreat. The weather was unsettled. We had only two days' food left and still a long way to go. The others were of sterner stuff and we finally decided to move up that day to the crest of the ridge just above the south col of Panch Chuli V. If the weather improved, we would be close enough to the top to make a bid for the summit and if it was bad, we still had time to retreat.

The snow in the basin was appallingly soft, but we plodded slowly up to where we could strike up the steep slope to the ridge crest. Here we dug a most spectacular campsite, cutting away a cornice so that the tents were perched on the crest, with a 2000-meter sheer drop on the east side and 500 meters of very steep snow down the other side to the basin on the west. That afternoon, with a huge rumble, a massive avalanche crashed down the west side of Panch Chuli V and swept the lower part of the basin we had walked up that morning. It was a dangerous place indeed.

I took on the chore of preparing breakfast each morning. We set the alarm for 1:45 A.M. There was still cloud around, but we at least got a glimpse of the stars. As I waited for the water to boil, I made my decision. The buttress above the camp was 200 meters high, of steep rock broken by snow-and-ice slopes. The map showed a kilometer from the top of the buttress to the summit. It was a long way to cover in a day. I was slower than the others and a team of five was much more cumbersome than a foursome. I decided to wait for them in the tent.

I snuggled back into my sleeping bag with a sense of relief as they set off, leaving the tents at 3:30. I looked out from time to time to see that their progress was very slow. They went around a corner, out of sight, at ten A.M. and were still some way from the top of the buttress. Sustad described the climbing as some of the best and hardest mixed climbing he had ever experienced in the Himalaya.

They reached the top of the buttress at midday. By that time, the weather had closed in and it was snowing and blowing. The climbing was much harder than they had anticipated, with ice for most of the way. It became obvious that they would be benighted. Despite talk of retreat, they kept on and reached the summit at three P.M. With no view, they started back down immediately, but downward progress was desperately slow. It was eight o'clock when they reached the top of the buttress. The iced-up ropes, stiff as hawsers, frequently jammed when they pulled down the doubled ropes. But the weather began to clear and it was at

PLATE 3

Photo by Graham Little

**Behind Panch Chuli IV on the left
rises PANCH CHULI V. The ridge
climbed is on the right skyline.**

eleven, when I first saw them from camp, that they also saw my welcoming head torch signal.

They worked slowly and methodically. Sustad later told me, "It was bloody cold, but in a strange kind of way, quite enjoyable. We took it slowly, backing up anchors all the way down, trying to make sure we didn't make a mistake."

It was 3:30 in the morning. They had been on the go for 24 hours and on their next-to-last abseil. In another half hour they would have been in the comparative safety of the camp, gulping down tea. Sustad, Renshaw and Saunders had all abseiled down. Venables removed the back-up anchors, which might be needed later on, and so he was now totally dependent on the angle piton driven into a horizontal crack in the rock. It seemed totally solid and had withstood the strain of the previous three abseils.

He started and had slid down the rope about 20 feet when the piton pulled out. He hurtled down, sparks flying from where his crampons struck the rock. He was sure that it was his end. As he flashed past the others, they also were convinced he'd be killed. Even so, Saunders lunged for the loose rope, which burned though his clothes and gloves as it came tight. What saved Venables from a further 300-meter fall to the glacier below, however, was the way the rope, which Renshaw had been feeding through the next anchor, coiled itself around Renshaw's leg.

Venables was hanging at the end of the rope, on the snow, after a fall of nearly 100 meters. There was complete silence for two minutes. Renshaw shouted down. No reply! He shouted again and heard a weak call. "I've broken my legs." It seemed a miracle that Venables was alive at all.

With his weight on the rope, they couldn't abseil. Saunders volunteered to climb down the rope, using prusik knots—a slow but safe method. Once he reached Venables, he tried to assess the injuries. His right leg was bleeding from a compound fracture and his left ankle was sprained or broken. There was no question of getting him across to the tents. We could only lower him straight down the slope and were lucky that there was a straight run-out to the glacier basin below.

Whilst Renshaw and Saunders organized a means of lowering Stephen down the snow slope, Sustad traversed the steep snow to the camp where I was waiting, desperately worried, to learn what had happened. Sustad and I dismantled the camp and carrying very heavy rucksacks, also started down the slope. We were unroped, since Renshaw and Saunders needed both ropes to lower Venables. Sustad and I were going to go ahead, find a safe campsite in the basin and pitch camp.

I was out in front, about 100 meters above the bergschrund. I was peering around to try to find a safe way past it when my foothold in the soft snow collapsed. Instinctively I grabbed my ice tools, which were planted in the snow, but they pulled straight out. I then got hold of my ice axe in both hands for a self-arrest, but the pick just cut through the snow. As I gathered speed, my crampons caught in the snow and I flipped over. Suddenly, I was cart-wheeling down the slope. I was vaguely conscious of being in mid air. I had shot over the bergschrund and was bouncing and rolling again. I tried to adopt a fetal position, hugging my arms and drawing up my legs, to avoid damaging my limbs. The motion became slower. And then it was still. Winded, frightened, pinned down by my heavy rucksack, I think I lay there for three or four minutes. Sustad, looking down at me, expected the worst. I flexed my arms and legs. They seemed OK, but I became aware of something wet on my face and of blood on the snow in front of me. I felt my face, which was sore over my left cheek, but the bone seemed solid. I shouted, "I'm OK," and struggled to escape from my rucksack and stand up.

I directed Sustad to a safe course over the bergschrund and continued down to find a safe site for a camp. It wasn't easy. The basin was quite narrow and surrounded by steep snow slopes with big avalanche cones at their bottom where fresh snow had sloughed off. We picked a spot almost in line with Venables's descent in a place where there was no avalanche debris. Having pitched the tent, we climbed back up to help the others lower Venables over the bergschrund. He was amazingly brave. The slightest tug or push on his damaged leg was agonizing, and yet he never complained. He was also wet and cold from being lowered down the snow.

As the angle eased, it became more difficult. We used one of the tents as a makeshift stretcher and hauled him down slowly. It was about midday when at last we reached the tent, were able to put Venables into a warm sleeping bag, feed him with hot drinks and inspect his wounds. There was a gaping hole just below his right knee and the knee itself was swollen and badly damaged. His left ankle seemed less severely damaged, but his chest was painful.

We assessed the situation. We now had practically no food and had been going for 36 hours with very little to eat. We could never get Venables back down the route of ascent and his only hope of rescue was by helicopter. Could a helicopter get in because of the altitude and the enclosed nature of the basin? We decided that Sustad and I would descend the next day to Base Camp and I would go all the way to Munsiary to start coordinating the rescue. Sustad would open a supply line from Base Camp for Renshaw and Saunders, who would stay to look after Stephen.

The next day, June 22, Sustad and I staggered exhausted into Base Camp at two P.M. to find the three porters Harish had promised to leave behind. They fed us huge quantities of rice, potato and tea. It started raining at four o'clock that afternoon and continued all night and into the next morning. I couldn't help worrying about the others high on the mountain. They were all at high risk of being swept by avalanche in the event of a heavy snowfall.

I set out in torrential rain at 5:30 on the morning of June 23, accompanied by Harsingh Sr., one of our porters. Initially there was no path and the route was like an assault course through steep water-logged jungle. We kept going through the day and made it down to the roadhead in nine hours to raise the alarm through the police radio net that same afternoon.

PLATE 4

Photo by Richard Renshaw

On PANCH CHULI V after the accident. Venables is being lowered while Saunders supports him.

The response of the Indian Air Force was magnificent. The following morning, they sent a helicopter up from the nearest air base some hundred miles away, but there was too much cloud and they could not reach the campsite.

Meanwhile, Sustad went back back up the mountain with only a half-day's rest. He took with him one of the porters, who had little snow experience and was not acclimatized. As a result, Sustad climbed the first gully alone, carrying a heavy load to leave the food and gas cylinders on the shoulder at its top as they had arranged. "I don't think I've ever felt so tired," he commented.

We had agreed that Saunders and Renshaw would go down to pick up the supplies on the morning of June 25. "It was one of those occasions when instinct takes over," Saunders told me. "Although it would have been logical to wait till the early morning when the snow was better frozen, we set out at 6:30 P.M. on the 24th. We had had practically nothing to eat for four days and were so weak that if the food hadn't been there, I don't think we would have had the strength to get back up again." They collected the food, had their first real meal in four days and started back up. "Starting so early saved our lives," Saunders continued. "We'd just crossed the dangerous section where all the avalanche debris was, when what was left of the sérac on the west face collapsed. A huge avalanche swept our tracks all the way to the bottom of the basin."

They got back in the early morning, fed Venables and heard the helicopter again, but it could not get through the broken clouds. The helicopter returned in the early afternoon. The clouds had cleared and this time it was able to reach the basin. It was a fine piece of flying by Squadron Leader P. Jaiswal and Flight Lieutenant P.K. Sharma. It took them about a half an hour and several tries before they managed to maneuver the helicopter with one skid on the tent platform and the blades swishing inches away from the snow slope. Renshaw lay on the tent and gear to prevent it from being blown away by the slip-stream, while Saunders handled Venables to the open door of the helicopter.

Saunders said, "It was desperate. I heaved Stephen up onto the skid and pushed his upper body into the helicopter. He was screaming in pain, but I just had to ignore it. I got my arms under his legs and just heaved him in. The crew couldn't do a thing. They were both fully occupied in keeping the thing airborne."

Sharma told me afterwards that it was the most difficult pick-up they had ever completed and that they were nearly forced to turn back. Had they done so, it would have been desperately difficult to have rescued Venables.

I shall never forget the vast relief I felt when we saw the red jacketed figure of Venables as the helicopter flew towards the pad in Munsiary. Harish and I hugged each other in our relief. Three days of hellish worry were nearly over. I was not able to relax, however, for another two days until Sustad, Saunders and Renshaw reached the roadhead.

It had been a close thing. Not just Stephen Venables, but all five of us, were lucky to have come out alive. We had undoubtedly pushed our luck— continuing in worsening weather, running our food down to the minimum,

Photo by Richard Renshaw

PLATE 5

Helicopter picking up Venables at 5600 meters on Panch Chuli V.

trying to snatch one more climb at the end of a successful expedition. Yet this is the very nature of climbing. Without that element of boldness, very few Himalayan climbs, certainly ones tackled alpine-style, would be completed. We had got away with our lives, had had a successful expedition in terms of peaks climbed, but even more important, had had a very happy one, with the entire team getting on well together. In spite of everything, it was one of the best trips I have ever had in the mountains.

Summary of Statistics:

AREA: Panch Chuli Range, Kumaon, India.

ASCENTS: Sahadev East, 5750 meters, 18,865 feet. First Ascent, Northwest Snow Rib, May 28, 1992 (Bonington, Little).

　　Rajrambha, 6537 meters, 21,447 feet. New Route, Traverse of East Ridge over Menaka Peak (6000 meters) and down West Ridge and South Face, Summit reached on June 5, 1992 (Renshaw, Saunders, Sustad, Venables).

　　Panch Chuli II, 6904 meters, 22,650 feet. Fourth Ascent of Peak and Second of Route, Southwest Ridge, June 7, 1992 (Contractor, Devjani, Pasang Bodh).

　　Panch Chuli II. New Route, West Spur, June 8, 1992 (Bonington, Little).

　　Panchali Chuli, 5220 meters, 17,126 feet and Draupadi, 5250 meters, 17,225 feet. Both First Ascents via Panchali Glacier, June 20, 1992 (Kapadia, Contractor, Devjani, Kubram, Prakash Chand).

　　Panch Chuli V, 6437 meters, 21,120 feet. First Ascent, South Ridge, June 20, 1992 (Renshaw, Sustad, Saunders, Venables).

PERSONNEL: Harish Kapadia, co-leader, Muslim Contractor, Monesh Devjani, Bhupesh Ashar, Vijay Kothari, Wing Commander Anil Srivastava, liaison officer, *Indians*; Christian Bonington, co-leader, Graham Little, Richard Renshaw, Victor Saunders, Stephen Venables, *British*; Stephen Sustad, *American living in Britain*; porters Pasang Bodh, Yograj, Kubram, Prakash Chand, Suratram, Sundersingh, Revatram, Harsingh, Sr. and Harsingh, Jr.

Everest's Northeast Ridge

MOTOMO OHMIYA, *Sangaku Doshikai Club, Japan* and VALERI
KHRISHCHATY, *Kazakhstan**

O N MAY 17, 1982, BRITISH CLIMB-
ers Joe Tasker and Pete Boardman disappeared high on the northeast ridge of
Mount Everest. They were last sighted through a telescope by Chris Bonington
as they were working their way behind the Second Pinnacle. (See *AAC, 1983*,
pages 22-29.) In May of 1984, American climber Donald Goodman, standing
on the northeast shoulder of Everest, saw and photographed yellow and orange
objects on a small domed snowfield high on the pinnacled section of the ridge,
near the notch below the final Third Pinnacle. The next climbers to reach that
section of the ridge were Briton Harry Taylor and New Zealander Russell Brice
in August of 1988. They found the whole ridge knife-edged with cornices and
snow mushrooms. Just before reaching the Third Pinnacle, they cut down into a
gully to a small arête for a miserable bivouac. The next morning, they regained
the ridge in a white-out and climbed the last pinnacle, perhaps bypassing the spot
where Goodman had seen the objects. Goodman's snow dome was higher than
where in 1992 Pete Boardman's body was found, which was near the top of the
second pinnacle.

In the spring of 1992, a joint Japanese-Kazakh expedition attempted to
complete the ascent of the northeast ridge of Mount Everest, which has not yet
been climbed all the way to the summit. With a large number of 7000-meter
peaks and some 8000ers to their credit, the four Kazakhs were much more
experienced than the four Japanese, with the exception of the Japanese leader,
Otomo Ohmiya, who had climbed Kangchenjunga and several other Himalayan
mountains. For that reason, the Kazakhs undertook to prepare the route with the
help of two Sherpas. (A third Sherpa, who had originally been assigned to
that task fell ill and could not continue and this added to the load-carrying of
the Kazaks.)

Base Camp was established at 5200 meters on April 3. Camps I, II and III
(Advance Base) were placed at 5500, 6000 and 6500 meters on April 6, 7 and 8,
the latter on the Rabü La at the foot of the northeast ridge. The Kazakhs set to
work on April 9, stringing 4000 meters of rope and digging snow caves at 7090
and 7900 meters for Camps IV and V, which were established on April 15 and
30. Above Camp IV, at 7200 meters, they came upon signs of the 1982
expedition: two sleeping bags, two rucksacks, a notebook and other small

---

*This article has been put together thanks to detailed reports written by the co-leaders of this
joint Japanese-Kazakh expedition, and with the able assistance of Audrey Salkeld, *Alpine Club*.
Mr. Ohmiya's report was dictated to a friend on September 10 in the hospital where he was still
recovering from frostbite and injuries suffered on the mountain.

PLATE 6

Photo by Christian Bonington

Boardman, Tasker and Renshaw seen in 1982 photo of the Northeast Ridge of EVEREST approaching the First Pinnacle. Boardman's body was found near the top of the Second Pinnacle at the right.

items. Apparently hurricane winds had etched the snow away, revealing what had been in a snow cave. On May 15, near the top of the second pinnacle, the Kazakhs stumbled on a corpse, which has since been identified as that of Peter Boardman.

On May 16, they pitched tents at 8350 meters as Camp VI, nearly at the junction of the northeast ridge and the north ridge, which has become the normal route on this side of the mountain. Unfortunately they were storm-bound on May 17. Climbing without supplementary oxygen and with still doubtful weather, on May 18 they realized they could not push on to the summit. Two of them descended the ascent route while the other two went down via the North Col. They all rested at Base Camp for two days.

Meanwhile, three of the Japanese and three Sherpas set out from Advance Base on May 15, but they were storm-bound at Camp IV for several days. They were using supplementary oxygen for sleeping but not while they were climbing. This and lack of time at higher altitudes may have contributed to their imperfect acclimatization. One of the Japanese, suffering from the altitude, descended with one of the Sherpas. The upward progress of Ohmiya and his companion, Manabu Hoshi, was slow.

Although still not adequately rested from their previous efforts but knowing that the date for the end of the expedition was nearly upon them, the four Kazakhs left Base Camp on May 22, planning to sleep at Camps III, IV and V and to make their summit attempt, bypassing Camp VI, on May 25. Unfortunately, their plan could not be carried out. Ohmiya and Hoshi had continued along the fixed ropes slowly, sending Sherpas Dawa Tenzing and Nawang Shakya ahead. The Sherpas carried their loads to Camp VI and descended via the North Col. When night fell on May 23, the Japanese pair had not yet reached Camp VI. Notified by radio at Camp IV, the tired Kazakhs, revitalized by this news, set off for Camp V at 10:30 P.M. by headlamp. They reached Camp V at 5:30 on the morning of May 24, where they drank tea and rested until 7:30, when they climbed on. Ohmiya saw Boardman's corpse. He gives the following description: "I did not examine closely the body found on the route at 8200 meters on the Rongbuk side of the ridge. I saw a cheek, cap and shoulder on the snow. The cheek was mummy-like. The shoulder was covered with what looked like leather and not a down jacket. The color was light brown. Of course it could have faded from many years' exposure. Neither of us Japanese went close to the body or tried to dig it out. Only Kazakh Vladimir Suviga took photos."

At two P.M., the Kazakhs found Ohmiya alone and in a pitiful state three rope-lengths below Camp VI, after spending three nights out without a tent. Khrishchaty describes the rescue: "He was beside himself. We could hardly persuade him to climb up the fixed rope to the tent. He did not want to obey us and all the time tried to walk downwards. It was difficult to get him to Camp VI, where there were four oxygen cylinders which would be enough for his descent. Omiya's ropemate, Manabu Hoshi, was not with him. A hundred meters below Camp VI, we found Hoshi's Jümar on the fixed rope and his ice axe leaning against the rock. Hoshi was not in Camp VI, where he could have had oxygen. He had been carrying both rucksacks. He will remain forever on the slopes and we were too late to help.

"We didn't sleep the whole night. We kept a primus stove burning and melted pot after pot of snow. Ohmiya was utterly dehydrated and drank warm water with great pleasure. His face was badly frostbitten, his fingers would soon turn black, but he didn't notice that. He was conscious only for moments. We couldn't force the oxygen mask onto him. He kept on insisting that we needed to economize oxygen so that we could continue our summit bid together. But he didn't realize that Hoshi had been lost and that he was not with us.

"On the morning of May 25, we had trouble forcing Ohmiya to start down. He implored us, swore at us and insisted that he didn't want to climb down. What we didn't hear from him! We led him downwards along the route toward the North Col, tearing ourselves away from the alluringly simple way along the ridge to the not-too-distant summit. We figured we were only about five hours from the top, but we were not fated to finish the route.

"Two oxygen cylinders were not enough to get Ohmiya to the North Col. It was then that he began to understand reality. When the oxygen ran out, he nearly collapsed and our pace fell sharply. We couldn't get further than the North Col that day. The joint Austro-German expedition, which had worked on the route, offered us tents for the night. Ohmiya could not walk to the tents of the American team, which were set up not far below. Americans brought us food, because we had left most of our food and even necessary personal gear at Camp IV before setting out on the rescue. So we were forced to beg. Thank you very much, American lads and all the others!

"We fed Ohmiya and gave him drink before we ate ourselves. Then it seemed that I had just put myself into the sleeping bag when I heard someone outside speaking English with a German accent and striking the tent with a ski pole. It was morning. We were to get up and walk down from the North Col because in a short time the sun would warm the snow and threaten avalanches. The Austrian lad who had offered us his tent the night before came in and with a smile asked if we could add four or five kilos to our packs to get some of *their* stuff down! And he had seen how the day before we could hardly put one foot ahead of the other! I explained that we had worked to exhaustion for three days, had hardly slept for two nights and had a victim who could barely walk.

"Rescues! What can be harder? How wonderful when everybody renders assistance, understanding how difficult they are!

"We walked the last several meters into the camp below the North Col, staggering, at the end of the day. That was actually the end of our joint Kazakh-Japanese expedition. We walked downward from Everest, carrying away in our hearts the pain of the irreplaceable loss of Hoshi and also unrealized dreams of the summit and the hope to come back again some day."

Summary of Statistics:

AREA: Mount Everest on the Tibetan side.

ATTEMPTED ROUTE: Mount Everest via the Northeast Ridge to 8350 meters.

PERSONNEL: Motomo Ohmiya, co-leader, Manabu Hoshi (disappeared and presumably died near the high point), Yoichiro Taniguchi, Tsuyoshi Kokubo, *Japanese*; Valeri Khrishchaty, co-leader, Vladimir Suviga, Yuri Moseev, Viktor Dedi, *Kazakhs*.

Alone on Dorje Lhakpa

CARLOS BUHLER

ORJE LHAKPA IS A RELATIVELY UNEXPLORED BUT BEAUTIFUL PEAK in the Jugal Himal, in the southern part of the same group that includes Shisha Pangma. It is 55 kilometers northeast of Kathmandu, near the eastern end of the Langshisa Glacier. It is the southern-most of the three principal peaks near the head of that glacier. The other two are Gurkarpo Ri and Lengpo Kang. All three are worthwhile objectives, but Dorje Lhakpa is the most alluring from the Lanshisa side. It was off limits until 1981. Its first official and recognized ascent took place that year when the mountain was opened to joint foreign-Nepali teams only. A Japanese-Nepali team reached the summit via the west ridge. Over the following ten years, six teams attempted the climb with four achieving success. All climbed the same west ridge.

I applied for the peak in 1991 when the Ministry of Tourism explained the peculiarities of a joint expedition. I had two experienced Sherpa friends, Lhakpa Dorje and Nuru, who were interested in working with the expedition, and so the officials let me include our cook as the third required Nepali of our team. To make matters simpler, my Sherpa friends were not interested in going to the summit. In keeping with my idea that the most enjoyment comes from climbing with the smallest groups, I limited the number of non-Nepali climbers. Jon Aylward, from Yorkshire, England, had written to me about climbing in the Himalaya's less explored areas. The two of us were to be the entire "foreign" team.

I suspected that several unexplored ribs on Dorje Lhakpa would reveal brilliant climbs, but since it was hard to judge difficulties from our limited selection of photographs, we adopted a wait-and-see attitude. A promising line was the unclimbed buttress on the left of the northwest face. Another possibility was a direct route up the central part of the face itself.

Though Dorje Lhakpa can be approached in five or six days from the village of Dhunche, a longer walk does wonders for getting one prepared for a Himalayan peak. We decided to extend the approach by four days, beginning from Sundarijal, 50 minutes from Kathmandu. This trail took us up a beautiful ridge to the 4600-meter Laurebinayak Pass and led by the famous Gosainkund Lakes. From there we dropped to the village of Syabru, where we joined the Dhunche trail from the west. We continued up the Langtang valley and then up the Langshisa valley to a site on the Langshisa Glacier at 4780 meters directly below the north side of Kanshurum. Despite problems with getting porters to

19

PLATE 7

Photo by Carlos Buhler

The West Ridge of Dorje Lhakpa.

help us that high, we got to the site on April 2. It was a fabulous spot on the glacier with a full view of the northwest side of Dorje Lhakpa as well as full views of Gurkarpo Ri and Lengpo Kang.

During the final days of hauling loads up to Base Camp, Jon became fatigued and then somewhat ill. For several days after our arrival, he rested. Meanwhile, I teamed up with Lhakpa Dorje and made a quick single-day trip to a 5100-meter col at the foot of the west ridge.

Lhakpa Dorje and I then took two days of provisions and a tent to camp on a low shoulder of the west ridge at 5250 meters, just before the climbing steepens. Though Lhakpa's experience in the Himalaya is impressive, he was not comfortable without fixed rope on the hard, blue ice on the exposed ridge. He was happy to remain in the tent the next day while I climbed up to have a look around. Old ropes, originally anchored to snow stakes, were now dangling on top of hard ice. To facilitate a future descent, I reset some anchors to make use of the rope I could chip free from the ice. I climbed the 35° to 45° ice and passed nervously over large crevasses that crisscrossed the icy ridge. My high point was 6050 meters, a hundred meters above another large shoulder where Koreans and others had obviously camped. From my position there on an exposed, narrow ridge, the remaining 900 meters to the top left many unanswered questions. The knife-edge leveled out for about 200 meters before curving upwards at a 30° angle and running into unstable-looking séracs at 6250 meters. Above these blocks, the ridge ran straight up to 6400 meters, where it took a sharp turn to the left. It looked as though one could follow the ridge eventually to reach easier slopes toward the summit cone.

I descended the ridge to the tent and Lhakpa and I enjoyed a beautiful sunset. The next day, April 9, we returned to Base Camp, hoping that after these three days, Jon would be better.

I took a rest day and, on the 11th, Jon and I set off for an acclimatization hike toward the Dorje Lhakpa-Kanshurum col. Only an hour out of Base Camp, Jon realized that he was not yet feeling his normal strength. The disappointment was agonizing for him. We had no choice but to turn back. That afternoon, we agreed that the only course of action for him was to descend to Kyangin Gompa for a long enough period to recover. Our delightful cook assistant, Mingma, was willing to go down with him to interpret and keep him company.

I started thinking about whether the west ridge could be soloed. After Jon's twelve days of illness, there was no way of telling how long it would take him before he felt strong enough to climb. Furthermore, he would have to acclimate before he could do any sort of alpine-style climbing.

When Jon left Base Camp, I sensed that I should try the ridge while the weather was steady. There were a lot of fears I had to resolve before I could make the decision to try the route alone. My preparations would need to be simple. I would carry only what was essential. To reach the summit and descend in 55 hours I must solo terrain where I normally used a rope. The factor that would make it possible was that I would be carrying practically nothing the day I pushed for the top.

Sleep came that night more peacefully than I expected. I had familiar feelings unique to mountaineering situations. Before a difficult climb, my overriding emotion is a fear of being unable to handle every situation that might arise. That includes a fear of dying. Yet, it is more a fear of the "what ifs?" than the fear of being hit by a falling stone or of a rappel anchor giving away. At any rate, I usually don't sleep well before an important climb, but on the night of the 11th I slept reasonably well. I felt an illogical assurance from Lhakpa Dorje's offer to accompany me for an hour's walk from Base Camp. I didn't like leaving camp by myself. His act of companionship may have allowed me to sleep deeply. In any event, by 7:30 A.M. I was on my way.

* * * * *

It is April 14. The climb is finished. I lie in my tent with the radio bringing me news of the outside world: British elections, the acquittal of Los Angeles policemen for the beating of Rodney King, the severe struggles for democracy in the streets of Kathmandu. Though it all seems incredibly intense, I am dulled by exhaustion. Outside my tent stands the shimmering wall of the northwest face of Dorje Lhakpa. On the right border is the ridge I have just descended. I don't want to take in this spectacular view right now. I let my mind flow in an unobstructed stream. This is my reward for having completed this climb. It is an unfiltered, unprotected state of mind that flows like sparkling water out of a mountain stream on a summer day. Its soothing gentleness kindles relaxation and the release of anxiety.

As I descended the ridge at night some hours before, I had been like a little child with no strength left. I tried to choke down a biscuit as I stood in the lonely darkness. I was so thirsty! Small bits of ice in my mouth faked momentary relief. I needed strength to go on. The ridge wound its way into the shadows. Over the cornice at its end lay the two rappels to the base of the triangular ice face. My bivouac tent was there, offering safety and water. I lived for that arrival. I was wiped out but I could not let myself stop. Surrounded by the blue light of the moon, I faithfully followed the beam of my headlamp. I could make no mistakes. Employing both my hand tools, I negotiated short ice traverses between rock, clawing along until I reached a restful stance. I clung to the thought of lying in my bivy tent, safe from the verticality tugging at my heels. I made one rappel, impatient with the clumsiness I displayed to the stars and moon. After chopping a small platform for footing on the 65° ice, I drove in a solid screw for the second rappel. As I fixed the line, I felt a sense of satisfaction. I could still take precautions although my body wept for rest. When I reached the tent a few minutes later, it was 9:59 P.M. Barring a mistake, I would make it down the next day.

* * * * *

Twenty-four hours earlier, I had set my alarm for three A.M. and had set off from my 5950-meter bivouac at five A.M. In my ultra-light rucksack, I carried a liter of water, 100 feet of 6mm line, some shortbread, sunscreen, film and a camera. I exulted in the beauty of the sunrise. I climbed along the lengthy horizontal section of the ridge, staying to the right of the crest. I prayed that the séracs at 6250 meters would allow safe passage. My pace was comfortable though rapid. As daylight widened my world, I was surprised by the airiness of the ridge. It was much more exposed than the photos had revealed. Langtang Lirung caught the light of the sun before any of the other peaks. Its beauty left me dazzled. Alone, in a sea of peaks, I felt like a flea on the arm of a mighty giant.

As I approached the séracs, a yearning for the answer to my doubts made me impatient to reach them. A short, steep wall led me into a labyrinth of ice. Insecurity competed with my desire to go on. I climbed delicately up a shattered ice band and into a cluster of 30-meter-high séracs. The ice underneath was studded with crevasses and I stepped carefully to avoid them. After a tricky step over a bergschrund, I climbed the wall to my left. In another 50 meters, I found the remains of a camp. It was nine A.M. Had the previous team begun from this spot and not where I had bivouacked? Would this mean more hours of climbing than I had anticipated?

Beyond the séracs, I was barred by a crevasse running horizontally across the face of the ridge. I climbed up, stepped onto the lip and planted my tools in the soft snow above. But I could not make the move. Would the tools hold if the soft snow under my feet gave way? Losing precious time, I traversed along the edge of the crevasse, looking for a place I could cross. After a fruitless 20-minute search, I returned to my initial spot. I dug the tools in again and pulled hard to step up. They held and I panted a heavy sigh of relief.

Once across the crevasse, I continued climbing along the ridge's right face. Numerous smaller crevasses carved through the ice. In each case, I found a point where the edges came close enough to stem across and continue upward. I was making good progress when I frontpointed up a 55° sheet of ice which leveled out onto a shoulder at the place where the ridge made its steep turn to the left. Three more hours had elapsed.

I was completely unprepared for the view that awaited me when I stopped and surveyed the last 500 meters. From the shoulder I looked into a 200-meter-wide glacial amphitheater. The ridge I had hoped to climb became a sheer-sided knife-edge of crumbly rock circling to form the left side of the bowl. It was bare of snow. A three-meter-wide snow-covered bergschrund separated the shoulder from the basin. Another open crevasse cut across the middle of the bowl, barring access to the wall above. Yet, the real dilemma was above. As the walls swept up towards the base of the summit cone, an open, nasty bergschrund cut continuously across the entire face. Was there a route over the upper bergschrund? I ate and drank a bit. To cross the 'schrund immediately in front of me, I inched my way across a stable-looking snow bridge. Whoosh! Instantly, I was up to my waist in a crevasse. My reaction was a call for sanity. I had no back-up system and only a slight injury would put me out of the game. But another voice answered the first, suggesting I ignore the call for sanity. I chose to listen to the second voice and crossed the rest of the bridge. I was amazed at the determination I had. If I stopped now, I was letting doubt and uncertainty make decisions instead of logic and planning.

Entering the bowl rewarded my decision. What appeared to be an unmanageable crevasse actually had a simple snow bridge. I then had to deal with the wall above me. Refocusing my energy, I gained elevation rapidly. The complicated route I had chosen from the shoulder began to appear unfeasible. Again, I searched for a way up over the bergschrund. There was a possibility where the 'schrund split into two veins. There were two points on the 50° slope, about 40 meters apart horizontally, where each vein narrowed to a manageable meter-and-a-half break. I could see that a traverse along the lip of the bergschrund would take me to the narrowing of the lower vein. If I could get over the first break, I could traverse 40 meters to the left and deal with the second. From there it looked like a clear 55° slope to the base of the summit pyramid. Above, I knew I would have only one last bergschrund to cross.

After climbing to the lip of the enormous gap, I edged my way toward the veins fanning out to my left. Huge holes lay beneath me as I traversed. I concentrated on the climbing to avoid thinking of the exposure. I was in luck. I placed my axes in the firm ice and hauled myself up. Like several earlier passages, I knew I'd have to rappel this on the descent. Moving left was easy. With another move over the second vein, I was perched above the bergschrund. I could hardly believe it. The 55° face eased back and eventually I reached the summit cone. The last crevasse posed no problem. I crossed a long, slender bridge of ice with my hands gripping the top edge and my frontpoints on the face. I was doing things that I would have been reluctant to do with a solid belay at any other time. My desire to see this climb through was strong.

Fifteen minutes later, I was on top. There was little wind and not much cold. Clouds drifted across and obscured my view for a few minutes. I was amazed at standing alone on the summit. My watch read a few minutes after two o'clock. I sat and ate shortbread for strength. The south face of Shisha Pangma came into view. I appreciated those who had made quick ascents of it. Gurkarpo and Lengpo Kang emerged through the clouds.

I didn't stay long. The climb down would take all my strength. If I made no mistakes finding the route past the nasty bergschrund, I could reach the 6400-meter shoulder before dark. I knew that frontpointing down the ridge would last long into the moonlit evening. It didn't matter; I could go all night. "Slow and steady" would become my mantra until I reached the safety of my tent.

Descending the summit cone, I got confused and crossed a different snow bridge over the first crevasse. It would be easy to become disoriented looking for the twin veins. I followed my crampon indentations and came out exactly in the right spot above the 'schrund. The upper edge of the first vein came up suddenly under my feet as I descended facing in. I climbed up to a patch of ice to drive a screw for the first rappel. After the traverse right, the one snow stake I was carrying drove in firmly. My second short rappel went quickly.

I was back on the shoulder at four P.M. It had taken me five hours from there to the summit and back. With only a few hours of daylight left and fatigue tugging on every muscle, I started down with quiet resolve. Over and over, I repeated to myself that I could go on all night if need be. I reaped the benefit of old fixed lines, but I could not trust them to hold much weight. The sun dropped behind the horizon while I descended in a trance of activity. One set of frontpoints followed by another, two axe placements and a rest. Over and over into the darkness. I could eventually see light from the cook tent a mile below me on the glacier. I knew my friends had been watching me all day and were now worried. Thirst and hunger dominated my senses. I summoned the determination to continue without agonizing over my speed. It seemed like a journey without end.

By 9:45 P.M. I was descending the last meters of the triangular ice face. I stopped above the final 10-meter vertical wall, only minutes from my tent. I placed a screw and rappelled down. At 9:59, I was at my bivouac tent.

The next morning, I descended the ridge with the comfort of knowing I had negotiated that section earlier. To my utter surprise, in the notch where the west ridge ends in the col, Lhakpa Dorje stood waiting for me. He had come up from Base Camp early in the morning, knowing that I would descend and need a friend. It was one of those moments one never forgets: the coming together of two friends high on a Himalayan glacier. I hoped I would never climb a mountain by myself again.

Summary of Statistics:

AREA: Jugal Himal, Nepal.

SOLO ASCENT: Dorje Lhakpa, 6966 meters, 22,854 feet, via west ridge, April 13, 1992 (Carlos Buhler).

Russian-American K2 Expedition

ED VIESTURS, *Unaffiliated*

OUR EXPEDITION TO THE ABRUZZI Ridge of K2 consisted of sixteen climbers, a doctor and a Base-Camp manager. The climbers were two Russians, a Ukrainian, 12 Americans and an Englishman. The expedition was organized by the Russians and funded by the Americans. Dan Mazur was in charge of getting the members from the United States, who joined the team by paying a fee to the Russians. Some were experienced Himalayan climbers and some were not. Remarkably, everyone got on extremely well and most of the members fulfilled their specific personal goals on the mountain. Scott Fischer and I joined in April when our plans for the north ridge of K2 fell through because of a lack of funding.

The Americans met in Rawalpindi on June 8. Traveling overland, the Russians entered Pakistan via the Kunjerab Pass and their arrival was delayed until June 15. They were the first Russians to climb in Pakistan.

On June 11, Fischer, Thor Kieser and I with two American trekkers started for Base Camp, where we arrived on June 21. This was remarkably clean and deserted except for a team of four Swiss and a French woman, Chantal Mauduit. After their arrival in Rawalpindi, Vladimir Balyberdin, the Russian leader, Gennadi Kopieka and Ukrainian Aleksei Nikiforov dealt with the Pakistani bureaucracy and acquired necessary supplies. They and the rest of the team arrived at Base Camp on June 30. Two days before, on June 28, a Mexican-New Zealand-Swedish expedition had also reached Base Camp. Since we were all attempting the Abruzzi Ridge, we coordinated our efforts to fix the route.

On June 25, Kieser established Camp I at 6100 meters. Fischer and I followed on the 28th. We began fixing rope above Camp I, joined on July 1 by New Zealanders Gary Ball and Rob Hall. On July 2, we established Camp II at 6700 meters. During this time, the Swiss-French team gave up at 7000 meters because of deep snow on the Black Pyramid. The Swiss left the mountain and Chantal Mauduit joined us.

On July 7, Fischer, Kieser and I began fixing the route toward Camp III through the Black Pyramid, while others supplied Camps I and II. By July 17, the route was fixed to the top of the Black Pyramid, Balyberdin and Kopieka finishing the last ropes. Up to there, the route was pleasant mixed climbing, averaging 45°. Above, it was all ice and snow.

PLATE 8

Photo by H. Adams Carter

K2. Abruzzi Ridge on the right

All summer the weather was very unsettled with two or three days of good weather and then four or five days of snow and wind. Each time we went back up the mountain there was endless trail-breaking in new snow.

On July 12, in a small icefall at the base of the ridge Fischer broke through an ice plug, dislocated his shoulder and was incapacitated for two weeks. On July 15, Kieser, Neil Beidleman and I continued fixing rope above the Black Pyramid through the ice cliff and established Camp III in a small crevasse at 7410 meters. We eventually moved the camp 30 meters higher to escape spindrift avalanches.

On July 21, Balyberdin, Beidleman, Kieser, Chantal Mauduit and I left Camp III, hoping to establish Camp IV. The weather was so terrible that everyone except Balyberdin descended to Base. That day, Balyberdin bivouacked at 7500 meters. During the next three days, he inched his way higher, eventually reaching 8000 meters in deep snow and white-out, establishing no camp and going higher each day to acclimatize. He returned to Base on July 24. Again, the weather worsened and much snow fell.

On July 28, Beidleman, Kieser, Mauduit, Balyberdin, Kopieka and I left Base on our first summit attempt and were in Camp III the next day in a raging windstorm. Balyberdin and Kopieka continued on that day to camp at 7500 meters.

The next day, Beidleman and I descended to Base while Kieser and Mauduit remained at Camp III. The two Russians inched their way higher through storm and snow. Their climbing style is very different from ours and they push to limits beyond what Americans consider safe. On July 31, they reached the base of the summit pyramid in chest-deep snow and camped at 8000 meters. Nikiforov joined Kieser and Mauduit at the higher Camp III.

On August 1, Balyberdin and Kopieka reached the summit of K2 without supplementary oxygen at nine P.M. after climbing for 18 hours. Kopieka managed to descend to Camp IV for the night, but Balyberdin bivouacked below the summit, suffering no ill effects. The pair was back in Base Camp on August 3.

On August 2, Kieser, Mauduit, Nikiforov and Peter and Robert Green climbed to Camp IV, but the next day the Greens descended to Base. Kieser and Nikiforov set out for the summit at 5:30 A.M., followed at seven o'clock by Mauduit. She was climbing much faster than the men and passed them at the Bottleneck, getting to the summit at five P.M., the fourth woman to do so. Nikiforov summited at seven P.M., but Kieser had to turn back a few hundred feet below the top. On the way down, Mauduit, who was afraid of descending on her own in the dark, decided to bivouac at 8400 meters. Some three hours later, she was found by Nikiforov who convinced her to continue the descent with him. They got to Camp IV at seven in the morning where Kieser was waiting for them. The Ukrainian descended on his own to Camp III, where Fischer and I had arrived the night before. We plied him with liquids to help him rehydrate. Mauduit was snowblind and exhausted. It was with great difficulty that Kieser escorted her toward Camp III in bad weather. They had to bivouac at the edge

K2
8611

WEST RIDGE

RIDGE

SOUTH

Ice cliff
Hourglass

④

Shoulder

③

NORTHEAST

De Filippi Glacier

House Chimney

②

ABRUZZI

①

SOUTHEAST

RIDGE

Jumar slope

GODWIN - AUSTEN — GLA

To Base Camp

K2

PLATE 9

Watercolor Painting by Dee Molenaar

Abruzzi Route on K2.

of the shoulder that night. Fischer and I had tried in vain to climb up to them that day.

On the morning of August 5, Fischer and I braved the weather to meet the other two struggling down the mountain. Just below the shoulder, we felt the potential avalanche conditions were so great that we decided to wait. Just then, a spindrift avalanche swept over Fischer, who was leading. After a 200-foot slide, I managed a self-arrest and held Fischer. We traversed off the slope and eventually met up with Mauduit and Kieser. We assisted Mauduit to Base Camp over the next two days.

Due to time constraints, many of the Americans had already left the mountain. During breakfast at Base Camp on August 7, Berlyberdin announced that the expedition was over and that with the "summer season" past there was no more possibility of climbing the mountain. Americans Fischer, Charlie Mace, Mazur and I and Briton Johnathan Pratt were stunned and committed to staying longer. With the assistance of the liaison officer, the leadership was officially changed to Mazur. The remainder of the team left.

The weather was horrendous until August 11. The upper mountain was scoured by a raging jet stream. That day, three Mexicans, Mace, Pratt and Mazur climbed to Camp II. On the 12th, Fischer, Hall, Ball, three Swedes and I climbed from Base Camp to Camp III, where we met those from Camp II. On August 13, everyone except Pratt, Mazur and one Swede went on to Camp IV.

The morning of the 14th was bad and Mexicans Ricardo Torres and Adrián Benítez began their descent to Base Camp. At a small ice step at 7775 meters, rather than down-climbing, they set up a rappel from a ski pole as anchor. Torres rappelled first. As Benítez rappelled, the anchor pulled out and he fell 1000 meters to his death. He probably died instantly since after he stopped falling, he never moved. Pratt and Mazur spent the next two days trying to get to him, but the snow conditions were too dangerous and they descended to Base.

The weather on the 15th was still bad and so the Swedes and the remaining Mexican descended. At midnight, it looked good enough for an attempt on the summit. Fischer and I left Camp IV at 1:30 A.M. on August 16, roped together. Mace left shortly after and soon caught up. All of us were without supplementary oxygen. Hall and Ball followed about an hour later, using oxygen.

We three climbed steep, firm snow up the Bottleneck, but higher the snow conditions worsened: deep and soft or breakable crust. We traded leads often. At the top of the Bottleneck, the New Zealanders quit as Ball had fallen ill. We continued in warm, snowy weather, breaking out of the clouds into sunshine 200 feet below the top. When we arrived on the summit at noon, we became the first Americans to complete the Abruzzi Ridge. After a half hour on top, we descended in storm and white-out, getting to Camp IV at five P.M. The storm worsened in the night and our tent was partially buried by a spindrift avalanche.

On August 17, Americans and New Zealanders began our descent. We managed to pick our way down the shoulder, following wands we had placed on the ascent. Ball began to weaken from pulmonary emboli complicated by pneumonia. We Americans arrived at Camp II at four P.M. and the exhausted

PLATE 10

Photo by Ed Viesturs

Shoulder and Summit Pyramid of K2 seen from 25,800 feet.

Kiwis at ten P.M. Ball was so much worse the next morning that he had to be helped at each rappel. By the time we got to Camp I, he could no longer walk. That day, Pratt, Mazur and three Swedes climbed up to Camp I with oxygen for Ball and then, as a team, we lowered him by midnight off the mountain. On August 19, he was helicoptered to the hospital in Skardu, where he recovered uneventfully.

Pratt and Mazur made one more unsuccessful attempt. K2 had lived up to its reputation as "The Savage Mountain."

The New Zealanders found a human foot in a sock and boot at the foot of the south face, halfway between the usual Base Camp and the bottom of the Abruzzi Ridge. This must have been Dudley Wolfe's, lost in 1939. None of the Sherpas who died in the same year had such big feet. No subsequent expedition used boots with iron hob-nails.

This was the first successful team on the Abruzzi Ridge since 1986, despite some 20 attempts. We put six of our team and one other onto the summit without oxygen. Balyberdin was the first Russian and I the first American to reach the summits of the three highest peaks in the world and both of us without the use of supplementary oxygen. Only five other people have achieved the three peaks. Now 72 people have climbed K2, one of them twice. For Fischer, this was his second 8000er.

Summary of Statistics:

AREA: Karakoram, Pakistan.

ASCENT: K2, 8611 meters, 28,250 feet, via the Abruzzi Ridge. Summit reached on August 1, 1992 (Balyberdin, Kopieka); on August 3 (Mauduit, Nikiforov); and on August 16 (Fischer, Mace, Viesturs).

PERSONNEL: Vladimir Balyberdin, leader, Gennadi Kopieka, Yelena Kulishova, Base Camp manager, Yuri Stefanski, expedition doctor, *Russians*; Aleksei Nikiforov, *Ukrainian*; Neil Beidleman, Doug Colwell, Scott Fischer, Peter Green, Robert Green, Larry Hall, Thor Kieser, Charles Mace, Daniel Mazur, Gayle Olcott (f), Kelly Stover, Ed Viesturs, *Americans*; Johnathan Pratt, *British*; and, after the departure of her expedition, Chantal Mauduit, *French*.

Run For Cover—Trango Adventure

GREG CHILD

T RANGO TOWER, OR NAMELESS Tower as it is also called, is a strangely symmetrical 20,470-foot granite shaft of the Baltoro Mustagh. I first read about it in 1976 when *Mountain* published Martin Boysen's account of the first ascent on the southwest face, a 3000-foot sheer wall. He also described the attempt in 1975. On this, Boysen nearly died when his knee wedged in a crack at 19,000 feet. He hung there for three hours until he hammered a piton into a saw-edge and hacked into his breeches and his flesh, then popped like a cork backwards onto the rope. It was certainly one of the most ungainly epics of mountaineering.

I first met the tower in 1983 when I went to the Baltoro with Doug Scott and team. We climbed a 2000-foot big-wall route on nearby Lobsang Spire. It occurred to me that nothing could be cooler than to climb a big-wall route on Trango Tower. Three expeditions then began in which the tower slapped me around like an unwanted suitor.

In 1986, I arrived at the Dunge Glacier with Tom Hargis and Randy Leavitt. The British route, which lies above the Trango Glacier, was still the only route up. The east face was unclimbed. We got there just after Pole Wojciech Kurtyka had given up on it. We headed up the steep wall, using portaledges to bivouac. We found hard free and aid climbing. The problem was that Hargis and I had been on the top of Gasherbrum IV a week before. We were in no condition for Trango Tower. Our food was down to potato powder and porridge, and my gums bled from vitamin deficiencies. When a truck-sized wart of snow bombed Leavitt on day three, we retreated.

In 1989, I was back on the Dunge with Mark Wilford. Kurtyka had completed his route in 1988; in 1987, Slovenes had added a route to the south face (formerly the Yugoslav route; it must now be called the Slovene route); and French Swiss had climbed the west pillar. We tried the northeast pillar, a smooth sheet of rock similar to modern nailing routes on El Cap. During the thirteen days we spent on it, we reached half height, got trapped by two three-day storms and got both wet and hypothermic. Falling ice was so constant that we slept in our helmets. Climbing alpine-style, we had no fixed ropes for escape. It was either climb it in one shot or go down for good. I remember the ugly day we left the portaledge, frozen fast to the wall like a car rammed into a snowdrift. We bailed out on icy ropes with cold hands, *but* with the intention of coming back another season.

35

In 1988 and 1989, Wolfgang Güllich and friends freed most of the Slovene route and added one beside it called "Eternal Flame." Spaniards had added a new route left of the British one in 1989.

In 1990, I got lucky and climbed K2 from China, but as I looked across the miles to the Trango group, basking in a honeyed glow of sunshine, I was stung by a premonition; our route was being scooped. Sure enough, Takeyasu Minamiura was passing our abandoned portaledge and on his way to the summit on a 40-day solo climb. On top he unfurled a parapente and stepped into the air. On Trango you pay your money and take your chances. A crosswind dashed Minamiura into the cliff and he plunged down. But luck had a change of heart, and his chute snagged, bringing him to rest on a ledge 200 feet down. When he called Base Camp by radio, his Japanese friends launched a rescue, jümaring up the decaying ropes of the 1976 first ascent. By the time he was down, he had spent 49 days on the tower.

When Mark Wilford and I were back in the Trango Glacier Base Camp on July 29, 1992, there were seven routes up the tower. We figured we could find a line untouched by human hands and enjoy a few days on the wall in better weather than the tempest of 1989. We set off on a jigsaw of cracks on the eastern margin of the south face. We shared a bivouac ledge at 18,600 feet with four jovial Korean Americans. (See Climbs and Expedition Section.) On August 13, they summited via the Slovene route, then left their fixed rope, telling us, "The next ascent will be lucky. They'll have fixed rope all the way."

Our route followed cracks and flakes. We climbed about 60% free at 5.11, A3+. Two bolts for belays and four rivets to connect cracks were our only drilling. We occupied a bivouac ledge at nearly 20,000 feet on two occasions and we fixed rope to this ledge. For a time, we were joined by Rob Slater, who had climbed some big walls on El Cap in the past, but in recent years a career in high finance had whittled his climbing down to cameo appearances. Rockfall, icefall and storms that smear the wall and ropes in wet ice are the norm on Trango Tower. I didn't begrudge him when he said one morning, "I'm not going back up there. I don't want to end up buried in a shallow grave."

Wilford and I returned to the route, looking forward to an uneventful climb. On the morning of August 23, we woke to clear skies and clipped our jümars to the ropes to head to the summit 2000 feet above. A whoosh of falling rock and a shadow streaking across the wall sent us scattering like mice spooked by a hawk. A table-sized block slammed into the snow 80 feet to our right. A second later, more debris ripped through the air and exploded nearby. We looked up and saw a fresh scar of rock 1000 feet above. A plate of rock had fallen away to expose a gaping cavern. Out of this commenced an exodus of boulders and ice which rained onto the slope beside us.

The rocks clattered down perilously close to our fixed ropes on the wall. We stood for minutes, watching to see if anything struck the ropes. Risks escalated every minute, so we headed up. Though we knew it was dangerous, the temptation to reach the summit that day was great. We judiciously noted that the rocks were striking just short of our ropes. A wad of ice frozen to the first hundred feet of rope slowed me to a crawl as I scraped it away with a piton. Rockfall was so close I could taste it. Each falling rock had a unique sound, some

PLATE 12

Photo by John Middendorf

TRANGO NAMELESS TOWER from Great Trango Tower.

sounding like helicopters, others sputtering like poorly tuned Volkswagens, and still others zooming like incoming artillery.

At eleven A.M, we sat on a ledge at the top of our fixed ropes, relieved to be above the rockfall. Above me, Mark was leading a new pitch, getting up nearer the summit, 800 feet higher. Suddenly, vibrations began to well up through the cracks and flakes around me. The wall shuddered as in an earthquake. The ledge seemed about to collapse. Mark, clinging to the rock with his fingers, stared down with a look of alarm. Then, a roar like the sonic boom of a jet filled the air and a cloud of granite dust rose up the wall and darkened the sun. Tons of rubble roared off down the approach gully above the Dunge Glacier.

As the dust cleared, I saw the team of parachutists who were climbing Great Trango Tower with the intention of base jumping off. They were far away and looked like ants on a sugar cube. They stood in their tracks, convinced we'd been squashed. In fact, we were 100 feet from the edge of an enormous geological event. A slab of rock 30 feet thick, 500 feet high and 200 feet across had collapsed, grinding everything beneath it to grey dust. We shouted to let them know we were alive. Then we headed on.

Our route surmounted a giant triangular snowfield and then joined the Slovene line for the last four pitches. We passed a pile of parachute cord—no doubt Miniamiura's—when we got slightly off route. We arrived on the summit at nightfall in time to see Masherbrum and the silhouettes of Broad Peak and the Gasherbrums in the last alpenglow.

The next day, after a frigid bivouac without sleeping bags on the ledge at 20,000 feet, we decided that our route was too dangerous to descend. We executed some diagonal rappels and joined the Koreans' fixed ropes, removing them as we went. At the bottom, Mark took a risk and jümared our ropes to remove all but a 300-foot section. He expressed a conviction that Trango Tower was angry at climbers, and the thought prompted us to make amends by filling a haulbag with the trash of past expeditions and taking down more than 3000 feet of rope left by various teams.

In all the eons it had taken to shape this mountain, it seemed uncanny that the day we chose to climb to its summit, it should fall down, and uncanny that the rockfall should wait until we were safely above it. Moreover, early in the climb, we had considered climbing directly up the section of wall that had collapsed. Little more than the toss of a coin had made us climb the route we finally chose. Little more than the toss of a coin had saved our lives.

Summary of Statistics:

AREA: Baltoro Mustagh, Karakoram, Pakistan.

NEW ROUTE: Trango Tower (or Nameless Tower), 6239 meters, 20,470 feet, via a new route on the south face, "Run For Cover," VI or VII, 5.11, A3+, 22 pitches. Route preparation started on August 5, 1992. Summit reached on August 23, 1992 (Greg Child, Mark Wilford).

Broad Peak Central from China

Oscar Cadiach, *Centre Excursionista de Tarragona, Spain*

D URING A THIRD SUMMIT ATTEMPT frustrated by bad weather, five of us were trapped for four days at Camp III at 7350 meters. Out of food and fuel, we had no choice. We plowed our way down technically difficult terrain to Advance Base. Jordi Magrinyà and I in particular were in bad physical shape. Jordi kept on down to Base Camp.

Four of us remained at Advance Base at 4400 meters. The atmosphere there was worse than pessimistic, but there flickered a spark of hope. No one uttered a word about the mountain. We had already said it all: the different possibilities, how much time was left, fear that a new attempt would fail. This was our last chance—if the weather would cooperate. Reflexion, concentration, rationalization. Everyone was locked in his thoughts, even forgetting to eat.

Three days before the camels were scheduled to arrive to take us out, the weather cleared. At Base Camp, Jordi would have to persuade the camel drivers not to leave and abandon us. It was August 1. We agreed to climb the upper part of the North Gasherbrum Glacier early in the afternoon when the sun no longer baked the east face. This was a zone of cavernous crevasses; we had already had some rude surprises despite always going roped.

On the steep face leading to Camp I, just before the rock section, Enric Dalmau was jümaring ahead of me. I heard a thud and violent cursing. What had happened? A grapefuit-sized rock had struck him full on the leg. Luckily nothing was broken. We treated the swelling and the pain in Camp I at 5700 meters, while taking a hot drink and a bite to eat. Soon we continued on to Camp II.

At one in the morning, we got to Camp II at 6350 meters, eight hours after leaving Advance Base. I had looked forward to sinking into my sleeping bag, which I had left open in the tent to dry. What a disappointment! The ice which had formed on the inside of the tent had melted in the recent sunny weather. The resulting swimming pool had frozen in my bag. Alberto Soncini lent me his half sack and a jacket. I shivered for the rest of the night sandwiched between him and Lluis Ráfols.

On August 2, the weather continued to be fine. We first had to climb those fatiguing 1000 meters to Camp III at 7350 meters. The route through and over the séracs was complicated and technically difficult. On previous tries, we had

PLATE 13

Photo by Kurt Diemberger

**East Face of BROAD PEAK
CENTRAL.**

COLOR PLATE 3

Photo by Leo Dickinson

Rock Avalanche on the South Face of the TRANGO NAMELESS TOWER.

PLATE 14

Photo by Kurt Diemberger

North Gasherbrum Glacier in Sinkiang, China. BROAD PEAK rises

left rope fixed on the hardest and steepest places, which included spots of 70° ice. On the first two attempts, we had not pushed through to the plateau but had placed "Camp II½" short of where we wanted our highest camp. On the third attempt, we finally had moved to Camp III, a safer place some 150 meters higher, on the plateau above the séracs, which gave us the most difficult climbing on the mountain, but all food and fuel there had been used up.

Above Camp II½, we reached the ridge crest and out of the fog emerged a wide crevasse full of chaotic blocks of ice. Dominating the crevasse was a 30-meter-high, vertical ice wall which looked at first glance unclimbable. Lluis immediately attacked it, while Enric belayed and I filmed. Alberto reconnoitered in vain for other possibilities up the 90° wall. Lluis continued up the ice on artificial aid, no mean feat at 7300 meters. Finally the ice cliff was split by an ice chimney, which gave access to Camp III at 7350 meters. The campsite was buried under more than a meter of snow. While searching for the camp, one of the tents was ripped to pieces by crampons. Luckily, we had brought a replacement. We did not get the camp set up again until late that night. The next morning, we were incapable of an early start.

Lluis preferred resting by exploring the plateau. The other three of us found ourselves around midday at the base of the final wall with a burning sun that was frying us. However, long wisps of clouds began to appear in the sky up at about 11,000 meters, no guarantee of continuing good weather. We halted, drank something and discussed plans. Alberto and Enric opted for going for the summit that same day. I agreed, although we had not foreseen this possibility. We realized that it would mean an unprotected bivouac, completely without gear. Broad Peak was offering us a terribly hard opportunity but we wanted to take advantage of it. I called Lluis by walkie-talkie who immediately proposed to cross the "plateau" and join us. Our tracks let him catch up to us before we got to the final difficulties. He joined us just before dark.

We were now on Broad Peak Central's uppermost northeast face, which was furrowed by several 65° to 70° couloirs. We four, now reunited and roped, sought the most direct and safest way to the summit. As night fell, we climbed in the light of our headlamps. The batteries of mine had given out the night before, but the others still worked for a while. Then the cold got to Alberto's and Enric's. We kept on by the light of Lluis'. That too finally gave out and we continued in black obscurity. We placed and removed ice screws by feel and climbed by instinct.

It was two o'clock in the morning. At 8000 meters, we had just surmounted the last ice pitch and sensed that we had emerged on a wide and gently angled ridge that almost seemed like a plateau. We didn't have to think twice to grub a small platform out of the ice. At first the wind caressed our faces, but soon our bodies were shivering till our bones rattled. From time to time, they called us from Base Camp on the walkie-talkie. The hours stretched out to eternity.

When morning finally came, we took stock. We were on the edge of a plateau that rose gently to the summit a few meters higher. We looked at our watches. It was seven o'clock Beijing time, but only four A.M. in Pakistan. The first rays of

PLATE 15

Photo by Oscar Cadiach

Ice wall below Camp III on the East
Face of BROAD PEAK CENTRAL.

the sun tentatively shone on our backs, but they gave no warmth. The wind left us stiff and rigid. Like zombies, we got to our feet, plowed through by the cold, and began the first and the last steps upwards. Slowly, at the end of a few minutes, we stepped onto the summit. We felt nothing special, or rather, yes, we felt the cold! K2 behind us; the main summit of Broad Peak ahead of us. There we could make out tracks, yesterday's perhaps. The Gasherbrums. We were looking at them with our own eyes . . . . and from our summit! Finally! It was incredible. Before calling on the radio, I huddled to protect myself from the wind and to catch my breath. Down there, our companions were jubilant; up here an embrace meant it all!

We were neither hungry nor thirsty. Everything in our packs was frozen. So as not to get out of practice, we had bivouacked nearly on the summit. We knew it was dangerous to take off our gloves for photos, but finally we did it . . . . one, two, three . . . . Let's get going. The clouds will catch up with us. They already cover the Baltoro Glacier, Concordia, the Godwin Austen Glacier. They threaten to envelop everything and quickly.

We didn't start the descent on the ascent route, not wanting to rappel down where we had climbed. We lost altitude, heading for the north peak. Soon we felt recovered from that $-30°C$ bivouac without sleeping bags, stove or drink.

We slabbed around a gendarme and came back onto the face, but not before we had seen yellow tents at the Pakistani K2 Base Camp, perhaps belonging to the Russians or Mexicans. It came to our minds that we should cross the Sella Pass to visit them and offer them some of our food in exchange for caviar, titanium ice screws or a bottle of tequila. We knew we couldn't, since the camels were awaiting us and the camel drivers had issued an ultimatum: they would wait only until seven A.M. on August 6.

We halted in a hollow, sun-lit and windless, to eat a bite. We took off face-masks and mittens. We tried to call Base Camp on the walkie-talkie, but the batteries had gone dead. The sky clouded over and it began to snow. Nonetheless, we found a passage at 7800 meters that led us to our tracks of yesterday. To get there, Lluis and I set up a 25-meter rappel on a sérac. Since the anchor hardly seemed secure, I set in another one. I got set to descend. Uaaahhh! The ice screws popped out and I fell head over heels onto some snow blocks that kept me from plunging over the edge. I shouted up to my companions that they had better fix the anchor.

Despite our exhaustion and the bad weather, we descended to the "plateau," where we met the Sherpas. We picked up Camp III and got to Camp II just before dark.

Finally, the four of us could rest in a tent, drink and shelter ourselves in down bags. The next morning, one of our companions discovered a hornets' nest in his feet, deep frostbite. But we had to keep on down. By afternoon, we were at Advance Base. With 20-kilo packs, the walk down the glacier to Base Camp was torture, but we made it in the moonlight by five in the morning. We embraced Jordi Magriñà, Kurt Diemberger, Jesús Elena and radio-operator Joan

PLATE 16

Photo by Oscar Cadiach

Exit from Ice Wall below Camp III on East Face of BROAD PEAK CENTRAL.

Gelabert, as well as our interpreter Zhang and our liaison officer Thong La, who had arrived with the camel caravan.

As a prize, the camel drivers had brought a water melon from Kashgar. But as a punishment, they made us continue on for eight hours to Durbin Jungle, where the Chinese helpers provided us with a sumptuous banquet.

We finally began to get the idea that Broad Peak was giving us a beautiful memory, a dream that had taken faith and will-power to make into reality.

Chronology:
June 6, 1992. Departure from Islamabad, Pakistan for Khunjerab Pass and Kashgar.
June 9. Arrival in Kashgar.
June 11. Arrival at Quqia and the Mazar Pass, where the camel caravan started.
June 16. Crossed the Aghil Pass (4800 meters).
June 17. Base Camp established on the side of the North Gasherbum Glacier at 4350 meters, higher than in 1991.
June 28. Advance Base established at 4850 meters.
July 7. Camp I established at 5750 meters.
July 10. Camp II established at 6300 meters.
July 11. First summit attempt stopped at Camp II by bad weather.
July 14. Second summit attempt halted at Camp II½ (7200 meters) by bad weather.
July 19 to 27. Third summit attempt in which the route to the Camp III at 7350 meters was worked out. Stopped by lack of food and bad weather.
August 1 to 5. Climb to the summit.
August 5 to 11. Return with camel caravan to Mazar Pass.
[See also the report of the 1991 reconnaissance in *AAJ, 1992,* pages 268 to 270.]

Summary of Statisitics:

AREA: Karakoram, Xinjiang, China.

NEW ROUTE: Broad Peak, c. 8016 meters, 26,300 feet. Third ascent via a new route from the North Gasherbrum Glacier via East Face and then Northeast Face. Summit reached on August 4, 1992 (Cadiach, Dalmau, Ráfols, Soncini).

PERSONNEL: Jordi Magrinyà, leader, Oscar Cadiach, Enric Dalmau, Jesús Elena, Lluis Ráfols, Joan Gelabert, radio operator, *Spanish;* Alberto Soncini, *Italian;* Kurt Diemberger, *Austrian,* who carried on considerable geographical exploration in the region; Tenzing, Nawang and Mingma, *Sherpas.*

Mountaineering in Mongolia

EDWARD R. WEBSTER

"IT'S A COMBINATION OF MONT Blanc and Scotland with the remoteness of the Himalaya," mused Julian Freeman-Attwood upon our first sighting of Mongolia's Taban Bogdo mountains. After five plane rides, two spine-destroying days bouncing in the back of a truck along endless dirt roads and a one-day approach by camel, horse and foot, on June 6 we arrived in a snowstorm at our 3100-meter Base Camp beside the Potanina Glacier, Mongolia's longest *muson gol* or "ice river."

Mongolia is the essence of remoteness. Western culture has considered Mongolia as the literal and figurative end of the world since Jenghiz Khan's marauding reign marked the beginning of the Mongolian Empire in 1206. For centuries since, Mongolia, like Tibet, has remained a land of myth and mystery. In 1921, it presaged Tibetan history by falling under communist domination, Russian in this case. Since Mongolia gained full independence in 1990 from the then USSR, its economy crumbled, leaving it one of Asia's most distant and obscure backwaters, reachable only with difficulty by plane (sometimes) or train from Moscow or Beijing.

I never imagined Mongolia would offer such mountaineering. The sub-ranges of the Altai, particularly the Taban Bogdo Range ("the Mountains of the Five Gods") on the Mongolian-Russian-Chinese border in the country's north-western corner and the Monke Chajrchan Range ("His Eternal Grace") further south, contain many 3000- and 4000-meter-high glaciated peaks. While the major summits were climbed by joint Mongolian-Communist Block expeditions in the 1960s and 1970s, there remain many unclimbed, technically hard mountains, especially in the more rugged Taban Bogdo, home of Mongolia's highest peak, Huiten (4374 meters).

Our summer-long expedition was part of a larger effort, the Mongolia Amarasanaa Expedition, led by Colonel John Blashford-Snell and organized by Operation Raleigh in London, England. It usually runs six trips a year to various exotic countries. It aims to give an international, but mostly British, group of young adults the opportunity to visit the world's untraveled regions. In combining the best of the Peace Corps and Outward Bound, each "venturer" undertakes *two* projects, one medical or civic and one adventure. Julian Freeman-Attwood,

49

Photo by Ed Webster

PLATE 17

"Almas" or "Yeti" tracks on
Aleksandrov Glacier, Mongolia.

Tilman's modern reincarnation, Lindsay Griffin, another British expedition veteran and I headed up the mountaineering group. I was the sole American among the 40 British staff members.

We had several free days exploring the Taban Bogdo before the first venturers arrived. Our warm-up climb, just west of Base Camp across the Potanina, was Hadat Chajrchan (Rocky Peak; 3884 meters). We romped up the east-face icefield, found good conditions, roped up for one pitch and were on the summit five hours after leaving camp.

Our next goal was a new route up the range's most striking peak, 4073-meter Mosun Sum (Snow Church), which was first climbed by the 1967 Polish-Mongolian Friendship Expedition. Lindsay, our thorough researcher, had somehow discovered an article about Taban Bogdo in a 1967 Polish mountaineering journal, *Taternik*. The Poles had achieved the first ascents of several major summits and appeared to be the only group to have pioneered any hard technical ascents. Their Taban Bogdo map became our Bible. On June 10, we made the five-hour approach to Snow Church, crossing the Potanina and hiking up the Aleksandrov Glacier to its head. We doubted that anyone had visited this sanctuary since the Poles climbed Sniezna Cerkiew. (The map was, of course, all in Polish!) Late that afternoon, we visited two cols behind camp where we looked down at the Przhevalski Glacier, which perhaps no humans had ever trodden. It was named for the Russian explorer, Colonel N.M. Przhevalski, who in 1878 discovered the world's only surviving species of wild horse, subsequently named Equus Przhevalski in his honor.

Unsettled weather kept us tentbound until June 12 when we started across the glacier as the sun's first rays illuminated Snow Church's sharp, icy fang. Quite curiously, Lindsay, who was leading, stopped dead in his tracks. "Did I give either of you permission to go out last night?" he finally shouted. What was he talking about? Then we saw them, a line of unmistakable footprints coming up the glacier for several miles. They passed in front of us, then disappeared over the left of the two cols we had investigated two days before—into China onto the Przhevalski Glacier. "I can't imagine who, besides ourselves, would want to go there," quipped Lindsay. Like excited schoolboys, we nearly ran across the glacier to investigate the mysterious footprints.

The prints were approximately eight inches long, slightly curved and primate-looking, showing five toes with evidence of claw or nail marks. They were about two or three inches deep, frozen in the fresh, crisp snow, in excellent condition and less than a day old, we speculated. The odd thing was that they appeared to be made in sets of three: left, right, right, or right, left, left. Had we discovered the world's first triped, or were we looking at prints left by a primate who walked with one hand on the ground like a chimpanzee?

According to Britain's Scientific Exploration Society, there are more Yeti sightings in Mongolia than in any other part of Asia. Mongolians believe that the *Almas*, their word for Yeti or Abominable Snowman, is a primative human rather than an animal. Male Almas are six to eight feet in height. The females, five or six feet tall, have pendulous breasts. Their bodies are covered with reddish-grey fur and their heads are somewhat pointed. They eat almost any-thing. They don't appear to speak but emit a high-pitched squeak or a shrill cry. There are countless stories of Almas falling asleep in Mongolian yurts. Another story describes the female Almas' habit of carrying off male hunters! Had we found the footprints of the Almas? It seemed so.

We continued our climb up the "Ice Diamond," the north face of Snow Church. Lindsay, the ice machine, led us left over the bergschrund. Then we angled back right, forging a line up the center of the prominent 1500-foot polished face. It was magnificent ice climbing, sustained at 50° increasing to 60°, and quite exposed. I asked Lindsay for the lead at one point, but he was a man possessed and so he led the entire ten pitches. After angling left onto the summit ridge, just when we thought success was ours, Lindsay discovered bad windslab, suspect layers of snow, ice and air. We traversed left but sank hopelessly into thigh-deep depth hoar clogging an avalanche-prone gully. Unable to afford an accident this far from home, with black clouds massing overhead, prudence was the wisest counsel. We regained the tents at nine P.M., having descended the mountain's east ridge to conclude our 15-hour day.

It was an interesting concept, teaching students to be mountaineers in a place so isolated and unknown as Mongolia's Taban Bogdo. Our first group of ten venturers, young men and women, were English and Scottish, plus one Mon-golian woman, Bolormaa, from the capitol Ulaan Baatar. Assisting us were Andrew Herrod, a British Army paramedic, and Colonel Jantsan Tsangid, a veteran of five previous Tabana Bogdo expeditions, one of Mongolia's few Masters of Sport in Mountaineering.

We climbed a host of peaks with the venturers, nearly all by new routes. In four days of perfect weather, we had our most productive spell, climbing the north face and east ridge of Selenge Chajrchan (3922 meters), the lengthy frontier ridge on the Mongolian-Chinese border, a rock route, Midas Ridge, (IV, 5.9), unclimbed Midas Peak (unsurveyed) and Sunset Peak (3790 meters), and the snowy south ridge of P 4152, a sub-peak of Huiten, where we found more suspicious tracks, this time melted.

Our final climbs with this group included the icy east face of P 3763, a sub-peak of Burget Chajrchan (4068 meters), the first ascent of Independence Day Peak (unsurveyed), a sub-peak of Tsoorchon Chajrchan Ola (3786 meters) or Dappled Mountain—where we found upon our return across the glacier snow leopard tracks that hadn't been there in the morning—and Irves Chajrchan or Snow Leopard Peak (3805 meters)—where we discovered an even bigger set of tracks and recently molted tufts of snow leopard fur.

Between instructing our two groups, Julian, Lindsay and I decided to explore the Przhevalski Glacier. We had been told by radio from our main Base Camp in Hovd that our departure date was advanced to August 1. Because there was no aviation fuel in Mongolia, we would have to drive back to Ulaan Baatar on a thousand miles of dirt road. If we were to climb Huiten, it was now or never.

We hiked to Snow Church on July 9, camped and then climbed a small snow peak beside Yeti Col (3794 meters), which Lindsay had soloed before Julian or

Photo by Ed Webster

Near the top of the South Ridge of Mount Huiten, Mongolia.

I stumbled out of bed. Next, we frontpointed down the west side of Yeti Col and wallowed in horribly mushy snow to our advance camp below the south face of Huiten. We decided to attempt the 1300-meter-high south ridge, which began as rock, but ended in a lovely snow-and-ice arête. Following a day of bad weather, we left camp at midnight on July 12, crossed a small glacier and ascended an endless talus slope to a prominent rocky shoulder. Mindful of loose blocks, we traversed along a horizontal ridge. Lindsay and I roped up at the base of the first icefield, while Julian continued soloing.

At dawn, we reached the elegant upper ridge, which Lindsay led, frontpointing left just below the fragile, slightly corniced ridgeline. Surrounding us was completely uninhabited mountainous terrain, with unclimbed 4000-meter peaks to the south and west, and to the north the green plain of southern Siberia. In short, it was the grandest alpine view one could ask for, all the better because so much of it was an honest-to-god blank on the map. When the difficulties eased, we unroped and hiked to Huiten's summit (4374 meters), which we reached at 8:30 A.M. The weather was glorious. We admired the views of Mongolia, China, Russia and distant Kazakhstan. We climbed a subsidiary summit further southeast but determined the northwestern summit was the higher of the two by four meters.

We reversed the route, roped, reaching the horizontal rock ridge at 1:30 P.M. Taking fate into our own hands, we split up and continued down the mountain by which ever route we preferred. Julian reversed our original ascent. I glissaded a 2000-foot snow gully to the west, then circled around on moraines and met him at the tents at 3:30. We were exhilarated and completely knackered. Unfortunately, by six P.M., Lindsay had not returned. Alarmed, we suspected an accident and left to look for him.

As we had parted, Lindsay said he intended to follow the path of least resistance down the rocky shoulder. We hiked to the shoulder's base and began to shout. Seconds later, we heard an agonized scream, yelling for help, 2000 feet higher. We ran uphill, completely out of breath, periodically shouting his name. Julian found him first. While Lindsay was descending the talus, several rocks had given way. An 800-pound boulder landed on his left leg, breaking it in two places and trapping him. It was now eight P.M. He had been alone and expecting death for five hours.

In excruciating pain, Lindsay had fought off passing out. Taking the climbing rope and knotting it, he threw the knotted strands above him. They wedged between other boulders. He passed another loop under the boulder and constructed a 6:1 pulley, taking some of the rock's tremendous weight off his broken leg. Utilizing Lindsay's two ice axes, Julian and I managed slowly to lever up the boulder, chocking it in place with smaller rocks, then made our own 6:1 pulley with the rope to hoist the huge rock a few inches more. At 11:30 P.M., Lindsay's leg was free!

We now had to get him to the base of the mountain, to a level spot where — here in Mongolia? — we hoped a helicopter could land. While Julian descended to get a tent and other provisions, Lindsay and I began the long crawl down the

PLATE 19

Photo by Ed Webster

North Face of Mosun Sum or "Snow Church."

mountainside in the dark. Luckily, I had a headlamp. While he slid forward on his buttocks, propped up by his arms and hands, I crept backwards blindly, holding his splinted leg in a "comfortable" position. When I slipped on loose stones and twisted the leg, Lindsay screamed in bloodcurdling agony. Blood slowly dripped from the top of his left boot. Worried that he might bleed to death, I dared not stop. We crawled all night down the 2000-foot rock-strewn slope, only reaching the tentsite at four P.M. the next day. Leaving Lindsay stabilized and with plenty of supplies, Julian and I climbed over an unclimbed col and reached Base Camp at 2:30 A.M. on July 14, concluding a sleepless 50-hour marathon climb and rescue.

At 5:40 P.M. on July 15, a Mongolian-piloted, Russian-made helicopter arrived at Base Camp, having flown a thousand miles one way from Ulaan Baatar! I went in the helicopter with Dr. Jan Kennis and George Baber, the expedition deputy leader, while Julian manned Base Camp. The helicopter was running perilously low on fuel. The Hovd province had released fuel from their national reserves just to get the helicopter this far! We flew up the Potanina Glacier, circled the back side of Huiten and by my hand gestures, the Mongolian pilot, Byamaaglin Jambadorj, located Lindsay in his tiny tent.

The helicopter couldn't land by the tent but let us out instead on the Przhevalski Glacier. Thirty minutes later, we reached Lindsay, who was extremely relieved to see us. We resplinted his leg and prayed the helicopter could land to pick us up. After a thunderstorm passed, it did, settling into a snowbank 600 feet away. Slipping on wet boulders and plunging into the snow, George, Jan and I stretchered Lindsay to the waiting 'copter. Lindsay screamed with pain as we inadvertently twisted his broken leg. The roar of the whirring blades was deafening, and George, an RAF pilot, shouted, "Don't stop! Keep going! Don't stop!" as we staggered forward in a scene reminiscent of Vietnam. Finally, we raised the stretcher to the helicopter doorway, slid Lindsay inside and all jumped in. We lifted off, and everyone was immediately in tears, sobbing and hugging each other.

After dropping me at Base Camp, the helicopter continued to the nearest airport at Bayan Olgei, where it arrived with three minutes of fuel remaining. The dashboard light had been flashing for 20 minutes. The next morning, the pilot traded five bottles of vodka to some Russian pilots for enough fuel to fly to Hovd. From there, an SOS Learjet evacuated Lindsay to Hong Kong for surgery —making an emergency landing at the airport which had been closed due to an imminent typhoon!

Following the accident and rescue, Julian and I climbed with our second group of venturers. Our energy was spent after the trauma of the rescue, the weather was much less cooperative, and we managed only three peaks, including the Triple Border Peak, Taban Bogdo Ola (4104 meters), which marks where the borders of Mongolia, Russia and China converge. We had enjoyed a memorable expedition, the Mongolians were hospitable to us, Lindsay was safe in the hospital, and it was time for steak and chips and pints of bitter.

Summary of Statistics:

AREA: Taban Bogdo Range, Altai Mountains, Mongolia.

FIRST ASCENTS AND NEW ROUTES: Hadat Chajrchan (Rocky Peak), 3884 meters, 12,783 feet, via east-face icefield, June 8, 1992 (Lindsay Griffin, Julian Freeman-Attwood, Ed Webster).

Mosun Sum (Snow Church), 4073 meters, 13,363 feet, via ice diamond on north face, June 12, 1992 (Griffin, Freeman-Attwood, Webster).

Selenge Chajrchan, 3922 meters, 12,867 feet, via north face, June 26, 1992 (Griffin, Bridget Cowan, Richard Bruton).

Frontier Ridge, including several previously unclimbed summits, June 26, 1992 (Freeman-Attwood, Claire Gosney, Colonel Jantsan Tsangid).

Midas Peak, Unsurveyed, and Sunset Peak, 3790 meters, 12,435 feet, June 26, 1992 (Webster, Vanessa Carter, Tom Nichols).

Selenge Chajrchan, via east ridge, June 27, 1992 (Webster, Carter, Tsangid).

P 4152, 13,622 feet, sub-peak of Huiten, via south ridge, June 28, 1992 (whole group).

P 3763, 12,346 feet, sub-peak of Burget Chajrchan (Eagle Peak), via east face icefield, July 4, 1992 (Freeman-Attwood, Gosney, Tsangid).

Independence Day Peak, Unsurveyed, sub-peak of Tsoorchon Chajrchan Ola, via east ridge (Griffin, Andrew Herrod, Joanne Grant) and via north ridge (Webster, Bolormaa, Katie Allen) both on July 4, 1992.

Irves Chajrchan (Snow Leopard Peak), 3805 meters, 12,483 feet, July 5, 1992 (Griffin, Herrod, Webster, Allen, Grant).

Lindsay's Lump, 3794 meters, 12,382 feet, July 10, 1992 (Freeman-Attwood, Griffin, Webster).

Huiten, 4374 meters, 14,350 feet, via south ridge, July 12, 1992 (Freeman-Attwood, Griffin, Webster). The Chinese name is Najramdal.

Malcin Chajrchan (Herdsman Peak), 4027 meters, 13,212 feet via east-face icefield, July 28, 1992 (whole group).

Sam Ford Fiord— Baffin Island

Jonathan Turk

$\mathbb{A}$ WEEK BEFORE WE LEFT, I called a friend in Iqaluit and he advised, "This is the worst ice year in several decades. I don't know how you are going to get into Sam Ford Fiord. You should have come last year. Or maybe try next year." But there was no turning back. Conrad Anker and I had received a Shipton-Tilman grant from Gore to explore and climb in a remote region of Baffin Island's east coast. We had already shipped our kayaks and bought non-refundable tickets.

The Arctic coast is ruled by ice. You can travel over the ice before breakup or on the water after breakup. But the ocean is nearly impassable in between, when it is a maze of floating pans too small to walk on and too thick to float through. A logistic nightmare arises because the climbing season is three months long and breakup can vary by three months from one year to the next.

Much of the rock climbing on Baffin Island is concentrated in the Weasel Valley in Auyuittuq National Park, near Pangnirtung. However, the granite batholith that forms Mounts Thor and Asgard also extends along the entire eastern border of Baffin Island, the world's fifth largest. There are tens of fiords and thousands of kilometers of rock walls. I became interested in Sam Ford Fiord, north of Clyde River, during a winter dog-sled trip in 1984. There are six published accounts of climbing expeditions, but no one had attempted technical big wall climbs.* Steve Sherrif, Gray Thompson and I traveled to Clyde River in 1989 but were barred from Sam Ford Fiord by bad ice. We swung south and completed two fine climbs in Inugsuin Fiord. (See AAJ, 1991, page 187.)

Conrad and I had planned to fly north in mid July, after breakup, and hire an Inuit to ferry us to Sam Ford Fiord by speedboat. We dreamt of a luxurious Base Camp from which we could travel around the fiord by kayak. But the ocean was

---

*J.M. Wordie, "An Expedition to Melville Bay and Northeast Baffin Island," *Geographical Journal*, 86, 1935, p. 279.
P.D. Baird et al, "Baffin Island Expedition, 1950: A Preliminary Report," *Arctic*, 3, 1950, p. 131.
E. Whalley et al, "Baffin Island, 1973," *Canadian Alpine Journal*, 57, 1974, p. 23.
K. O'Connell and E. Whalley, "Baffin '77," *Canadian Alpine Journal*, 61, 1978 p. 51.
K. O'Connell, "Midnight Sun Mountaineering," *Summit*, April/May, 1979, p. 16.
E. Whalley et al, "Baffin Island ACC Alpine Climbing Camp," *Canadian Alpine Journal*, 63, 1980, p. 29.

Plate 20

Photo by Jon Turk

**Paddling through ice in Sam Ford
Fiord, Baffin Island.**

still ice-covered when we arrived on July 16. A local hunter, Sam Palituq, suggested we travel part way by snow machine. Numerous open-water leads posed problems, but he told us, "We jump them . . . until they get too wide. Then you continue on your own by kayak."

We couldn't fit all our gear into the kayaks, so we left behind two large duffels containing most of the pitons, a large haul bag, water jugs, ice-climbing gear and hammocks. We left town on July 18 with two snow machines, one driven by Sam and the other by his friend Amos. Our kayaks were lashed to a long wooden sled called a *komatik*, pulled behind Amos' skidoo; we rode on a second one pulled by Sam. When we came to a lead, we disconnected the komatiks and pushed them across while our guides backed up, revved full throttle, hit the water like a flat skipping stone and drove over the gap. Any hesitation and the machine would have sunk to the bottom of the ocean. The first leads were half a komatik length across, about ten feet. They grew to a full komatik length as we proceeded up the coast. We kept going.

Amos hooked a ski on a chunk of pressure ice and it broke. The skidoo careened to a halt and the komatik plowed in from behind, puncturing the gas tank. I stood aghast, sure the two men would return to town. But no! Amos pushed the komatik out of the way, leaned back over the leaking gas tank and lit a cigarette to think our problems over. I stepped back. Conrad ventured some advice, "You don't think you'll blow us all up with that cigarette?"

Sam assured us, "You guys worry too much. Gas tanks only blow up in the movies."

Amos unbolted the wear bars from the good ski to patch the broken one. Since no one had a drill, Sam shot holes in the ski with his rifle and passed bolts through the holes to fasten the splice. A few hours later, we reached a lead nearly two komatik lengths across, too wide to jump. Sam and Amos drove to the shore, pried a few smaller floes loose and herded them into the lead. Then they jumped their skidoos from the solid ice across the floating floes and over open water again to the other side. Conrad and I followed with the komatiks. Finally, at a large opening near the entrance to Sam Ford Fiord, Sam shook his head. "Too wide!" So we unloaded and parted company.

We paddled across the leads and dragged the boats over the ice. We were alone in the Arctic. No ground-based transportation could follow us, and the nearest rescue aircraft was far away.

Snow fell that night, changing to rain by morning. We pulled the heavily-laden kayaks through thick slush in a cold drizzle. By evening, we had covered four miles. Fortunately, conditions improved. We dragged 35 miles to our Base Camp in Swiss Bay in four days. Only the last mile was open water. Rolling hills dominated the outer fiord, but the inner sanctum was walled with granite.

A prominent buttress loomed across the valley from Kigut Peak and so we called it Kigut Buttress. We climbed an obvious chimney/crack system just north of the prow. After four pitches of lower fifth-class slabs, the rock steepened. The remaining eleven pitches were mainly 5.8 to 5.10 with a few short stretches of easy ground. We completed the round-trip from camp in a continuous 20-hour

Photo by Jon Turk

COLOR PLATE 5

Paddling through Heavy Ice in SAM FORD FIORD, Baffin Island.

push. Much of the route was clean rock climbing, but a few wet, ugly chimney pitches detracted.

Originally, I had planned this expedition with Mugs Stump, but those dreams ended with his tragic death on Mount McKinley in May. Conrad and I wanted to do a Mugs Stump Memorial Climb, one that was aesthetic enough to remember our friend by. While we were proud of Kigut Buttress, a 5.10, Grade V, we weren't ready to go home yet.

Within a few days, the ice melted in the narrow neck of the fiord near our Base. We paddled northwest into Walker Arm. The first good campsite there was dominated by a 4500-foot-high, free-standing pinnacle. The lower slabs were icy and wet, but a valley curved around to a high saddle and from there a nearly vertical prow led to the summit. We scrambled up a scree gully from the saddle and climbed three pitches of relatively easy broken rock. Conrad then led a 5.11 finger crack and I flailed along as second. That pitch and the next four were clean, airy climbing on steep rock. We had found what we were looking for. The final three pitches were more moderate, over steps and ledges. The route went free except for one short pendulum. We named it Stump Spire.

On our rest day, we began to get the fly-in-the-bottle feeling. The Ice God had given us passage into the interior of Sam Ford Fiord, but as the season progressed, the large floes broke into smaller mobile chunks, and we feared that they would block the exit passage. The Ice God seemed to take the form of a mischievous little boy who watched us crawl into the bottle and now gleefully inserted the cork to trap us. With two good climbs behind us, uncertainty ahead and low pressure moving in, we started our retreat.

Think of our exit passage as a checkerboard with 64 squares. The ice had broken apart and only a small amount had melted or beached on the shore. Therefore, there was enough ice to fill 63 squares. When we paddled out of Walker Arm, a south wind blew the ice northward, leaving the only open space in front of us. We rode out a scary squall and pulled to shore at the first available camp. Thick ice barred passage onward.

"Oh boy!" I told Rad. "We're going to be here for a week." But that night the wind shifted and moved enough ice southward to leave one square of open water in front of us again. We continued until we were again stopped by an impenetrable, dangerous mass of dense floes. The next beach lay less than a mile away, but we couldn't move even another hundred yards. We camped on a small rock ledge. Although I admitted that I had been wrong the day before, I assured Rad that this time we were really stuck for a week. But a wind from the north made me a liar again as it pushed another six miles of ice out of the way.

Our route home led north, south and east as we followed the convoluted coastline. Each day we faced odds of 63 to 1 in favor of being blocked by ice. But each evening the wind changed direction and cleared a passage in front of us. Some days we traveled only a few miles, but we always made some progress. This incredible luck held for nine days until we reached the outer coast beyond. Here the sea ice was crisscrossed with leads but not broken apart. We dragged on good ice and paddled in the leads. When the ice was too thin to walk on but too

PLATE 22

Photo by Jon Turk

SAM FORD FIORD, Baffin Island.

thick to paddle through, we straddled the kayaks and waddled with them between our legs. When we broke through, we merely dropped into the cockpit. Sometimes we sat in the boats and pushed along with our hands, like paraplegic beggars in New Delhi. But every day we made progress and returned to Clyde River on August 13, after four-and-a-half weeks on the land.

Summary of Statistics:

AREA: Sam Ford Fiord, East Coast of Baffin Island, Canada.

FIRST ASCENTS: Kigut Buttress, Grade V, 5.10, July 26 and 27, 1992.

STUMP SPIRE, Grade V, 5.11, 11 pitches, July 30 and 31, 1992.

PERSONNEL: Conrad Anker, Jonathan Turk.

PLATE 23

Photo by Jon Turk

**Anker climbing on STUMP SPIRE
above Sam Ford Fiord, Baffin Island.**

The Great Canadian Knife — Logan Mountains

GALEN A. ROWELL

$\mathbb{I}$N 1972, JIM McCARTHY TOOK ME to a place he described as paradise on earth. We were on our way back from failing on the 4000-foot southeast face of the Mooses Tooth in the Alaska Range, and I did not expect to be impressed by more rock walls because I knew we had left the land of huge glaciers with outsized Yosemites poking through them far behind us. As Jim flew his Cessna 180 ever deeper into the eastern Yukon, the mountains were the kind normal people describe as rugged, gnarled, or impassable, but climbers aren't normal people. Nothing about the peaks of the Mackenzie Mountains quickened my pulse or hinted at the impossible. Green valleys curved in gentle arcs without the straight lines I had come to associate with great climbing.

As we crossed the imaginary boundary of the North West Territories, the simplicity of forms remained unchanged. Everything appeared neatly in its place as if we were flying over a huge Japanese garden. Then came the Cirque of the Unclimbables in the Logan Mountains. Vertical granite erupted from unbelievably green meadows fringed with snow and ice. Jim guessed that fewer than twenty-five people had ever set foot in Fairy Meadow below Lotus Flower Tower, which he had climbed for the first time by its most prominent face just four summers earlier. As we flew out of the cirque, Jim took me into a side valley that housed the southeast face of Proboscis, by far the steepest and most sheer of the region's big walls. He had climbed it in 1963 with Layton Kor, Dick McCracken and Royal Robbins on a grant from the AAC. The purpose of the AAC sponsorship was to bring rock climbers closer together with the club's mountaineers by making possible an ascent that would involve extreme technical rock climbing on a major mountain wall. I had no idea that two decades later I would be introducing younger climbers to Proboscis with a somewhat similar idea of blending today's most extreme rock techniques with ascents of the great wilderness walls of North America. Our new goal was to free-climb these routes.

Back in the summers of 1972 and 1973 I had failed to get up any major big walls when I climbed with Jim in the Cirque. Storms hampered us, as did the black lichen blankets and green-welded cracks on all but south faces that had lots of sun exposure. We gave up on the nose of Parrot Beak Peak even though it

PLATE 24

Photo by Galen Rowell

"Great Canadian Knife" on Mount Proboscis, Logan Mountains, North West Territories.

faced the same way as nearby Lotus Flower Tower because it was enough in the shadow of its neighbor to foster biological diversity beyond our wishes. We also backed off several other big walls that looked appealing from a distance. We felt it wasn't worth grunting our way through hanging ecosystems just to bag a first ascent. I know that a far better climbing experience was there, because I had personally found it on an eight-pitch route on Sir James McBrien with knobby white rock that looked the same as what we had seen from his plane on Proboscis.

Nearly two decades later in 1991, Todd Skinner called me to ask what I knew about the face of Proboscis. Jim McCarthy had told him in glowing terms that Proboscis might be just the wilderness wall he was looking for to have continuously extreme free-climbing, yet not require a single move of direct aid. Jim had described clean vertical granite with protruding feldspar knobs like those of Tuolumne Meadows in Yosemite. I seconded the description and told Todd how great the face had looked from the air and how much better the rock looked than what I had seen on fabled Lotus Flower Tower. We planned an expedition on the spot a year in advance.

Knowing how such a momentary high can fade like autumn leaves, I sent Todd and his long-time partner Paul Piana something to ponder over the winter: an exhibit print of my best aerial of the face. To the best of our knowledge the face had never been repeated. I assumed that we would follow the crack systems done in four days by the first-ascent party with pitons for direct aid on anything above 5.8. I saw no other obvious route.

Having climbed with Todd and Paul on the first free ascent of another Robbins wilderness wall route in 1990, I knew that our climb was likely to be highly controversial. We would not be following the old ethic of starting from the bottom and leading each pitch on sight. When I had climbed the north face of Mount Hooker in Wyoming with Todd and Paul in 1990, we had done the hardest pitches in modern sport climbing tradition. Most all of the 5.13 and 5.14 sport climbs that have been done in recent years involve gymnastic sequences of moves that were first figured out, rehearsed, and memorized with a safety rope from above, often over a period of weeks or months, before they were finally led from below. Natural holds are previewed and brushed clean on rappel. Necessary fixed pitons and bolts are usually placed before the final lead. Since the hardest routes by their very nature seek out apparent blankness that avoids continuous cracks into which camming devices or pitons might be placed for protection, bolts are used far more often than on older, less difficult routes.

Thus the best rock climbers of the nineties are even more divided than those of my era in the sixties and seventies, which is less remembered for its comradeship than for its incidents of bolt and route chopping. However, today's antagonists are far less likely to be operating in the same arena. One discrete group trains almost exclusively for competition, while another pursues adventure on ultimate rock walls. They meet in passing on short sport climbs. Todd and Paul dreamed of merging the two by finding just the right wall to become, depending on one's point of view, either the world's most continuously difficult alpine free-climb or the world's biggest sport climb. They believed they could do it without destroying the sense of adventure of a big wall or causing more impact than traditional ascents of big faces that have always used pitons and bolts where necessary. In the history of mountaineering, every new technique used for short ascents of rock or ice in ideal conditions has eventually worked its way up to use on climbs of the world's biggest and most remote faces. Why shouldn't they be first, as they had already been on the first free-climb of the Salathé Wall of El Capitan? Why wait for someone else to drill bolts before attempting a free ascent?

One day in late July 1992, I hopped into my old Chevrolet Suburban in California, picked up Todd and Paul en route, and drove to the Yukon. The Far North revealed itself slowly through a progression of changes as we detoured through Glacier, Waterton Lakes, Banff, Jasper, and Mount Robson parks. Days became longer, sun angles lower, and vegetation less complex as species dropped away with each passing mile. Here was the beginning of the simplified sub-arctic landscape that gives the Cirque of the Unclimbables a sense of paradise on earth.

I'd flown to the Far North a number of times in recent years without realizing how radically northern British Columbia had changed since I'd driven through it two decades before. The wild sheep, goats, elk, moose, and bears I had photographed beside the roads were all but gone, as were most of the old-growth forests. The Bowron Valley clearcut near Prince George is one of the few efforts of our species visible from space. If aliens have seen this 75-mile swath and haven't tried to contact us, it's because they've rightfully concluded our planet lacks intelligent life.

As we continued north up the Cassiar Highway, where I had driven through endless virgin forest the year it opened in 1974, virtually all the lower valleys were clearcut. Only after we crossed into the Yukon were the trees consistently standing. Our travel by car ended abruptly at a mineral exploration camp beside a remote lake on the Campbell Highway, a euphemistic name for a narrow dirt road that heads north from Watson Lake. We had arranged a 150-mile flight into the Cirque with Warren LaFave of Inconnu Wilderness Lodge, but decided to spend a couple of days at his lodge when he made us an offer we couldn't refuse. Did we want to spend a day or two surveying the climbing potential of the region by helicopter? He introduced us to Jet Ranger pilot John Witham, who was the nearest town's Justice of the Peace, coroner, dogcatcher, and ex-mayor, as well as one heck of a Country Western singer. Under stormy skies the next day we chased caribou and rainbows over intensely green valleys and scouted unclimbed rock walls in several ranges hundreds of miles away. We found several fine faces in the thousand-foot range, but nothing that approached the awesome Half Dome-like wall of Proboscis rising out of verdant splendor.

The exact view in the photo I had enlarged for Todd and Paul passed before our eyes as John's helicopter dropped us into the valley below Proboscis. To our surprise, a Spanish team was on the face ahead of us. We were reasonably certain that no one else had tried it since McCarthy's first-ascent party in 1963. Todd

PLATE 25

Photo by Galen Rowell

**Paul Piana on the third pitch (5.12b)
on the "Great Canadian Knife,"
Mount Proboscis.**

walked a few hundred feet to the left with Paul and began eyeing a wild, vertical corner that projected out from the cliff. I thought the route looked ugly and unclimbable.

"The rock is perfect!" Todd called out to no one in particular as his fingers ran over feldspar crystals that projected out from the granite just enough for extreme finger and toe holds.

"But look at that hideous slime in the crack," I remarked as my eyes followed a single line draining melting snow from the upper face.

"Not that *inside* corner," Todd laughed. "I'm looking to the right where that *outside* knife-edge merges with the face again. It goes for over a thousand feet like that. I checked it out in that picture you sent me."

"But there are no cracks," I said, searching the projecting rib for natural protection possibilities with eyes trained for route-finding in the sixties.

"That's the point! This is just what we've been looking for. It's got 'Route of the Nineties' stamped all over it. No one's ever free-climbed a natural feature this big and steep that wasn't a crack, but with that edge to hold onto and all these little crystals to stand on, it's worth trying. It's the wildest line I've ever seen in my life, either in photos or on real rock. I can tell you one thing, I won't be able to live with myself until we find out if it goes."

Todd and Paul were eager to invest weeks of preparation if necessary to climb the knife-edge with direct-aid and rig ropes from above to work out the hardest moves. The next morning Paul led the first pitch up a wet 5.10 crack, ripping out familiar hanging ecosystems of moss and flowers to make upward progress. After 160 feet, the soggy crack merged abruptly into clean rock that stretched upward as far as we could see. For the rest of that day and the next four days, Todd and Paul worked on three steep pitches up tiers of little overhangs. They used a combination of free-climbing, sky hooks on crystals, direct-aid anchors in discontinuous cracks, and an occasional drilled bolt to gain the top of each pitch. Bolts were placed extremely frugally, and on the rare occasion when one wasn't in line with the final free-climbing route, the hole was drilled long so the shaft could be driven in after use and capped with gravel and moss.

The second pitch immediately forced all Todd's cards on the table. It began with a maze of possible moves up crystals so small Todd couldn't see them at first. "I had to mark all the possible crystals I might use with chalk, then begin slowly erasing those I couldn't use until I found the right combination. Some of the crystals I had to use were so small I could only locate them with my fingers to know for sure they were there. Without a mark, I can't find the next hand hold fast enough to move my foot before it slides off one of those little guys. I think I'll only be able to lead this section when the weather is cloudy and dry, but not too cold. It's got to be warm enough to hold on with my fingers, but without direct sun that will soften my boot rubber so it won't hold my weight on those tiny crystals. Putting the whole thing together on one lead is going to be a real mind drain. It starts off with 5.13, then keeps going and going with complex 5.12 and no rest spots for the full 165 feet. And if it rains hard before I try it, it'll wash away the chalk and I'll have to prep it all over again."

**Paul Piana on the fourth pitch (5.12d)
on the "Great Canadian Knife,"
Mount Proboscis.**

I was aware that some of the extreme preparations Todd and Paul have used for their hardest free climbs have been controversial in the past, but I was impressed by how rigidly they followed their chosen ethic. They pushed their limits so hard that they took too many falls to count during preparations, yet every pitch on the final ascent was led clean without a fall. One might argue over whether chalk marks are clever tools to access the hidden natural character of a cliff or visual direct aids, but in no case did I see holds altered or any kind of real direct-aid used for the final ascent of any pitch. I bring this up because after Todd and Paul free-climbed the Salathé Wall, rumors that they hadn't really done it all free made it into print. To the contrary, Todd told me, "We were so paraniod about being watched through spotting scopes every inch of the way up the Salathé that we were scared to go to the bathroom."

I can't lead 5.12, so I spent all the early days photographing and watching Todd and Paul work out the route up to the seventh pitch, from where we planned to go for the top in one push. Paul spent two days working out both the third and fourth pitches. On the first section he was able to hold onto the sharp edge of the corner with his left hand while he pulled on tiny crystals with his right to gain just enough purchase to walk his toes up the wall. The pitch was continuous 5.12, but no harder. The fourth pitch, however, began with a ten-foot overhang that required a complex series of finger pulls and dynamic moves into a lieback. Paul rated this part 5.12d, but didn't up the rating for the pitch even though it continued for another 150 feet of vertical and overhanging 5.11. It was somewhere here that Paul first suggested, "If we ever make it up this blade, let's call it 'The Great Canadian Knife.'"

We talked about other names and Todd quipped that if we succeeded we should rename the whole place "The Cirque of the Freeclimbables." Our positive energy was soon interrupted by a major rainstorm that brought both the Spaniards and our team back to Base Camp for two days. We learned that they were using direct-aid in cracks that stayed wet for days after every thunderstorm. They no longer had any intention of pushing their whole route free. Our route, on the other hand, dried out minutes after a storm because it projected out from the wall without cracks that seeped water from above.

Several days before we were ready to make our final push, the Spaniards succeeded in repeating the original route with some minor variations and a bivouac on the summit ridge after a twenty-hour push from the base. They decided not to do the final few pitches to the true summit. After they left by helicopter, we prepared our route to the sixth of 22 pitches and began free-climbing in earnest. Preparing the route had taken up nine climbing and two storm days.

Todd and Paul flawlessly free-climbed the first four pitches over two successive days, during which we returned to the base to sleep. Finally, Todd was ready to try what he thought might be the crux of the route, the fifth pitch up he called "a pure textbook arête." With his left hand on the edge much of the time, he moved up with "quiet feet" from one tiny crystal to another toward spots where he had rehearsed letting go for a brief moment to move his hand higher or clip a bolt. Ten minutes seemed like an hour as he clung to the face in total concentration to negotiate just twenty feet. Somehow, he kept going when it seemed his fingers would no longer hold him, a technique he equates to "a spiritual lessening of gravity when something kicks in from the ozone. You feel like you're faking it for a few moves, but you don't fall." He breathed a sigh of relief when the difficulty eased back from 5.13b into eighty feet of 5.12 with no possibility of a rest until a two-inch ledge at the end of the pitch.

Meanwhile, I had been using the fixed ropes strung for prepping the route to take photographs. It feels quite bizarre to be on a big wall watching a companion from three feet do a hard lead and be right there with him when he mantles up, ties off, smiles broadly, and gulps a Powerbar, our only food for the final three-day push we had now begun.

When I asked Todd what he thought of the lead, he said he had to think about it because no one move or sequence stood out. Difficulties were just piled one on top of another. He later told me, "That pitch was something you might dream of finding on the ground, but never in your wildest fantasies would you ever think of it being up here 600 feet off the deck in the middle of a continuous arête. It's the best of this kind of climbing I've ever done."

A re-energized Todd continued leading up the sixth pitch to the highest point where the route had been prepared. The climbing was 5.12 with a crux that required a traverse into a dripping short crack. Then Paul took over for what he thought would be an easier lead that began with underclings and liebacks up a solid flake with a crack behind it. As he started out, he said he'd love to have the pitch in his backyard. After the crack ended abruptly, Paul finished the pitch on 5.12 crystals yet again.

Paul's lead brought us to the first ledge large enough for a person to sit on, but we still couldn't see a decent bivouac ledge anywhere around us. We appeared to be in a system of cracks that led continuously for more than a thousand feet to the summit ridge, and we expected the difficulty to ease up considerably.

Todd insisted on leading the single crack above us, but a hand-jam quickly widened into a continuous six-inch off-width that stayed the same width inside and out or up and down. He intensely disliked the inelegance of thrutching his way up off-widths, but he did so without whimpering or attracting vultures as he drew blood. In fact, he felt so strong at the top of the 160-foot lead that he took the next unchanging six-inch off-width too.

I was eager to get a lead in somewhere in this section of off-widths that were in the 5.10 and 5.11 range, but darkness was coming on too fast. It was midnight by the time we set up Portaledges under a nearly full moon. I fell asleep in total comfort, looking forward to leading free-climbing within my abilities in just a few hours.

In the middle of the night I awoke to the sound of rain on my wind fly and imagined the worst. The thought of retreating down a thousand feet of wet ropes to end up at the bottom like a drowned rat made me shiver. Todd later told me that he never let himself think about defeat. "All I could do was tuck back in and hope

we didn't get wet. It wasn't going to end our effort because we had a month's supply of food. If we had to, we'd wait for a better period and start the entire thing again."

The morning was windy and damp, but by noon we were heading up rather than down. The brief storm had passed, our face was dry again, and I felt glad to be doing the next lead, even though it was a strenuous 5.10 off-width. Paul drew yet another off-width filled with moss that took hours to clean before he could lead it from below. Ideally, we had hoped to do the final push entirely free without any more prepping of pitches, but the vegetation in the cracks was prohibitive as well as slow to clean. It was late in the day by the time I continued up a 5.10 corner that I hoped would end on a broad set of ledges we thought we had seen from across the valley. Instead of flat ledges, I found tiers of ramps that sloped off into space like pagoda roofs. Since we'd left our Portaledges far below in hopes of climbing more quickly and reaching a level place for our final bivouac, we decided to keep climbing into the night.

While Todd climbed on, darkness came and snowflakes began to fall. He found no place to belay, so we tied on an extra rope until he had free-climbed a total of 330 feet above us. When Paul and I jümared up the rope with headlamps at one in the morning, we found ourselves perched on a knife-edged ridge that dropped 2000 feet to a glacier on the other side. With the wind roaring and the temperature down into the teens, we tied ourselves to anchors and waited out the night lying down as best we could, heads hung over one valley and feet dangling above the other.

For a second night in a row the weather raged at night and cleared after dawn. To our surprise, we had six more pitches of climbing along a spectacularly narrow ridge to reach the true summit. By mid-morning we were on top in the warm sun, gazing down into magical Fairy Meadow at the base of Lotus Flower Tower and wishing we could be there. Our helicopter was due the next morning and the meadow was across a sheer ridge from the valley below our face.

On the summit Todd and Paul seemed uncharacteristically restrained about discussing what we had just done. In their minds, alerted by a little incident of falling off the top of El Capitan at their moment of triumph on that free ascent, our climb wasn't over yet. As we made our way down, Todd asked Paul if the climb would be a success when we got back to camp. Paul replied, "Not till we're back in Wyoming alive."

The next morning John Witham picked us up from our Base Camp right on schedule. Instead of our expected hour-and-a-half flight, however, we were in the air for less than five minutes. He landed in Fairy Meadow right where I'd camped on my first visit in 1972. To our complete surprise, a victory banquet in our honor was served to us in the meadow below Lotus Flower Tower by a lady chef he had flown in 150 miles from a mining camp just for the occasion. We began with wine, worked our way through hot soufflé, and devoured the ice cream like eager children. That night we soaked our tired bodies in the Inconnu Lodge hot tub before heading south by road.

Todd must have considered the climb a success as soon as we crossed the Canadian border back into Montana. He used the past tense to say, "What we just did may be one of a kind in the world. There may not be another piece of rock so well suited to hard free-climbing. That 800-foot section of 5.12 and 5.13 is the most continuously difficult stretch I've ever heard of on any big wall, alpine or not, without a move of direct-aid. Even on El Capitan, the hard pitches weren't all in a row like that. What shall we try to free-climb next year?"

Summary of Statistics:

AREA: Cirque of the Unclimbables, Logan Mountains, North West Territories, Canada.

NEW ROUTE: "The Great Canadian Knife," Southeast Face of Proboscis, VI, 5.13b, August 13, 1992 (Paul Piana, Galen Rowell, Todd Skinner).

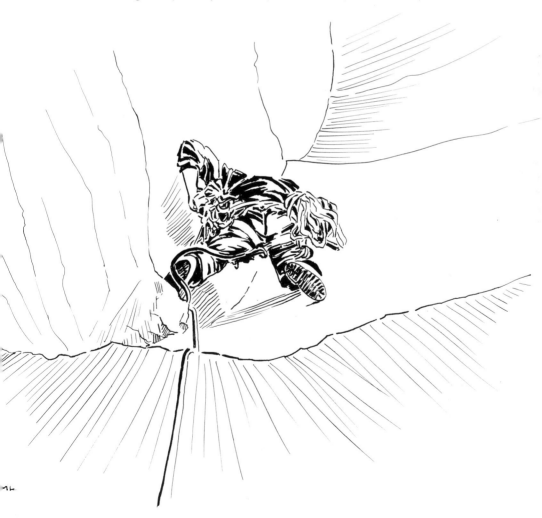

Count Zero on Huntington

CLAY WADMAN, *Unaffiliated*

I N 1991, I SAT IN BASE CAMP with my friends Gordy Kito and Ritt Kellogg while Jay Smith and Paul Teare climbed the Phantom Wall. (See *AAJ, 1992*, pages 50-58.) We had been stormbound for ten days when they arrived. The weather remained unsettled and we slowly strung out every bit of rope we had. We had the support of a grant from the American Alpine Club Fellowship Fund and the thought that someone was interested in our success pushed us on.

After 27 days on the glacier, we had climbed eleven pitches and fixed seven ropes on a prominent buttress on Huntington's west face. The climbing was difficult (5.9, A3+) up steep, snow-covered granite. With time we grew to understand the buttress with more detail. It seemed to grow in its beauty as well as its mystery. It was hard to grasp its size or to guess under which snow-laced features we might find a bivouac.

In the end we retreated. I remember watching Ritt's enthusiasm crash as we returned to camp after pulling the ropes. He had never had a moment of doubt that we would climb the buttress. He always remained quietly psyched, bounding with energy. A sad postscript was Ritt's tragic death on Mount Foraker this summer. He was a person with a truly good heart. The mountains will miss his laughter.

* * * * *

By May of 1992, I had made all the proper sacrifices: job, relationship with all the usual sort of Mark Twight memorials. All the signs looked bad. It had been a brutal season for Denali. The weather was bad. I felt exhausted and unfit. To top things off, my partner Bruce Miller had smashed his index finger while working on a flagstone patio. His finger swelled so much that on the drive to Seattle we drilled a hole in the nail with a 1/16″ bit to relieve the pressure.

From that point on, things turned around. We were in the air less than an hour after arriving in Talkeetna. Once again we flew with Jay Hudson, landing on the glacier on June 1. The weather had been bad in May but seemed to be clearing now. The buttress was dry and upon closer reconnaissance appeared to have thin ice runnels plastering some dihedrals to the left of the line Gordy, Ritt and I had tried. About 1000 feet up, the two lines intersected at our high point of the previous year.

On our second day, we fixed three pitches, stringing out all our rope. Climbing up the series of exfoliated flakes with rock shoes and a chalk bag, we

PLATE 29

Aerial Photo by Bradford Washburn

**Upper part of the West Face of
HUNTINGTON.**

reached the bottom ice runnel. Two days of weather kept us in the tent. I welcomed the chance to sew up the last little tears in my gear, to eat and to rest before the climb.

On June 5, we woke to clear skies. We had packed and repacked, trying to limit our loads to an absolute minimum. With three days' food and five fuel cannisters our commitment was set. Leaving the security of camp at eight A.M., we were at the top of our ropes by ten o'clock. After jümaring in double boots, I was able to clamp on my crampons at the top anchors and traverse up into the narrow runnel. Bulging to 90°, the ice laced the deep north-facing corner above us. The corner rose for 50 meters before it stopped. Some rock climbing linked us to a second corner system. We resorted to hauling after a brutal struggle up the first lead. Steep, sustained ice climbing with short mixed sections took us to a sling belay at the high point of last year. As I belayed, I looked towards the quick draw and pin that I had rappelled off twelve months earlier. At that time, I was certain I would never return.

Now, as the sun set, we were breaking into new terrain. The next pitch, the crux, climbed through the bottleneck of the buttress. This golden overhanging section of the wall is split on its left side by a sort of hanging corner system. Once above this, we entered a straight-in gully that divides the prow of the buttress. Bruce took a fall on this pitch when a crystal broke on the edge of the crack into which he was camming his tool.

As night set in, we established ourselves in the upper gullies. Vertical ice interrupted the flow in places, but the ice stayed thick and consistent. By three A.M., we had climbed nine pitches. Too exhausted to continue, we carved a minute platform for our tent. Perched 1500 feet off the glacier, the pre-dawn colors of the sky began to reflect on Hunter's northern flanks several miles to our west.

By eight A.M., we were up and moving. Clouds had moved in and it was snowing steadily. Our best guess was that we were close to the top of the buttress. After simul-climbing 450 feet of 60° ice, we found ourselves on a knife-edged cornice. What had appeared from below to be the rising snow-fields of the Colton-Leach route was in fact a deception. Below us, the far side of the buttress dropped away in a giant gash to the steep ice gully of the Colton-Leach route.

After a brutal pitch of unconsolidated snow, we reached a final step of rotten rock, climbing up and out of the clouds. Below us, a sea of softly lit clouds stretched out to Mount Hunter. Topping out at about six P.M., we joined the Colton-Leach route at mid height on the face. Below us dropped our "Ice-Breaker Buttress," an 18-pitch variation to the Colton-Leach route.

Simul-climbing for another hour, we placed our bivouac as high as possible before entering the thinner runnels of the upper face. A good meal in the sun and twelve hours of sleep put us in good shape for the top.

With packs as light as could be hoped for, we left camp at about eight o'clock the next morning. The early morning cold took its toll on fingers and toes, but by midday we were high on the face. As we entered the feature referred to as the

PLATE 30

Photo by Bruce Miller

Jümaring on "Count Zero o
Huntington."

"snow arête," the climbing slowed considerably. What had looked like two or three pitches stretched out to six. We were traversing a series of flutings. The north side of these was unconsolidated sugar snow several feet deep over brittle ice or worse, rock. The south side was calf-pumping blue water-ice. By evening, we had reached the far side of these snowfields, but we were exhausted.

As we debated rappelling, I scouted an unlikely traverse. Linking a thin strip of névé, I was able to push through to a series of exit ramps. Two more pitches took us to the ridge crest by eleven P.M. Now, as night set in, the cold cut through me. On the ridge, a soft breeze off the south face froze every bit of moisture. Continuing up what at that point was the Harvard route, Bruce found a tiny bivouac. By two A.M., we were wrapped in our sleeping bags, cooking our last Ramen. The cold kept us awake all night. Another 18-hour day had made apparent how minimum our supplies actually were. With no safety buffer, we prayed for one more day of clear weather.

After staying in the tent until the sun hit at eleven the next morning, we slowly packed camp. Crystal blue skies laced with far-away cirrus clouds beckoned us on. Tying our jackets around our waists, we simul-climbed the steep icefields leading toward the summit. After crossing a snow plateau at the crest of the French ridge, we climbed three pitches of corniced ridge to the top. We spent half an hour taking in the view and eating our last two cookies before heading down.

In Nick Colton's account of Huntington, he had said it took them only a few hours to descend. Jay Smith and Michael Covington had separately described the rappels down the Harvard route to us as straightforward. Nonetheless, as we rappelled off ice screws towards the lip of the face below us, I felt terrified, as if something was sure to go wrong. Ancient anchors and slings appeared and I kept thinking of Roberts' book, *Mountain of My Fear*. I checked and rechecked my rappel rig.

On our sixth rappel, the anchors disappeared and so we continued straight down, leaving a nut and a sling. Below us, the tremendous south face, the Phantom Wall, yawned for thousands of feet into the dark and chaotic depths of the lower Tokositna Glacier. Then, the next rappel took us to a Japanese fixed line, bleached white and stiff over the years, backed up by a marginal 0.5 tri-cam. Slowly Bruce lowered out of sight on a 50-meter rappel, half of it free-hanging, that took us to an ancient Japanese camp, desecrated by a dozen bolts. We knew we were finally on route.

Night was upon us and in the cold everything began to freeze. Our ropes, drenched from rappelling, turned stiff and my gloves froze. Bruce lent me his extra glove liners, saving me from frostbite. Finally, we were approaching the Stegosaurus. As I rappelled down the final wall, one of the ropes wrapped around a large block. When I flipped it, the entire block gave way. I examined the rope and found it had been cut through to the core in several places. I prusiked back up and we began to do 25-meter rappels.

The night passed. Bruce rappelled on our single rope with the packs and belayed me while I climbed down. We rappelled over the bergschrund off our final ice screw at three A.M. The walk to camp took an hour, enlivened by a harrowing rappel off a small dead man in deep powder. We rested for two full days before finding the resolve to jümar up and clean our fixed rope.

Summary of Statistics:

AREA: Alaska Range.

PARTIAL NEW ROUTE: Mount Huntington, 3731 meters, 12,240 feet, West Face. "Count Zero," an 18-pitch Direct Start to the Colton-Leach Route. Summit reached June 8, 1992 (Bruce Miller, Clay Wadman).

PLATE 31

Photo by Clay Wadman

Steep ice on "Count Zero on Huntington."

From the Sea to P 12,300

WALTER R. GOVE *and* WILLIAM PILLING

PPROACHED FROM THE WEST, the northern Fairweather Range rises out of the Pacific Ocean. Paralleling the shoreline is an old terminal moraine which acts as a natural dam that forms a large lake at the foot of the Grand Plateau Glacier. Covered with a rain forest, the moraine is rich in wildlife. The lake, which has a surface elevation of 85 feet, is the home of large icebergs. From the lake it is possible to wend one's way 35 miles on foot up a complex glaciation system to the top of the Grand Plateau at 8000 feet. The ice on the east side of the plateau flows to Glacier Bay via the Ferris and Margerie Glaciers. On the south side, Mounts Fairweather (4663 meters, 15,300 feet) and Quincy Adams (4133 meters, 13,560 feet) jut up, posing a formidable barrier. To the west is P 11,105 (3355 meters), with a high ridge connecting it to Fairweather. Because of the tremendous snowfall and the northern exposure produced by Fairweather and its flanking peaks, few environments in North America are more arctic than that of the Grand Plateau.

Gove commences: The northeast border of the Grand Plateau is formed by three major peaks. Mount Watson (3815 meters, 12,516 feet) is on the western end and Mount Root (3920 meters, 12,860 feet) on the southeastern end. P 12,300 (3749 meters) is nestled in between, at the head of an impressive cirque. I originally saw these peaks in 1968 while making the first ascent of the west ridge of Fairweather (*AAJ, 1969*, pages 304-7). In 1974 seven of us landed on the lake at the foot of the Grand Plateau Glacier. We climbed to the plateau and made the first ascents of Watson and P 11,105 (*AAJ, 1975*, pages 43-46). In 1977, Loren Adkins, two others and I used the same approach to make the first ascent of Root and new routes on P 11,105 and Fairweather. However, we failed in our attempt on P 12,300. The day before our pick-up, we walked to the ocean (*AAJ, 1978*, pages 397-402).

Loren and I returned in 1990. Our intent was to make the first ascents of P 12,300 and the east-northeast ridge of Quincy Adams. Landing on the lake was now prohibited and the importance of experiencing the environment through which we passed was much clearer. On the morning of May 28, 1990, Mike Ivers landed us at low tide at the point on the beach to which we had walked in 1977. The rain forest had changed little, but the four miles of shoreline, which had been open gravel bars and small hummocks, had become a tangle of alders interspersed with an occasional cliff. The signs of bear, moose and wolf were everywhere. As we pushed our way through the alders on a bear trail, we met a Brown Bear. Fortunately, he chose not to confront us.

We reached the plateau on schedule. However, it slowly became clear that we could not make our summits, for Loren could not muster the inner drive and determination so essential for such a serious climb. Twice we reached the bergschrund on P 12,300. It was an intimidating place. Loren would not go on. Finally, he said, "Walt, what is friendship and mountaineering about?" My answer was to begin the descent. My frustration was strong and my anger discernible, but I knew the core of my frustration was my ego and I slowly let it go. And we had a glorious time. Free from the pressure to make a summit, we took the time to watch the colors of the sunset hours merge into the colors of the dawn. We explored the boundaries of the plateau, climbing the nunatak separating the Ferris and Margerie Glaciers (P 9000) and the one separating the north and south forks of the Grand Plateau Glacier (P 8880).

The desire for summits dies hard, and I was back in 1992 with Bill Pilling. The previous year, we had made a kayak-mountaineering ascent of Mount Abbe (*AAJ, 1992,* pages 81-9). We were to be out 23 nights. Although our time was limited, I felt it sufficient for our basic goals as the weather on the plateau tends to be better than at lower elevations.

Two issues had to be addressed. As my feet had been badly damaged by frostbite, they needed special protection. This was solved by adapting Foot Fangs to fit bunny boots. And, we had to have a better approach. Following the climb of Abbe, I had camped with my family on the wilderness beach south of Yakutat and my son had made his way to the lake at its outlet. A kayak approach looked plausible.

On May 19, Mike Ivers deposited us on the last section of sandy beach north of the outlet. One can land only at low tide and because of the tides, he left us off after ten at night. There were only two campsites available, one on a bear trail and the one we chose, which was ten feet from the trail.

The next day, we ferried our loads to the lake. We followed the moraine to the outlet of the lake, about two-thirds of a mile, and then went upstream two-tenths of a mile to the lake. On the moraine we walked along a bear trail expressway. The bushwhack to the lake was nasty. There we assembled my kayak. Having loaded it, we set forth. It was a cloudless day. The Fairweather Range was magnificent and we took pleasure in being the first to paddle across the lake. At the end of our ten-mile paddle, darkness was upon us.

Although we worked at a hard, steady pace, it took us five days from the beach to reach 3400 feet. We had fallen behind our optimistic schedule. I felt some frustration, Bill more. Our need to be in the mountains was similar, but Bill was in a stage of life when summits were more important. And at times, I had caused modest delays due to my relative inefficiency.

The next camp was at 5300 feet. The route meandered through serious crevasses and then up a snow chute where there was risk of avalanche. Instead of sledding our gear, it was now on our backs and, even with two carries, our loads were heavy. To get back on schedule, Bill wanted to do two carries in one day. I was skeptical but said little. I led through the crevasses and Bill led the entire chute. Breaking trail, he was working harder than I, but I slowly became

PLATE 32

Photo by Walter Gove

P 12,300 from Mount Watson.
The route ascended the lighted snow
ridge, rising from the lower right
to the summit.

exhausted by my effort to keep up. It was clear that I was unable to do what Bill wanted. In a safe place, I insisted that we talk. I told him that he would have to adapt to the limits of my ability. Tears ran down my cheeks as I spoke. Bill is a kind and sympathetic person, and seeing my anguish, he comforted me. But his frustration was clear. We talked that night about life and mountains, about the ways climbing enriched one's life and the social costs incurred. This conversation became a dialogue that continued throughout the climb. The next day, we made the second carry to the camp at 5300 feet.

Pilling continues: The next day, Walt saved my life when I fired through a snow bridge and fell thirty feet into a hidden crevasse. His prompt belay kept me from slamming into the ice ten feet below my stopping point. Covered with ice water and buzzed with adrenalin, I chimneyed out, without bothering to take off my snowshoes. Prusiking just seemed too slow. Our trip was not turning out as planned. I had to accept that we would have time enough on the plateau to attempt only P 12,300. It was time to let go of my overachiever's alpinism and learn just to be in the mountains.

In the next few days, we moved our equipment across a long, easy traverse between 5300 and 6500 feet and up a steep snow couloir to 7000 feet. After the hard carries up the couloir, postholing the whole way, I felt stoked and ready to go all the way to the plateau that day. But Walt did not want to push on much farther. My muscles themselves seemed angry at being held back. To deal with my frustration, I focused on the fact that in the mountains there is no sin in having limits, only in denying them. I added some weight to my sled and pulled harder.

Camped on the north side of the nunatak which partially blocks the entrance to the plateau, we weathered a storm with 50-mile-per-hour winds. Our weather radio reported 14 inches of rain in Yakutat during the first day of the storm. Late on the second day of bad weather, Walt insisted that we start out for the plateau. Visibility was a fiction, and I whined about avalanche conditions. But Walt knew the way, was confident that the slope angles would be safe. He led us to the edge of the plateau by dark.

We spent another day waiting out the weather, listening to the wind thunder on the lower buttresses of Mount Watson. Thick clouds threatened to keep us in camp for a third night, but Walt had a feeling the weather would clear. His persistence and feel for the mountains paid off, for the clouds moved out just before sunset and the peaks surrounding the plateau appeared. In silence, we sledded our loads in the blue and gold light to a camp at 9000 feet on the arm of the plateau between Watson and Root.

From our high camp we could at last see P 12,300, a fine steep pyramid. The steep corniced ice arêtes which form the skyline were quickly ruled out as routes. The safest and most direct route to the top was the west face. This appeared to be in the same category as the north face of Robson in length and technical difficulty.

The next day we watched as avalanches cleared the face. It snowed again that night and it was late in the afternoon when the sun was fully on the face before the new snow sloughed off. By eight A.M. of the following day, we were over the schrund wall. We climbed hard, frozen 55° snow to the crest of a rib in mid face. Above, we headed up eight pitches of 55° ice to a point just right of the apex of the face. One exposed pitch along the corniced ridge put us on top in the late afternoon.

Our summit was the size of a small kitchen floor, situated in the wildest alpine panorama I have ever seen. In comparison, the view from Denali is tame. To the north, we could see St. Elias, Augusta, Cook, Vancouver and Logan. To the east, there were uncountable ranges and glacier systems. Glacier Bay dominated the southeast, and Root and Fairweather bulked gigantically to the south. The west ridge of Fairweather fell steeply into the sea. The sea: it defined the whole western horizon. P 11,105 looked like a ship under sail against the water. Only 15 air miles from us, we could see the individual waves breaking on the beach where we had been dropped off. Somehow, this spot was suspended between the awful, immense simplicity of the sea and the infinite articulations of rock and ice.

We started our descent in the early evening, and the sun had set by the time we finished our last rappel down the ice. The wind had been rising all day, and the final half of the descent was unpleasant and scary in the dark, as we moved without headlamps in the sloughing and blowing spindrift. My night vision is poor, and Walt saved the night by leading the descent and finding our filled-in steps. By the time we reached camp, it was morning again. After a full day's rest, we leisurely broke camp and headed back to the beach.

Three days later, we stepped off the bare ice of the glacier and onto the dry till of the lakeshore. There was life everywhere. Walt and I couldn't have been happier—we had let go of our petty ambitions on our way into the range and were connected to what was important to climbing and to our lives.

As we packed camp the next morning, I injured my back and was unable to stand or walk because of the pain. As Walt assembled the kayak, I stretched to alleviate the pain. Paddling actually helped my back, and by the time the kayak was disassembled, I was able to carry a pack. We spent the night relaying loads to the landing site. I remember little of the night except pain, the sea breeze blowing through the Sitka spruce and my fear of walking at night on a bear's trail. As Walt returned for the final load, I sat on a log on the beach. The sand was laced with fresh wolf, bird and bear tracks. A huge orange moon was sinking into the Gulf of Alaska. A fox walked up and began pulling equipment out of Walt's pack. I softly asked the fox to be more considerate. He looked at me with interest, walked up, sniffed my parka pocket and then returned to foraging on the beach.

Gove concludes: In the Fairweather Range, one engages in serious mountaineering in a rugged wilderness environment. For me, and for Loren and Bill, those who reach the summits of the mountains surrounding the plateau after having been flown there have not climbed those mountains. To truly climb a mountain, one starts at its base. In the Fairweather Range, this means the ocean. Starting there means that the arctic zone of the plateau brings forth an intensity of awareness, for it differs so from what has come before. The transition on the return is even greater, for one is returning to the life of spring. The sight of leaves and flowers, the rich odors in the air, and the song of the birds, particularly the trilling of the variate thrush, which goes on hour after hour, are forever imprinted on one's mind.

Summary of Statistics:

AREA: Fairweather Range, Southeastern Alaska.

FIRST ASCENTS: P 9000+, 2743 meters, June 9, 1990 (Loren Adkins, Walter Gove).

P 8880, 2707 meters, June 12,1990 (Loren Adkins, Walter Gove).

P 12,300, 3749 meters, June 4,1992 (Walter Gove, William Pilling).

PLATE 33

Photo by Walter Gove

West Face of P 12,300. The route diagonaled up the face from the bottom right.

Great Gorge of Ruth Glacier is deeper than the Grand Canyon

Bradford Washburn

WHAT MAY BE THE deepest gorge in North America was measured successfully for the first time in the summer of 1992 by scientists from the Geophysical Institute of the University of Alaska, Fairbanks.

The Great Gorge of the Ruth Glacier on the south side of Mount McKinley was found to be nearly 9000 feet deep, making it deeper than the steepest valleys in the Grand Canyon and in Yosemite National Park. The measurement includes 3770 feet of ice of the Ruth Glacier, which fills the bottom of the gorge at the foot of Mount Dickey, combined with the height of the 5200-foot vertical walls surrounding it. Devoid of ice, the walls of the gorge would rise to nearly 9000 feet, one of the greatest defiles in the world.

It may be helpful to consider the difference between a gorge and a canyon. A canyon is wider than it is deep, while a gorge is deeper than it is wide. For example, the Grand Canyon of the Colorado in Arizona drops 5300 feet from the rim to the canyon bottom, but it measures from four to thirteen miles across from the Northern to the Southern Rim. The Great Gorge of the Ruth Glacier drops about 9000 feet, but the ice measures only about a mile across from the cliffs on one side of the glacier to those on the other. The thickness of the ice was measured on the surface of the Ruth Glacier directly below the summit of 9545-foot Mount Dickey. The Moose's Tooth on the opposite, eastern side of the gorge rises to 10,335 feet.

The 40-mile-long Ruth Glacier drains the southeastern slopes of Mount McKinley as it flows through the granite-walled Great Gorge. Every flake of snow that falls on this flank of McKinley and the southern side of Mount Silverthrone flows downward and is squeezed through that mile-wide gorge. From the first time I saw it, I knew it had to be terribly deep, but I had to wait for 55 years to find the depth of the Great Gorge. I suspected it would be among the deepest in the world.

On August 9, 1937, I made a photographic flight around and over Mount McKinley with pilot Estol Call of Anchorage. It was on that flight that I got my

91

PLATE 34

Aerial Photo by Bradford Washburn

GREAT GORGE of the RUTH GLACIER. McKinley rises in the background.

PLATE 35

Photo by Bradford Washburn

**Eastern edge of the GREAT GORGE
of the RUTH GLACIER.**

first glimpse of the Great Gorge and it was an experience I'll never forget. The Ruth is McKinley's most spectacular glacier and the wilderness through which it flows is the most dramatic in North America. From that moment on, I was fascinated with the Ruth Glacier.

At my instigation and with my help at gaining funding, researchers set out to find the bottom of the gorge two years ago. First, they tried to determine the total depth of the ice by using conventional ice radar instruments to measure the thickness of the Ruth Glacier. These are regularly used in Antarctica. That didn't work, primarily because the gorge is so deep and so narrow that radar echoes bouncing off the *side walls* mixed with signals from the *bottom* and produced a confusing jumble of noise. Also, Alaskan glacial ice is warmer than that in Antarctica. It therefore contains more water, which weakened the signals. The scientists returned home with no record of the ice's depth, but with a visceral conviction that it was very, very deep.

In 1992, the Alaskan scientists tried again. Associate Professor Keith Echelmeyer of the Geophysical Institute, graduate students Ted Clarke and Keri Petersen and research technicians Chris Larsen and Kent Swanson returned to the Great Gorge with dynamite and seismic geophones. These were planted at various spots in holes near the surface of the ice. Small explosions sent out sound waves that moved through the ice to the bottom of the gorge and bounced back to be picked up and timed by the geophones. Through this process, the scientists were able to determine the depth and shape of both the gorge and its glacier. The 9000-foot-deep gorge is U-shaped and less than a mile wide. The ice which is contained within it is in places more than 3800 feet thick — and it is significantly deeper on its west side than on its east.

It is now my hope that others will carry out more studies of the Ruth Glacier and its dramatic valley to record the depths of snow that accumulate at the head of it and to determine the rate at which the glacier flows both above and below the Great Gorge. Last summer, Dr. Echelmeyer also measured how fast the glacier flows *through* the Great Gorge, using a satellite-based GPS surveying method. He found that the ice moved an average of 3.3 feet per day, which is relatively fast for a glacier, much faster than the old and deteriorating Muldrow Glacier, which averaged only 0.46 feet (5.5 inches) per day during the last sixteen years.

PLATE 36

Photo by Monique Dalmasso

ARATITIYOPE. The route followed the left skyline (north ridge), turning left onto the East Face four pitches from the top.

COLOR PLATE 6

Photo by Galen Rowell

Todd Skinner and Paul Piana bivouacking on the "Great Canadian Knife," Logan Mountains, North

Climb to the Stone Age—Venezuela

RICK RIDGEWAY

T HE WAY I CAME TO ORGANIZE a journey to the upper Orinoco—crossing the Casiquiare Canal, continuing up narrowing tributaries and finally hacking overland through an untracked and uninhabited jungle to a granite spire which rises more than 2000 vertical feet over the most removed fastness of the Amazon Basin—had its roots 16 years earlier on the slopes of Mount Everest. I was then a member of the American Bicentennial Expedition. One day on the Lhotse Face, while assisting the CBS film crew, it occurred to me that they were doing the same thing I was: climbing the mountain. But there was *one* difference: they were being paid for it.

Back in California, I called the film's director, Mike Hoover, and told him I wanted to get into the film business. "All you need are good ideas," he said. I had these. In fact, I had a file in my cabinet labeled "Good Ideas." In it were notes from Baron Alexander von Humboldt's *Travels in the Americas,* published in 1802, in which he described in the upper Orinoco mountains with vertical sides and flat tops. These quartzite mesetas, or *tepuis,* were the inspiration for Conan Doyle's *Lost World.* I told Hoover it would make an interesting film to climb one. I started serious research, and a six-month flurry of letters led to the National Geographic photographer, Robert Madden, who had been commissioned to photograph the southern sector of Venezuela's Amazonas Territory. "There's one peak the Indians call Aratitiyope. It's like a shark's fin, or like a needle when viewed on end," he said. "It's by itself in the most remote part of the region, and it looks different from the others, a different kind of rock." He gave me the approximate coordinates. On a geologic map of the Guayana Shield I found the region blank white other than the cryptic notation: "Area of Reported Granitic Domes."

I wrote a proposal. Hoover sent it to ABC and soon I was in Caracas organizing the expedition. There I found a French expatriate who had been hired twenty years earlier to survey the region. He had seen Aratitiyope from the air. He knew the area as well as any non-Indian on earth. He said it would take a couple of months just to get there.

With a limited budget and time, we opted to climb a tepui called Autana that had the advantage of being on the edge of the known world. Our trip was successful, the film launched me on a career, but Aratitiyope was still there. Then came the report in the mid 1980s that the same French surveyor had led Jean-Marc Boivin to the mountain and Boivin and his team had climbed it. Later, in an interview in *Mountain*, Boivin said that of all his climbs and adventures—and his was an extraordinary list—nothing had equaled the ascent of Aratitiyope.

And so, last year when John Wilcox told me he needed one more film to complete an adventure series for ESPN, I dusted off the Aratitiyope proposal. Once again I had the green light for the Lost World. I soon found a young Venezuelan, Kike Arnal, who had been with Boivin. I needed two colorful Americans and so I took on Todd Skinner and Paul Piana. I needed a beautiful French woman climber and called Monique Dalmasso; she asked if there were many mosquitoes. I said, "Of course not," and she signed on. For film crew, I got Mike Graber, veteran of our Autana climb, Paul Sharp and the accomplished Swiss climber and sound recordist, Marie Hiroz. Four climbers, four camera crew, including me as producer and director.

In Caracas, we chartered a DC3 older than I am (and I'm not too young) and flew to the jungle mission of Esmeralda on the upper Orinoco, under the shadow of the great tepui, Marahuaca. We hired porters from two tribes: the more Westernized Yekuana and the wild Yanomami. We were warned not to take too many Yanomami as we were going to an uninhabited region certain to be bountiful of fish and wild animals. The Yanomami might at any time drop their loads and head off through the jungle after game.

Even drawing from the two tribes, however, we could not retain enough porters. We had anticipated this and exercising "Plan B," we took off in the DC3 and flew south one hour to Aratitiyope, where we parachuted food and climbing gear into the base of the peak and then returned to Esmeralda.

We hired four *bongos*, the long, narrow dugouts favored on the Orinoco and started downstream to gain entry to the remarkable Casiquiare Canal—a natural waterway connecting the rivers Orinoco and Amazon—then up-river on the Siapa and its tributaries. Eight days later, this brought us to an uninhabited region where the nearest Yanomami villages were over 80 airmiles away, villages only recently discovered by anthropologists. This was a journey, as Conrad wrote, that was "like traveling back to the beginning of time."

Kike had been on many jungle expeditions. He had never seen an area as wild as the greater Aratitiyope. Each night for our dinner we took caiman of record size; they were delicious. Every day we saw the elusive and angelic *tonina*, the fresh-water dolphin of the Amazon. There were turtles, anacondas, toucans, monkeys, macaws. Even the Yanomami were impressed.

We were also impressed with the Yanomami. Watching them in the evenings hunt for our daily fare was like watching a wild animal stalk its game. It was a sight that made you tingle. On the journey to Aratitiyope, our head porter—a quick and perceptive man whose Spanish was excellent as a result of working as an informant for anthropologists, invited us to spend the evening in a remote and traditional Yanomami village. This was a chance to step back in time into the

Stone Age and look into the mirror of an age that as human beings we all shared in some ancestral past.

The visit was also an occasion for a party. We wanted to show our Yanomami hosts our appreciation for their hospitality, but Kike warned us against disrupting their cultural balance with Western artifacts. Then we had an idea: we would cook them a meal they would never forget. The Yanomami responded, dressing in their finest feathers and body paint. The party was a big success: tuna casserole for 100.

That evening in the village was one I shall always treasure. I lay in my hammock trying hard not to sleep. I didn't want to miss anything. For the Yanomami, night is simply an alternative of day. People are up all hours, tending fires, caring for children, chatting. About midnight, one fellow rose to give a speech to anyone who would listen. The village shaman injected through a long blowpipe up his nose the powerful hallucinogenic *epene* and was up all night chanting. In the predawn, a strange bird I had never heard called from the surrounding jungle. Then, at first light, like roosters crowing at dawn, the entire village—a hundred odd people still in their hammocks—started passing gas. In the middle of this cacophony of farting, from a nearby hammock, came another sound I had never heard, nor will ever forget: a man farting a song. A jolly song, morning reveille, time to get up.

Back on the river, the tributaries became too narrow and overgrown, so Kike climbed a tree to fix a bearing on Aratitiyope. We started overland. It was not easy. The jungle floor was a confusion of narrow watercourses, slick with moss. Kike and the Yekuana headman held the lead, carrying full loads while at the same time opening the trail with razor-sharp machetes. In another week, we arrived at the base of the mountain.

Not without incident. Monique had slipped and sprained an ankle. (Later we would learn it was broken.) Todd and Paul alternated carrying her piggyback. Our river journey and march had taken longer than anticipated. The Yekuana had used their last shotgun shells and the Yanomami their last arrows. We were down on food and needed the parachuted load.

We searched for two days and found nothing, absolutely nothing. Most of the climbing gear and much of the food was in the parachute. But we had anticipated this. Exercising Plan C, we decided to abandon our intentions on the broad, absolutely vertical east face. Dividing into two groups, Kike and the porters would continue the search for the parachute while Todd and Paul, accompanied by film crew Mike, Marie and me, taking such minimal food and gear as we had, would make a quick attempt on the French route.

The French had climbed the most ascetic and aesthetic line on the mountain, the steep, direct north ridge. It was an attractive consolation. Jungle rock, however, has two drawbacks. Most routes are vegetated, actually an understatement, and the rock, because of a lack of freezing and thawing, is monolithic, with few cracks. The first two days found us often deep in grungy chimneys, but Todd and Paul did manage to push onto the smooth corner of the true north ridge,

Yanomani Indian on the upper Orinoco River.

Kike Arnal and Mike Graber on the Casiquiare Canal during the approach to Aratitiyope.

stringing together several pitches of difficult face climbing on granite polished by eons of tropical rains.

Rain, however, was a problem, or I should say, lack of it. We were at the end of the dry season, and on day four we ran out of water. We had anticipated this probability, however, and exercising Plan D, we pulled from our packs lengths of surgical tubing to use as long straws to suck water from the central reservoirs of the many bromiliads clutching the steep rock. These bromiliad pools also harbored large colonies of aquatic insects that wiggled on the way down. To put a positive spin on things, it was easier to think of these refreshments as a kind of protein drink.

By day five, positive spin was becoming increasingly difficult. We were now out of food. Mike and Marie were protesting about heavy loads on few calories. I was becoming Fitzcarraldo-like in my demonic desire to finish the climb and the film. But Todd and Paul only grew calmer and more focused.

The crux, naturally, came just before the summit. The French route took a chimney around the right side of a huge summit caprock that was too slimy to climb. (If Skinner couldn't climb it, how did Boivin?) We traversed to the left. With no supplies whatsoever in our kit, the cowboys climbed a flaring 5.12 chimney and continued into the night by dimming headlamp, hooking up blank A4 granite. They rappelled back to our bivouac ledge at two A.M., reporting that only one or two pitches remained to the summit.

There was rain, thunder and lightning that night. The next morning, peeking from under our single lightweight nylon sheet, Skinner looked out over the jungle canopy 2000 absolutely vertical feet below us, slapped his knee and in Wyomingese said to Piana, "Gawd damn, can you believe it? Another day and we're still alive."

"Ya know," Paul replied. "We might just pull this off. Just barely . . . but just barely is more than enough."

By ten A.M., we were on top, admiring a pair of scarlet macaws flashing yellow, blue and red over the green backdrop. We were out of everything: water, food, climbing gear, energy. But we had anticipated this possibility. Exercising Plan E—a logistical achievement of paramilitary complexity to impress even General Schwarzkopf—an hour later, a helicopter whisked us off the summit and the others from the base and flew us back to the mission, where the next day the DC3 carried us 900 miles, and across many centuries, back to Caracas.

Torre Central del Paine— El Regalo de Mwoma

Paul Pritchard, *England*

T HIS IS THE STORY OF four friends, myself, Simon Yates, Noel Craine and Sean Smith and our new climb on the east face of the Central Tower of Paine.

* * * * *

My ascender hits a fraction point, a peg in the corner that I am in, and I am shocked back into the night. Yes, this is outrageous. It's two A.M. and I've been sliding up this line of fixed rope since the previous afternoon. The headlamp beam forms a mirror upon the wall. In this mirror I see the past, no present and appalling visions of the near future. Below, the rope fades, limp, into the darkness. Above, the rope disappears, taut as a hawser, into the constellations of the southern night sky. Way below, Sean follows. I know he's thinking about the state of the fixed line. In this dark, it is impossible to see how much more damage our violent and eternal companion, the wind, has made to our frail cords in the past five days of storm.

* * * * *

Five weeks earlier, we had arrived in Chile's Paine National Park, joyful and naïve. We had partied with an American team. They had been successful on the south face of the Torre Central and gave us good advice about big-walling here. And we partied with Pepe, the local horseman who was to help us carry our kit to Base Camp. Pepe and his family live in tents in this grey and blue wilderness and as they say themselves, have no use for the law. Pepe, a man of great wisdom and few teeth, was to become our teacher of customs and politics in Chile. He had seen many expeditions come and go. "Very few climbers leave this place having climbed a summit," he had said.

Within three days, we had a snow hole dug below the 1200-meter-high east face of the Torre Central. We knew now where we wanted to go. The steepest, smoothest and highest part of the face was split by a fine crack for more than a kilometer. We were in awe, but we all agreed that we had to attempt this most aesthetic of lines.

In apparently typical fashion, the weather was diabolical, and we spent our first week doing battle with the initial 300-meter apron, which was out of sight beneath a lot of unstable powder snow. Spindrift and wind-blown ice made life very uncomfortable. It was obvious: we had come on holiday by mistake.

We clambered onto a sloping ledge, just below where the face gets really steep and set up a multi-story portaledge camp. We had been warned against using ledges in Patagonia due to fierce winds. Indeed, a past expedition to the South Tower was aborted when a large chunk of ice fell right onto a ledge camp. But we were much too lazy to walk continually up and down the valley and the overhangingness of the wall seemed to offer some protection. In fact, we hardly ever saw rockfall on this face and huge pieces of ice seemed to fall horizontally. The ledge was the high point for a Spanish team who had made two expeditions to get there. They had abandoned nine haulbags full of gear there: sponsorship flags, a barrel with hundreds of rotting batteries inside, transistor radio, fluorescent strip lights, very bizarre things. We thought—with this much gear it's no wonder they got no higher.

Noel and I set to work on the 100-meter spire above the camp. Although too overhanging to hold snow, there was much ice in the cracks. Noel took the first fall of the trip, a 30-footer, unzipping bashies on an aid section, and I ended up climbing an icefall in my Sportiva slippers.

The next day, while Simon and Sean worked hauling, we two crag-rats set about the great scoop, the formidable feature of the spire. Once again, Noel tried to climb in rock slippers, but the intense cold forced him to lower off halfway up the pitch and don double boots. Very little free climbing was done after this point. I led two consecutive pitches up a rotten, choked-up chimney, unzipping the second pitch twice. Each time I fell, I bounced off a ledge and landed on top of Noel. He was a little worried, for his belay was of the same wobbly pins as my placements. Most of the belays in this area were hanging on a blank shield, often without the slightest foothold, 50 meters above the last belay. The exposure was now beginning to be unreal.

Christmas passed in a series of hideous storms and epic retreats down frozen, ice-encrusted ropes. Weathering one 40-hour tempest on our unbelievably cramped ledge was to prove a particularly good insight into human relations when confronted with fear and poor personal hygiene. Through the maelstrom, Noel shouted quotes from his book of quantum physics and I made long cigarettes from its pages. As we pondered Schrodinger's cat, the ledge began to fly like a kite and the seams of the tent began to split. Cooking in a minute tent was a dangerous procedure and used up valuable oxygen. It was infinitely preferable to be the cook than the one who went outside to collect the snow.

I wriggled back into the tent with two pots of snow. "Come on, Noel. Eat your snow." "But, Daddy, we've had snow for the last three days!"

The day dawned calm and wondrous. Two carbon-monoxide-poisoned figures jümared laboriously back to the high point. Noel led what was to be the most difficult pitch of the climb, a huge overhanging corner with a stack of loose filing cabinets neatly slotted above it. I was belaying directly below in the funnel-shaped corner. To pass these blocks, Noel first had to expand them from below with a pin, a very dangerous maneuver, and then delicately aid up on micro nuts. That pitch required eight hours. One of the mind games used in these periods of intense fear was totally to convince oneself that one had no body

PLATE 39

Photo by Olaf Sööt

East Face of TORRE CENTRAL DEL PAINE. "El Regalo de Mwoma" route is marked.

weight whatsoever. With this form of meditation, even the most dreadful RURP placement could be made to work. I ran out another pitch, a hairline crack up a smooth, overhanging shield and arrived at the base of an immense coffin-shaped chimney. It was getting late and we could see Sean and Simon starting the long jümar a couple of thousand feet below. It was time to switch shifts.

For three more days of varied leads up the coffin and a second corner system, we persevered in very bad weather. By now the 24-hour attention to knots, carabiners and general safety was becoming stressful. Everyone had his close calls. But the view over the ridges into the surrounding valleys got better by the day, a little like climbing the oak in the backyard until you can see into the next-door garden.

Sean added to the air-miles collected when he stripped his gear out of the iced-up chimney which split the monster overhang below our top bivouac. An air-fall without danger. As Sean and Simon prepared to spend the night up high, Noel and I rested at our portaledge camp, waiting nervously for a midnight start on the ropes. As we dossed and discussed relativity, we were startled by twanging on the fixed rope a few feet below our bed. This was weird because, aside from our friendly condors, we hadn't seen a soul in this valley for a month. The smiley face of our American friend, Steve Hayward, popped up and we all laughed. He'd jümared 350 meters to come and have a big-wall party. We salivated as he unpacked wine, beer, chocolate, bean burritos, real cigarettes and mail from our Base Camp manager and coach, Hanneke.

The middle of the next morning we joined the other half of the team at the top bivouac. Simon was leap-frogging bashies up a thin seam above. We were pitifully low on carabiners and had nowhere nearly enough to clip every piece. At last, 140 feet out, Simon found a good friend placement and weighted it confidently. For no known reason, it instantly ripped and Simon bounced and somersaulted down the corner to come to rest upside down and just above our heads. He was angry, shaken, and more than a little battered. Noel re-led the pitch, throwing caution through the window (in Paine the wind is too strong), and I swung through into the grossly overhanging chimney above. Massive bands of water ice hung above us and demanded care to surmount. And suddenly, all was different. I was confronted with the summit block and lesser-angled ground. Euphoria set in. I screamed and yelped and sent Noel up the next pitch, a hidden crack which took some penduluming to find. In darkness, we fixed our haul line and a lead rope and returned to the bivouac with tidings of great joy. Dinner was cold porridge and rehydration salts.

The day dawned unusually warm but very windy. Water was dripping onto us. We didn't pay much attention to this retrospectively ominous sign and within an hour a massive thaw was upon us. We jümared through waterfalls in the overhanging chimney. The nylon gardening jackets which we had found in Noel's mum's garden shack had worked well until this point but were no match for this torrent of melting ice. Simon led half a pitch and retreated bitterly cold and in pain from the previous day's plummet. Sean, who had decided to go to the top in his canvas hiking shoes, now had frozen feet. Also, the fact that we had no

PLATE 40

Photo by Paul Pritchard

Simon Yates jümaring above the portaledge camp on East Face of the TORRE CENTRAL DEL PAINE.

food or gas, fuelled our decision to bail out. After sliding down a kilometer of deteriorating rope, we sprinted for Puerto Natales, a fishing village, only a day away.

It was a depraved team of hillbillies who hit town. Manic stares behind scruffy beards and innane gruntings passing as language worried the restaurant staff, who timidly placed endless plates of salmon in front of the savages, fearful of losing their hands. Sean and I visited the Mylodon Disco (a sound mountaineering decision). It was here, I think, when reality became an obscure concept. A short while earlier, we had been 150 meters below the summit of the Torre Central with all its sickly heights and violent winds. Now we were jumping to throbbing music below spinning lights of all colors. Velvet mylodons on the walls, señoritas, fluorescent liquids. All I was capable of was screaming.

And so, sated, we headed back to our mountain.

Noel was becoming increasingly agitated. He had told his Oxford University bosses that he was going on a short holiday to Chile. He wanted to get back to his laboratory, pronto. I stole his passport in an effort to get him to stay, but he played his trump card and pulled out a second passport. Damn! We were sad to see him go. He had done more than his fair share of the graft and he deserved another crack at the top. True, the chances were slim. Simon also made a decision not to go back to the mountain. He wasn't happy with the state of the fixed rope and his fall had shaken him. Fair enough, I thought. There's no honor in death, only image enhancement.

When my ascender hit the fraction point in the corner, I wearily removed the top clamp and replaced it on the rope above the peg. I raised my leg in its foot loop and slid the clamp upward. With an effort, I took my weight on my leg, unclipped the chest clamp and replaced it above the peg. And so on and so forth.

At nine A.M. Sean and I were both together at the top of the ropes. The wind blew hard, making shattering cracks as the gusts exploded through the gendarmes above. At this moment, the sky was blue. We had left our cabin in the forest a day earlier at 3:30 P.M. We had been moving fairly continuously ever since. Over a few hours I led another 60-meter pitch of aid with some tenuous free climbing in plastic boots. I took a large air-fall from a roof when I stripped a nut from a rock-ice sandwich. There was no place for emotion here, only judgmental corrections and an awareness that any injury could have catastrophic consequences. Since the monster thaw, all the cracks had become choked with hard water-ice, making the placing of gear difficult and frustrating. At the end of the pitch, I arrived at a snowfield and above I could see old fixed ropes running up toward the summit. Ecstacy set in once again, but this time it was certain. Just below, condors contoured the wall, shadows flitting from corner to face. Sean led through, and after an hour of mixed gullies and frozen, frayed lines, we wallowed onto the top.

How odd! After 21 days on the wall we could, at last, look west. Lago Paine, La Fortaleza, El Escudo. They appeared as hurriedly as they disappeared while the clouds shunted past with a fast-forward velocity. We were unable to stand and our eyes watered, from the wind rather than with tears of joy. On the first abseil, the ropes stuck fast and so Sean had to reclimb the top pitch to release them. This wasted a lot of time and we didn't get back to our top bivouac ledge until midnight. I instantly dozed off while Sean made endless brews to rehydrate us.

With the first light came a horrible storm, which made the already desperate task of cleaning a kilometer of rope and dismantling a camp by only two people even more desperate. Our ropes spiraled and twisted above us in the updrafts, searching for crevices and flakes to hook onto and forcing us several times to cut them.

We descended the glacier in the night, front-pointing on 20° ice to avoid being swept away by the wind. It was two very addled boys who staggered back into the forest in the early hours. Rejoicing didn't commence until five days later.

We named our climb "El Regalo de Mwoma" (The Gift of Mwoma) after the Tehuelche god who lives in those frozen steeples.

And we do feel honored to be granted such a gift.

Summary of Statistics:

AREA: Paine Group, Patagonia, Chile.

NEW ROUTES: Torre Central del Paine, 2460 meters, 8071 feet, East Face between the 1991 German and the 1974 South African Routes. Summit reached on January 16, 1992 (Pritchard, Smith).

Paine Chico, 2670 meters, 8760 feet, West Face, February 12, 1992 (Lloyd, Pritchard). (See *Climbs and Expeditions* Section.)

Torre Norte del Paine, North Summit, c. 2200 meters, 7218 feet, West Face to the right of the Italian 1992 route, February 14, 1992 (Lloyd, Pritchard). (See *Climbs and Expeditions* Section.)

PERSONNEL: Noel Craine, Paul Pritchard, Sean Smith, Simon Yates, *British*; Philip Lloyd, *South African*.

Cordillera Sarmiento in Winter

JACK MILLER

The islands, fjords and mainland along the southwest coast of South America are legendary for collecting storms. Rolling off the Roaring Forties and Furious Fifties of the South Pacific and Antarctic oceans, they dump precipitation in enormous amounts (one station commonly reports over 8 meters—more than 300 inches—per year). This results in lush rain forests at sea level and healthy glaciers that lie not much higher. Some of the world's fine mountains are found there—when they can be found.

My travels and climbs in this wet zone, over the last 30 years, have ranged from the Darwin Range in Tierra del Fuego to San Lorenzo, 15° of latitude further north. Over time I learned there are pockets within this wet zone that are even wetter, viewed as a perpetual cloud cap, and sure to be centered over some orographic attraction. The Cordillera Sarmiento* is one. Of the several hundred days I'd been, theoretically, within sight of the range, I had glimpsed its peaks only twice, in 1974 and 1976. Even camping during our three-week siege, in January 1976, across the Fjord of the Mountains from these peaks failed to reveal more than their lower escarpments and tongues of glaciers that must descend from massive fields of ice (see *AAJ 1977*, pages 57-72). Ridgeway and party in November, 1989 *(AAJ 1991*, pages 95-98) reported the same unceasing overcast.

Then, one day in February 1990, as I was driving a road some 55 miles to the east, they came clear! I dropped all else, rented a plane and overflew the range, all 40 miles of it, both sides. The photos created an excitement that resulted in grants from The Shipton/Tilman Fund of Gore and Associates and *National Geographic Magazine*. With support from Ladeco Airlines, several equipment manufacturers and donations from friends we raised enough for a modest expedition of six men for six weeks.

Over the years Patagonian locals told me that austral *winter* offered the best chance of clear days and low winds, and the scant climate data bore that out. The trade-off would be short days and colder temperatures. In the winter of 1992 we

---

* Not to be confused with well-known Monte Sarmiento, south of the Strait of Magellan.

109

arrived in Puerto Natales, a fishing village 120 miles north of the Straits of Magellan, to learn that June and July had brought some clear, some calm days, even some clear *and* calm days. We were on the right track.

As companions in these explorations, I'd chosen Pete Garber, Rob Hart, Phillip Lloyd, Gordon Wiltsie and Tyler Van Arsdell. Although they had climbed widely in mountains around the world, only Pete had experience in this climate. They were astounded when first stepping ashore into the super-rain forest. Gordon declared "I've never seen a place like this!" which quickly translated to "How the hell do we stay dry?"

That was August 16. We had arrived from Puerto Natales on a 50-foot wooden motor sailor, the *Trinidad*. Early in our 70-mile voyage we abandoned "dry" Patagonia and all of man's activities, except fishing and some rudimentary logging. Even place names on the map stopped, at the edge of "wet." Every map, every book, every person we consulted gave us reason to believe the range was essentially unknown.

Base Camp centered around a smallish 8x16-foot tent that could withstand Antarctic winds, but not, we soon learned, Patagonian rain. We mounted it atop a plywood platform on posts; thus we'd brought our own level and firm ground with us, for such clearly was not to be found anywhere in those boggy forests or along the steep ridges which soar directly off the beach. Our sleeping tents were draped over planks on the bog or on bedrock too exposed to support soil and its spongy mosses. Large stands of old growth *Nothofagus*, or southern beech, protected us from the ferocious winds.

Our 1990 air photos suggested not only this location but also the best ridges for approaching the icefields which overhang the fjords. By August 29, we were camped at 4000 feet, three in a snow cave and three in a Himalayan Hotel tent, until it blew away. By comparing our air photos with views during open moments between storms, we located the route through the lower icefalls and crevasse fields.

Of the 45 days in the range we were graced by several brief periods of clear weather but only had four days which might be called "good." August 30 was one. We rapidly skied our flagged route, and beyond, up steep but trouble-free glacial slopes. Before noon, we topped "The South Face" and stood in awe at the view.

Those readers who have been atop an unclimbed peak in a virgin range on a clear day can imagine our ecstacy. Magnificent peaks spread out to the south and north of us, none with names, or even mapped. The block-faulted nature of the mafic olivine/serpentine bedrock, anomalous throughout the Andean cordillera, resulted in peaks mostly steep-sided, often vertical. By dint of weather and remoteness, all will be difficult climbs; some, such as "Angel Wings"—two overhanging summits in the form of shadow-hands wings—will push moun-taineering limits.

Once our initial rapture passed we took surveys with compass and a compact Garmin G.P.S. (Global Positioning System) computer which read our position accurately off military satellites. Then our afternoon passed in a virtual orgy of

PLATE 41

Photo by Jack Miller

"Fickle Finger of Fate," Spire Fjord, Chilean Patagonia.

peak-bagging, our skis taxying us across the glaciers to "Gremlins Cap," "Jaco," and "Elephant Ears," summits encrusted in rime. Even as dusk came on, young Pete mirrored our reluctance to descend out of this paradise by scrambling around on vertical ice with his front points. The perfect mountain day ended with our ski descent down the rolling glaciers to camp.

The following day, also good, allowed us to split into two groups, Gordon and I went south to scout the route up the ranges's highest peak, "Peak 66" (given by previous estimates as 6600 feet, although our surveys put it closer to 7000). This we accomplished as the wind was coming up and cumulus lenticularus were building. Given just one more good day, we could climb the peak—but we never got it.

The other four came in at dark, having skied several miles across the entire northern icefield of the range to climb two peaks, named tentatively "Taraba I and II." Their summit views looked almost straight down into Taraba Sound, the large inland sea which borders the Sarmiento range on the west.

Storm held us in the snow cave for five days, frustrating any further exploration. One attempt aborted abruptly just outside our cave when winds picked up 220-pound Pete and tossed him like a rag doll. Finally we descended in hellish winds and nasty rappels to the fjords, then motored in our small inflatable boat to Base Camp on treacherous seas. We made it in time for our radio schedule with the *Trinidad*.

As we sailed out of the Fjord of the Mountains, the weather lifted and gave us clear views of the range. For the first time I saw the one peak that Dan Asay and I had climbed, blinded by storm, in 1976. It was the highest of three rock towers we called the "Three Furies," with an altitude of approximately 4000 feet. Rounding Cape Earnest into the shipping lanes, we had full view of Monte Burney, climbed by Eric Shipton in the early 1960s on his third attempt.

Sailing into the unknown Taraba Sound, we explored all five major fjords that pierce the range from the Sound. At the head of one we discovered a glacial lake whose emerald green waters captured icebergs that calved off two immense piedmont glaciers. Gordon pointed out that if this were the Himalaya, thousands of pilgrims would pay homage to it each year for its sheer beauty.

We eventually settled on one fjord, "Spire Fjord" for locating our second Base Camp to explore the range's central icefield and attempting the spectacular spire that dominates the fjord. We came to know it as the "Fickle Finger of Fate."

Moderate scrambling on ice got the team to the base of the vertical "Finger." Only 50 meters of climbing remained to the top, but the infamous "hongo" ice (which we dubbed "elephant ears"), the lacy rime inter-lensed with wind-blasted snow, frustrated Phillip's first attempt to lead it. It was nearly three weeks before weather permitted another try. On October 1, in an eleventh-hour attempt, he and Pete reached the summit. The following day the *Trinidad* motored in and returned us to civilization.

Summary of Statistics:

AREA: Cordillera Sarmiento, Chilean Patagonia.

FIRST ASCENTS: (All names are unofficial and altitudes are estimated) South Face, 2125 meters, 6970 feet, August 30, 1992.

Jaco, 2039 meters, 6700 feet, August 30, 1992.

Gremlins Cap, 1992 meters, 6550 feet, August 30, 1992.

Elephant Ears, 1920 meters, 6300 feet, August 30, 1992.

Taraba I and Taraba II, 1890 meters, 6200 feet, August 31, 1992 (Garber, Hart, Lloyd, Van Arsdell).

Fickle Finger of Fate, 1342 meters, 4600 feet, October 1, 1992 (Lloyd, Garber).

PERSONNEL: Jack Miller, leader, Peter Garber, Rob Hart, Phillip Lloyd, Gordon Wiltsie, Tyler Van Arsdell.

PLATE 42

Photo by Jack Miller

CORDILLERA SARMIENTO from the Fjord of the Mountains.

The Mountains, My Perspective

ROBERT M. MCCONNELL*

I HAVE BEEN ASKED TO REFLECT about where we stand on protecting the mountains we love so much. The first thought that comes to mind is that we have turned an important corner in this effort. Alpinists today are increasingly aware of how fragile mountain environments are and how great an impact our adventures can have if we are not careful. The stories of trashed-out approaches and the photos of tents pitched on piles of garbage in base camps have caused many to reconsider the role they have played in creating these problems. The growing trend to close climbing areas in many countries and to close entire mountain ranges in others has brought home the need to address the problem now.

Today we face another challenge. Awareness is not enough. Awareness must be translated into action. We must each adopt a personal commitment to leave as little trace as possible of our passing through the mountains. That personal commitment should be part of our planning for every trip. A plan to deal with packaging, food scraps and human waste as it is generated at each stage of the trip from approach to return is essential. In order for the plan to work, it should be shared with and agreed to by the entire team and your support staff before departure.

Human waste is probably the toughest issue to address and so I'll start with it. There are those among us who seem to romanticize stepping behind a bush or digging a cat hole when they squat to contemplate the meaning of life. Anything else seems to get in the way of their enjoyment of the great outdoors to hear them tell it. Well, they are living in a fantasy world, as least as far as popular climbs are concerned. The fact is that in too many places, there aren't any more bushes to step behind without stepping in someone else's previous deposit. All too often there isn't anywhere to dig without digging into what someone else left behind.

So what is the answer? Over the long term, solar or composting toilets should be purchased, installed and maintained on approaches and in base camps. We

---

*The author is a co-founder and director of the Everest Environmental Project, led the 1990 and 1992 Everest Environmental Expeditions, co-chairs the American Alpine Club Conservation Committee, is the American delegate to the International Commission for Mountain Preservation and is writing a book for the American Alpine Club about environmentally sound expeditions.

Tibetans rummaging through food left by a Spanish expedition at the Everest Base Camp.

who use these areas are going to have to pay for this. Near term, plan to bring along five-gallon plastic buckets with sealing lids for use as "porta-potties" while on the approach and in base camps. The buckets fit neatly in a duffel bag and make great packing places (before use) for things you don't want to get wet or broken. One bucket per person is enough. On the way in, find farmers who want your manure for their fields. Often they will want the bucket even more. As long as the buckets are sealed, for a bit of extra pay, porters, yak herders and others you rely on will carry it to where it can be used. Not as romantic as a bush, but then, there are other ways to work out romantic fantasies. Try it. The bucket approach will work and make base camps much pleasanter.

By thinking before you leave, you can minimize the amount of packaging you bring. You can rely as much as possible on buying food in local centers when you travel in developing countries. This eliminates even more packaging and stimulates the local economy. One way to do this is to send your support staff a shopping list. Have them confirm what they have bought before you leave so you can fill in around the edges. This thought process is critical because most packaging becomes garbage during a trip.

In nearly all mountainous areas, wood is a precious commodity. Climbing expeditions and trekking groups should *never* burn wood, which takes years to regenerate and in many places rarely grows back. This also causes devastating erosion. Campfires, for all their romantic appeal, are *taboo*. Wood must not be used for cooking. It is easy enough to insist that visitors to the mountains use portable cooking stoves to prepare their food. It is more difficult to enforce this prohibition of cooking and heating fires on the porters. They must be given stoves and instructions in their use. Fuel has to be rationed to them so that they don't burn it all up in a short time. This prohibition can be enforced if there is a clear understanding with the sirdar that absolutely no wood may be burned.

Another issue that needs advance planning is "toxic" waste. I use the term to mean anything that cannot be safely disposed of in remote areas. Again, minimizing the amount you bring is an important first step. Solar rechargers can reduce the number of batteries you need for extended trips. The batteries you do use and any medical waste you generate should be brought out of the mountains. Your plan should include how you will pack out with you anything that won't burn or decompose.

When planning is finally done and the trip is underway, the personal commitment to leaving as little trace as possible of your passing should be part of your thought process every day. The higher you go, the tougher this becomes. But no one can justify leaving a mess behind with the argument that a climb is too far out on the edge to do it right. Doing it right means doing it in such a way as to leave no trace of your passing.

Fortunately, the greater number of people and therefore the biggest problems are at the base camps and on the approaches. Anywhere you are supported by local transportation, whether it is porters, yaks, camels or trucks, the answer is easy. You pay for the round trip use of the transportation, you bring enough burlap or woven plastic bags for all the garbage you will generate and you bring out whatever won't burn or decompose. And take care of what other thought-less people have left. Anything less is no longer acceptable. Those who object to the extra cost, to supervising those you hire and the time it takes should look to other sources of personal challenge, spiritual growth and enjoyment rather than climbing.

The last issue I want to address is what happens when someone else screws up. Some of what I have said will be unacceptable to some climbers. I welcome their thoughts and the opportunity to debate these issues. However, all of us realize a base level of unacceptable behavior. You may not be able to define it, but you know it when you see it. Here is an example. This photo was taken near Annapurna in 1991. The day is fast approaching when this type of behavior will result in those responsible being banned from the mountains, forever. And well it should.

PLATE 44

Photo by Robert McConnell

KOREAN GRAFFITI.

Medical Therapy of High Altitude Illness

Colin Kerst Grissom, M.D.

E WERE CLIMBING UNROPED on steep terrain near the top of the West Rib of Denali. We had made good progress initially after an early start from our camp at 16,000 feet, but the higher we climbed, the slower we moved. I took comfort in the fact that my four partners were leaning on their ice axes and panting every few steps because I was doing the same with increasing frequency. It had been a week since we had started up the initial couloir that gained the West Rib from the head of the northeast fork of the Kahiltna Glacier, and we were all feeling the effects of the altitude. As we neared the summit plateau at 19,000 feet, I noticed that one member of our expedition was starting to stagger. By the time we reached the easier terrain of the plateau, he was slurring his speech and complaining of a headache. It was clear that he could not go on, and by the time we stopped to help him into a sleeping bag, he was nauseous and had vomited. After resting a while and sipping on a hot drink, he was able to descend the West Buttress with us. Subsequently he recovered uneventfully after a night's rest several thousand feet lower.

The above scenario occurred on my first trip to Denali in 1982. That was my first big mountain and I wasn't yet a doctor. In the eleven years that have passed since then, I have seen many climbers with altitude illness on big mountains in various parts of the world and I have returned to Denali several times to work as a doctor at the 14,000-foot medical camp on the West Buttress. I often reflect on that experience on the summit plateau in 1982 and wonder what would have happened if we had not been able to descend. In retrospect, the ill member of our group had severe acute mountain sickness (AMS) that was progressing to high altitude cerebral edema (HACE). If we had not been able to descend because of bad weather or because he had become incapacitated, it would have been imperative to have other treatment options at our disposal.

Descent is still the standard treatment for severe altitude illness, but other pharmacological options are available as an aid to descent or for use as definitive treatment when weather and terrain conditions preclude descent. Climbers need to be aware of the options for treating the spectrum of altitude illness from mild to severe because medical care is not immediately available on a high mountain in a remote area. Having the ability to recognize altitude illness in yourself or your partner, and having the knowledge of the appropriate intervention, may save a life. This article will present for climbers the most recent knowledge regarding pharmacological treatment of acute mountain sickness (AMS) and the more severe high altitude pulmonary edema (HAPE) and high altitude cerebral edema (HACE).

Acute Mountain Sickness. Acute mountain sickness is the most common form of altitude illness and is seen a few hours to a few days after ascent to altitudes over 2500 meters (8200 feet). In the milder forms, the symptoms include headache, dizziness, decreased appetite, nausea, difficulty in sleeping and decreased energy. Swelling of the hands and swelling around the eyes caused by fluid retention are also observed in some individuals. The milder form of AMS usually resolves within a few days if ascent is halted.

More severe AMS primarily affects the brain, but it may also involve the lung. A person may have difficulty with balance and walk as if he or she were drunk: a condition called *ataxia* in medical terms. This is due to increased swelling in the brain, called cerebral edema. When the amount of swelling in the brain becomes severe, high altitude cerebral edema results. In severe AMS, a person may also experience shortness of breath after minimal exertion. This is caused by a lower blood oxygen level than normal, which may be due to increased fluid in the lung that is interfering with the diffusion of oxygen from the lung to the blood. It is not yet known whether this represents a mild form of HAPE, but some individuals with severe AMS and shortness of breath do develop HAPE.

AMS is most certainly a precursor to HACE and may be a precursor to HAPE. Because both increased brain fluid and increased lung fluid occur in AMS, it is not surprising that as AMS progresses to more severe high alitude illness, HAPE and HACE sometimes occur together.

The best prevention for AMS is gradual ascent. Climbing high and sleeping low and limiting the rate of ascent to 1000 feet (300 meters) per day at higher altitudes are both effective in allowing the body adequate time for acclimatization. Gradual ascent may not be practical, however, during an alpine-style ascent of a higher mountain. In this case, a prolonged acclimatization period before the alpine-style ascent is recommended.

Acetazolamide (trade name Diamox) is the drug of first choice to prevent AMS and acts by increasing breathing and improving the oxygen level in the blood in individuals climbing to high altitude. Acetazolamide may be taken starting the day of ascent at a dose of 125 mg twice a day. This lower dose of acetazolamide (125 mg or half a 250 mg tablet) is recommended because recent studies suggest that it is as effective as the higher dose and will result in less diuresis (increased urination resulting in fluid loss). Acetazolamide should be continued during the ascent but may be stopped after one or two days at the same altitude. Upon further ascent, acetazolamide may be restarted again to prevent AMS at higher altitudes.

Acetazolamide is recommended for prevention of AMS in those individuals who experience symptoms recurrently upon ascent to high altitude. For individuals without a history of recurrent AMS on ascent to high altitude, acetazolamide may be taken prophylactically (to prevent AMS) or may be taken once symptoms occur to treat AMS. (See discussion of treatment of AMS below.) Many climbers prefer to continue taking 125 mg of acetazolamide prior to sleep at altitudes higher than 13,000 feet (4000 meters) because it prevents periodic breathing during sleep at high altitude. This breathing pattern disturbs the sleep of some individuals and results in periods of low oxygen levels in the blood during sleep for everyone. Acetazolamide should not be taken by those allergic to sulfa drugs.

Dexamethasone (trade name Decadron) is an alternative to acetazolamide for the prevention of AMS. The dose is 4 mg every 6 to 8 hours starting the day of ascent. Dexamethasone is a steroid and may cause many of the side effects of this class of drugs, including depression or euphoria, bizarre dreams and fluid retention. Dexamethasone is not an anabolic steroid, the kind used by some athletes to enhance performance. Unlike acetazolamide, the use of dexamethasone for more than a few days is not recommended because of more serious long-term effects of the drug (after weeks to months of use, weight gain, decreased bone density, and suppression of the normal hormone system occur.) Dexamethasone is a good option for prevention of AMS in those individuals allergic to sulfa drugs. One instance where a combination of acetazolamide and dexamethasone might be used for prevention of AMS is in rescue workers transported to altitudes greater than 10,000 feet (3000 meters) where more than one day at the higher altitude is anticipated.

Acetazolamide or dexamethasone may also be used to treat, as opposed to prevent, AMS. This means that the drug is not used until the symptoms of AMS occur. As for prevention, acetazolamide is the recommended drug for the treatment of AMS because of the fewer side effects and because it increases breathing, which aids in acclimatization. (The primary mechanism of acclimatization during the first few days at altitude is increased breathing.) The recommended dose for the treatment of AMS is 250 mg twice a day, higher than that recommended for prevention. The higher dose of acetazolamide will cause a greater fluid loss from urination, which may be beneficial. This is because fluid retention is part of the complex reactions in the body that lead to AMS. If increased urination requiring frequent trips out of a warm sleeping bag at night prevents adequate sleep, then a dose of 125 mg in the evening and 250 mg in the morning may be preferable for the treatment of AMS. When used for treatment, acetazolamide may be continued until symptoms resolve, then stopped and restarted again if symptoms recur at a higher altitude. Dexamethasone may also be used to treat AMS at the same dose as used for prevention, 4 mg every 6 to 8 hours, until symptoms resolve. An assured cure for AMS is descent to a lower altitude, which is recommended if symptoms progress suggesting the development of HAPE or HACE, but in mild to moderate cases, drug therapy will shorten the duration of illness and make further ascent possible. Analgesics, such as ibuprofen or acetaminophen and anti-nausea drugs are appropriate adjuncts to the therapy of AMS.

High Altitude Pulmonary Edema. I awoke from a restless night's sleep in our well-sheltered camp placed in the bergschrund at Windy Corner, an exposed area at 13,000 feet on the West Buttress of Denali. I felt weak and tired, as if I had the flu. As we packed up camp, I was breathing a lot harder than usual. Just shouldering my heavy pack was an ordeal and we hadn't gone far out of camp that morning before Kitty and John had taken the bulk of my load. The climbers' camp at 14,000 feet (4275 meters) was just a few hours away, but at the rate I was moving it would take us most of the day to get there. As we moved higher, I had to stop more frequently because of coughing episodes and to allow myself to gasp for more air. It was 1985, I was young and fit, and I had HAPE.

HAPE is a condition where the tiny air sacs in the lungs, called alveoli, fill with fluid, which impairs the diffusion of oxygen from the lungs to the blood. As my own case illustrates, HAPE is characterized by increasing shortness of breath both at rest and with exercise and a dry cough that progresses to a cough productive of a pink, frothy sputum. A climbing partner who is moving slower than usual, breathing with more difficulty and coughing may be developing HAPE. As the lung fluid increases, the affected individual may be able to walk only short distances without resting, and gurgling may be heard if the ear is placed against the chest wall. A purplish discoloration of the lips and fingernails caused by a low oxygen level in the blood may also be observed. Death may occur within hours if HAPE is left untreated.

The best treatment for HAPE is early recognition and descent to a lower altitude. At the first indication that HAPE is developing, descent should be undertaken while the individual can still walk, rappel or down-climb under his or her own power. Descent of as little as 2000 or 3000 feet (650 to 1000 meters) usually results in marked improvement and may be life-saving.

Oxygen, if available, is also an effective treatment for HAPE; 3 or 4 liters per minute should be administered via nasal cannula in milder cases, and 8 to 10 liters per minute administered via facemask in more severe cases. Experience treating climbers with HAPE at 14,000 feet on Denali suggests that treatment with oxygen for a few hours or overnight results in enough improvement so that the individual may descend on his or her own. An oxygen tank may also be placed in a pack for use while descending. A portable hyperbaric chamber (Gamow Bag) is also effective treatment for HAPE but should never be used in a situation where it delays descent. When an ill climber comes out of the Gamow Bag, he or she is still at the same altitude and HAPE may continue to progress. The most useful situation for a Gamow Bag or oxygen in treating HAPE is when descent is impossible because of weather or terrain conditions.

A recent development in the prevention and treatment of HAPE is the use of the drug nifedipine (trade name Procardia) that lowers blood pressure in the circulation to the lung. Nifedipine has been shown to be beneficial in preventing HAPE in those individuals who recurrently develop HAPE upon ascent to high altitude, and it has been shown to be effective in treating HAPE once it occurs.

Lowering the blood pressure in the circulation to the lung appears to decrease the amount of fluid leaking from the blood into the alveoli. Nifedipine, however, may also reduce blood pressure in the rest of the body to the point where an individual feels dizzy or might pass out. Because of these serious potential side effects, nifedipine should only be administered by a physician. Oxygen, if available, should always be used first to treat a climber with HAPE. Nifedipine might also be useful as a supplement to oxygen therapy in a climber who is incapacitated with HAPE and cannot descend. In this case, nifedipine might improve climbers with HAPE enough so that they can descend on their own. Nifedipine should not standardly be used to prevent HAPE either, except by those climbers who recurrently develop HAPE after ascent to altitude. Most climbers with a history of HAPE in the past, though, will not have recurrent HAPE on subsequent climbs if a gradual ascent is undertaken, and thus they do not need to take nifedipine.

High Altitude Cerebral Edema. High altitude cerebral edema should be suspected in persons who have progressive deterioration in their level of consciousness. Individuals with AMS who walk as if they were drunk and become increasingly confused and disoriented are developing HACE. Left untreated, HACE will progress from drowsiness to coma, and ultimately death. Immediate descent to a lower altitude is imperative in someone with HACE. Oxygen, if available, is helpful but is no substitute for descent. Dexamethasone is also helpful at a dose of 4 mg by mouth or injected intramuscularly every six hours. Although dexamethasone has never been studied in a controlled fashion in individuals with HACE, it is very useful in decreasing cerebral edema from certain causes in hospitalized patients. Isolated reports on the use of dexamethasone to treat climbers with HACE suggest that it has helped, and it is therefore recommended as a treatment for climbers with HACE.

* * * * *

Summary. Although various effective treatment options for high altitude illness have been discussed, there is no panacea. The best treatment for high altitude illness is still prevention, a gradual ascent allowing time for acclimatization. When altitude illness does occur, descent is the first treatment option that should be considered. In more severe forms of altitude illness, such as HAPE and HACE, descent is imperative if the conditions permit. Mild to moderate AMS, however, may be treated and resolved while staying at the same altitude. Of the drug treatment options available, acetazolamide and dexamethasone may be used to treat AMS. For HAPE, descent is the treatment of first choice, while oxygen or a portable hyperbaric chamber (Gamow Bag) may be used as a temporizing measure. In the right situation as judged by a physician, nifedipine is also effective treatment for HAPE. For HACE, immediate descent and the administration of dexamethasone are recommended, while oxygen may be used if available.

REFERENCES

1. Bärtsch P et al, Prevention of high altitude pulmonary edema by nifedipine. *N Engl J Med*, 1991, 325:1284-9.
2. Grissom CK et al, Acetazolamide in the treatment of acute mountain sickness; clinical efficacy and effect on gas exchange. *Ann Int Med*, 1992, 116:461-5.
3. Hackett PH, Rennie D, The incidence, importance and prophylaxis of acute mountain sickness. *Lancet*, 1976, 2:1149-1154.
4. Hackett PH et al, Dexamethasone for prevention and treatment of acute mountain sickness. *Aviat Space Environ Med*, 1988, 59:950-4.
5. Hackett PH, *Mountain Sickness: Prevention, Recognition and Treatment*. New York, The American Alpine Club, 1984.
6. Houston CS, *Going Higher: The Story of Man and Altitude*. Boston, Little, Brown and Company, 1987.
7. Larson EB et al, Acute mountain sickness and acetazolamide; clinical efficacy and effect on ventilation. *JAMA*, 1982, 288:328-32.
8. Levine BD et al, Dexamethasone in the treatment of acute mountain sickness. *N Engl J Med*, 1989, 321:1707-1713.
9. Oelz O et al, Nifedipine for high altitude pulmonary oedema. *Lancet*, 1989, 2:1241-4.
10. Schoene RB, Pulmonary edema at high altitude; review, pathophysiology and update. *Clin Chest Med*, 1985, 6:491-507.

Climbs and Expeditions, 1992

The Editorial Board is extremely grateful to the many people who have done so much to make this section possible. Among those who have been very helpful, we should like to thank in particular Kamal K. Guha, Hari Dang, Harish Kapadia, H.C. Sarin, Józef Nyka, Jerzy Wala, Tsunemichi Ikeda, Sadao Tambe, Taleh Mohammad, Trevor Braham, Luciano Ghigo, César Morales Arnao, Vojslav Arko, Franci Savenc, Paul Nunn, José Manuel Anglada, Jordi Pons, Josep Paytubi, Carles Capellas, Xavier Eguskitza, Elmar Landes, Colin Monteath, Claude Deck, Annie Bertholet, Fridebert Widder, Silvia Metzeltin Buscaini, Zhou Zheng, Ying Dao Shin, Karchung Wangchuk, Dolfi Rotovnik, J.D. Swed, Lloyd Freese and Tom Eliot.

METERS TO FEET

Unfortunately the American public seems still to be resisting the change from feet to meters. To assist readers from the more enlightened countries, where meters are universally used, we give the following conversion chart:

meters	feet	meters	feet	meters	feet	meters	feet
3300	10,827	4700	15,420	6100	20,013	7500	24,607
3400	11,155	4800	15,748	6200	20,342	7600	24,935
3500	11,483	4900	16,076	6300	20,670	7700	25,263
3600	11,811	5000	16,404	6400	20,998	7800	25,591
3700	12,139	5100	16,733	6500	21,326	7900	25,919
3800	12,467	5200	17,061	6600	21,654	8000	26,247
3900	12,795	5300	17,389	6700	21,982	8100	26,575
4000	13,124	5400	17,717	6800	22,310	8200	26,903
4100	13,452	5500	18,045	6900	22,638	8300	27,231
4200	13,780	5600	18,373	7000	22,966	8400	27,560
4300	14,108	5700	18,701	7100	23,294	8500	27,888
4400	14,436	5800	19,029	7200	23,622	8600	28,216
4500	14,764	5900	19,357	7300	23,951	8700	28,544
4600	15,092	6000	19,685	7400	24,279	8800	28,872

NOTE: All dates in this section refer to 1992 unless otherwise stated. Normally, accounts signed by a name alone (no club) indicate membership in the American Alpine Club.

Summits of the Seven Continents Climbed by Women. The first to succeed in climbing to the summits of all seven continents was 54-year-old Texan Richard Bass when he reached the top of Everest in 1985. He completed the "smaller" series, which included Mount Kosciusko, the highest in Australia. Canadian Pat Morrow made his last ascent, Vinson Massif, in 1986 and became the first to complete the "big series," which includes Carstensz Pyramid, the highest point in Australasia. Since then, more than twenty men have completed the achievement. It was not until 1992 that a female, 54-year-old Japanese climber Junko Tabei, scaled the highest point of all seven continents. On June 28, she ascended Carstensz Pyramid (Puncak Jaya). Her first conquest was in 1975, when she climbed Everest. This was followed by Mont Blanc (1979), Kilimanjaro (1980), Aconcagua (1987), McKinley (1988), Elbrus (1989), Vinson Massif (1991) and Carstensz Pyramid (1992). At the time of publication, it is likely that a second woman will have become the second woman to have completed the series. Dr. Christine Janin is now in Argentina, planning to climb her last, Aconcagua.

JÓZEF NYKA, *Editor, Taternik, Poland*

UNITED STATES

Alaska

Denali National Park and Preserve Mountaineering Summary, 1992. The 1992 climbing season on Mount McKinley was record setting in the number of climbers and mountaineering fatalities. This year marked the most intense period of rescue in the mountain's history. Twenty-two rescue or recovery missions involving 28 climbers were conducted by the Talkeetna ranger staff and volunteers. There were eleven fatalities in 1992, the largest number for any year to date. There have been 75 deaths on McKinley since 1932, and 72 of those have occurred in the last 25 years. Rescue costs incurred by the National Park Service totaled $206,000, double those for 1991. The military costs associated with the rescues was $225,345. This brings the total for search and rescue to $431,345. The National Park Service and the Korean Alpine Federation joined in an effort to reduce the high percentage of South Koreans involved in rescues which have occurred in the last two years. District Ranger J.D. Swed made a nine-day visit in November to Seoul, Korea, meeting with members of alpine and climbing clubs and climbing-school directors. He gave programs on the severity of the McKinley environment, difficulty of ascent and statistics involving Korean climbers. Swed stated that the Korean Alpine Federation is dedicated to educating Korean climbers who wish to attempt McKinley. A long-range plan to improve communication, education and to exchange climbers was proposed. The National Weather service accurately predicted in early May "the worst storm to hit the mountain in ten years." This brought in excess of 60 inches of snow at the 7200-foot Base Camp in a 24-hour period and winds over 110 mph at 14,000 feet! This halted most summit attempts for several weeks and brought about a number of rescues. Both guides and climbers assisted the mountaineering rangers at the 14,200-foot ranger station during these rescues, which were carried out under intense weather conditions. In the ten days from the start of the storm, seven people died and six were rescued. For the second year, the Aerospatile Lama helicopter, piloted by Bill Ramsay, was used for rescues, including a bold rescue of three Koreans at 17,700 feet on the Cassin Ridge. For the first time, short-haul technique was used for rescues when two Americans at 11,000 feet on the East Buttress were extracted. U.S. Army CH-47 Chinook helicopters were used to establish and remove the 14,200-foot ranger station. The 210th Air National Guard and Chinooks from Fort Wainwright assisted in rescue support. 11,070-foot Mount Spurr, 100 miles southwest of McKinley, erupted on June 27, causing glacier landings to be halted temporarily at the 7200-foot Base Camp. Expeditions beginning their climbs were informed of the possibility of walking out if the ash continued to fall on the glaciers, prohibiting landings. In the winter of 1991, data was collected from an automatic censor device placed near 19,000 feet above Denali Pass by the Japanese Alpine Club. This instrument monitored a low temperature of $-72.4°$ F on February 6, 1991. From November 1990 through February 1991, the temperature remained at $-60°$ F or colder for a total of 30 days. The wind-monitoring instrument was destroyed by high winds and those data were lost. The National Park Service conducted four 24-day patrols on Mount McKinley and numerous backcountry .and hunting patrols in the park. We continue to staff a ranger station in Talkeetna, where climbers register for their expeditions. Registration is required for all climbs and expeditions on McKinley and Foraker. Commencing in 1994, all climbers will be required to preregister by February 15 of the year they plan to climb. Climbers and backpackers planning trips into other areas are encouraged to register. A strong emphasis is set on maintaining self-sufficiency and on conducting self-evacuations whenever possible. Environmentally sound sanitation procedures are a high priority in keeping the pristine wilderness of Denali National Park and Preserve.

Interesting Statistics: In 1992, 1081 climbers of 291 expeditions from 23 countries attempted 10 different routes on McKinley. This is 133 more climbers than in 1991, and the most on record with a total of 19,028 user days. 73% (831) attempted the West Buttress. Americans made up the largest segment with 634 climbers (59%). The rest of the countries represented were Switzerland (68), United Kingdom (58), Germany (56), Japan (44), Korea (40), Canada (37), France (24), Italy (18), Austria (17), Australia (16), Norway (9), Mexico (8), Netherlands (8), Spain (6), Taiwan (6), Sweden (5), Scotland (4), China (4), CIS (3), Finland (2), Slovenia (2) and Argentina (1). [The five new routes done are described in the "Climbs and Expeditions" section.] *Acute Mountain Sickness:* 105 cases (10%) of climbers reported symptoms of AMS. 55 (52%) were mild, 40 (38%) were moderate and 10 (9%) were severe. *Frostbite:* 38 cases (4%) reported frostbite. 21 (55%) were mild, 11 (28%) required physician care and 6 (16%) required hospitalization. *High Altitude Pulmonary Edema:* 12 cases were reported, of which 9 were treated at the 14,200-foot ranger station with oxygen and advice to descend and 3 required hospitalization. *High Altitude Cerebral Edema:* 4 cases were reported of which 2 were treated on the mountain and advised to descend and 2 required hospitalization.

Accidents: *Frostbite, helicopter evacuation:* On May 6, Mountaineering Ranger Ron Johnson and Student Conservation Aide Keith Nicholson climbed from 11,000 feet to the 14,200-foot camp on the West Buttress of McKinley. The temperature was −15° F and the wind 30+ mph. Nicholson was wearing polypropylene glove liners and shell mittens. He contracted frostbite on his little finger and thumb of his left hand and on all finger tips of the right. A full recovery with no tissue damage has occurred. *Frostbite, AMS, HAPE, HACE, helicopter evacuation:* On April 25, Daryl Hinman, Robert Rockwell and Tom Roseman attempted McKinley from the Muldrow Glacier. Due to cold weather, altitude, high winds, fatigue, pulmonary edema (HAPE) and cerebral edema (HACE) and the loss of supplies, they became incapacitated at 17,500 feet below Denali Pass on the West Buttress side. On May 10, Hinman climbed down to the 14,200-foot ranger station for help. The National Park Service Lama helicopter picked up Ranger Johnson and VIP (Volunteer in the Park) Julie Culberson and flew to 17,200 feet, where they loaded Roseman and Rockwell into the Lama. Both had frostbite while Roseman suffered from pulmonary and cerebral edema. *Fall on headwall, helicopter evacuation:* Also on May 10, Paul Kogelmann and Timothy Hagan fell 500 feet down the headwall from 15,800 feet. Ranger Johnson and Culberson in the Lama landed at 15,200 feet and loaded Hagan into the helicopter, which flew to the 14,200-foot station to off-load Johnson and Culberson and pick up Roseman and Rockwell. The Lama then flew to the 7200-foot Base Camp. Roseman, Rockwell and Hagan were flown by fixed-wing aircraft to Anchorage. *Abandonment by fellow climbers, rescue by NPS ground team:* On May 10, Edwige and Frédéric Sement and Philippe Berthois spent the night at 17,200 feet without a stove. This had been cached at 16,200 feet on the West Buttress. On the afternoon of May 11, F. Sement and Berthois attempted to descend to 16,200 feet for the stove but turned back in the face of high winds and poor visibility. They decided to descend to 14,200 feet via the Rescue Gully and to return that evening to 17,200 feet. Because Mme Sement was too tired to descend, she was left at 17,200 feet, where there were no other parties. Sement and Berthois arrived at 14,200 feet, notified Ranger Johnson that they were too tired to climb back to 17,200 feet and that Mme Sement did not have a stove. A weather forecast predicted a severe storm. Johnson, VIP Matt Culberson and volunteers Mike Wood and Willy Peabody ascended the Rescue Gully. Mme Sement was found in her tent in good condition. The rescue team with Mme Sement descended to 14,200 feet. The expedition was issued a citation for Creating a Hazardous Condition and for making inappropriate decisions which exposed rescuers to life-threatening hazards. This expedition also reimbursed the NPS for rescue costs. *Fall on Cassin Ridge, fatalities, body recovery by helicopter:* On May 10, Italians Giovanni Calcagno and Roberto Piombe arrived at the base of the Cassin Ridge.

They intended to climb and descend the ridge in two or three days. On May 15, the NPS ranger station at 14,200 feet received a report that a body had been seen the day before at the base of the South Face. On May 16, Rangers Jim Phillips and Daryl Miller flew in the Lama to the South Face, where they recovered the body of Piombe. The body was sling-loaded to 7200 feet and flown out by fixed-wing aircraft to Talkeetna. Calcagno's body was located at 15,400 feet on the first rock band on the Cassin Ridge just off route. His body was not recovered. *Fall on South Face, aircraft evacuation:* On May 11, Koreans Song Seong-Woo and Lee Seung-Hwan were descending a new route they had nearly completed on the South Face. Due to bad weather, the pair had decided to descend to their Base Camp and wait. While rappelling, Song fell 1000 feet to the bottom of the South Face, on the east fork of the Kahiltna Glacier. Lee saw Song falling past him and assumes that the rappel rope broke. Song was found unconscious with a head injury. Another Korean party assisted in bringing Song to the 7200-foot Base Camp. Song remained semi-conscious, suffering from facial wounds and having respiratory difficulties. The Alaska Air National Guard, hampered by poor weather, arrived at 7200 feet on May 13 and evacuated Song to Anchorage. He remained hospitalized for three weeks, where he slowly regained consciousness. *Frostbite, AMS, helicopter evacuation:* On April 28, three Koreans flew in to climb the Cassin Ridge. They started with 15 days of food. By May 9, they had reached their high camp at 17,700 feet. They planned a summit attempt the next day, but strong winds made them decide to construct a snow cave. While working on that, their tent blew away with most of their food, fuel, clothing and climbing gear. To wait out the weather, for over a week they rationed themselves to one cup of rice and a quart of water a day. The weather finally improved, but they were too weak to continue in the cold and wind. The leader, Kang Hyun-Doo, had frostbitten fingers and AMS. They began distress calls, saying they had no food or fuel and that their leader had AMS. The weather remained poor and it was not until two P.M. on May 17 that the Lama could get to the 7200-foot Base Camp then to attempt an airdrop at 17,700 feet. The helicopter experienced extreme down-drafts and was forced back. When the winds subsided, the Lama departed with Ranger Jim Phillips aboard. The Lama landed and picked up one Korean and flew him to 14,200 feet, returning to pick up the climbers, one at a time. An Army Chinook delivered them to 7200 feet and a Pavehawk flew them to Anchorage. Kang suffered frostbite on all fingers and three toes. The other members had minor frostbite. *Crevasse fall, aircraft evacuation:* On May 17, in a whiteout Koreans Jang Duk-Sang, Kang Seong-Yu and Seo Dong-Choon at 15,000 feet on the West Buttress were preparing a campsite on a snow bridge, which suddenly collapsed. Kang and Seo fell 60 feet into the crevasse. Jang was uninjured and able to descend to 14,200 feet and notify Ranger Johnson. VIPs Matt and Julie Culberson and volunteers Jim Wickwire and John Roskelley were sent to the site. They found that the collapsed snow bridge had exposed a crevasse 40 feet wide, 200 feet long and 60 feet deep. They saw Kang in the bottom of it, buried chest-deep. Matt Culberson and Roskelley rappelled and dug Kang out. They also located Seo. Brian Okonek and Bruce Blatchley arrived with a sled litter. Seo was worked free and extricated from the crevasse. He was conscious, but hypothermic with suspected internal injuries, injuries to his lumbar spine and pelvis and lacerations to his tongue. He was lowered to 14,200 feet. Kang was uninjured. On May 18, a break in the weather allowed Seo to be flown to 7200 feet and to be transferred to a helicopter and flown to Anchorage. *HACE/HAPE fatality at 14,200 feet:* On May 17, a Swiss expedition was camped at 14,200 feet on the West Buttress. The expedition leader, Roli Merz, notified Ranger Johnson that a member was having difficulty breathing. Johnson and Matt Culberson were led to Alex von Bergen's tent. Von Bergen was cyanotic and his pupils were fixed and dilated. Johnson notified Dr. Mike Young, who arrived at the scene. CPR was initiated by Matt and Julie Culberson after a pulse was not detected. Von Bergen remained pulseless and unresponsive and was pronounced dead. The body was removed from 14,200 feet by the Lama and flown to Talkeetna. An autopsy determined that von Bergen had died from pulmonary and cerebral edema. *Fall on Orient Express, three fatalities, bodies removed by helicopter:* At midday on May 20, Koreans Yung Soo-Yang, Hong Sung-Tak and Jin Seong-Jong were killed when descending the Orient Express route. They had started their ascent on May 3 and in ten days had ascended to 14,000 feet. From May 14 to 17, strong winds kept them tent-bound. The weather improved on the 17th and they ascended to 16,200 feet. On May 20, the Culbersons discovered their bodies at 15,800 feet on the Orient Express. Their bodies were recovered by helicopter. *Crevasse fall, fatality, helicopter evacuation:* On May 4, Terrance "Mugs" Stump and his clients Nelson Max and Robert Hoffman began climbing the Japanese Ramp on the South Buttress. On May 20, Stump and Max reached the summit via the Southeast Spur in extremely adverse weather. Max suffered frostbitten feet on the descent. On May 21, Stump and his clients began the descent from the high camp at 16,000 feet on the ramp. First on the rope was Hoffman, followed by Max with Stump at the end. They came to a large crevasse. Hoffman stopped near the edge of it, unsure how to proceed. Stump approached from uphill, passing Max and Hoffman. He was standing on the uphill lip of the crevasse when they heard a crack and Stump suddenly disappeared into the crevasse, pulling on fifteen feet of slack rope between him and Max. Max attempted to self-arrest and was pulled about 20 feet before stopping. The rope between him and Stump went slack. Feeling uneasy on the uphill side of the crevasse, Max cut the rope and tied it to a ski pole. They traversed around and approached from below. Max rappelled into the crevasse but was unable to locate Stump. He described the debris as a large volume of very hard blocks of dense snow and blue ice. The crevasse was at least 60 feet deeper from the bottom of the large blocks wedged into it. Because of the perceived danger, their condition, the weather and the low probability of survival, Max and Hoffman abandoned their efforts to recover Stump. On May 21, another expedition heard distress calls from Max and Hoffman and got a message to the National Park Service. The pair suffered frostbite and were assisted to 11,400 feet. The Lama transported them to 7200 feet and thence they were flown by fixed-wing aircraft to Anchorage, where Max was hospitalized with frostbite on both feet. The Lama returned to the accident site with Rangers aboard. The crevasse was wedged with big chunks of snow and blue ice, as Max had described it. Because the accident had occurred 25 hours earlier and the exposure of the rescuers to excessive hazards, a recovery effort was not initiated. *Fall above Denali Pass, helicopter evacuation:* On May 28, Germans Gerhard Seibert and Christoph Mach ascended the upper West Rib. They decided not to make a summit attempt and to descend the West Buttress route. As they descended to Denali Pass, Mach was ahead when Seibert fell. Seibert suffered head lacerations and was unconscious. Mach set up a tent and began to call for help on their CB radio. On May 29, Ranger Daryl Miller and VIPs Billy Shott, Mike Abbott and Dr. Colin Grissom left 14,200 feet and reached the climbers at 19,400 feet. VIP Andy Lapkass had joined them at 17,200 feet. Seibert had regained consciousness but had double vision. Mach had a frostbitten left hand. The rescue team lowered the two climbers to 17,200 feet, where the Lama landed and took them to 7200 feet. A 210th Air National Guard Pavehawk flew them to Anchorage. *Fall on the Messner Couloir, four fatalities, body recovery by helicopter.* On May 31, Canadians Alain and Christian Proulx, Alain Potvin and Maurice Grandchamp fell about 3000 feet to their deaths from 19,300 feet in the Messner Couloir. They had left the 17,200-foot camp on May 30. They were not seen again until the next evening as they descended the summit ridge at 20,000 feet. The weather was deteriorating. Then the weather cleared and a search plane with Ranger Roger Robinson aboard took off. Robinson saw the four traversing between 19,200 and 19,300 feet on the Messner Couloir. Robinson notified Ranger Miller at 14,200 feet, who could view them with binoculars. Minutes later, the climber at the back of the rope fell, dragging the rest of them down some 3000 feet over the rock bands and through the hourglass of the couloir. They stopped above an icefall at 15,800 feet. A rescue team set out, but visibility was down to 25 feet and the snow unstable. On June 1, the visibility had improved and the rescue team reached the accident site. The Lama recovered the bodies using a grappling hook. *Avalanche on East Buttress, short-haul by helicopter:* On June 6, Bob Archbold and Allen Sanderson ascended from their 11,000-foot camp on the East Buttress. They finally decided to descend because Archbold was not comfortable with the route. While descending, they saw an icefall avalanche start at about 13,000 feet. This struck them and carried them down. Sanderson was uninjured and observed the slack rope below him reaching into a crevasse. Archbold had been carried 150 feet down and 60 feet into a crevasse. He managed to free himself and his pack and then jümar out of the crevasse. He had a bad head wound and lower leg pain. They descended to their 11,000-foot camp. Sanderson was able to contact a pilot with his CB radio. The NPS responded in the Lama and performed the first short-haul extraction to a staging area on the Ruth Glacier. It actually took less than three minutes from the 11,000-foot camp to the Mountain House on the Ruth. Both climbers were flown to an Anchorage hospital. *Avalanche on Mount Foraker, two fatalities, one self-evacuation:* [This is covered in the "Climbs and Expeditions" section.]

DENALI NATIONAL PARK AND PRESERVE
1992 MOUNTAINEERING SUMMARY

	Expeditions	*Climbers*	*Successful Climbers*
Mount McKinley			
West Buttress	213	831	429
Cassin Ridge	23	56	17
East Buttress	2	8	0
Muldrow Glacier	3	18	0
Muldrow Traverse	3	8	2
South Buttress	2	8	4
West Buttress Traverse	8	38	16
West Rib	31	90	47
Southwest Face	5	20	0
Pioneer Ridge	1	4	0
	291	1081	515
Mount Foraker	8	26	2
Mount Hunter	21	51	4
Mount Huntington	3	8	2
Moose's Tooth	8	21	2

Administrative Notes: A special recognition must be made to the VIPs and others who assisted in search-and-rescue missions. A portable radio repeater was once again installed in the Ramparts, west of the lower Kahiltna Glacier. This was an integral part of communications between the Talkeetna Ranger Station and the mountaineering patrols. For more information or to request mountaineering information and/or registration forms, please contact the Talkeetna Ranger Station, PO Box 588, Talkeetna, Alaska 99676. Telephone: 907- 733-2231.

J.D. SWED, SOUTH DISTRICT RANGER, *Denali National Park and Preserve*

McKinley West Buttress Variant. On June 11, Bruce Normand and I climbed a new variant on the right side of the southwest face of the Direct West Buttress. It involved twenty belayed pitches of water ice of Alpine Grade III. We completed the climb in 15 hours round-trip from the 14,200-foot camp on the West Buttress.

JACK TACKLE

Plate 45

Photo by H. Adams Carter

MOUNT FORAKER, showing Pink Panther Route. X = Accident.

McKinley South Face, New Route Attempt and Accident. On April 26, six South Koreans departed from the 7200-foot landing strip, heading for the south face of McKinley off the east fork of the Kahiltna Glacier. Over the next few weeks, they pioneered a new route between the Japanese Direct and the American Direct routes. They fixed rope to 15,600 feet on the new route. On May 10, Song Seog-Woo and Lee Seung-Hwan placed a camp at 16,300 feet. Due to a forecast of an impending storm, the lack of food and inadequate protection for the camp, they decided to descend to Base Camp. After descending some 3000 feet in five hours, Song suffered a rappelling accident and a 1000-foot fall but fortunately survived. The accident is covered above.

ROGER ROBINSON, *Denali National Park and Preserve*

McKinley Climbers' Memorial. A memorial dedicated to climbers who have died on McKinley has been established in Talkeetna, Gateway to Denali. Through the end of 1992, 75 mountaineers representing 13 nations have lost their lives on North America's highest peak, including a record 11 people last year. Another 20 have died on nearby mountains. Built by Ace Ebling, a retired Air Force sergeant who tends Talkeetna's cemetery, the climbers' memorial features a 30-foot-high cedar telephone pole painted white to symbolize McKinley's snow and ice. Two chainsaw-carved climbers complete with ice axes, crampons and rope are ascending the pole, which is topped by a raven figure. The finished product will also include a 10-by-24-foot mountainscape which shows McKinley, Foraker and Hunter as they appear on the horizon from Talkeetna. That mountain silhouette, also made from telephone poles and painted white, will be surrounded by a garden of forget-me-nots. A list of all who have died on McKinley and the surrounding peaks will be put on permanent display nearby. Those wishing to contribute to the upkeep of the memorial may send donations to the Talkeetna Cemetery Association, PO Box 38, Talkeetna, Alaska 99676.

BILL SHERWONIT, *Anchorage, Alaska*

Foraker Tragedy, Pink Panther Route. Our original plan was for Tom Walter, Ritt Kellogg and me to join forces on June 13 at the Kahiltna Base Camp to try an unclimbed route on Hunter, the ridge just south of its west ridge, which Walter had attempted two years before. Kellogg and I flew in on June 3. After reconnaissance, an unsuccessful attempt on Hunter from the west and some doubtful weather, we two were joined by Walter on the 13th as planned. We were all discouraged when we studied the unclimbed ridge. Ritt and I had had a good look at it while descending the west ridge. Two years ago, the crux for Tom had been getting to the base of the ridge up a heavily crevassed glacier. A new obstacle now presented itself; the glacial headwall exit off the ridge had turned into a broken icefall, possibly as a result of last summer's earthquake. We decided on the Pink Pather route on the east face of Foraker as an alternative.

Although much of the east face is exposed to avalanche danger from hanging glaciers and cornices, it seemed free from objective danger, would provide challenging mixed climbing and could be done quickly with bail-out options. On the evening of June 14, with six days of food we were below the S-shaped couloir at the foot of the face, but we waited there to see what the weather would do. By the morning of the 16th, three inches of snow had fallen, but we quickly climbed the 2000 feet of the couloir with running belays. The couloir ended with a rotten ice pitch and was followed by several rock bands. We put in two-thirds of the entire route before we dug in. On the night of the 16th, it snowed two more inches. We were able to make a break for it at midday on the 17th and pushed through a ridge section in a whiteout. The final obstacle was a long, steep rock buttress. Because clouds were obscuring the view, we dug in. By mid morning of the 18th, the weather improved. The demanding climbing went well. As we were finishing the technical difficulties, visibility decreased to 50 meters and the wind picked up. We had ahead the final exposed slope/ridge, 1400 feet of 60° to 65° ice, where the route meets up with the southeast ridge. Feeling strong, we continued with running belays, but discovered honeycombed, unprotectable ice. Digging in, bucket-seat belays or climbing unroped seemed unacceptable alternatives. Speed appeared to equal safety. For a couple of hours, we climbed steadily upwards, on ice all the way. The first I knew of the avalanche was when it hit me. According to the rangers, we were 200 feet below the southeast ridge; an ice axe was sighted here twelve days later from a helicopter fly-by. Tom Walter was leading and Ritt Kellogg was bringing up the rear. I don't remember seeing or hearing anything from either of them. Self-arrest proved useless against the overwhelming force of the avalanche. I was quickly flipped headfirst onto my back. I blacked out seconds later. We slid 1200 feet back to the top of the final buttress before the rope between me and Tom snagged on a rock. When I came to, it was morning, clear but windy. By now it was the 19th. I must have been unconscious for four to six hours. There was no sign of the avalanche; the slope was too steep and windswept. Tom was not far from me, the rope having caught near its middle. I worked my way over to him and discovered he was dead. His entire face was covered by a thick layer of snow, which could not be brushed away. His body was rigid and there was no pulse. Below him was evidence of considerable blood loss. I yelled in vain for Ritt whose rope disappeared over a steep section. In my present condition and the buffeting wind, I could not go to him. I replaced my lost left crampon with Tom's and struggled to remove his pack. I then cut the loaded rope and was shocked when Tom slid away. The only refuge in sight was a horizontal chair-sized rock 20 feet away. While getting there, I realized my left foot and shoulder were injured, my neck was stiff and my head ached. I slept not at all that day and night, anchored to my axes, with Tom's bag and bivouac sack. I knew I was hypothermic from my full-body shivers and I craved water. When the wind lessened, I emerged. It must have been the 21st. Equalizing my axes, I fixed the 7mm rope going to Ritt and rappelled down. He was 140 feet below, upside down, with his face hidden behind an armor of snow like Tom's. When I attempted to unravel Ritt's body

MOUNT HUNTER from the southeast. Foraker rises at the left.

from the rope tangle, it bounded down 25 feet and shock-loaded the static rope, yanking me off my feet. I pulled out the tent, fuel and food and drank the water. Securing the body to axes, I cut the rope and ascended. From Tom's pack, I grabbed food and fuel and stuffed it into mine. As I readied to begin the descent, I noticed my helmet had been shattered on the same side that my head ached and I left it behind. I had to descend the southeast ridge. There were glacier jumbles to negotiate, headwalls to rappel and traverses under hanging glaciers. With my injuries, it felt harder than it probably was. It took me four long periods of climbing, plus some rest and waiting for clouds to clear. Needless to say, my faith in God was being reaffirmed. I reached our skis just before the weather closed in for four more days and made it to Kahiltna Base Camp at five A.M. on the 24th. I had two things to do: I had to get a call to NOLS before Tom's wife, Lisa Johnson, flew in that evening and I had to get some sleep. I slept till noon and then hurried to the Base Camp manager's tent to inform her of what had happened. From that point on, I got caught up in a river of support from rangers, other climbers, NOLS, friends and family. I suspect the avalanche came from an isolated pocket of wind-deposited snow. No fracture line was visible later to the rangers in the helicopter. No snow had fallen on Foraker for twelve days, and the five inches that fell over the 48 hours before the accident had given us little cause for concern. The slope was ice and wasn't going to avalanche under our feet.

COLBY COOMBS, *National Outdoor Leadership School (NOLS)*

East Kahiltna Peak Attempt. On May 2, Jamie Kanzler, J.P. Gambetese and I began skiing up the east fork of the Kahiltna Glacier to the southeast face of East Kahiltna Peak (13,440 feet). What caught our eye was an S-shaped couloir toward the west end of the face that topped out on the south ridge. On May 7, we left our Base Camp at 9400 feet to ascend the couloir and to attempt the fifth recorded ascent of the peak. Less than 100 yards from the tent was a crevasse maze, and Gambetese plunged into a hidden one. An interesting evacuation followed. We started up the couloir. Kanzler led a pitch where the couloir necked down to an ice-filled crack in beautiful granite. Halfway up, suspicious windslab on depth hoar crystals forced us to deviate into mixed terrain over a rock tongue as the weather deteriorated.Our delays put us onto the south ridge at 11,800 feet at dusk in poor weather. We were able to dig a small snow cave in a small snow pillow to escape sub-zero temperatures, wind and snow. In the morning, we descended the south ridge, releasing windslabs, luckily none more than a couple of inches thick. A second attempt on May 10 also failed.

TERRY KENNEDY, *Dirty Socks Club of Montana*

Hunter, Southeast Spur Attempt, 1991. Jay Hudson, our pilot, dropped Jim Graham and me off on the seldom-visited south fork of the Tokositna Glacier on April 22, 1991. We believe that no one had been here since 1980 when Pete Athans, Peter Metcalf and Glenn Randall successfully climbed the incredible

PLATE 47

Aerial Photo by Bradford Washburn

Upper slopes of BARRILLE on the left and McKinley in the background.

southeast spur (*AAJ, 1981*, pages 22-28). Because of deep powder, no landings in eleven years and a drastically changed glacier, Jay needed a light plane. We had to fly in separately in Jay's Super Cub. Then, knee-deep powder and no skis or snowshoes provided a longer approach than anticipated. We were hoping to traverse the peak and descend the southwest ridge where Jay had planted a cache. Two days of slogging brought us to the couloir which leads to the crest of the spur. We had 14 days of food. From a waist-deep trench, we got to the firmer snow of the couloir. In the 1000-feet of step-kicking in 45° to 60° snow, we found some exposed fixed line probably left by John Waterman on the first ascent (*AAJ, 1979*, pages 91-97). Mixed pitches brought us to a spot on the ridge for our tent. The next day, Graham led a steep and overhanging dihedral (A1), time-consuming because of our scant rock rack. The following day, we prusiked the dihedral and climbed four more slow, difficult, mixed pitches. In near darkness, we chopped a ledge for our bivouac. The next part of the ridge was narrow, somewhat level and corniced. In heavy powder snow, we didn't need crampons but a snowblower. Without any exposed ice, we couldn't even pretend to protect the thin, airy climbing. We headed back to our last ledge. That night, we awoke to a shaking, trembling world. I grabbed the rope which linked us to a large rock horn and held on. Suddenly it stopped. We poked our heads out and watched the cirque fill with powder from all the snow and ice avalanches tearing down the slopes. Avalanche debris covered the glacier below for several miles. Our campsite was covered by huge ice chunks. The couloir we had climbed had a huge cone of debris at its base. We learned later that the epicenter of the 6.4 earthquake was 40 miles away from us. We began a series of blind rappels down the west side of the ridge. Except for one snow anchor, we used our expensive rock anchors. Several times, all we could find on these vertical cliffs was a single nut placement. On the glacier, we headed back to our now buried airstrip. Excellent walking on the avalanche debris let us travel in a few hours what had previously taken several days. With no radio and with poor flying weather, we sat in the tent for three days before Jay spotted our message stamped in the snow and picked us up.

MARK KIGHTLINGER, *Unaffiliated*

Hunter, Barrille and P 6000+. Julie Brugger and I made the third ascent of the north buttress of Hunter to the summit via the Stump route. It was in excellent condition during the nine days it took to climb it. We summited on June 3. We took another five days to descend the west ridge in bad weather. We then made the second ascent of the 1988 Austrian route on the east face of Barrille in two days, reaching the summit on July 4. The route was of good quality except for the entire section between the first and second towers, which was either rotten or under a watercourse. We also climbed a new route on P 6000+, the small wall a half mile north of the east face of Barrille (III, 5.10c). This 8-pitch route is easily accessible from the Mountain House and climbable during marginal weather when bigger things may be out of shape.

ANDREW DE KLERK, *Mountain Club of South Africa*

PLATE 48

Aerial Photo by Bradford Washburn

MOUNT HUNTER from the north.

P 9070. On April 20, David Barlow and I made the first ascent of P 9070, southwest of Mount Hunter. We made a glacial approach to the west of a small icefall on the north side and then an ascent to the col separating this peak from Thunder Mountain. From there, we ascended the east ridge to the summit. This was our second attempt as our first attempt was repulsed by a storm.

GEOFF HORNBY, *Alpine Climbing Group*

Huntington, West Face, Count Zero Route. The ascent of a difficult new route on the west face of Mount Huntington by Clay Wadman and Bruce Miller is described in a full article earlier in this *Journal.*

Mount Brooks, Northwest Ridge. From August 21 to 23, Clarice Dickess, Ian McRae, C. Michele Morseth and I climbed the northwest ridge of Mount Brooks. Starting from the Traleika Glacier, we gained the ridge via a 1700-foot couloir, thereby bypassing some rock towers. The ridge steepened until a 45° ice face led to a good bivouac on a prominent shoulder. On the upper part of the ridge, we encountered a loose rock band. The northwest ridge offers a more challenging alternative to the popular north-ridge route, which we used for the descent. We had a magnificent concert of howling wolves on the approach, a horrific wind on the hike out and, most significantly, the booming sound of Mount Spurr erupting 200 miles away on the eve of the climb. Apparently, the acoustic wave from the eruption was echoing off the upper flanks of Mount McKinley.

RANDY WAITMAN, *Alaskan Alpine Club*

Kichatna Spire, East Buttress. On June 9, Koreans Yu Hak-Jae, Shin Dong-Seok and Han Tai-Il completed a new route (VI, 5,10, A3) on the east face of Kichatna Spire. The 4500-foot high face had excellent cracks and chimneys. There was severe rockfall in the first 650 feet and a difficult, slightly overhanging chimney filled with ice and snow near the first bivouac site. They took nine days to do the climb. The other members of the party were Lee Bong-Yoon, Shin Sang-Man and Kim Jung-Bo.

Mount Steller, Eastern Chugatch Mountains. In 1991, our expedition, shortened by weather delays on the fly-in and awed by the complexity of the route, had diverted away from Mount Steller and we instead made the first ascent of P 8263, eleven miles to the north. On May 18, 1992, we flew over the vast icy wilderness of the Bagley Icefield toward Steller. Paul and John Claus landed Bob Jacobs, Gil Anderson, Mark Bowling and me at 7250 feet on a tributary of the Steller Glacier, below the northwest ridge of Steller. The next day, we found and gently crossed a bergschrund on a snow bridge and gained an arête which led steeply to the ridge at P 8761. From the ridge we were treated to spectacular

PLATE 49

Photo by Robert Wesson

Northwest Ridge of MOUNT STELLER.

views of the Gulf of Alaska, the Bering Glacier and our first sight of the summit ridge of Steller and the icefall guarding its western flank. The following day, we retraced our steps and camped at 8550 feet. Our third climbing day found us heading along the northwest ridge, using pickets to protect the steep climb to P 10,096. Beyond the peak, the ridge broadened, allowing access to the upper glacier west of and below the summit ridge. The next day, we repeated the climb up the ridge, crossed a tricky schrund and dug in a high camp on the upper glacier at 9650 feet. A rest day was followed by four days of snow, wind and zero visibility. Finally, at noon on May 27, the sky cleared and we reconnoitered the crux of the climb, the steep snow-and-ice west face. Later, at camp, our dinner was interrupted by the roar of an avalanche sweeping the face below the summit ridge, 100 yards south of our route. Early the next morning, we gingerly retraced our steps. Rising above a schrund, the 500-foot face gradually steepened from 45° to nearly 60°. Protecting with pickets, deadmen and a screw, we gained the airy crest of the summit ridge and climbed to the summit at 8:30 A.M. on May 28. We planned for our descent the next day but awoke to falling snow. At midnight it cleared. The descent was marked by one crevasse fall, thigh-deep snow on the arête and a rappel over the changed schrund at its base.

ROBERT WESSON

P 6520, Lake Clark National Park, 1991. During a three-week stay in Lake Clark National Park, on August 7, 1991 I climbed P 6520 by the east ridge. The rock was very loose near the top. The peak lies about two miles east of the northeast corner of Two Lakes. Bad weather and high water at river crossings prevented other ascents.

DANIEL BLODGETT, M.D.

Mount Hajdukovich, Delta Mountains, Alaska Range. Almost 22 years to the day of the first ascent, twin parties converged on the top of Mount Hajdukovich to achieve the second ascent of the north summit and the first of the slightly higher south peak (2926 meters, 9600 feet). We started on March 14 by flying out of Sawmill Creek east of Delta for a ski landing near the peak. However, weather separated the group into two climbing teams. The northern party of Stan and Carol Justice, Tad Fullerton and Franz Mueter began their ski approach from the woods at 2000 feet on the Little Gerstle River. The southern party of Ken Leary (married to a Hajdukovich descendant), the author and Hank, a 70-pound Siberian husky, started from 5500 feet on the Gerstle Glacier. We skied with sleds down a little icefall to the glacier confluence at 4000 feet. We cached skis and sled before heading east up a snow ramp paralleling the unnamed glacier that drains the south basin of Hajdukovich. We camped at 6580 feet alongside an icefall that avalanched the following morning. That day, March 16, we hurriedly curved through the basin's crevassed ice-steps, cramponed up a rocky snow slope to the 8200-foot col and traversed over a steep dome to climb the south ridge onto the main summit. In extremely rare perfect weather, we had climbed a new route on the peak in five hours from camp. But already there, to our amazement, were Justice and his party, who had just ascended from camp at 6000 feet on the north side to repeat the first-ascent route to the north summit and had then traversed over the top of the impressive east face to make the main summit's first ascent. That party descended its ascent route. We others retraced our steps, keeping Hank on the rope as "middleman." His special canine harness saved him twice in crevasse falls. By late on March 18, we had descended back to the Gerstle Glacier and skied 25 miles out its valley to the nine-trestle Gerstle River Bridge of the Richardson Highway, meeting all kinds of skiing conditions. Justice's group remained on the mountain on March 17 to climb a 40° snow-and-ice rib on the north face of Hajdukovich's north peak. We were privileged to make these new climbs in the memory of a multi-talented native of Montenegro who had come into the country as a guide, trapper and pioneer more than 80 years ago. A Yugoslav flag unfurled on the summit went to the Hajdukovich family still in Fairbanks.

PHILIP S. MARSHALL

Bona and Churchill, Wrangell-St. Elias Mountains. A considerable number of people have been climbing in the Bona-Churchill group. Dave Custer believes that a total of 22 climbers in five separate parties attempted Bona in May and June, of whom some 15 reached the summit. In early June, Custer's group, consisting of John Arnason, Suzanne Lorenz, Tamar More, John Rhodes, Frank Ziegler and himself, was landed by plane on the Kutlan Glacier at 10,000 feet and camped at 12,000 and 14,500 feet. Despite doubtful weather, they climbed Bona, Churchill and the prominent bump southeast of Churchill, often called Churchill's Chin.

Ice Climbing above Nabesna, Wrangell Mountains. On April 2, Harry Hunt and I drove to the town of Nabesna, north of the Wrangell Mountains, to climb several frozen waterfalls we had scouted in January when we had snowshoed up canyons to check out possible routes. We had discovered several Grade III, IV and V climbs, but the weather on the earlier trip was too cold for ice climbing (−25° to −35° F). In April, the days were longer and the temperatures warmer (0° to −7° at night and up to 25° in the daytime). The canyons we climbed in did not get any sun. All the climbs were on hard, boilerplate ice, sometimes brittle and hollow. We arranged to stay in a log cabin in Nabesna, with a wood stove. We walked down a hard-packed snowmobile trail to the east side of White Mountain to look at three climbs. Our main objective was a two- tiered waterfall up in a narrow canyon a short hike from the cabin. It was about 200 feet high. The lower curtain was a 100-foot pitch of Grade III or IV ice depending on the line taken. This brought us to the crux: a 65-foot section of vertical ice with a couple of ledges 30 feet up. At the top of the last steep step were 40 feet of rambling Grade II or III ice below a snow gully. The ice in the crux was candlesticked, hollow and brittle. We rated the climb Grade V. Just to the right is a Grade III or IV ice curtain, which Harry led up the center and then on the right. On April 4, we drove back down the road to milepost 36.5. We had seen ice in a hidden canyon to the south. It was a hard two hours across the valley and up a narrow stream gorge to the climb on the right up the canyon. The lower part consisted of three 15- to 25-foot sections of Grade II or III ice. Then a snow slope took us to the base of a 40-foot-high, free-standing pillar, easier ice for 20 feet and another steep curtain of candlesticked ice. The lower pillar was about six feet wide and three feet thick. If you hit the ice with your tools, it produced a sickening hollow sound. The upper steep section was sustained vertical ice for 40 feet and fun to climb after the lower pillar (Grade V). There are at least ten climbs in the area that range from Grade II to V. More ice will probably be found but be harder to get to.

DANNY W. KOST, *Unaffiliated*

Mount St. Elias Ascents and Attempts. A number of expeditions entered the St. Elias Mountains via Yakutat. Eleven expeditions with 43 people climbed in Wrangell-St. Elias National Park or Glacier Bay National Park. Only four groups and ten climbers were successful. This is on a par with the average success rate in the area, caused predominately by the weather. The unpredictable and highly wet, windy, snowy conditions make difficulties. An early March expedition to Mount St. Elias was stopped by snowfall of 25 to 30 feet in a ten-day period. Another party never made it out of Yakutat because of the weather and flew south after waiting for five days. After starting on March 3, Alaskans Dave McGiven, Leo Americus and John Bauman gave up on the east ridge of St. Elias when new snow turned the climb into an exercise of survival. Englishman Dean James and Scot Alex McNab on May 22 successfully climbed St. Elias by its south ridge. A commercially guided group led by George Dunn failed to get up St. Elias by its south ridge, but all eight reached the summit of Haydon Peak. Tom Hafnor, Bobby Derry, John McKinney and Jim Chisolm hoped to climb St. Elias but the air taxi was unable to get into the area. They opted for Mount Logan instead, but weather kept them from the summit there. Some of the other expeditions in these two parks are described below. Climbers are invited to contact the National Park Service Yakutat District Ranger Station. They are encouraged to submit a voluntary registration form for climbs. For forms or other information, please contact National Park Service, Yakutat District Ranger Station, PO Box 137, Yakutat, Alaska 99689. Telephone: 907-784-3295.

RICK MOSSMAN, *Wrangell-St. Elias National Park and Preserve*

Death of Pilot Mike Ivers. Mike Ivers, owner of Gulf Air Taxi and the pilot for most of the expeditions in this area, died in a plane crash on July 29. He was attempting to haul rafting parties and their gear out of Glacier Bay National Park. He was alone in the plane at the time of the accident. He will be missed by the climbing and rafting community.

RICK MOSSMAN, *Wrangell-St. Elias National Park and Preserve*

Mount St. Elias as a Coastal Peak. Mount St. Elias (5489 meters, 18,008 feet) is *much* nearer the ocean than before. The Tyndall Glacier has retreated into a newly created fjord and tidewater is only twelve miles from the summit of St. Elias. The glacier has retreated well over six miles since I photographed it in 1938.

BRADFORD WASHBURN

Mount Tittmann, St. Elias Mountains, 1991. Mount Tittmann (3525 meters, 11,565 feet) was probably the second-highest, named, unclimbed mountain in Alaska. The few climbers who had seen it had considered it ominous and forbidding. It sits within seven miles of the Canadian border, just north of the Chitina Glacier and 30 miles northwest of Logan. It was named for O.H. Tittmann (1850-1938), a former International Boundary Commissioner and a leader of some of the early USGS boundary survey parties that explored the US-Canadian border. In the fall of 1990, I flew to a small landing strip near the Canadian border and hiked alone up the Ram Glacier to reconnoiter. During my first night at high camp, I got a foot of new snow. The second night saw three feet of snowfall. However, I did pick a possible route up the west face of Tittmann to where it joined the southwest ridge at about 10,500 feet. I hiked out in a rainstorm with avalanches roaring down both sides of the Ram Glacier canyon. In June, 1991, I guided a St. Elias Alpine Guides group of four to attempt the route. Our high camp was at 7800 feet near the base of the route. Steep snow and ice led to the bergschrund at 9300 feet. From there it was mainly 45° slopes steepening to 70° to under the huge cornice at the top of the face. We traversed left under the cornice and up over several séracs to reach a small basin under a rock tower at the ridge junction. Because of the weather, this was our high point at 10,500 feet. After the failure in June, Bruce Blatchley and I flew to the Ram Glacier landing strip at 2500 feet on July 28, 1991. It took two days to hike up the rock-covered Ram Glacier to high camp at 7800 feet. Despite doubtful weather, on the 31st we kicked steps to 8800 where the route steepens. At 5:30 A.M. on August 1, we started back up the route. From the end of the steps at 8800 feet, the snow was thigh-deep, wet, unstable snow. The final pitch under the cornice again involved tunneling through soft snow. Finally, at 1:30 P.M., we reached the basin below the rock tower and rested. At 3:30, I crossed the bergschrund under the tower on a snowbridge, which disappeared in a puff of snow. I fell only a few feet and did a back-flip out of the schrund. I had to find a new snow bridge. I picked a tricky ramp of hollow ice and crusty, layered snow to the left. The first fifty feet were on vertical ice and then the angle eased to 70°. I climbed to a corniced sérac with a curtain of icicles hanging from it. I broke off icicles to crawl upward, swung out over space, and eased my way around the corner, hanging on my ice tools with no protection. I climbed the final eighty feet to the cornice on crusty, loose snow and through it to the ridge crest. It took us five hours to reach the summit and return along the corniced ridge in a whiteout with high winds. The descent was tricky and we finally reached our high camp at 8:30 A.M. after a 27-hour summit day.

DANNY KOST, *Unaffiliated*

Fairweather Ascent and Lituya and Crillon Attempts. On May 21, Scot Alex McPherson and Brazilian Adriano Petrachi completed the ascent of Fairweather by the Carpé route. Also members of the party were Alaskan John Thompson and Canadian Keith Carter. Germans Urban Gebhard, Fritz Rodun and Günter Zimmermann made an unsuccessful attempt on the southwest ridge of Lituya. Dave Williamson, Jayson Faulkner, Kevin and Jim Haberl failed in their attempt on Crillon's north ridge.

RICK MOSSMAN, *Wrangell-St. Elias National Park and Preserve*

P 12,300, Fairweather Range. A full article appears earlier about the ascent of P 12,300 from the Pacific Ocean to the Grand Plateau and then to the summit.

Washington—Cascades

Colchuck Peak. On August 9, Keith Hertel and I did a new but unpleasant route on the clean-looking face and slabs on the east face of the northeast buttress of Colchuck Peak, left of the standard northeast-buttress route. We climbed the Colchuck Glacier almost to its top directly below the northeast summit. Scrambling led up to the slabs, but they consisted of rotten rock. We kept going up and left for 500 feet until a jam-crack and open-book let us get onto a wall on the left side of the face. Steep climbing up cracks, short walls and large loose flakes led to a small roof, after which the hard climbing ended. Five hundred feet of easy fifth class led to the northeast summit. We placed one bolt. (IV, 5.10d, A0.) Colchuck's west face gave much better climbing. On October 11, after an approach via Mountaineer Creek, Donna McBain and I did this climb by a large gully which splits the bottom half of the left face of a large yellow wall. The crux was a steep section of cracks and ramps on the right side of the gully which led to easier slabs above. The upper 700 feet are broken, offer variations and end in a beautiful amphitheater of pinnacles just below the summit. (III, 5.8.)

STEVEN C. RISSE

Katsuk Peak, North Face Couloir. On May 3, my brothers Gordy and Carl and I climbed a 1200-foot couloir that splits the left side of this face. We made running belays by looping slings around horns, but some of the anchors were

PLATE 50

Photo by Bart O'Brien

**Peter Cummings approaching
previously unclimbed Sierra Towers.**

questionable. Snow flukes, rock protection or second ice tools would have been useful. At the top of the couloir, we swarmed up 60° powder snow and then squeezed through a narrow slot to pass a cornice. We scrambled along the south side of the west ridge to reach the summit, which offered great views of the North Cascades. (II, Class 3.)

LOWELL SKOOG

California

Climbs in the High Sierra. The publication of R.J. Secor's *Climber's Guide to the High Sierra* stimulated both a significant amount of new-route activity and a reporting of older routes that were omitted from the new guidebook. Among the new routes done in 1992 were four previously unclimbed summits east of Morro Rock in the Angel Wings-Hamilton Dome area of Sequoia National Park. There is a tremendous amount of unclimbed granite in the region. The climbing possibilities are certainly more extensive than in many other better-known Sierra climbing areas, including Bubb's Creek, the Gorge of Despair and Glen Aulin. Peter Cummings and I spent several days climbing the following new routes: *Granite Creek Dome*, identified as P 9326 on the Triple Divide Peak quad, is three miles south of Hamilton Dome. The route follows the west ridge (5.6). We also ascended three spectacular towers on the south side of Eagle Scout Creek and shown on the Triple Divide Peak quad collectively as *P 9550*. We named the central tower "Periscope Dome." The route is five pitches long and begins on the east side, just left of a big chimney. A 5.7 face leads up to a bushy ledge at the base of an overhanging chimney. This short 5.8 pitch leads to a blocky ledge which we followed around to the south side of the dome, where a 5.6 ramp leads to a steep 5.9 jam-crack. From there we proceeded north to the spectacular summit block. We descended via two rappels down the east ridge. We also climbed *Eagle Scout Creek Dome,* the largest tower on this side of the canyon. Numerous excellent crack systems exist on this formation. The first-ascent route follows easy corners on the left side of the east face. Two pitches of 5.5 flakes lead to the summit ridge, which may be scampered along to the high point. *Eaglette Pinnacle* was the final summit done by Peter Cummings and me in June of 1992. This 200-foot spire can be ascended via a 5.7 off-width on the west side. It is located between Periscope Dome and Eagle Scout Creek Dome.

The following routes were all completed over the last several years, but the information has just filtered in. *Cockscomb Peak*, east face of South Tower (I, 5.10a): Rick Cashner and Alan Swanson completed this route in September, 1987. The climb begins at a knobby 5.10 crack that leads to a pedestal. The second pitch follows a wide curving crack to the summit bulge, which is overcome by a thin 5.9 crack. *Eichorn Pinnacle,* Erratic Route (III, 5.10a): Cashner and Swanson climbed this route in September, 1991. It begins up a ramp of grainy rock (5.8) to the base of a low-angle, right-trending corner. The short second pitch follows the corner to a steep, left-facing dihedral (5.4). Sustained 5.10a climbing up the dihedral leads to an exit on the right above a large, loose flake. This is followed by a nice pitch up a thin crack (5.8) to a ledge beneath a knife-edged ridge. The crest of the ridge is followed (5.6) to the base of a flake with a wide crack. The last pitch climbs the wide crack (5.9) and continues along the ridge, bypassing gendarmes, to the summit. *SAR Dome*, west face (II, 5.10c): This summit, 1.5 miles southwest of Wildcat Point near Tuolumne Meadows, was first ascended in September, 1990 by Alan Swanson and Urmas Franosch. It is best approached from California Falls. The four-pitch route climbs the obvious dihedral on the west face. The first pitch is the crux, but each of the four pitches has some 5.10 climbing. Protection up to four inches is needed. *Blacksmith Peak,* far right side of northwest face (III, 5.10d): Swanson and Franosch made the first ascent in September, 1990. It climbs slabs on the right side of the face to a thin curving crack that leads over a bulge. The route continues up a flaring crack to a corner with a scary roof. This second pitch ends in a prominent dihedral. It wanders up and left over loose flakes to a belay. A short pitch leads to the base of an overhang, which is bypassed by a poorly protected, difficult layback to a belay in a corner 40 feet above the overhang. Two more pitches lead to a long dihedral, followed by a short headwall. Above this, a knife-edged ridge leads to the summit. *Santa Cruz Dome*, southwest face (II, 5.9): This lies 1.1 miles north-northeast of Tokopah Falls. It was first climbed in 1980 by Alan Swanson, Nick Badyrka and Val LeCon. It begins up a 5.7 chimney to the base of a smooth ramp, which is climbed past two bolts. The third pitch features some wild overhanging chicken heads to a steep face. The last pitch continues up the face with two bolts to the rounded summit. *Cheba Spire,* (II, 5.9+): Alan Swanson and Corey Hicks made the first ascent in August, 1988, climbing three pitches on the south face. *Carson Peak,* Saint's Way (5.9): The first ascent was made in April, 1992 by Dean Rosenau and Doug Nidever. They climbed snowfields from the base of the northwest face to the Y-shaped couloir, followed the left branch of the couloir and climbed the upper narrow chute that splits the headwall above. They followed the crest of the ridge to the summit. *Fin Dome*, east face, left side (I, 5.6): Rick Spitler, Don Spitler and Kevin Babitch made the first ascent in August, 1975. They started on the left side of the face, traversed up and right to a left-facing corner and climbed the corner to a large ledge in the middle of the face. One more pitch led to the top. *Painted Lady,* west rib (III, 5.7): David Babitch and Rick Spitler climbed this nine-pitch route up a prominent rib on the right side of the peak when it is viewed from Rae Lakes. They started up the center of the rib and emerged onto the west face after four leads. They continued up the face as directly as possible to the summit. *Horse Creek Tower,* northwest face (II, 5.8): Alan Swanson and Rich Kropp first climbed this route in July, 1985. The tower is a half mile north of Matterhorn Peak. The three-pitch route is marked by a prominent guillotine flake at the top of the second pitch. *North face* (II, 5.7): In May, 1975, Dean Gillman, Don Spitler and David Babitch started just to the left of the center on the north face and climbed three pitches of assorted cracks and corners to the top.

BART O'BRIEN

Cragtree Crags, East Summit, 1991. Extending west from Mount Chamberlain and above both Crabtree Lakes is a long ridge containing a number of faces, arêtes and buttresses. Just west of the scree-filled gully that separates Mount Chamberlain from this ridge is a face, marked with two very prominent lines. Several hundred feet down and right from these wide fissures is a Yosemite-like crack system that runs from fingers to fists. The system ends abruptly below obvious overhangs about 200 feet off the ground. The third pitch skirts the overhang on the left and continues up loose orange rock to a belay in a chimney dihedral. Three-and-a-half more pitches lead directly to the east summit of the Crabtree Crags. Dave Harden and I climbed this wall in July, 1991.

BART O'BRIEN

Mount Chamberlain, Mount Whitney Area; Incredible Hulk, Little Slide Canyon; Outguard Spire, Little Slide Canyon. In September, Julie Brugger and I climbed a new route to the left of the Fiddler-Harrington route on the north face of Mount Chamberlain (V, 5.11a; 13 pitches.) The line follows the dihedral and thin-crack system on the left side of the wall. We found two rappel bolts on the first two pitches. In August, we two climbed what we think is a new route (IV, 5.10a; 10 pitches) to the left of "Positive Vibrations" on the west face of the Incredible Hulk in Little Slide Canyon. Exact details about climbs on the wall seem sketchy; whether ours was new or not is irrelevant because of the quality of the climb. We climbed cracks and corners up an obvious cracked break on the right side of the wall. We rappelled the route. Also in August, Julie Brugger and I climbed a new six-pitch route (III, 5.10c) up cracks a few feet to the right of the southeast arête of Outguard Spire, also in Little Slide Canyon. We descended the southwest arête en rappel.

ANDREW DE KLERK

Bath Mountain, Tulainyo Tower and Mount Whitney. In September, Kenn Kenaga and I climbed a new route up the south side of Bath Mountain, just left of the southeast buttress. Low on the south face are two dihedrals; our route started on the left one above a small formation at the base of the wall (where we also did some one-pitch routes naming it "Bath Dome.") We exited from the dihedral to the left on the fourth pitch and climbed to the top of a shoulder. Third-class climbing led up and right to the base of an east-facing headwall, which we climbed in its center for three or four more pitches to the summit. The first pitch on the headwall was the crux. (III or IV, 5.10a.) In July, Steve Untch and I made what we believe is the first free-ascent of the east-face direct on Tulainyo Tower, one of the finest we have done in the Sierras. There are several difficult off-width cracks, with the crux on the fifth pitch. One needs some extra protection in the 3" to 4" range. (IV, 5.10d.) In September, Bruce Binder and I climbed what we believe is the first free-ascent of the old Direct East Face on Mount Whitney.

There was previously only one aid pitch, and the gear is mostly fixed in this section. (IV or V, 5.10d.)

PATRICK BRENNAN

Third Pillar, East Edge of Mount Dana Plateau, Tuolumne, 1990. In September, 1988, Miguel Carmona and Eric Klosterman climbed the first three pitches of this line on the pillar, which is drawn on page 47 of Reid and Falkenstein's *Rock Climbs of Tuolumne Meadows.* There were no signs of other climbers on these pitches and no bolts at the base of the headwall, where they turned back, not having enough gear or time to attempt the headwall. Carmona, a Spaniard living in Los Angeles, came back with me in September, 1990 and we reclimbed the three pitches. Upon arriving at the headwall, we found two anchor bolts at its base and another bolt 30 feet higher. The bolts were close to a good crack and not necessary. The line up a thin knifeblade crack showed no signs of having been climbed. At the top of the fourth pitch, we found two more anchor bolts close to a good piton crack. There is a drilled hole higher up the pitch. We continued up the line and completed the pitch to the base of the summit tower. Two more pitches of 5.9 mixed with aid got us to the top. (IV, 5.10b, A2+.) The route starts up a right-slanting ramp just right of the obvious dihedral at the base of the pillar. We are not sure if the first ascent was done previously. We don't claim ours to be the first and we don't know who placed the five bolts. The line is very esthetic and worth doing.

ALOIS SMRZ

"Four O'Clock Rock," 1991. In June of 1991, we did a route on the rock buttress north of the north buttress of Three O'Clock Rock, for which we suggest the name, "Four O'Clock Rock." We reached it via the Square Creek Pass Trail. The route begins on the extreme right edge of the formation and follows cracks and seams, with occasional face moves, on the right side of four pitches. The third pitch has two variations and the last pitch finishes in a widening crack with a small tree in it. Protection is bolts, small camming devices and nuts. (II, 5.10b.)

ROBERT COBB *and* SCOTT PRESHO

P 3129, Northeast Buttress. On November 7, Chris Breemer and I arrived at the base of Mount Morrison to find its north face out of condition, or at least out of condition for us. Rather than to go home without accomplishing anything on such a warm fall day, we decided to attempt a route on P 3129 (10,266 feet; .7 mile northwest of Morrison). We chose the easiest looking line, the northeast buttress, and climbed seven rock pitches of varying looseness and difficulty, the hardest being 5.4. The fourth and fifth pitches are the highlight of the climb as

PLATE 51

Photo by Steve Porcella

**Cameron Burns on the CORN DOG,
Arches National Park, Utah.**

they cross an extremely narrow arête not visible from below. There is roughly 1000 feet of air on either side. Most of the route is somewhat loose 4th class.

JOHN M. CLIMACO

Utah

Corn Dog, Park Avenue, Arches National Park. On December 20, Cameron Burns and I climbed the Corn Dog in the Park Avenue area. The tower sits on an extremely narrow, sandy base. While we were on it, we had the feeling it might topple over at any moment. A pitch of 5.6, A1 was required to reach the base of the tower. The tower had no true cracks and the rock was extremely soft, typical of Arches sandstone. Drilled baby angles and a few 5-inch bolts allowed us to pat the summit with our hands. We dared not stand on the summit because it was composed of loose sand. (II, 5.6, A1.)

STEPHEN PORCELLA

New Mexico

New Routes in New Mexico, 1991-3. In January, 1993, I made several new ice climbs around Questa, New Mexico. Luke Laeser, Mike Lyons and I climbed *Eskimo Pie* (II, WI 4+/5, A0; 3 pitches), one of the finest ice routes in the state. It rises above Highway 38, opposite the Moly Corporation Mine. We three then climbed a one-pitch route, *Hershey Squirts* (I, WI 4+). The second pitch never formed enough ice to allow climbing. Then Michael Horan and I climbed *Droplet* (I, WI 2) on the north side of the highway. Unreported from March, 1991 was the first ascent of *Church Rock* (II, 5.9+; 2 pitches), a prominent New Mexico landmark, by Mike Baker, Bob Rosebrough and me. Later, on the second ascent, Rosebrough placed two drilled angle pitons on the second face pitch, which were not used during the first ascent. Laeser and I climbed the tower *King Rudi*, near Ghost Ranch, on April 18, 1992 after several days of effort (III, 5.8, A2). Laeser and I made what we believe was the first ascent of *Bennett Peak*, (III, 5.8, A1) in the Four Corners area on August 8, 1992. Our route started up a gully on the west side of the main summit of this huge plug south of Shiprock. We then rappelled into a couloir and climbed a pitch to the three main summits. The peak is described in Herbert Ungnade's *Mountains of New Mexico.* Last year, I reported a route by Baker and me on Ford Butte's south summit. The first ascent of the north summit had been made by Mark Dalen and a partner in 1971. Laeser and I climbed the first route on the east side of *Venus Needle* in September, 1992 (III, 5.9, A2+; 2 pitches.)

CAMERON M. BURNS

Idaho

He Devil Peak, East Ridge, Seven Devils Mountains. On July 24, I climbed He Devil Peak by following the crest of the east ridge from the He Devil-She

PLATE 52

Photo by Steve Porcella

Timebinder (IV, 5.11) on the PROW
Bitterroot Mountains, Montana.

Devil col to the summit of He Devil. Three short fourth-class chimneys were encountered, the last of which was blocked by an overhanging chockstone. My route is a delightful scramble and offers a much more enjoyable way of reaching the summit than the regular east-ridge route. The latter, as described in the guidebook, is little more than a talus trudge.

WALT VENNUM

Montana

Lost Horse Buttress and Unnamed Tower, Bitterroot Mountains. Five separate attempts were made on this route before it was finally completed. Most were foiled by bad weather. Rod Sutherland began this route on the south face in July, putting up eight pitches. We started between two large rock flakes that lie on the lower apron of the buttress. Six pitches of thin, often run-out 5.8 slab climbing gained a small ledge below the prominent dihedral on the headwall. The seventh pitch was a full rope-length of 5.0 to 5.7 climbing and traversed west up flakes to a small belay stance protected by a bolt and a pin. The next pitch started off with 5.9 face climbing, followed by some thin crack A2, an east-slanting flake-and-crack system and finally ended at a bolt and pin belay stance on a 2-inch ledge. In August, Bruce Anderson and I regained the high point just as we were hit by a cold, rainy Montana storm. Rather than to rappel nine pitches that involved a now dangerous, wet traverse, we decided to continue on. Bruce led the ninth pitch (5.8, A2), which traversed to the right and up good flakes and cracks to a large ledge. I led the 10th pitch, which followed up a shallow, crackless corner to an east-facing wall with a good crack. An exposed eastward traverse brought us to the crux of the route, a large overhanging roof with widely spaced, marginal placements (A2+). After turning the roof, we continued up to a bush and then to the east and to a belay on a small sloping ledge. The last, short pitch went through a second smaller roof, traversing west and then east over loose rock to gain the plateau on top. (IV, 5.9, A2+.) In September, Rod Sutherland and I became intrigued with a crack that split the major roof of the Unnamed Tower. The first pitch (5.8) started up a rotten, blocky gully. The second pitch moved onto the face and ascended steep rock with thin, discontinuous cracks (5.10). The third pitch (5.8) followed up a corner to a large tree. The fourth pitch, the crux, went up a left-facing corner and through the roof, which I led over, following shallow, poorly protectable cracks (5.10s-R) up the face to a right-facing corner system. We traded leads for the last three pitches of 5.8 crack climbing to finish the route. (IV, 5.10c.)

STEPHEN PORCELLA

The Prow, Bitterroot Mountains. In unusually dry weather, I spent eight days finishing the first free-ascent of the 900-foot south face of the Prow. With the help of Steve Porcella and later Ralph Grana, *Timebinder* (IV, 5.11) links four different routes put up in four different decades. We started left of a white alcove near the center of the base of the spire. The first pitch face-climbed a bolted slab (5.9+) to a crack up and right and to a stance near a large ponderosa. Then a short pitch up a wide crack led to a comfortable ledge. The third pitch headed up another bolted slab (5.10) to a shoulder just right of large roofs. In the middle of this slab is a seam. The intimidating 300 feet above the shoulder had never been attempted and provided Steve and me with difficult route-finding. The fourth pitch diagonaled left (5.9) above the roofs up a series of right-facing corners past a tooth of rock. From the top of this tooth, we climbed through a small roof with cracks (5.10) to a ledge. The fifth pitch ascended a steep bulge to the right (5.10) and then a series of exposed finger-cracks. We belayed on a ledge 20 feet above the final thin finger-crack. The next pitch climbed the right of the Red Tower (5.10), which received its first free-ascent by Bruce Anderson and Keith Schultz in 1988. At the top of the Red Tower, we connected with the original ascent line on the spire, put up in 1977 and 1978 by Tom Shreve, Cory Macalnay and Pete Herbine. Above the tower, we climbed the slab with cracks (5.9), turned the roof on the right and belayed on a ledge. The final pitch was a vertical headwall of orange granite. We started up a strenuous flake (5.10+) to reach a good hand-and-finger crack which ends at a band. We traversed left to a finger-crack which bulges at its end (5.11). We then traversed right on an exposed ledge to belay in a notch near the summit. To descend, we scrambled north and then walked off to the east.

CRAIG KENYON, *Dirty Socks Club*

Wyoming—Wind River Range

Mount Hooker. After a previous unsuccessful attempt on Mount Hooker's northeast face, Craig Luebben and I hiked from Big Sandy Lodge into Hailey Pass. On August 30, we made a complete girdle-traverse ascent of Mount Hooker. A perched block on pitch 3, an exciting arête switch on pitch 5, a thin tip layback led masterfully by Craig on pitch 8, the crux 9th pitch (5.12−) and an amazing summit hike the width of the wall on Der Major Ledge comprised the highlights of the ascent. The route ascends a right-leaning ramp for two pitches to the start of the large left-facing dihedral on the left side of Hooker's northeast face. The route then follows this dihedral (or just to its left) for six pitches until it meets Der Minor Ledge. A difficult, heel-hook traverse followed by a classic left-facing dihedral leads to Der Major Ledge. This ledge, a couple of feet wide at first, narrows and then expands to Winnebago-size as one traverses to the summit.

TIM TOULA, *Exum Mountain Guides*

New Fork Lakes Buttress, 1990. About six miles up from the New Fork Lakes Trailhead lies a large south-facing granite wall to the left above the trail, visible from the road driving into New Fork Lakes. I have heard it referred to as the China Wall. Left of this wall and split by a gully sits a smaller, unnamed buttress.

On September 13, 1990, Jacob Valdez and I put up a nice four-pitch route. We climbed steep talus to the start of the route, a finger/hand crack splitting a face just left of a left-facing dihedral. The first pitch is the crux. The remaining three pitches round off the day with interesting 5.9− to 5.10+ climbing for a total of 500 feet.

TIM TOULA, *Exum Mountain Guides*

CANADA

Yukon Territory

Mount Logan, Altitude, Ascents, Attempts. Using GPS equipment, a joint Royal Canadian Geographical Society, Geological Survey of Canada and Canadian Parks Service determined that Mount Logan is 5959 meters or 19,545 feet tall. The 1992 climbing season was characterized by generally poor weather during the spring. The arctic low pressure system brought high winds, cold and more than average precipitation during March, April and May. The rest of the climbing season experienced fairly normal weather. Twelve expeditions were on Logan's King Trench route, half of which were successful. From May 10 to June 15, Mike Schmidt led the Geological Survey of Canada expedition, which worked on determining the height of Logan and placed ten members on the summit. The other members were Lisel Currie, Sue Gould, Leo Nadeau, Charlie Roots, Roger Laurilla, Karl Nagy, J.C. Lavergne, Pat Morrow, Lloyd Freese, Rick Staley, Kevin McLaughlin and Al Bjorn. Canadians led by Steve Smaridge climbed from May 17 to June 6. Two reached the west summit or Prospectors Peak and one made the main summit. Other Canadians led by Dwayne Congdon were on the mountain from May 21 to June 6, two also reaching Prospectors Peak and one the main summit. From May 24 to June 12, Americans John Halloran, Bill Hoyt, Rob Michaels, John Watson, Paul Fotinos and Dean Morrison completed the ascent. Americans Jack and Tom Bennett, Warren Grill, Jefferson and Jerrold Wagener, Dave Peterson, Greg Borges, Ihor Zalubniak and Mauro Conzatti reached the summit in June. Also in June, Alaskans Jim Sayler, Larry Hartig, Dolly Lefever, Tom Bringham and Judith Terpstra climbed to the top. Three expeditions were on the east ridge. Canadians led by Robert Tomich got to 5000 meters in May. An international group on June 1 placed Swedish leader Peter Fredman, Swedes Mårtin Källström, Nils Mörck and American Craig Hollinger onto the east summit. From May 17 to June 5, Canadians Hugh McReynolds, Fred Richie, Anthony Meier, Robin Janfield, Danny Denkowycz, Michael Friar, Michael Perkins, Joseph McCauley, Jim Brian, Randy Huber, J.A. Oakes, K. Deroche and Mike Vattheuer all got to the east summit. Italians Claudio Kerschbaumer, Mauro Girardi, Paolo Ribiani and Nello Fontanella attempted a variation to the west of Hummingbird Ridge from

May 14 to 23. Two of the team managed to get to 4725 meters before getting stranded and requiring a helicopter rescue.

ANDREW LAWRENCE, *Kluane National Park Reserve*

St. Elias, Kennedy, Queen Mary, Peak East of McArthur and Steele Attempts. Alaskans John Bauman, Dave McGivern and Leo Americus attempted a winter ascent of Mount St. Elias via the Abruzzi route from the Newton Glacier from March 4 to 23. Due to extreme snow accumulation, they were forced to retreat from 3350 meters. Mike Fischesser, Bill Proudman, Diana McAdams, Joe Lackey and Nej Mulla attempted the east ridge of Kennedy from April 28 to May 10 but failed because of bad weather and deep snow. Soft snow prevented Britons John and Lauriann Owens, Gregory Davies, Ian Clarke, Dominic Williams, W.S. Hotten and John Westerman from climbing Queen Mary from the north from July 3 to 16. Canadians Jim Elzinga, James Blench, Don Serl, Phil Whelan, Ron Van Leeuwen, Phil Schmitt and Glen Roane attempted an unnamed peak east of McArthur from June 6 to 17. The expedition was cut short when two members were injured in a fall into a crevasse. From April 7 to 21, Canadians Paul Langevin, Steve Oates, Mike Wynn, Chris Bradley and I attempted to climb Steele via the south and southeast ridges. High winds, cold and deep snow forced us to retreat from 4100 meters.

ANDREW LAWRENCE, *Kluane National Park Reserve*

Point 465 179 on McArthur, East Ridge. On May 18 and 19, Grant Stathem and I climbed a new route on the south buttress of Point 465 179 on the east ridge of McArthur. We had 5000 feet of very pleasant climbing on good granite with little objective danger (V, 5.9, A2, ice up to 70°). Despite appearances, the route was relatively easy with only 15 pitches needing belays. Careful route-finding up ramps, ice hoses and the odd boulder problem avoided most of the imposing steep walls. Combined with a straightforward descent down the east ridge to a glacial basin on the south, this is a highly recommended acclimatization route before heading for Logan.

BRUCE KAY, *Canada*

Peaks in the Upper Donjek Glacier Area, St. Elias Mountains. In June and July, 13 members of the Toronto Section of the Alpine Club of Canada enjoyed 16 days of continuously perfect weather amid the mountains that surround the upper Donjek Glacier. These peaks, ranging from 3300 to 3700 meters, form the divides between the Kluane, Kaskawulsh, Hubbard and Donjek Glaciers. Previous mountaineering was limited to brief forays by the Arctic Institute of North America (AINA), its predecessor, the Icefield Ranges Research Project (IRRP) and Parks Canada personnel, whose ascents are noted below. We placed Base Camp at 2800 meters on the Donjek Glacier. We climbed 17 peaks, 14 of them first ascents and the other three by new routes. Some of the peaks involved

PLATE 53

Photo by Bruce Kay

Point 465179 in McArthur Group, Yukon Territory. Ascent was up gullies on the left; descent was in the right couloir.

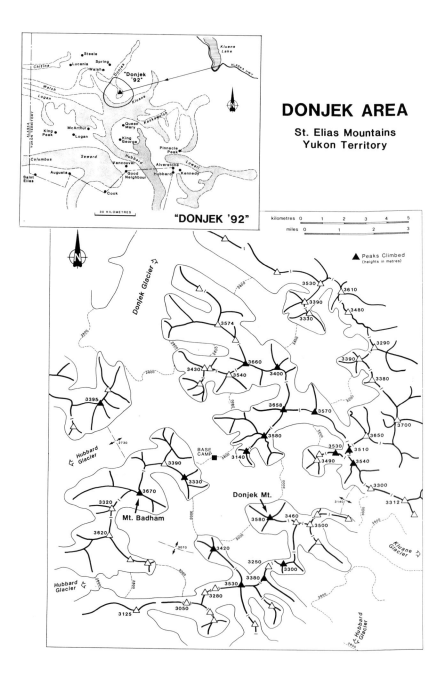

DONJEK AREA

St. Elias Mountains
Yukon Territory

"DONJEK '92"

excellent mountaineering. The northwest ridge of Donjek Mountain, Mount Badham's east face, the north and east ridges of P 3658, the northeast ridge of P 3580 and the southeast ridge of P 3660 were especially attractive. These ascents had interesting approaches, involving technical climbing, to reach the ridges, which themselves required thoughtful work so that the climbs did not deteriorate into "epics." There are many challenging ridges for future parties. Our party consisted of Paul Geddes (PG), Don Hamilton (DH), Willa Harasym (WH), Yan Huckendubler (YH), Wally Joyce (WJ), Mark McDermott (MM), Bill McKenzie (BM), Gary Norton (GN), Joe Piccininni (JP), Glynis Peters (GP), Rob Rick (RR), Ted Rosen (TR) and Roger Wallis (RW). We and our predecessors made the following ascents, all of which were firsts except where noted: *Mount Badham* (3670 meters), first ascent on July 24, 1972 via southwest ridge by Gary Gray, Gail Ashley, Joe LaBelle; second ascent in May, 1988 by a Parks Canada party including Lloyd Freese and Andrew Lawrence via north ridge from the col with P 3390, gained from the east; third ascent on June 28 via Parks Canada route by PG, WH, TR, GN; fourth ascent on July 3 by a new route, the east face and southeast ridge by BM, RW, YH, GP; fifth ascent on July 3 via Parks Canada route by RR, MM, JP; *P 3395* on July 9 via southeast ice face by BM, RR, YH, GP; *P 3330* on June 28 via south ridge by RW, DH, WJ, BM, YH, GP, RR, JP, MM; *P 3420* on June 27 via northwest ridge by TR, GN, PG, RW; second ascent on June 30 via same route by YH, GP, WJ, RR, MM, JP; *P 3530* in 1964 from IRRP station at 8400 feet on the Kaskawulsh-Hubbard divide by the long south ridge that joins the northeast ridge at about 10,000 feet by Gerald Holdsworth, Fred Erdmann; second ascent on July 10, 1972 via west ridge by Ashley, Gray, LaBelle, Denis Soloman, Susan Krieckhaus; third ascent on July 4 via north approach to east ridge by RW, DH; fourth, fifth and sixth ascents on July 5, 6 and 8 via the same route by PG, WH, BM; TR, GN; and GP, YH, RR; *P 3380* on July 8 via north approach to southwest ridge by WJ, DH, GP, YH, RR; *P 3300* on July 3 via northwest ridge by GN, TR; *Donjek Mountain* (3580 meters), first ascent in mid-August, 1965 from IRRP station on the Kaskawulsh-Hubbard divide via southern approach to east ridge by Takeo and Kikuko Yoshino; second ascent on July 21, 1966 from IRRP camp to central south rib by David Bittenbinder, Donald Stockard, David Johnston; third ascent on June 30 via northwest ridge by RW, BM; fourth and fifth ascents on July 1 and 5 via same route by PG, WH; and TR, GP, YH, RR, JP, MM; *P 3540* on July 6 via northwest ridge by PG; *P 3510* on July 2 via north ridge by YH, GP; *P 3530* on July 4 via east ridge by TR, GN; *P 3570* on July 1 via south slope and east ridge by GN, TR; *P 3658* on July 1 via east ridge from P 3570 by GN, TR; second ascent on July 8 via north ridge gained from west by BM, PG, RW; *P 3580* on July 6 via northeast ridge gained from east by BM, PG, RW; *P 3140* on July 7 via southwest slope and south ridge by WH, PG, WJ, GP, YH, TR; second ascent on July 7 via northeast ridge gained from east by RW, JP; *P 3400* on July 2 via a rib on the south slope by BM, PG, WH; *P 3660* on July 2 via southeast ridge from P 3400 by BM, PG.

ROGER WALLIS, *Alpine Club of Canada*

Mount Steele, North and South Gemini Peaks, Crag Mountain, P 10,478, Mount Sulzer, P 11,000, P 10,400, P 8590, P 8335 and Traverse from Kluane Lake, Yukon Territory to Chitistone River, Alaska. Betty Fletcher, Markus Kellerhals, Peter Stone and I arrived at Kluane Lake on May 4. We approached Doug Makkonen of Trans North Turbo Air for placement of our food caches. When the weather cleared, he would come find us, pick one of us up and place the food caches. We set off. Doug in his helicopter located us on the evening of the third day and and placed the caches with Kellerhals. With packs on our backs, we had set off from the Alaska Highway at Kluane with a foot of new snow on the ground. We skied along a track into the bush that parallels the Donjek River for 10 or 15 kilometers. The days that followed found us sometimes skiing, sometimes sledding, sometimes walking, other times wallowing along the Donjek valley to the junction with Steele Creek. We skied up Steele Creek and onto the marginal moraines of the Steele Glacier. On May 14, we moved out onto the Steele Glacier and arrived at the foot of the east ridge of Mount Steele and our first food cache the next day. Six days later, we stood on the summit of Mount Steele (4975 meters, 16,322 feet). After a day's rest at the camp at the base, we headed up the Hodgson Glacier. We crossed the next day to the Trapridge Glacier. Unfortunately we then had to descend to the rubbly Hazard Glacier before a gentle climb brought us to the junction with the Wood Glacier. A marvelous descent, below the icy flanks of Mount Wood, led us to the Brabazon Glacier. We skied up the Brabazon to the foot of a small, broken glacier lying below and east of the Gemini Peaks. We ascended this until it became a collapsing mass, spent a day storm-bound and then broke out once again into high country via a snow gully. That afternoon we climbed both North and South Gemini Peaks (3360+ and 3421 meters, 11,024+ and 11,224 feet). The next day, May 30, we arrived at the Nesham Glacier and our second food cache. The following day, we skied down the Nesham to the Klutlan Glacier. Back to ice and rubble, we made our way to Camp 23 below Crag Mountain. We ascended Crag Mountain (2793 meters, 9162 feet). The next day more skiing, in surroundings that can only describe the beginning of time, took us across the Alaskan border to our third and final cache. With ten day's food and supplies, we continued through séracs, wandering past turquoise pools, until we got to vast tracts of smooth glaciers that if followed would lead to the base of Mounts Churchill or Bear. We left the Klutlan by heading north via a small unnamed glacier and reached the head of the Russell Glacier. We climbed P 10,478 from here and then descended 2000 feet. At last in the land of big, deep, safe snows, we spent the next couple of days peak-bagging. The first day saw us up Mount Sulzer (3330 meters, 10,926 feet) and the 11,000-foot peak three miles south-southeast of Sulzer. The following day, after a snowy start, Stone reclimbed P 10,478 and Kellerhals and I set off to climb P 10,400 seven or eight miles south of Sulzer, a marvelous looking peak. We climbed the east ridge to the summit, switching back and forth from one side of the corniced, haystacked ridge to the other, a short but breathtaking climb. On June 9, with crazy-carpet sleds in tow, we effortlessly glided eleven miles to the junction of the main branch of the

Russell Glacier. From here it was easy traveling, under the watchful presence of Castle Mountain to Chitistone Pass, heather, color and smells. The following day dawned beautiful and although we were tired, we headed off and climbed P 8590 and P 8335, three miles south of the pass. On the 11th, we carried skis for all but 15 minutes. The hike down from Chitistone Pass to Chitistone Gorge was most definitely one of the highlights of the trip. Our senses responded to every smell, color and sound. The crossing of Falls and Toby Creeks provided some intensity to the final day, June 12. An ice bridge just below the Chitistone Glacier made crossing the Chitistone River easy. However, just five minutes after we were all across, the old ice collapsed. We stared at each other, knowing that this late in the season we should have gone up onto the glacier and not taken the chance. We crossed Toby Creek just before lunch and were picked up by Gary of McCarthy Air.

DAVID E. WILLIAMS, *Alpine Club of Canada*

Mount Steele. In June, Bertrand Poinsonnet, James Larabee, Steve Tyler and I repeated the 1937 Washburn-Bates route which leads from the Dennis Glacier to the broad ridge between Steele and Lucania. We skied 13 kilometers from our landing east of the peak, establishing at 10,200 feet a camp below the route, which is essentially a rib of ice of moderate to low angle on the south side of Steele. After putting in camps at 12,200 and 14,200 feet, we were easily able to climb Steele. We then put a camp below Lucania's northwest face, hoping to finish our objective the next day. After five days of poor weather, we left without much of an attempt. During correspondence with Brad Washburn, I became aware of confusion about the 1937 route. A much-used Canadian map, commemorating the centennial, shows several routes. It is in error, marking the south-southeast ridge as the Washburn-Bates route. That ridge leads directly to the summit of Steele. The original route, more to the south, does not. It is possible, due to the map, that the Washburn-Bates route had not been repeated for 55 years.

WILLY HERSMAN

Mount Manitoba, First Ascent. During the 1967 Canadian Centennial Celebration, a range of unclimbed peaks was found in Kluane National Park and given the name of the Centennial Range. Twelve were named after the provinces and territories of Canada, and a further one was called Mount Centennial. The largest peak in the area, on the border with Alaska, was named Good Neighbor Peak in recognition of the friendly relations between the USA and Canada. The Alpine Club of Canada spear-headed an ambitious attempt to climb all these peaks by organizing an enormous expedition of over 60 climbers, who were transported into this remote area by plane and helicopter. The expedition was a tremendous success with many fine first ascents. Five of the peaks, including Mount Manitoba, were not climbed, mainly because of bad weather and dangerous conditions encountered during the nearly 24-hour daylight in July. (See *Canadian Alpine Journal, 1968,* and *Expedition Yukon,* edited by Ed. M. Fisher, 1972. The *Canadian Alpine Journal, 1992* has a fine summary article about climbing in the St. Elias Mountains, which includes this area.) On May 17, 1992, in the 125th year of the Canadian Confederation, climbers from the Manitoba section of the Alpine Club of Canada made the first ascent of Mount Manitoba. We eleven members were dropped off by ski plane on the Logan Glacier at 60°48′N, 140°29′W, on May 9. We traveled six days to reach Base Camp at 60°57′N, 140°47.7′W along a previously untraveled route along the Logan, Walsh and Prairie Glaciers. (The 1967 party was dropped by helicopter close to the base of the mountain.) We first crossed to the Walsh Glacier, continued for three days on the south and then the north side of the Walsh Glacier and finally ascended seven kilometers for two days up the inappropriately named Prairie Glacier, which is anything but flat. Base Camp was in a stunningly beautiful location at the junction of four glaciers and surrounded by Mounts Centennial, Ontario, Manitoba, Saskatchewan (still unclimbed) and Alberta. The first attempt at night on May 15 in bad conditions almost ended in disaster when four of the party were swept down the slope for 300 feet by an avalanche. They tumbled head-over-heels over old hardened avalanche debris but only one person was injured, a broken rib. The successful attempt started from Base Camp at five P.M. on May 16, again in light snow. After we waited four hours in a snow cave, the weather cleared and we started ascending a prominent couloir on the southwest face at 10:30 P.M. This is probably one of the routes attempted in 1967. The couloir led straight to the summit, but the last pitch was very steep with dangerous sugar snow held in place by a thin sun-melted crust. The successful climbers were Tibor Bodi, Dr. Robert France, Pat Dillistone, Jeffrey Aitchison and I. A second attempt on the same route was turned back by dangerous accumulations of snow in the couloir.

PETER W. AITCHISON, *Alpine Club of Canada*

Hubbard. American Peter Videler, and Netherlanders Imke Grijpma, Bart van der Meulen and Martine de Bruyne climbed Hubbard via the Cathedral Glacier from July 4 to 21.

ANDREW LAWRENCE, *Kluane National Park Reserve*

Canadian Rockies

Waterfall Climbs, Canadian Rockies. On March 22, I made what is perhaps only the second on-sight solo of the formidable Canadian Rockies' alpine waterfall "Slipstream," taking four hours for the Grade V ascent. Marc Twight made the first on-sight solo in the winter of 1988-9. Earlier in the season, on December 24, 1991, I made an on-sight solo of a route on the Upper Weeping Wall, referred to in the *Canadian Alpine Journal, 1992* on page 80 as "Nasty Habits-Left," attributed to "unkown climber(s), winter 1991/2." My route followed the initial 100 meters of steep thin ice of Nasty Habits and then, after a snow bench, ascended the large ice flow 100 meters left of Nasty Habits (IV, 4+, 200m). I also made what is probably the first on-sight solo ascent of Bourgeau Lefthand, which overlooks the Sunshine Ski area (IV, 5, 185m). Barry Blanchard had soloed the route in the winter of 1990/1, but had, I believe, previously climbed the route roped up. On December 22, 1991, I made an on-sight solo of Lower Weeping Wall Right-Hand (III, 5,125m). While soloing Canadian waterfalls has become more common, these solo ascents are rarely on-sight efforts, i.e. the climber confronts the route not having climbed it roped with a partner. The rehearsal removes a psychological barrier for the soloist. Conversely, the on-sight soloist faces the unknown and must learn its charac-teristics while climbing alone and unroped. I feel that, given the technical edge today's climbers have gained through ultra-modern ice gear and training, on-sight soloing of established lines conserves the elements of adventure and commitment.

ROBERT CORDERY-COTTER

Petrie and Peaks at the Headwaters of Ovington Creek, Hart Ranges. From August 1 to 8, the British Columbia Mountaineering Club organized a climbing camp in the Hart Ranges of British Columbia's northern Rocky Mountains. Eleven climbers were helicoptered to the headwaters of Ovington Creek. During the first half of the trip, the party made the second ascent of Mount Petrie by a new route, the glaciated northwest face, and climbed P 2470 (8104 feet; 2½ kms west of Petrie) via west ridge, P 2750 (9022 feet; 3½ kms north of P 2470) via south ridge; and P 2800 (9186 feet; 5 kms northwest of Petrie) via south face and ridge. All the unnamed peaks appear to have been previously unclimbed and were class 2 or 3 rock scrambles. Bad weather prevented any further climbing.

MICHAEL FELLER, *British Columbia Mountaineering Club*

North West Territories

Proboscis, Logan Mountains. Paul Piana, Galen Rowell and Todd Skinner climbed and filmed a difficult new route on the left side of the southeast face of Proboscis. A full article appears earlier in this *Journal.*

Proboscis, Logan Mountains. In August, Spaniards José María Codina and Joaquín Olmo climbed the southeast face of Proboscis. They fixed rope on the lower half of the 700-meter-high wall. Their route probably mostly followed the 1963 first-ascent route, which had not previously been repeated.

Canadian Arctic

Peak North of Mount Tyr. From July 14 to 19, Walter Obergolser, Reinhard Siller, Claus Obrist, Karl Hofer and I climbed a difficult new route of 17 pitches

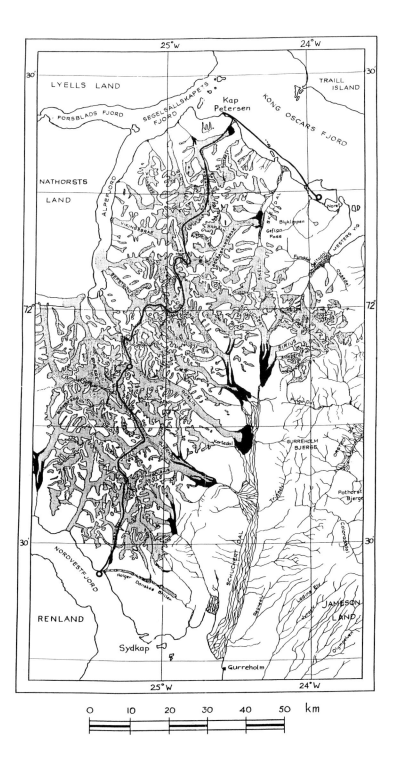

on the peak north of Mount Tyr (VI, 5.7 to 5.12a, A0). We ascended the north face of the buttress on good rock and descended the route with 16 rappels.

HELMUT GARGITTER, *South Tirol*

Climbs Above Sam Ford Fiord, Baffin Island. A full article on an expedition to this remote Arctic area appears earlier in this *Journal*.

GREENLAND

Scottish Staunings Alper Expedition. We completed a south-to-north traverse of the Staunings Alper. The journey was about 150 kilometers and followed the glacier systems on a route as close as possible to the east-west divide. We were Britons Mandy Wilson, Bob Neish, Paul Thompson and I as leader and French climbers Eric Flamand, Florence Germaine and Jean-François Haas. We flew from Akureyri, Iceland at the beginning of May and landed on skis on the sea ice at Storm Pynt, Nordvest Fjord. A food dump was made halfway along the route by the plane which landed on a tributary of the Roslin Gletscher. Hauling pulks, we took 18 days to make the northerly point of the traverse, Kap Petersen on Kong Oscars Fjord. The route, linking most of the major glaciers, crossed eight cols, two of which had not previously been crossed. One, formerly called False Col, connects the Bersaeckerbrae and the Skjoldungebrae. The other, which we named Alliance Col, connects the head of the Main Gletscher directly with the uppermost tributary of the Roslin Gletscher. We climbed three peaks: 1. The peak east of Alliance Col was climbed by its east ridge from the col by three members, climbing unroped. Two members ascended the south face on skis. A cairn was found on top. 2. Three of us made what we believe is the first ascent of the peak east of Crescent Col on skis from Gully Gletscher. It is the highest point on the ridge running south from Knoxtinde dividing the upper basins of the Gully and Schuchert Gletschers. 3. Four climbed Lambeth, south of Col Major, by two routes. From Kap Petersen, we skied 32 kilometers across sea ice to the airstrip at Mestersvig.

JOHN PEDEN, *Alpine Club*

Staunings Alper. The "High Altitude Astronomers' Expedition" consisted of Britons E. Knobloch, D. Smith, Canadians L. Murdock, C. Pritchet, S. Tremaine, H. Yee and me from Norway. We flew to Mestersvig on July 24 and returned to Akureyri, Iceland on August 8. We established Base Camp on the Skelbrae after crossing Gefion Pass. Soft snow hindered our approach up the Edinbrae. On July 30, we moved camp to the Kishmul Glacier, after which the weather became fine. The whole party climbed a snow gully terminating near a summit north of P 1603. On August 1, we reached the col of P 1603 (or

Richmond Peak?). Here the party split and Knobloch, Tremaine and I gained the summit (c. 1700 meters). Four went to Glamus Col, but conditions were not favorable for moving camp across the Bersaeckerbrae. Therefore, we retreated down the valley and made a new camp on the Bersaeckerbrae. From here, the whole party climbed Harlech (c. 1900 meters) via the standard route. We also explored the glacier up to Dunnottar, looking for a food drop which a Scottish expedition had failed to reach because of soft snow.

SVERRE AARSETH, *Alpine Club*

Peaks in the Lindberg Bjerge; Cathedral and Other Peaks in the Lemon Bjerge. Our expedition was composed of Gary Baum, Luke Bartlett, Luke Hughes, Robin Illingworth, William Pelkey, Michael Woolridge and me as leader. We landed at 68°54'N, 32°08'W. Our objectives were to begin a man-hauled sledge journey in the Lindberg mountains some 30 miles inland, continuing through the Lemon Mountains and finishing on the coast, to explore and climb some peaks in each range and to undertake botanical fieldwork. We climbed a dozen virgin summits, to some of which we gave unofficial names. Altitudes were measured by altimeters. We climbed the following: *Lara's Peak* (2840 meters; 68°53'N, 31°13'W), a straightforward snow ascent on skis for all but the final 100 meters; *Karen and Rosie Peaks* (3100 meters, 68°58'N,31°25'W), a dual summited mountain, approached via southeast ridge; *Snebordet* (68°57'N, 30°64'W) via southwest arête; *Tarongaborg* (68°67'N, 31°09'W) straightforward snow ascent from north; *Trillingerne North* (68°48'N, 31°27'W) via steep snow on east and *Trillingerne Central* (2040 meters; 68°47'N, 31°47'W) via west ridge; *Horseshoe* (1790 meters, 68°39'N, 31°54'W) traverse. There seems to be confusion about which mountain really is the *Cathedral* (2600 meters, 68°35'N, 31°52'W), first ascent via east ridge and subsequent ascent via snow gully on south face. Chris Bonington climbed in the region in 1991 and in *AAJ, 1992* pages 150-1 describes what he and his group thought must be the peak. Our party feels that the peak named many years ago by Wager as the Cathedral lies a mile further into the range than the difficult peak attempted by Bonington and that it is clearly the highest in the region. It should be noted that Bonington's peak marked as 2660-meters-high Domkirkebjerget on the 1:250 000 map is not the highest point in the Lemon Bjerge. We propose the name of "Minster" for P 2660, which is in fact lower than our 2600-meter-high Cathedral, some distance to the northeast; *Cymbrogi* (68°35'N, 31°40'W) snow ascent of northeast flank mostly on skis; *Sara's Peak* (2970 meters, 68°35'N, 31°48'W) via snow gullies on south and a final difficult section on granitic gneiss; *Mitre Peak* (68°35'N, 31°55'W) via east face; *Coxcomb* (1970 meters, 68°32'N, 31°53'W) via east-facing snow gully to left edge of northeast face; *Chisel Southeast* (68°27'N, 31°47'W) via snow gully on south to snow ridge; and *Pyramiden* (68°28'N, 31°03'W) from Black Cap Pass via north ridge.

PHILIP BARTLETT, *Alpine Club*

Perserajôq, West Greenland. Italians made the second ascent of Perserajôq (2259 meters, 7412 feet). Rising on the Qioqe Peninsula at 71°25′N, 52°00′W, it is possibly the highest mountain on the west coast. The first ascent was made by Piero Ghiglione, Carlo Mauri and Giorgio Cualco in 1960. This second ascent was made up the northwest buttress. The summit was reached on August 6 by Duilio Ginepro, Gaetano Magnano and Enzio Vecchi.

Ketil Attempt and Ascent of Pingasut, South Greenland, 1991. A French expedition composed of Vincent Buffin, Bruno Lambert, Emmanuel Ratouis, Isabelle ??????, Bruno Martel and Alain Hoffman climbed above Tasermiut Fjord in July of 1991. In unstable weather, they first fixed rope on 16 pitches on the lower 500 meters of the Barrard route on the 1500-meter-high west face of Ketil (2010 meters, 7595 feet). On June 6, 1991, they all bivouacked on a ledge at the end of the fixed ropes, hoping to climb the following day to the summit. The next day, they overcame many of the problems of this very serious route. At the end of 33 pitches, they felt that they had come to the end of the difficulties, but it was ten P.M. and time to bivouac. During the night, the weather went bad and they had to rappel down without reaching the summit. Buffin, Lambert, Martel and Ratouis then turned to Pingasut (1600 meters, 5250 feet), which lies between Ketil and Tasermiut Fjord. On July 20, 1991, they completed in 11 hours the ascent of the southwest face. An article, complete with photos and topos, appear on pages 64 to 69 of *Vertical* of July 1992.

Ketil, South Greenland. Our expedition to Ketil's west face above Tasermiut Fjord was organized by two French guides, Michel Pellé and me, in collaboration with "Terres d'Aventure." The team included Belgians Lut Vivijs and her husband Jan Van Hees and Frenchmen Yves Le Bissonnais and François Martin. Having arrived at Base Camp on July 9, we made what was probably the third ascent of the Barrard route on July 22, thanks to exceptionally good weather. Sixteen pitches were fixed with rope and then after three days' rest, we climbed the route in two days. The descent was accomplished by rappelling down the face. The weather remained good till the end of July. The exploit of Le Bissonnais should be noted, since he lost one leg at the age of 17 and is now currently leading 5.10.

ERIK DECAMP, *Club Alpin Français*

SOUTH AMERICA

Colombia

Sierra Nevada de Cocuy, Cordillera Oriental, 1991. Our expedition was composed of two women, leader Isabel Suárez and Rosario Rivas, and Carlos Dávila and me. Suárez had in December of 1990 climbed the difficult north face

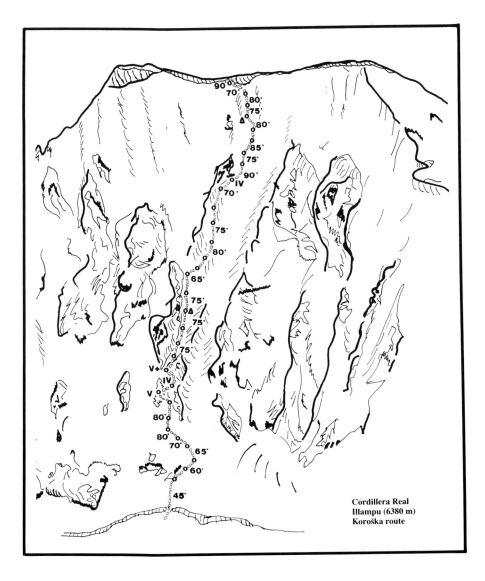

Cordillera Real
Illampu (6380 m)
Koroška route

of Ritacuba Negro in this same sierra. From the town of Güicán and Hacienda Ritacuba, we walked over the Los Verdes pass and descended onto the eastern (Orinoco) side of the range. On December 12, 1991, we climbed the fine pyramid of Pico Blanco (5096 meters, 16,720 feet) by the much receded west glacier. In a storm on December 26, 1991, we also climbed Pico La Aguja (c. 5100 meters, 16,733 feet), previously known as Pico Sin Nombre.

JOSÉ BETANCOURT, *Mérida, Venezuela*

Venezuela

Climb to the Stone Age. Earlier in this *Journal,* there is an article about exploration in the untracked jungles of the Orinoco River and the ascent of the sheer face of Aratitiyope.

Peru—Cordillera Blanca

Huascarán Sur, North Face, 1991, Correction. On page 152 of *AAJ, 1992*, a report on the climb of the north face of Huascarán Sur may have implied that a new route had been ascended. In 1985, Sharon Wood and I climbed the line which Kozjek followed almost exactly, except that we climbed straight up the final rock headwall while it appears that he diagonaled up from left to right and joined Benoît Grisom's solo route at the top . (See *AAJ, 1986*, pages 80-86.)

CARLOS BUHLER

Artesonraju, Southwest Face. On June 8, Andrej Gaspari and Štefan Mlinarič climbed a new fall-line route on the southwest face of Artesonraju directly to the summit, which they have named in memory of Marija Frantar. They descended the Austrian route on the south face.

FRANCI SAVENC, *Planinska zveza Slovenije*

Bolivia

Illampu and Condoriri, Cordillera Real, New Routes, 1986. Stanko Mihev, Robi Jamnik and Andrej Gradišnik climbed in the Cordillera Real in 1986. From July 1 to 3, 1986, they climbed a 1200-meter-high route on the northwest face of Illampu (6368 meters, 20,993 feet). The route follows the middle of the wall, left of the main couloir and was very steep except for the first 200 meters. (UIAA V on rock and steep ice.) On July 17, 1986, Mihev and Gradišnik climbed a 700-meter-high route on the south side of Condoriri (5648 meters, 18,531 feet). They started at the lake called both Chiar Krota or Lago Condoriri, reaching the plateau via a snow couloir on the rock buttress between the commonly followed couloir and the cascade icefall. They crossed the plateau and climbed to the col

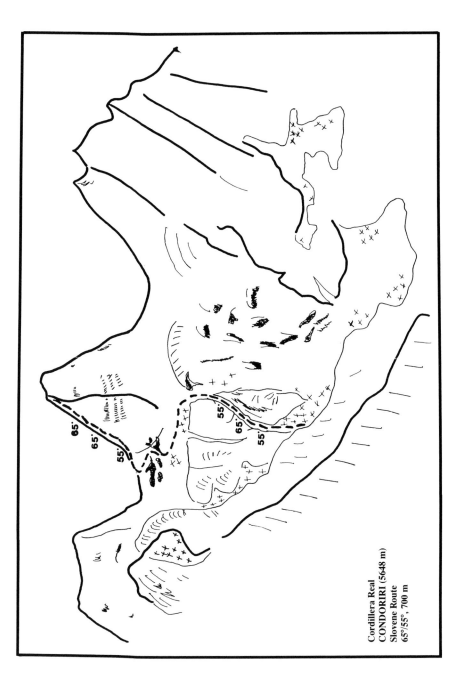

Cordillera Real
CONDORIRI (5648 m)
Slovene Route
65°/55°, 700 m

between Condoriri and its west wing (Ala Oeste) to ascend the southwest ridge to the summit of the Ala Oeste.

IRENA KOMPREJ, *Planinska zveza Slovenije*

Nevado de las Vírgines. Late in May, Bolivian Mario Miranda and Americans Stan Shepard and I probably made the first ascent of the Nevado de las Vírgines, part of the Khori Chuma group, the southernmost of the granite peaks. This is a 5500-meter (18,045-foot) fluted ice wedge forming the high point of a ridge walling in the second valley southeast of Mina Viloco. The construction of a dam and viaduct in this valley made it possible to drive to our camp at Laguna Choco Kkota at 4450 meters. We began at four A.M., worked our way through moraine, an icefall of barest blue ice, and continued up bare ice to the bergschrund—more blue ice which provided a good lead on steep boilerplate. By now it was late afternoon. Shepard set a belay and I led out to the summit on a 100-meter rope. I summited at sunset and we picked our way by headlamp back down the mountain and its interminable moraine. We bivouacked briefly at five A.M. when our last batteries gave out. Soon after sunrise, we arrived back in camp, 27 hours after starting. A word of warning: many Bolivian peaks have lost their agreeable snow cover and present much hard ice.

DAKIN COOK, *Unaffiliated*

Cordillera de Quimsa Cruz. In June, I made two forays from La Paz into this range south of Illimani. In the first, I attempted the west side of Nevado Vila Collo (5400 meters) but did not scale the last 200 meters of ice polished by wind and drought. I also entered the Huallatani and Laramcota Glaciers in search of routes to peaks, but the drought of the last several years had altered the surface of those glaciers. In my second campaign, I reached the mining settlement of Viloco on the northeast side of the range. On June 26, by the north side and east ridge I made the first ascent of P 5160 (16,929 feet), which lies east of Cerro Negro; I named it Jisca Jaque ("Small Rock Peak" in Aymara) The rock was excellent. On June 29, I climbed to the gap between Nevado Cori Chuyma and its western neighbor, P 5300 (17,389 feet), a long ridge with many points. I traversed the two highest summits, located at each end of the ridge and called it Curumiña ("Precipice Peak" in Aymara.) Snow storms in early July blocked roads to the mining villages and prevented further climbs.

EVELIO ECHEVARRÍA

Chile—Northern Andes

Llullaillaco. On September 18-21, Rodrigo Jordán, Juan Sebastián Montes, Claudio Lucero, Cristián García-Huidobro, Christian Buracchio and I climbed one of the summits of Llullaillaco (6723 meters, 22,058 feet), where we found pieces of wood which probably were used by the Incas in sacred ceremonies 700 years ago. The nearest trees are more than 300 kilometers away.

DAGOBERTO DELGADO, *Club Alemán Andino, Chile*

Ojos del Salado: Permit, Hut and Road Conditions 1991-2. In late December, 1991, Ken Nolan, Jean Aschenbrenner, Dan Smith and I drove across the southern Puna de Atacama to the Chilean-Argentine frontier near the Ojos del Salado, assisted by Chilean Gastón Oyarzún. A travel permit issued by the Chilean authorities is necessary to enter the border region. This is obtained from the Dirección Nacional de Fronteras y Límites del Estado, Ministerio de Relaciones Interiores, Bandera 52, 4° Piso, Santiago, Chile. Without this, climbers are refused entry to the Ojos del Salado area. On December 31, 1991, Nolan, Aschenbrenner and Smith climbed Cerro Mulas Muertas (5895 meters, 19,340 feet) from camp on Laguna Verde at 4000 meters. The once impressive Hostería Murray, the hut previously used as Base Camp for climbing the Ojos del Salado, has been leveled by fire. The 17-kilometer road from the police checkpoint adjacent to the Murray ruins to the hut at Camp I is driveable in summer conditions but quite sandy, which can be troublesome to vehicles without large tires. The standard north-face route utilizes solid *refugios* at Camps I and II (5200 and 5800 meters). Running water can normally be found near each hut. The summit of the Ojos del Salado (6885 meters, 22,590 feet) was climbed by the entire party on January 4. The steep summit block, which contrasted with the otherwise mundane volcanic slopes found below, was ascended by a loose 4th-class arête where a short section of fixed rope was placed.

CHARLES D. HUSS, M.D.

Tocorpuri Group, 1990. Our expedition was composed of Austrian Theo Dowbenka and Germans Ludwig Albrecht, Ludwig Esenböck, Josef Hümmer, Josef Knott, Rolf Thorenz and me. We ascended by their normal routes Licancabur (5921 meters, 19,426 feet) and San Pablo (6092 meters, 19,987 feet) in northern Chile and Tupungato (6550 meters, 21,490 feet) in the central Chilean ranges. After Licancabur, we also made on December 28, 1990 the first modern ascent of the rocky summit of P 5183 (17,004 feet) in the Tocorpuri Group, southeast of the Tatío geysers. On the top we found a wooden stick, about a meter long.

HERBERT ZIEGENHARDT, *Bayerische Naturfreunde*

Chile—Central Andes

Yeguas Heladas and Nevado Juncal, 1991. I joined Frenchmen Patrick Gabarrou, François Marsigny, Fred Vimal and Italian Giorgio Passino in November 1991 and together we traveled up the valley to the usual Juncal Base Camp at the foot of the glacier north of Juncal at 2800 meters. Above us rose the unclimbed northeast face of Yeguas Heladas to its 4790-meter (15,715-foot) summit. (First ascent of the peak in 1942 by Chileans Edgar Kremer and Herbert Wünsche.) We decided on this as our first objective. After several mixed and ice pitches, a narrow 60° to 80° couloir divided the face in the center and took us halfway up the wall. Then we turned left on a steep snow ramp. From there to the top was mixed terrain. Next, we climbed the north face of Nevado Juncal, which is technically not difficult. On the first day, we climbed steep couloirs to bivouac at 4500 meters. Despite poor weather the next day, we continued on to bivouac at 5700 meters and reached the summit (6110 meters, 20,046 feet) the following day. We bivouacked again that night at 5700 meters on the descent. After this, all but I moved on to Patagonia. In early December, I returned to climb Juncal by the same route with Chilean Andrés Zegers, with the idea of ascending from Base Camp to the summit and back in one day. We left camp at one A.M. on December 5, 1991. I was standing on the summit 11½ hours later. Andrés had reached 5835 meters. We started the descent together and got to Base Camp at five P.M.

RODRIGO MUJICA, *Chile and American Mountain Guides Association*

Torre San Andrés, Torres del Brujo Range, 1991. Chileans Waldo Farías and Christián Heitmann climbed the spectacular Torre San Andrés (3050 meters, 10,007 feet) in the first half of February of 1991, reaching the summit on February 10. The granite spire lies west of Cerro Palomo. From the Río Tinguirirca, they ascended the Ríos Azufre, Portillo and San Andrés. After an approach on the glacier, they first spent six days preparing the route and were three days and nights on the final push to complete the eleven pitches (5.10, A2). [Tragically, Heitmann died five months later while descending from another difficult mountain, Punta Zanzi. He was 24 years old.]

RODRIGO MUJICA, *Chile and American Mountain Guides Association*

Cerro Altar, South Face Solo. On April 7, I made the second ascent of this face. It was mixed climbing. The crux was a UIAA VI-pitch on very rotten rock. Cerro Altar rises to 5222 meters or 17,132 feet.

DAGOBERTO DELGADO, *Club Alemán Andino, Chile*

Cerro Punta Negra, South Face, 1990. On December 9, 1990, Christian Buracchio and I climbed the beautiful ice couloir at the right side of the south face to the summit ridge and summit (4090 meters, 13,419 feet). The good ice was angled at 45° to 50°. (UIAA III.) [The couloir was first climbed in 1951. Two climbers were killed in it in 1960. —*Editor.*]

DAGOBERTO DELGADO, *Club Alemán Andino, Chile*

Argentina—Northern Andes

Picos de Ansilta, 1991. The Picos de Ansilta are seven high mountains north of Mercedario. Their access is from the city of San Juan but the peaks are seldom ascended because they demand a long approach. On March 25, 1991, Humberto Campodónico and Mauricio Manzi climbed Pico 2 (5886 meters, 19,312 feet), also called Cerro de Ansilta, the highest in the group. They then camped in the depression between Picos 1 and 2 and the following day climbed Pico 1 (5413 meters, 17,759 feet), making the second ascent by a new route. This peak is also called Manzuelo. Months later, in the southern winter, the same two climbers headed for Pico 3 (5557 meters, 18,233 feet). Winter weather meant swollen rivers, snowstorms and wind. On July 16, 1991, they climbed a gully with waist-deep snow that left them on the north side and east ridge, which they used to reach the summit. This was the first winter ascent. In November, the same two, with Eugenia and Luis Gómez, Adrián Manzi and Alejandro Quenan drove to Barreal and hiked to camp in the Quebrada Negra. On November 23, 1991, they completed the second ascent by a new route of Cerro Tridente (4641 meters, 15,226 feet), via the east side; they traversed the three summits. Campodónico and Mauricio Manzi stayed on. They placed a high camp north of Tridente and on November 25 climbed Pico de Ansilta 4 (5116 meters, 16,786 feet), traversing from the col with Tridente. This peak is also called Fidel Díaz.

MARCELO SCANU, *Grupo de Montaña Huamán, Buenos Aires*

Cerro Arenal and Other Ascents, 1991. In the Olivares group, west of the city of San Juan, on August 8, 1991 Humberto Campodónico made solo the first winter ascent and the third ascent of the peak of Cerro Negro Aspero (5500 meters, 18,045 feet). On September 29, 1991, a group of nine men and two women led by Luis Gómez ascended Cerro de la Fortuna (4376 meters, 14,358 feet) by a new route, the south side. From there, Campodónico alone traversed on to the summits of El Bronce Oeste and El Bronce (4000 and 4033 meters, 13,124 and 13,231 feet). On December 7, 1991, eight climbers from San Juan headed for the region near the Agua Negra international pass. That same day, they continued up to the gap between the twin peaks of Agua Negra and up the southeast ridge of Cerro El Arenal or Agua Negra II (5000 meters, 16,404 feet). Only Campodónico reached the summit; the hurried climb and the altitude affected all the others.

MARCELO SCANU, *Grupo de Montaña Huamán, Buenos Aires*

Cerro Tres Quebradas, West Peak. Our Italo-Argentine expedition had as members Italian scientists Francesco Matelli and Claudio Scala and Argentines Orlando Bravo, Juan Abregui, Rodolfo Alonso, José Paliza, Daniel Villagra and me. Between January 21 and February 12, we followed the route of the 1937 Polish expedition to the Puna. After several days on foot and horseback, we reached the Polish Base Camp in Tres Quebradas. A group led by my father, Orlando Bravo, explored the long Polish route to the Nevado Pissis. Meanwhile Agregui, Mantelli, Villagra and I on January 29 climbed P 5980 (19,620 feet), which sits on the border with Chile. This had first been climbed in 1965. This is the western of the twin peaks of Nevado de los Patos and is also called Cerro de Tres Quebradas. The higher summit (6250 meters) lies entirely in Argentina.

CLAUDIO BRAVO, *Club Andino Tucumán, Argentina*

Agua Negra Region, New Peaks. Using as a base a small populated place called Guardia Vieja, situated at 3000 meters on the new international road to Chile, we climbed for 20 days among the peaks near Agua Negra Pass. We were Miguel Beorchia, Luciano di Giovanni and I. On January 11, we hiked up the Quebrada de las Trancas and placed camp at 3500 meters below the northwest ridge of P 4221 (13,848 feet). On the 12th, we climbed the ridge, shifting near the top to the southwest side. We christened the mountain Bífida de las Trancas. We then traversed to the south summit (c. 4210 meters) and descended to Guardia Vieja. On the 14th, we drove to the abandoned hut of Quebrada Sarmiento, near the Chilean border. That same day we climbed P 5058 (16,595 feet), which we named Cerro de la Quebrada Sarmiento. Descending southward to a col, we then ascended P 4700 (15,420 feet). All were first ascents. Beorchia had to return to San Juan, so 16-year-old di Giovanni and I climbed Cerro El Bronce, a second ascent from the frontier police checkpoint. Descending eastward, we also climbed El Bronce Central (4000 meters, 13,124 feet), a first ascent and continued on to the next peak El Bronce Oeste, a third ascent. I then pushed on alone and reached the top of yet another peak, Cerro de la Fortuna (4376 meters, 14,358 feet), by a new route from the southeast, a third ascent. I descended to rejoin di Giovanni and for a rest at Guardia Vieja. On January 18, we climbed a c. 5000-meter (16,404-foot) peak northeast of the Agua Negra Pass. On the summit we found a solid cairn but no documents of the previous visitors. [This may have been Cerro Andrés, (5025 meters, 16,486 feet), climbed by the boundary commission in 1904.] Near Guardia Vieja we examined petroglyphs.

MARCELO SCANU, *Grupo de Montaña Huamán, Buenos Aires*

New Altitudes in the Northern Argentine Andes. Various peaks in this region have new officially corrected altitudes, generally lower than previously given ones. In Salta, we have new altitudes for the Volcán Socompa, 6031m; Volcán Salín, 6022m; Volcán Arácar, 6095m; Volcán Quehuar, 6102m; Cerro Acay, 5716m; Cumbre del Libertador General San Martín o Cachi, 6380m. In Cajamarca, Volcán Antofalla, 6409m; Volcán Gallán, 5912m. In the region of the Ojos del Salado, Cerro El Muerto, 6488m; Cerro Solo, 6205m; Cerro El Fraile,

6062m. In La Rioja, Volcán Veladero, 6436m; Cerro General M. Belgrano or Nevado Famatina, 6097m. In San Juan, Cerro El Toro, 6160m; Cerro Olivares, 6266m; Cerro Olivares del Límite, 6220m.

MARCELO SCANU, *Grupo de Montaña Huamán, Buenos Aires*

Argentina—Central Andes

Cerro San Juan, 1991. This high peak lies northwest of Cerro Alma Negra, in the Mercedario group. Silvia Tejada, Humberto Campodónico, Luis Gómez, Mauricio Manzi, Manuel Maurín, Iván Nobre and Fabián Olivieri from the city of San Juan placed camp in the upper valley of the Colorado River. On January 8, 1991, they headed for Alma Negra, but having mistaken the route, they climbed instead P 5850 (19,197 feet), a first ascent. They named the peak Cerro San Juan.

MARCELO SCANU, *Grupo de Montaña Huamán, Buenos Aires*

Aconcagua, Northern Valleys, 1991. From January 13 to 18, 1991, Austrian Theo Dowbenka and Germans Josef Hümmer, Josef Knott, Rolf Thorenz and I as leader climbed and traversed Aconcagua, but we took a long way over desolate valleys to do so. We started at the Plaza Francia at the foot of the south face of Aconcagua. We then crossed the 4800-meter-high pass, the Portezuelo Relinchos, and dropped northeast down the Relinchos Creek. We contoured part of the Relinchos Glacier, headed north to cross a gap between P 5116 and Cerro Ameghino, finally to descend into the dry Quebrada Vieja Alta. Ascending this valley, we met the former Ventisquero de las Vacas Sur, a glacier that has now disappeared. At 5700 meters, we found the wreck of a rescue helicopter. We then climbed Aconcagua up the Polish Glacier and descended the normal route to Plaza de Mulas and Puente del Inca.

HERBERT ZIEGENHARDT, *Bayerische Naturfreunde*

Argentine—Chilean Patagonia

Cerro Catedral, Bariloche. In the lake district near the Chilean frontier, Bariloche enjoys a much more favorable climate than further south in Patagonia. The Cerro Catedral massif has a multitude of rock towers (up to 250 meters in height) of excellent granite, which have made this the rock-climbing center of the Argentine. After Daniel Anker and I stopped by when returning from southern Patagonia in 1989, there has been an explosion of new routes, many established by Rolo Garibotti.

MICHEL PIOLA, *Club Alpin Suisse*

Cordillera Sarmiento. A full article on this nearly unexplored range that rises from Chilean tidewater appears earlier in this *Journal*.

Color Plate 8

Photo by Tommy Bonapace

Ridge between Bífida and Cuatro Dedos.

Attempt to Traverse the Southern Patagonian Icecap from North to South.
Spaniard José Carlos Tamayo and Argentines Gabriel Ruiz, Marcos Couch,
Alberto del Casillo and Alexander Portella attempted to make the first complete
traverse of the 400-kilometer-long Southern Patagonian Icecap. This has been
attempted a number of times but today still remains incomplete, although the
most successful, Shipton and companions and later New Zealanders, came
within 100 kilometers of reaching their objective, the Fiordo Ultima Esperanza.
The Argentine-Spanish party set out supply dumps from Calafate near the Fitz
Roy-Cerro Torre group in late March. They gathered in Coihaique and the next
day flew to Caleta Tortel to begin the traverse in the Fiordo Calén on April 4.
Thirty-one days later, on May 5, they had covered 145 kilometers in a straight
line on the map—and many more because of necessary deviations—and had
reached the first of their supply dumps near the Paso del Viento near Cerro Torre.
The rough weather of oncoming winter persuaded them to give up their attempt.
A full article appears on pages 20 to 29 of *Desnivel* of October 1992.

Cerro Cristal. Ugo and Benigno Balatti, Giuseppe Alippi and I had hoped to
climb Cerro Campana, which rises north of the Glaciar Moyano, but the weather
in late 1991 made this impossible. As a consolation, on January 3 we climbed
Cerro Cristal (2200 meters, 7218 feet), which lies south of the glacier, by its
northwestern flank. There were pitches of 70° snow and ice and a rise of 800
meters. The first ascent was made on February 17, 1968 by Argentines Jorge
Skvarča and Mario Serrano, but ours was probably a new route.

ENRICO LAFRANCONI, *Club Alpino Italiano*

New Altitudes in the Chaltén (Fitz Roy) Area. The maps of the Instituto
Geográfico Militar Argentino which were published last year now allow a more
exact determination of altitudes in this region. An Argentine publisher, Zaguier
and Urruty, has come out with a map in color with a scale 1:50,000 made from
the IGM maps. This map is bilingual in Spanish and English. Altitudes from
north to south are Gorra Blanca (3907m); Marconi (2210m); Cerro Dumbo
(2484m); Cerro Loma Blanca (2218m); Gran Gendarme (2255m); Aguja Pollone (2313m); Pollone (2579m); Cerro Eléctrico (2257m); Pier Giorgio
(2719m); Aguja Guillaumet (2579m); Aguja Mermoz (2732m); Cerro Rincón
(2465m); Domo Blanco (2507m); Aguja Val de Viois, 2653m; Chaltén (Fitz
Roy; 3405m); Aguja de la Silla (2938m); Aguja Cuatro Dedos (2281m); Aguja
Bífida (2394m); Cerro Stanhardt (2730m); Torre Egger (2673m); Cerro Mocho
(1953m); Cerro Torre (3102m); Poincenot (3002m); Aguja Rafael (2482m);
Aguja Saint Exupéry (2558m); Aguja de la S (2335m); Cerro Mojón Rojo
(2163m); Cerro Techado Negro (2152m); Cerro Adela Norte (2825m);
Cerro Adela (2938m); Cerro Adela Sur (2840m), Cerro Ñato (2797m); Cerro
Doblado (2665m).

MARCELO SCANU, *Grupo de Montaña Huamán, Buenos Aires*

FITZ ROY
3441 m. East Buttress "El Corazon"

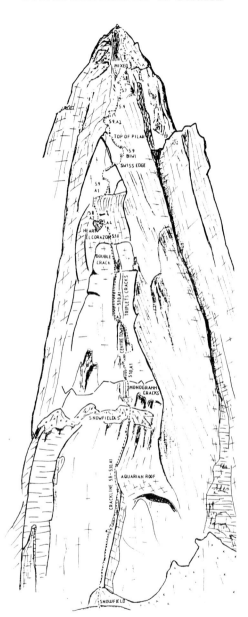

Fitz Roy, East Buttress, El Corazón Route. On December 13, 1991, Michel Pitelka and I reached the Río Blanco Base Camp below Fitz Roy. Our objective was the aesthetic line on the 1300-meter-high east buttress of Fitz Roy. The bad weather during December did not allow us any opportunity for climbing. During that time, we carried climbing gear and food to a great ice cave near the face. On January 14, we finally were able to put in a full day's climbing. After twelve hours, we reached the top of the icefield, a quarter of the way up the wall. From there on we were in new terrain; we found evidence of a number of previous attempts up to this point. The next day, we climbed to the prominent Center Tower, halfway up the route. In the rest of January, we climbed during one day of bad weather and one of good to where rock had fallen out to leave a heart-shaped scar, 850 meters up. The climbing up to there was superb, despite iced cracks. One 5.10, 150-meter-high dihedral without a single break as well as a slightly overhanging, 60-meter-high pitch up the finger crack of the Double Crack were marvels of nature and a treat for any rock climber. At the beginning of February, the notorious Patagonian weather again reigned over Fitz Roy. With 200-kph wind squalls, we fought our way up to the top of the buttress. Attempts to continue on to the main summit were defeated by continual bad weather and new snow. Not until the change of the

EL CORAZON

PLATE 54

Photo by Michel Pitelka

**East Buttress of FITZ ROY,
El Corazón Route.**

moon did hope for weather smile upon us. After a bivouac on the wall, we climbed to the summit on February 20 with radiant weather. We descended our new route along which we only left gear at the rappel points—two bolts and a carabiner at each—and eight pitons. Otherwise we left the wall as we had found it. Three old fixed ropes, left by previous parties, are still on the bottom of the route. In the 2½ months, we climbed on eight days. Without iced cracks, the route could probably be climbed free with UIAA difficulty of VI to VII. We had nine pitches of A1 to A4. There were 40 pitches, some 60 meters long. For the route, one needs two 60-meter ropes, a small assortment of pitons and nuts, Friends N° 0 to 4, 1 skyhook and 3 bathooks, 2 copperheads and a Rurp. The bottom of the wall can be threatened if there is much new snow or by ice falling from the icefield, but is generally lovely crack-and-dihedral climbing on superb rock. We were admirably supported on the last attempts by Ruth Baldinger, who in January came close to climbing the Argentine route with friends. They had to quit two pitches from the summit icefield because of the weather.

KASPAR OCHSNER, *Schweizer Alpen Club*

Bífida, East-Southeast Spur. After our group of eleven was thwarted by bad weather from climbing Cerro Campana, we moved south to the Cerro Torre region. Eventually, only four of us, Casimiro Ferrari, Manuele Panzeri, Luciano Spadaccini and I were left. From the Maestri Camp, we moved up under the east-southeast spur of Bífida. During two days of miserable weather, we climbed 300 of the 750 meters toward the top, but soaked to the skin, we descended on January 5 to the Maestri Camp. Despite terrible weather, we tried to advance but were blocked by high winds and falling snow. Spadaccini had to leave. We other three finally set out on January 15. From our bivouac at the foot of the spur, in splendid weather on the 16th we quickly climbed the fixed ropes. We bivouacked 300 meters from the summit. The dawn of the 17th was excellent, but after climbing 200 meters, it clouded up from the west. However, we continued and got to the summit at ten P.M. with strong winds and falling snow. When we descended to the bivouac site, we found the tent destroyed by the wind. We had no choice but to continue the descent in the dark by the light of a single headlamp. We rate the climb as UIAA V to VI, A1 to A2.

CORRADO VALSECCHI, *Club Alpino Italiano*

Bífida, Ridge Between Cuatro Dedos and Bífida, and Cerro Grande. Gerold Dünser and I were based at the Bridwell Camp near Laguna Torre from January 20 to March 24. Our objective was to climb the Egger-Maestri route on Cerro Torre, but knowing how important good weather was, we kept off it except for a one-day attempt, which ended with bad weather. There is a crack system on the east face of Bífida below the north and south summits, which rises some 800 meters. On January 29, we climbed a little more than halfway up the face, where an iced off-width crack stopped us. After a warm bivouac, we climbed up and right, crossing both the Ferrari and the first-ascent routes. By mid-afternoon we were on the north (main) summit, but we had to rappel directly off in a blinding snowstorm. On the ridge between Cuatro Dedos and Bífida, there are three impressive rock spires. On March 14, we first reached the col between Cuatro Dedos and the first of these towers, climbing the 200 meters of the east face on rock and then a snow ramp. Heading south, we found lovely slabs and cracks and rappels off the towers. At dark, we had climbed the third tower, from which we rappelled first to the south and then to the east. (VI+, 21 pitches, 12 hours.) On March 18, Dünser and Brazilian Bito Meyer started up toward the compressor route on Cerro Torre, but the single-day good weather soon ended. That same day, I ascended solo Cerro Grande by the 60° north face and descended the east ridge. I later found that in January of 1991 two Swiss had climbed the mountain: Werner Stucki solo by the north face and Thomas Villars by the east ridge. They descended the east ridge together.

TOMMY BONAPACE, *Österreichischer Alpenverein*

Punta Herron Attempt via West Buttress. Andrea Sarchi, Odoardo Ravizza and I arrived at Base Camp at Piedra del Fraile on October 25. Despite bad weather between October 28 and November 2, we managed two carries to the Paso Marconi at 1500 meters. When the weather cleared on November 5, we made a third carry to the pass and headed south with sleds for 13 kilometers along the Southern Patagonian Icecap to just below the west buttress of Punta Herron, a northern foresummit of Torre Egger. There we dug a snow cave, which served as Advance Base. On November 8, we climbed 150 meters of difficult rock, fixed rope and descended. On the 9th, we climbed another 50 meters higher but could find no bivouac site. We did discover the pack of Paolo Crippa and Eliana Zordo, who were killed on this route in 1990 and to whom we dedicated our climb. On November 10, we climbed three more pitches to reach the large ledge that cuts across the buttress. After climbing a little higher, we returned to bivouac on the ledge, where we could stretch out and eat amply. We spent a fatiguing day on the 11th, ascending 200 meters. Rather than to descend, we spent a miserably cold bivouac there. On November 12, we climbed three more pitches to reach the top of the buttress and a col, which gave access to the final north face of Punta Herron. However, fatigue and uncertain weather suggested caution and we gave up the climb and descended.

MAURIZIO GIAROLLI, *Club Alpino Italiano*

El Mocho and Punta Val Biois. After their climbs of Yegua Helada and Juncal, Frenchmen François Marsigny, Patrick Gabarrou, Fred Vimal and Italian Giorgio Passino traveled to the Cerro Torre-Fitz Roy region. Despite the usual bad weather, Marsigny, Gabarrou and Passino managed to make the second ascent of the Grassi-Rossi-Pe route, *Todo o Nada*, on El Mocho. Shortly before they were to leave, they turned to a new route which had been called to their attention by the Swiss Kaspar Ochsner. This was above the Piedras Blanca Glacier on the east face of Punta Val Biois, the rock spire between Fitz Roy and Aguja Mermoz. A superb, very narrow ice gully of 70° to 90° rose for 450 meters nearly to the top of granite needle. On January 9, Marsigny, Gabarrou and Vimal climbed ten 50-meter-high pitches, six of which were extraordinarily steep. In places the gully was only a meter wide.

Cerro Torre. Dan Cauthorn and I departed Chaltén on January 3 and began the long, arduous trudge to the west side of the Torres. Enduring winds seldom blew less than 60-mph and frequently gusted to 100-mph. After establishing Base Camp on January 8, we started up the 5000-foot-high west face of Cerro Torre on the 11th. The attempt was soon aborted by violent weather. At noon on January 13, we started again, even though the Torres were still socked in, gambling that the abrupt change in wind direction (it had just shifted from northwest to southwest) would bring a lull in the storm. We bivouacked that night in an ice cave at the base of the "Helmet" as a 30-hour spell of clear, relatively calm weather commenced. The next day brought a wealth of spectacular ice climbing. The 160 feet of vertical and overhanging rime on the Helmet pitch were one of the hardest, scariest things I have ever led. We bivouacked a second time on the summit ridge, 150 feet below the top, without sleeping bags, bivy sacks, stove, water or food. We topped out on the morning of January 15 with clouds boiling around us as the storm returned in earnest. Twenty feet of overhanging, unclimbable sugar snow kept us from surmounting the uppermost ice mushroom capping the summit tower, which changes dramatically in size and shape from year to year. Twenty-three rappels and lots of downclimbing got us back to Base Camp at midnight. Ours was the fourth ascent of the Ferrari route. It is an exceptionally superb line, certainly one of the most remarkable ice climbs on the planet.

JONATHAN KRAKAUER

Cerro Stanhardt and Traverse to Punta Herron, 1991. From October 26 to 29, 1991, Ermanno Salvaterra, Ferruccio Vidi and Adriano Cavallaro made an extraordinary traverse. Bivouacking before reaching the summit, they climbed Cerro Stanhardt via the Bridwell route and rappelled six rope-lengths south into the col betweeen Stanhardt and Punta Herron for a second bivouac. Over the next two days, they climbed Punta Herron by a new route (400 meters, V and VI), the northeast spur, which included three steep ice pitches and a summit mushroom, and then rappelled back 28 rope-lengths to the col and to the glacier. They filmed the entire climb, for which they received the UIAA Prize at the Trento Film Festival in April, 1992. Punta Herron is a foresummit on the north of Torre Egger. It was first climbed by Bruno De Donà and Giuliano Giongo in 1980 when they descended from Torre Egger.

SILVIA METZELTIN BUSCAINI, *Club Alpino Italiano*

PLATE 55

Photo by Olaf Sööt

Cerro Torre, Torre Egger and Cerro Stanhardt.

Don Bosco, South Face Ascent and Ski Descent, 1991. Italian Tone Valeruz is well known for his extreme ski descents. On January 14, 1991, he made a new route solo on the south face of Don Bosco (2515 meters, 8251 feet), taking only three hours to climb the 600 meters from the glacier to the summit. Part of the ascent was on 80° ice. He descended some of the route on skis, but was forced to climb down a part of it on foot.

Cerro Cervantes, Second Ascent, 1991. Our expedition was composed of Eduard and Ina Koch, Ferdinand Hujer, Kunibert Ochsenfeld, Christine Wieloch and us two. On November 29, 1991, from El Calafate and the Buscaini Camp, the Kochs, Hujer, Ochsenfeld and Wieloch climbed Cerro Cervantes (2383 meters, 7819 feet) from the northwest. Meanwhile, we two ascended a 1350-meter pass, north of Cervantes. From Calafate, we went by bus to Puerto Natales in Chile. On December 8, 1991, those who had climbed Cervantes made the first ascent of Punta Chocolate (1700 meters, 5677 feet), a rock peak north of Punzón in the central part of the Cordón Barros Arana. We other two, joined by American Steven Hayward, ascended the Ascensio valley. We made the second ascent of a 1750-meter-high peak east of the Ascencio Pass on December 20, 1991. Italians had climbed it on December 20, 1987 and named it Cerro Edoardo. We have suggested to the authorities that it be renamed Cerro Josef Koch, after an Austrian Andean pioneer of the 1930s.

GÜNTHER JÜLLICH *and* WILFRED SIEGEL, *Deutscher Alpenverein*

Cerro Cervantes. Sam Grubenhof and I arrived at Calafate on February 12. We hoped to find a way to the Glaciar Moreno and across the Brazo Rico to attempt Cerro Cervantes, which we believed was an unclimbed 7819-foot (2383-meter) peak below which Bill Tilman had walked in his 1956 crossing of the Patagonian Icecap. While obtaining permission to climb in Los Glaciares National Park, we learned that Cervantes had been climbed twice (1990 and 1991) and we met a local climber, Jorge Limos, who had made the first ascent. On February 13, we took a two-hour bus ride to the Glaciar Moreno snout and a half-hour boat trip across the Brazo Rico to the Base Camp of the Minitrekking Guides. From there, a pleasant three-hour walk along the right bank of the Moreno took us to a campsite which locals said had been used by Gino Buscaini. The following morning we quickly ascended 1000 feet to tree line and 2000 feet to the North Cervantes Glacier. Travel was easy until we reached a 500-foot, 40°, snow-and-ice slope in misty weather. We continued up in a whiteout until we reached what we thought was the summit. A brief clearing revealed the true summit further on, but the late hour and poor weather made us decide to retreat. Two days later, we completed the climb on Jorge Limos' easier route. After a brief visit to the Fitz Roy area, we made an attempt on Cuerno Principal del Paine but turned back at six P.M. at the base of the 500-foot summit tower in the face of a storm.

SILAS WILD

Paine Towers and Fitz Roy Regions in the Southern Summer, 1991-2. The weather from October 1991 to March 1992 was as usual changeable and harsh. Despite these "normal" conditions, at least eleven new routes were completed. Since periods of more than 24 hours of good weather are rare, such climbs have to be made in semi-heavy style, often using some fixed rope to avoid playing Russian roulette with the weather. To succeed in Patagonia, whether one uses fixed ropes or not, one needs moral strength and the will to climb in bad weather. This has been shown by such veterans as Fabio Leoni (six expeditions) and Mario Mànica (nine). It is not rare to have to wait out two or three months to be successful. The spirit between groups is normally excellent. On our arrival in January, however, we met the members of a victorious expedition dressed, curiously, in Spanish clothing. To understand this nebulous story, one must know that two-and-a-half years ago Spaniard José Luis Gallego and his team made an attempt on the Torre Central del Paine, which was beaten back by the cold. They left on the top of a projection a cache wrapped in plastic: 600 meters of fixed line, two climbing ropes, two portaledges, two sleeping bags, 150 carabiners, pitons and a quantity of clothing. Their route had been done, which is understandable, but the cache had been raided, which is not. A summary of the new routes done in the southern summer season of 1991-2 follows. In the Cerro Torre-Fitz Roy region, five new routes were completed. The ascents of the left side of the south face of El Mocho and the southwest face of the Aguja Poincenot by Jay Smith and Steve Gerberding have already been described on pages 164 to 172 of *AAJ, 1992.* Swiss Kaspar Ochsner and Michel Pitelka climbed a new line on the east buttress of Fitz Roy. Punta Val Biois, the spire between Fitz Roy and Aguja Mermoz, was climbed by Frenchmen Marsigny, Gabarrou and Vimal. Italians Salvaterra, Cavallaro and Vidi climbed the Bridwell route on Cerro Stanhardt, descended new terrain on the south spur and climbed Punta Herron by its northeast spur. These are described below in this *Journal.* Two Argentines who made the first female ascent of Guillaumet were Patricia Malatesta and Marcela Antonucci. In the Paine region, Vincent Sprungli and I climbed the east face of the Torre Sur and the west face of the Torre Norte. Two more new routes were done on the west face of the Torre Norte's northern summit after we left. Five routes now exist on the east face of the Torre Central del Paine: (from left to right) Spanish-American-Argentine (1992), Italian (1986), German (1991), British (1992) and South African (1974). Of the two new routes, the Spanish-American-Argentine is described below; there is a full article on the British. There were two new routes on La Catedral by American and Italian climbers, which are also described below. Italians climbed a new route on the southwest face of the Cuerno Principal del Paine. A Briton and a South African climbed the west face of Paine Chico.

MICHEL PIOLA, *Club Alpin Suisse*

Paine Towers, East Face of the Torre Sur and West Face of the Torre Norte. After the arrival of Frenchman Vincent Sprungli and me at the foot of the Paine

TORRE NORTE DEL PAINE "La última esperanza"

· Magnificent route on excellent rock running directly to the principal summit.
· Miserable weather on the first ascent from Belay 6 (R6) on,
  preventing a difficult free climb. Under good conditions, the whole climb
  should go free except for the A2 roof.
· First ascent: Michel Piola/Vincent Sprungli, February 14, 1992.
  500 m./TD sup./6b+, A2

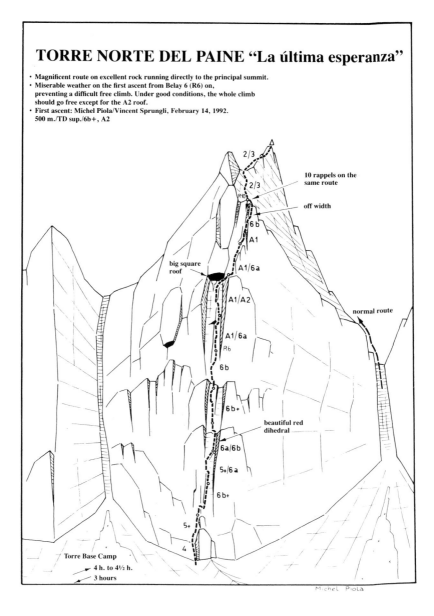

Michel Piola

Towers on January 18, we started the very next day to take advantage of each period of calm weather. The South Tower is the highest (c. 2500 meters, 8202 feet), the wildest and the most distant from Base Camp. It takes four and a half hours to reach the foot of the east face from there. Only two routes had previously been completed on the tower. There had been at least two tries made before on the 900-meter-high east face, including the attempt in 1985 by American Craig Peer and South Africans David Davies and Johnathan Gordon; they climbed to about 200 meters from the summit when Peer's leg was shattered by a falling rock, necessitating a dramatic rescue. (See *AAJ, 1986,* pages 87-95.) Their route was to the left of ours. Being only two and having only four weeks to spend, we placed a camp at the foot of the wall and for four days fixed ropes up to the steepest part of the wall (A3 and A4). Despite fog and falling snow on the morning of January 28, we climbed the 500 meters to our high point and continued on. By good luck, the weather cleared and we forced our way to the summit by eight P.M. The rock was very compact and called for numerous hooks, copperheads and knifeblades. The snow on the upper part softened so much that it was impossible at midday. We called the route "En el Ojo del Huracán" (In the Eye of the Hurricane). After evacuating the camp and all traces from the face, we turned to the west face of the Torre Norte. Only one route had previously been climbed on this tower, the south ridge. Although the east face of this two-peaked tower appears rotten, the rock on the west face is magnificent, but the wall is particularly exposed to the wind. Sprungli and I completed the 500-meter-high climb in 22 hours from Base Camp to the summit and back on February 14. We left in place only 3 pitons, 2 wedges and some nuts with slings, used for rappels. We called it "La Ultima Esperanza" (The Last Hope). After our departure, the face to the left of the north summit was climbed by two different new routes: by Italians Mànica, Leoni and Zampiccoli and by Briton Pritchard and South African Lloyd. [For these climbs, see below.]

MICHEL PIOLA*, *Club Alpin Suisse*

La Catedral, East Face. We saw a picture of La Catedral on a postcard. With no more information than that, John Catto, leader, Peter Gallagher, Max Kendall and I arrived in Patagonia on New Years Day, 1992, intent on making the first ascent of the striking east face. [The only previous ascent had been made by British climbers via the west face in 1971. See *AAJ, 1971,* page 432.] A week later, we had established Base Camp in the Valle del Francés. The face proved bigger and harder than we had imagined it, over 3000 feet high with no obvious weaknesses. Working from a snow cave at the base of the wall, we spent ten days slowly fixing lines up the beautiful white granite. Typical Patagonian weather kept progress to a crawl; we were continually buffeted by high winds and rain. After we had used up all our fixed lines, we began the waiting game for a spell

---

* For the ascent of the east face of the Torre Sur del Paine, Piola and Sprungli were given the prestigious award, the Piolet d'Or, for what was considered the best climb of 1992.

TORRE SUR DEL PAINE "En el ojo del huracán"

- Superb "Big-Wall" route with a very steep, compact technical central section.
- First part with good gray rock; second part with very solid magnificent red granite.
- First ascent: Michel Piola/Vincent Sprungli, January 28, 1992 after 4 days
  of preparation.

900 m./ED sup./6b et A4

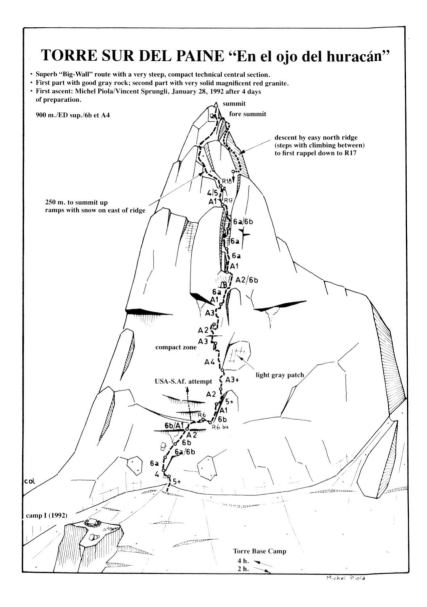

summit

fore summit

descent by easy north ridge
(steps with climbing between)
to first rappel down to R17

R18

4/5
A1   R17

250 m. to summit up
ramps with snow on east of ridge

6a/6b

6a

6a

A1

A2/6b

6a
A1

A3

A2
A3

compact zone

A4

light gray patch

USA-S.Af. attempt

A3+

A2   5+
R6   A1
6b/A1   6b
         R6 bis
      A2
       6b
      6a/6b

6a
4
      5+

col

camp I (1992)

Torre Base Camp
4 h.
2 h.

Michel Piola

PLATE 56

Photo by Fabio Leoni

LA CATEDRAL, Paine Group, Patagonia. Italian Route on left; American on right.

of settled weather. Fortunately, we didn't have to wait long. Four days of challenging climbing brought us to the summit on January 26. The east face is slightly concave; our route goes up the middle, following corner systems till we reached the summit ridge a bit left of the top. The climbing was mostly aid till the last few pitches where we were treated to delightful free-climbing on perfect rock. Another day was spent rappelling the route. (VI, 5.10, A4+; 29 pitches, 1000 meters.) We were followed by Italians. [See below.] They took a line to the left of ours, up a buttress that defines the left edge of the east face. Their route angled right at the top joining our route at our third bivouac and following it from there to the top.

CHARLES FOWLER

La Catedral, Southeast Face, and Torre Norte del Paine, West Face. Fabio Leoni, Danny Zampiccoli, Paola Fanton, Flavia Menotti and I spent January and February in the Paine region. We placed Base Camp at the foot of the southeast face of La Catedral in the Valle del Francés. We began the climbing on January 12. La Catedral is one of the most spectacular towers of Patagonia, but it is little known because of the difficulty of approach. Our route was very similar to climbs on El Capitan with cracks and dihedrals of an incredible steepness on beautiful rock. The climb begins immediately with very difficult pitches (VII+, A3+). In the first 700 meters of the 1000 meters of the ascent, there is barely a place to stand comfortably. We climbed on eight days with two bivouacs on the wall. At 3:30 P.M. on February 2, Leoni, Zampiccoli, Signora Fanton and I reached the summit in a strong snowstorm. On February 21, Zampiccoli, Leoni and I made a new route on the west face of the Torre Norte del Paine to the north summit of the peak; this route lies to the left of the new British-South African route. The excellent rock and difficulties not over VI+, A2 allowed us to do the climb in a single day, aided by ropes left on the face during an attempt by another expedition. [From another source, we learn that Signor Mànica was struck during the descent by rockfall which broke his leg. A difficult evacuation by helicopter followed.—*Editor.*] Because of climbers who seem to have little respect or love for nature, the incredible beauty of this region is being ruined by filth left at the camps and on the moraines and hundreds of meters of rope abandoned on the faces. This has happened in the last few years. In the very near future this little paradise will be destroyed. We did our best to remedy the situation. It would take little effort if all were to do their part.

MARIO MÀNICA, *Club Alpino Italiano*

Paine Chico, West Face and Torre Norte del Paine, North Summit, West Face. It had stormed for days and when it dawned fine on February 19, South African Philip Lloyd and I slumbered late. Not until nine A.M. did we awake with shock and horror and virtually run up to the massive apron and tower I had spotted from the east face of the Torre Central. We arrived at the base of Paine Chico's west

PLATE 57

Photo by Fabio Leoni

Climbing on LA CATEDRAL.

face at one P.M. and began ascending the now decomposing snow with avalanches thundering around the valley. It was very hot. After a couple of pitches of mixed climbing, we reached the smooth slabs and actually climbed baretopped. Seven long unprotected pitches followed an immaculate dike (5.10) until we got to a razor-sharp ridge leading to the final tower. It turned cold and it was late. I had to climb fast up a stunning overhanging corner capped by big roofs. This was a hard, very long pitch of thin hand-jamming, made all the more difficult with only three Friends of a useful size. Phil led one more pitch to the summit from where we descended in utter darkness through the whole night down an alpine ridge and couloir to the left of our route. After a rest day in glorious sunshine, February 21 dawned fine. This time we made the four-hour walk to the foot of the west face of the Torre Norte by 8:30 A.M. The day was cold but clear. We were to attempt the first ascent of the north summit by the superb pillar which sweeps up the right side of the west face. Three pitches of solid golden rock brought us to the first crux, a very overhanging constricted chimney which split the apex of a huge fin. After this, three pitches of hand- and finger-cracks led us to the main problem, an overhanging wall split by a finger flake. A dangerous traverse led rightwards to the flake, from where I had to climb fast to avoid pumping out. Higher, the crack was completely choked with ice and I had to traverse right to reach a crack line. After one more pitch in the crack, the angle eased and progress was fast, but the weather began to deteriorate. On top we met a team of Italian friends who had just completed a line to the left of ours. [See the account above.] We decided to rappel down their route with them and clean the fixed rope. Halfway down, the rope pulled off a loose block whick broke the leg of Mario Mànica, a gruesome compound fracture. The three-day rescue in appalling weather ensued with soldiers and helicopter.

PAUL PRITCHARD, *England*

Torre Central del Paine, East Face. A full article appears earlier in this *Journal* about the remarkable new route climbed by Britons on the east face of the Torre Central del Paine between the 1991 German and the 1974 South African routes.

Torre Sur de Paine, 1991. On November 1, 1991, Argentine Sebastián de la Cruz and Spaniard José Carlos Tamayo made the fourth ascent of the normal north ridge and the sixth to the summit of the South Paine Tower after fixing 300 meters of rope.

Torres del Paine, 1992-3. Three young climbers from Bariloche were the core of an expedition that climbed all three of the Paine Towers and made new routes on two of them. They were Teodoro Plaza, 20 years old, and Ramiro Calvo and Diego Luro, both 18. On December 3 and 4, they climbed a new route on the west face of the Torre Norte del Paine. On December 8, they repeated the

1963 Italian (Bich) route on the Torre Sur. They were then joined on a new route on the east face of the Torre Central by South African Phillip Lloyd, American Peter Garber and Argentine Nicolás Benedetti. Starting on December 10, they fixed 850 meters of rope and climbed 31 pitches between the 1963 British route and the 1976 South African one. On January 19, 1993, Calvo, Plaza and Luro reached the summit and descended, leaving the fixed ropes in place. On January 17, Lloyd, Benedetti and, for a second time, Luro climbed to the summit and cleaned the route on the descent. On January 10, Benedetti completed a solo ascent of the normal route on the Torre Norte. [This report was received as we were going to press. In the next *AAJ*, we hope to have more details. —*Editor.*]

VOJSLAV ARKO, *Club Andino Bariloche*

Escudo (Shield) and Torre Norte del Paine, 1992-3. Jerry Gore and I spent four weeks in the Paine region, enduring the expected storms before making two ascents in a five-day clear period over New Years. We established a tent under a boulder below the east face of the Escudo (Shield) and waited there for two weeks before making the first ascent of the north ridge. A 12-pitch, mixed approach-gully was prepared with 200 meters of fixed line. The ridge itself involved 12 pitches (5.10, A2) on often friable granite before we reached the summit ridge of shale and snow. The access to the very summit was barred by a notch of loose shale and, not wishing to resort to bolts, we descended from that point by abseil. The round-trip climb took 20 hours and was the second route on the mountain. Two days later, on January 1, 1993, we repeated the normal route on the Torre Norte del Paine with perfect, still weather.

ANDREW PERKINS, *Troll Safety Equipment, England*

Cuerno Principal del Paine and La Hoja, 1991. An Italian group composed of Franco Nicolini, Romeo Destefani, Claudio Kerschbaumer and Felice Spellini climbed a new route on the southwest face of the Cuerno Principal on November 6, 1991. It took them eight hours to complete the climb, which was mostly of UIAA V, VI and VI+ difficulty. On November 11, 1991, they repeated the 1982 route on La Hoja via the the central fissure of the west face and the south ridge. That climb took them 20 hours.

Aleta de Tiburón, Paine Group. After failing to climb Fitz Roy in early February, on February 28 Swedes Patrick Lind, Magnus Nilson and Americans Lorna Corson and I climbed the beautiful Aleta de Tiburón above the Valle del Francés by a crack system on its southwest side (III-IV, 5.8). We descended the route in 9 or 10 rappels after down-climbing the south ridge for about 500 feet.

NORM LARSON

ANTARCTICA

Pilot Peak, Lerrouy Island, and Mount Jules Verne, Pourquoi Pas Island, 1991. Our expedition traveled to Grahamland in the yacht Pelagic. We were American Skip Novak, Briton Hamish Laird, Kenyan Julia Crossley, Irishwoman Tara Machey, Belgian André Mechelynck and Italians Jacopo Merizzi and I. During the three months we were there, Novak, Merizzi and I made the following climbs: Pilot Peak (815 meters, 2674 feet) by its south ridge on February 5, 1991 and probably one of the most difficult climbs yet done in Antarctica, the south face of Mount Jules Verne (1633 meters, 5358 feet) on February 22 and 23, 1991. This TD+ climb was 36 pitches long and involved ice up to 80°. We made two attempts to climb 1100-meter-high Sharp Peak but were stopped both times by a big cornice 40 meters from the summit.

MARCO PRETI, *Club Alpino Italiano*

EUROPE

Les Droites, New Route, 1991. On October 3, 1991, Canadian Barry Blanchard and I climbed a new route on Les Droites. We left the Argentière Hut at 5:30 A.M. and crossed the bergschrund an hour later. The climb began in a small gully between the Couzy Spur and the rock *rognon* below the big ice slope that leads to the Col de la Verte. The 120-meter-high gully presents passages of 75° ice. We exited onto 50° ice and followed the slope's left edge close to the Couzy route for 400 meters. At 3550 meters (after climbing past the departure of the Couzy route), we exited left into a prominent ice gully, which we climbed for two pitches of 65° to 80° ice with poor protection on thin ice. We climbed two more pitches of moderate ice (55° to 60°) and entered another miniscule ice gully. Barry broke both his ice tools on the following pitch. The ice was thin, but pitons and medium-sized nuts gave protection. The next three pitches followed this system of ice and mixed ground more or less directly. The climbing was difficult and sustained (5.9 and 5.10 with "interesting" protection). At the top of the 8th pitch of new climbing, there were two options: to continue straight up in a chimney system to join the ice slope at the top of the Couzy route or to break right on an iced-up ramp for two pitches of mixed climbing. Pitch 9 was hard and Pitch 10 easier. We emerged on an arête bordering a deep couloir on the right. We climbed the rock directly for two pitches (5.7) and then turned to a small arête towards the left. We climbed a steep chimney to the summit ridge (5.9) and arrived on top at 6:30 P.M. We were at the Couvercle Hut at 11:30 P.M. The climb is difficult even by modern standards. With better ice conditions it might be easier. We were on the face for 12 hours, even though we climbed the first 500 meters unroped. It is not recommended for anyone who doesn't like long run-outs above nuts or tied-off ice screws.

MARC FRANCIS TWIGHT

Aiguille des Pèlerins, North Face. On April 21 and 22, Briton Andy Parkin and I climbed a new route on the north face of the Aiguille des Pèlerins (3318 meters, 10,887 feet). We climbed directly to the Col des Pèlerins and began about halfway between the Rébuffat route and Michel Piola's "Nostrodamus." We finally climbed it on the third attempt. The first was in November, 1989, when we ran out of daylight and were surprised at how difficult it was. The second was on April 11, 1992, when basically the same thing happened although we were two pitches higher. We finally accepted the idea that we would have to bivouac. We climbed 14 hours on the first day and slept at the top of the 8th pitch on one of the two "good" ledges that the route offers. We climbed on a 60-meter rope since the 5th and 6th pitches required at least 55 meters to reach reasonable belays. We climbed 12 hours on the second day. The first six belays are fixed and we left only one piton on the rest of the route. Technical data: 500 meters; fourteen 60-meter pitches: 90° ice, 5.9, A3. Pitch 1: 65° ice with one short vertical passage; Pitch 2: 60° ice; Pitch 3: 45° snow, then 70° ice; Pitch 4: 90° ice, 5.9, A2; Pitch 5: 90° ice, 5.9, A2 (harder than Pitch 4); Pitch 6: A2, 70° ice, 5.8 (a long, dangerous, loose pitch); Pitch 7: 60°-70° ice, 5.6; Pitch 8: 70° ice, then 5.7; Pitch 9: 80° ice, 5.9 (difficult protection); Pitch 10: 75°-85° ice (this pitch joins Rébuffat route for 20 meters); Pitch 11: A3 (loose; a 25-meter pitch); Pitch 12: A2, 5.9, 60° ice; Pitch 13: A.2, 5.7, 60° ice; Pitch 14: 45°-65° ice. 5.5 (big, loose blocks; very dangerous for both leader and belayer). This route is more difficult than the one we did on Les Droites, though half as long.

MARC FRANCIS TWIGHT

100th Anniversary of the Planinska zveza Slovenije. The American Alpine Club congratulates the Planinska zveza Slovenije (the Slovene Alpine Club) on the 100th Anniversary of its founding. Slovene mountaineering has a long history. The first ascent of their highest mountain, Triglav, took place in 1776, eight years before that of Mont Blanc. Slovene climbers are among the world leaders at this time. They have achieved notable climbs in recent years, such as the first complete ascent of the west ridge of Everest, the north face of Kumbhakarna, the south face of Lhotse, the southwest face of Kangchenjunga, Menlungtse and many others. They have continued to serve the whole moun-taineering community with the Aleš Kunaver Mountaineering School in Ma-nang, Nepal, which instructs Nepalese and others in climbing techniques. May they continue to prosper and have a brilliant future!

AFRICA

Mount Kenya, Diamond Buttress, 1991. A probable new route on the 500-meter-high rocky south face of Batian, the highest summit of Mount Kenya, was climbed on December 19, 1991 by Bulgarians Ivan Maslarov and Nikolai

Petkov. They ascended a 15-pitch high-quality route to the left of the Diamond Buttress Direct, which it joined in the upper part (UIAA VII, VII+, A2).

JÓZEF NYKA, *Editor, Taternik, Poland*

ASIA

American Ascents of 8000-Meter Peaks as of August 31, 1992. Gasherbrum I (Hidden Peak): July 5, 1958 by Andrew Kauffman and Peter Schoening (First Ascent). *Everest:* May 1, 1963 by James Whittaker. Numerous subsequent US climbs, giving a total of 64 US individual ascents by 57 men and 3 women. (Peter Athans made two repetitions and David Breashears and Ed Viesturs, one.) *Dhaulagiri:* May 12, 1973 by Louis Reichardt and John Roskelley, followed by further US ascents in 1987 and 1990. Total: 7 individual ascents (6 men and 1 woman). *K2:* September 6, 1978 by James Wickwire and Louis Reichardt. Further US ascents the following day and in 1990 and 1992. Total: 8 individual ascents (men). *Annapurna:* October 15, 1978 by Vera Komarkova (US Citizen of Czech origin) and Irene Miller. Another US ascent in 1988 by Steve Boyer. Total: 3 individuals (2 women, 1 man). *Makalu:* May 15, 1980 by John Roskelley. Further US ascents in 1987 and 1990. Total: 6 individual ascents (5 men, 1 woman). *Broad Peak:* June 28, 1983 by Stephen Sustad. Another US ascent in 1992. Total: 2 individual ascents. *Shisha Pangma:* September 30, 1983 by Glenn Porzak, Chris Pizzo and Mike Browning. Further US ascents in 1984 and 1987. Total: 10 individual ascents. *Cho Oyu:* May 13, 1984 by Vera Komarkova. Further US ascents in 1986, 1987, 1989 and 1991. Total: 9 individual ascents (5 men and 3 women). *Gasherbrum II:* July 11, 1985 by Theo Mayer. Further 3 men in 1987. Total: 4 individual ascents. *Nanga Parbat:* July 13, 1985 by Slawomir Lobodziński (US citizen of Polish origin). No further US ascents. *Kangchenjunga:* May 3, 1988 by Carlos Buhler. Further US ascents in 1989 and 1990. Total: 8 individual ascents (all male). *Lhotse:* May 13, 1990 by Wally Berg and Scott Fischer. No further US ascents. Total: 2 individual ascents. *Manaslu:* Remains unclimbed by US mountaineers.

The following nations (with dates of completion) have climbed all fourteen 8000ers: Germany (1983), Japan (1985), Switzerland (1986), Austria (1986), Italy (1986) and Poland (1987). The following (with the yet unclimbed peak in parentheses) have ascended thirteen 8000ers: France (Lhotse), Czechoslovakia (Shisha Pangma), United States (Manaslu), Spain (Lhotse) and South Korea (Annapurna). Then follow Slovenia (12), United Kingdom (11), Nepal (10), Russia (8).

XAVIER EGUSKITZA, *Pyrenaica, Bilbao, Spain*

Bhutan

Ganglagachu. A ten-member French expedition led by Philippe Allibert and Jean-François Tripard on October 25 climbed Ganglagachu (c. 6000 meters) in northern Bhutan, an "elegant," although not very difficult snow-and-rock peak. A photograph appears in *Montagnes Magazine* of January 1993 on page 12.

India—Sikkim

Chombu Attempt. A six-man Japanese team from Toyo University, led by Kenshiro Ohtani, was the first foreign expedition allowed to enter this part of Sikkim since World War II. They unsuccessfully attempted Chombu (6362 meters, 20,872 feet) via the Sebu La and the Chombu Glacier, west of the peak. They reached a high point of 5900 meters on October 29. A narrow ridge and loose snow stopped them.

HARISH KAPADIA, *Himalayan Club*

Nepal

Kangchenjunga Ascent and Tragedy. The famous Polish woman climber, Wanda Rutkiewicz, was last seen shortly after eight P.M. on May 12. On May 10, she and Mexican Carlos Carsolio, leader of a team of four Mexicans and two Poles, were climbing between destroyed Camp III at 7300 meters on the north face and Camp IV at 7900 meters when Wanda at eleven P.M. decided to bivouac. Carsolio continued on and got to the ice cave which was Camp IV at 6:30 A.M. Rutkiewicz arrived only at seven P.M. The pair left Camp IV at 3:30 A.M. on the 12th in good weather. According to Carsolio, she was climbing even more slowly than usual, and he went far ahead of her despite his having to break trail in deep snow while she could follow in his footsteps. "She was climbing extremely slowly," Carsolio reported later. "Maybe it was because she was 49 years old, or maybe because of her leg," which she had broken on Elbruz in 1981 and had kept bothering her. She had told him before going to Kangchenjunga, "I will not be quick. I don't want to take risks. I have a lot of respect for Kangchenjunga," which she had attempted with the Slovenes from the southwest in 1991. Carsolio reached the top alone at five P.M., the first Latin American to gain Kangchenjunga's summit. During the descent to Camp IV, he met Rutkiewicz three hours later between 8250 and 8300 meters. She was inside a wind hole, a kind of cave carved out of the snow by the wind, where she had stopped to bivouac an hour and a half earlier. "It was good protection for her," said Carsolio. "It was a very cold night, but clear and not windy." She told him she was cold, that her old down suit was not warm enough. She had her bivouac sack around her. She had no sleeping bag, stove, fuel or food, and she had taken from Camp IV that morning only a liter of water. She did have a headlamp, 20 meters of rope, extra gloves, extra goggles and perhaps some sweets. She planned to go for the summit the next morning. "She showed in her eyes determination to reach the summit," he said. "I think she felt this was her last chance to climb Kangchenjunga. I told her I was going to Camp IV for the night and would descend to Camp II and wait for her there." There was no food or fuel left at Camp IV. They were together for perhaps ten minutes; she was clear mentally. Then Carsolio went on down, never to see or hear from her again. A member at a lower camp watched the mountain on the 13th, the day when she should have gone to the summit, and saw no movement that day. But she could have left her bivouac during the dark early morning hours and would have been out of sight when she reached 8400 meters. Carsolio left Camp IV at noon on the 13th and spent that night and two more at Camp II at 6890 meters, waiting for Rutkiewicz. When she had failed to appear by the morning of the 16th, he left for Base Camp, leaving at Camp II a tent, sleeping bag, walkie-talkie radio (one of only two they had—the other was at Base Camp), food, gas and a thermos of water. At Base Camp, he and Arkadiusz Gąsienica and Andrés Delgado, who had been unwell and unable to go for the summit, had the other walkie-talkie open all the time, but no sound came from it. The three remaining members finally left Base Camp in very bad weather on May 21 with no idea of what had happened to Rutkiewicz. "It was difficult for us to leave the mountain," Carsolio said in Kathmandu, "but I am sure that she cannot have survived because of the bad weather and because she was extremely tired and without drink." This year on Kangchenjunga she had no problems with altitude sickness, nor had she succumbed to frostbite in April when two Mexican teammates, Carsolio's wife Elsa Avila and his brother Alfredo, did get seriously frostbitten and had to go home for medical treatment. Wanda Rutkiewicz had eight 8000ers already to her credit. She was the only woman to have climbed more than four of them. The first was Everest in 1978, when she became the first European woman and the third woman of any nation to ascend it. In 1991 she had conceived the ambitious plan to bag the rest of the 14 giant mountains in a year or a year-and-a-half. She wanted to attempt a second 8000er this spring; her name was on the list of the Romanian Dhaulagiri team. This summer she was to have been a member of an expedition to Broad Peak. Wanda Rutkiewicz will go down in history as one of the greats of mountaineering.

ELIZABETH HAWLEY

Kangchenjunga Attempt and Tragedy. Our expedition consisted of Hannes Grimm, Walter Hadersdorfer, Edu Koch, Dr. Gerhard Reif, Michael Saumweber, Karl Schrag and me as leader. On March 4, we left Basantpur with 156 porters. After traveling through Dhoban, Sokathum and Ghunsa, we got to Base Camp at 5100 meters at Pang Pema on March 19. From Gunsa on, because of the altitude, we had to make many carries with nine porters and 13 yaks. Colds brought from Europe weakened the team. We set up Advance Base at 5400 meters at the foot of the west-southwest ridge on March 20 and Camp I at 5750

PLATE 58

Photo by Michael Saumweber

North Face of KANGCHENJUNGA.

PLATE 59

Photo by Michael Saumweber

**KANGCHENJUNGA's North Face.
Full lines were climbed by Germans.
Broken lines show projected routes.**

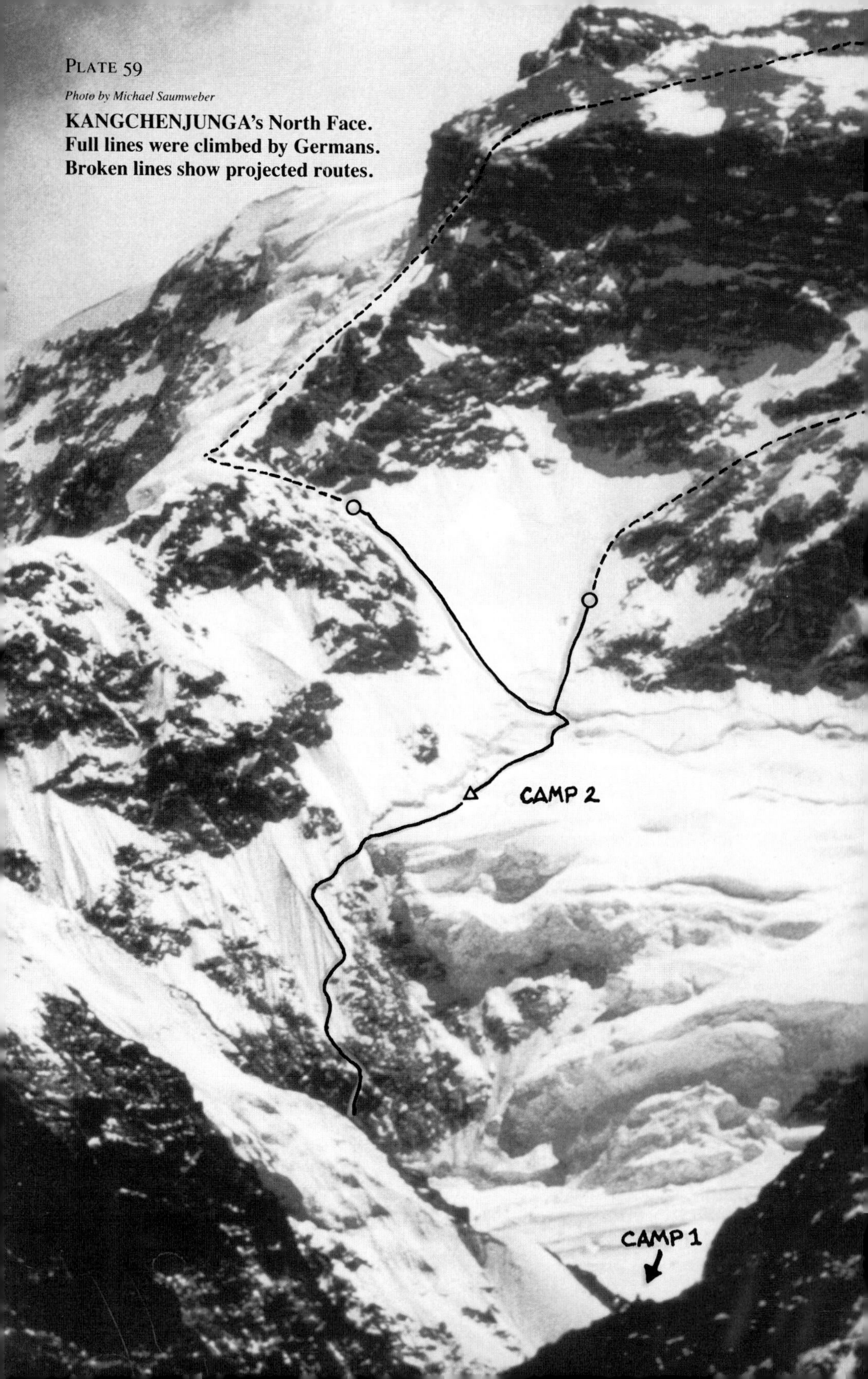

CAMP 2

CAMP 1

meters on March 25. We had problems with the lower wall on the 1983 Warth route because of blank ice and the high bergschrund. Vertical pitches had to be jümared. On April 5, Koch fell on the last rope-length below the glacial plateau. Despite a broken ankle, he descended under his own power to Base Camp, but he had to be helicoptered out. We placed Camp II at 6600 meters on April 7. We abandoned the Warth route on April 17 and Schrag and Dr. Reif climbed the Messner route almost to the north ridge at 7000 meters. We fixed rope between 6100 and 6600 meters and above 6700 meters. On April 23, sirdar Ang Phurba fell unconscious while cooking in a closed tent but was revived with oxygen. On the 25th, Grimm, Hadersdorfer, Lhakpa Nuru Sherpa and Ang Dorje Sherpa climbed to Camp II, hoping to establish Camps III and IV. At eleven P.M. Grimm and Hadersdorfer found the Sherpas unconscious and failed to revive them with oxygen. Despite strict warnings, the Sherpas cooked in closed tents. Their bodies were buried in a crevasse. We gave up the expedition. It is our opinion that the Warth route is the safest on the north face but it has very difficult rock and ice climbing. The Scott route is threatened by falling ice and rock and has avalanche danger.

WOLFGANG SINNWELL, *Akademischer Alpenverein, Munich, Germany*

Kumbhakarna. A team of six Canadians led by Ken Legg climbed the south ridge of Kumbhakarna (Jannu; 7710 meters, 25,294 feet), making the 20th ascent of the peak. Robert Driscoll and Michael White reached the summit on April 15.

ELIZABETH HAWLEY

Kumbhakarna Attempt. Four Swiss led by Hans Rauner attempted to climb Kumbhakarna (Jannu) by the south ridge. They reached 6500 meters on October 25.

ELIZABETH HAWLEY

Kumbhakarna East, East Face Attempts. Vanja Furlan and I again attempted to climb the east face of Kumbhakarna East (7468 meters, 24,502 feet), which we had tried in 1991. *(AAJ, 1992, page 4.)* After an approach march of ten days, we got to Base Camp at 5100 meters on April 28. We made two acclimatization climbs to 5800 and 6500 meters on Kabru in the first week of May. At 5:30 A.M. on May 12, we started from a tent at the foot of the face. We crossed the East Kumbhakarna Glacier and at 7:15 began the climb at 5500 meters. We climbed until midnight and bivouacked 800 meters up the wall in an ice cave in the central sérac. We had belayed 11 pitches (1 of UIAA VII, 2 of VII-, 2 of VI+ and 6 of VI). We left the bivouac at one P.M. and by nine P.M. had climbed another 600 meters. We bivouacked in a crevasse. We belayed 8 pitches (1 of VI+ and the

7100

2

1

5500

PLATE 60

Photo by Vanja Furlan

East Face of KUMBHAKARNA.

to by Bojan Počkar

eep ice at 7000 meters on JMBHAKARNA.

others of V to VI). On May 14, we were forced by a snowstorm to remain in the bivouac. Finally, at 6:30 A.M. on May 15, we proceeded in spite of unsettled weather. We decided to end the climb at noon at 7100 meters when we emerged from the face onto the southeast ridge. We had belayed seven pitches (1 of VII, 1 of VI+ and 5 of VI). At once we began the descent by rappeling the ascent route. At six P.M. we were back at the ice cave where we had had the first bivouac. We rested until eleven P.M. and continued the descent during the night. At six A.M. we were at the foot of the face. Dr. Matjaž Vrtovec was in support. A third Slovene attempt on the face, led by Dušan Debelak, was to have taken place after the monsoon. On September 20 during the approach, Damjan Vidmar drowned while bathing in the monsoon-swollen Kabela Khola. The expedition was abandoned.

BOJAN POČKAR, *Planinska zveza Slovenije*

Makalu Attempt. The great west face of Makalu had defeated top-class alpinists with its extreme difficulty at very high altitude. This season, a well-publicized, massively financed group of eight British members and one Australian under the leadership of Nick Mason did not make a fast alpine-style attempt but rather adopted the traditional siege tactics of Himalayan climbing. A British climber who was on another Makalu expedition commented, "Nick Mason's expedition was well organized, but they just didn't have the necessary Himalayan experience. Yet, they weren't *kamikaze*; they admitted the face was too much for them, and they got off it without anyone getting hurt." They reached no higher than 7000 meters on the face, then tried to scale the normal route from the northwest and managed to get to 8250 meters before newly falling snow and weariness caused them on May 14 to turn back.

ELIZABETH HAWLEY

Makalu Attempt. Our members included Americans Peter Getzels, Brad Johnson, Peter Carse, Dr. James States, Brian Cox and me as leader and Britons Adrian and Alan Burgess. Our objective was a light-weight ascent of the northwest-ridge first-ascent route without supplementary oxygen nor high-altitude Sherpas. We established Base Camp on April 6 at 17,500 feet just 20 minutes below the British Advance Base for the west face and next to a small painted mani wall. Camp I was placed at 21,500 feet on April 16, with a temporary acclimatization camp at 18,500 feet. Due to the new peak fees in Nepal, we were the only expedition on our route, which necessitated our fixing the entire route up to the Makalu La. Therefore, Camp II was not established on the col at 24,500 feet until May 13. It was our hope to reach the summit from this camp. On the evening of May 13, however, two or more feet of snow fell, making trailbreaking difficult. Most members withdrew by June 15. Brad Johnson made one final attempt on the 16th with the British west-face expedition, which a week before had switched to our route. This attempt also failed at

25,600 feet. I count the friendship and cooperation between our small American expedition and the much larger British expedition as one of the major successes of our trip. One last addendum: it should be stressed how important it is to change porters in Tashigaon on the approach. Lowland porters are definitely not up to the challenges of the relentlessly poor weather on the Shipton Col.

JAMES MCEACHEN

Makalu Post-Monsoon Attempts. None of the post-monsoon attempts on Makalu, all on the normal northwest side, was successful. French climbers Annie Beghin, Dr. Bruno Senechal and Dr. François Estève climbed to 7400 meters on September 20. Four Japanese led by Sadao Okada got to 8300 meters on October 2. Four Spaniards under the leadership of Juan José Rodríguez ascended to 7400 meters on October 7. An expedition led by Swiss Karl Kobler was composed of 11 Swiss and a Liechtensteiner. They reached 8100 meters on September 29.

ELIZABETH HAWLEY

Kangchungtse Post-Monsoon Ascents. An expedition of six Spanish Basques successfully climbed Kangchungtse (Makalu II; 7678 meters, 25,190 feet) by its south ridge. The summit was reached by the leader José Ramón Aquirare, Ramón Baztarrika and Mikel Saez on September 24. Japanese Shuichi Kaneko and Mrs. Tamani Kaneko climbed the same route to the top on September 25.

ELIZABETH HAWLEY

Kangchungtse or Makalu II Attempt. Our commercial expedition started on a really bad note. Britons Mark Miller, the original leader, Victor Radvills, who was going to be the third guide, were both killed in the Pakistani International Airlines crash outside Kathmandu in September. They had just unsuccessfully tried a new route on Nanga Parbat via Rakhiot Peak. The final expedition list included Scot Alexander Allen as leader, Englishmen Sean Smith, Fraser Andrew, David Soutar, Andrew Mayers, John Mitchell, Jonathan Vanderkar, and Americans Warren, Gabriel and Jonathan Kaplan. Unfortunately the Nepalese government did not accept my American Alpine Club endorsement because I am an Argentine citizen despite having lived in the United States for ten years. Since my name was not on the permit, I was not allowed to climb. Nine of us left Hile on October 11. Sandy Allen and Sean Smith flew from England and caught up with us. During the walk in, two members had to be evacuated: John Mitchell because of an allergic reaction to malaria pills and Warren Kaplan because of a lung infection caused by a fall which injured his ribs. We arrived at Advance Base at 5200 meters above the Barun Glacier on October 23. The bad weather during the walk in cleared but winter conditions set in: cold and high winds. The team ferried loads to Camp I at 5700 meters. The route got worse since the wind had blown all the snow off, leaving hard, grey ice. We benefited from fixed ropes left by the Japanese. Most members reached Camp II at 6400 meters. On November 7, Jonathan Kaplan, Allen, Nga Temba Sherpa and Dawa Tenzing set up Camp III at 7200 meters, just below the Makalu La. The next day extreme winds forced them down. We left Base Camp on November 11.

MIGUEL HELFT, *Out There Trekking*

Baruntse. Two expeditions climbed Baruntse (7129 meters, 23,389 feet) by the normal southeast ridge. On October 11, French climbers Michel Zalio, Guy l'Hermite, Mme Mariette Desplan, Mlle Christine Roux and Sherpa Kilo Temba reached the summit. On October 15, Germans Roland Brand, Helmut Chlastak, Peter Diesner, Eduard Kottmair, Andreas Kraus, Wolfgang Raiser, Frau Hildegard Reinwald, Austrians Hannes Neuwirt, leader, Frau Hannelore Neuwirt and Sherpas Pasang and Dorje got to the top.

ELIZABETH HAWLEY

Chamlang Attempt. Three Frenchmen under the leadership of Laurent Hallier attempted to climb Chamlang (7319 meters, 24,014 feet) by its north face but had to quit at 6400 meters on October 22.

ELIZABETH HAWLEY

Ama Dablam, Pre-Monsoon Ascents, Tragedy, Attempt. All four premonsoon expeditions to Ama Dablam were on the normal route, the southwest ridge. A pair of Americans, David Nettle and James Quirk, reached the summit on April 10. Seven Spaniards were led by José Joaquín Goñi. On April 19, the leader, his brother Carlos Goñi, Mikel Iraizoz and Iñaki Villanueva reached the summit. Carlos Goñi then rappelled some sixty meters. He was followed by his brother, who plunged to his death when the rappel anchor pulled out. The other two spent the night on the summit and then descended the next morning without a rope. The body of the dead leader was sighted at the foot of the mountain but could not be reached. An expedition of nine Britons was led by Ross Ashe-Cregan. Paul Higgins and Kami Tenzing Sherpa completed the 99th ascent of the peak on May 4. A group of nine Englishmen, an American and a New Zealander led by Robin Beadle made an unsuccessful attempt, reaching 6550 meters on April 24.

ELIZABETH HAWLEY

Ama Dablam. On March 31, Jim Quirk and I arrived at the beautiful Mingbo Valley Base Camp. After an abortive attempt that ended in storm at 21,500 feet on April 4, we regained the southwest ridge on April 8 and bivouacked at 19,000 feet. On the 9th, we climbed the long rock ridge to spend the night at the Red Tower at 20,000 feet. This lovely ridge has solid rock, fantastic exposure and a fair amount of technical 5th-class climbing. On April 10, we reached the summit in twelve hours. The technical crux was the steep, wide crack (5.9) that splits the base of the White Tower. On the upper glacial headwall and past the Dablam it was exceptionally dry and we found hard, brittle ice. Before leaving Base Camp, we made a thorough sweep of the surrounding area, collecting trash. When we arrived at Park Headquarters with two duffels of old cans, we were escorted to the superintendent who graciously thanked us and gave us a certificate of appreciation! This seems to be a rare occurrence. When we also donated our $5.00 "garbage deposit" to the clean-up fund, they were even more pleased. Most teams forfeit their deposit rather than bringing back their trash. I hope more expeditions will support the clean-up effort.

DAVID NETTLE, Unaffiliated

Ama Dablam, Post-Monsoon Ascents, Attempts and Tragedy. As has been the case in past post-monsoon years, many expeditions head for Ama Dablam (6812 meters, 22,349 feet). In 1992, they completed the 100th to the 112th ascents. Except for where noted, the route of ascent was the southwest ridge. A British expedition led by Henry Todd was also accompanied by two Poles. The summit was reached by Pole Ryszard Pawlowski and Briton Jeff Lakes on October 24, by Pawlowski again, Alec McNab, Paul Roberts, Phil Clark, leader Todd and Pole Krzysztof Pankiewicz on November 1 and by Ian Cotgrove and Pawlowski for the third time on November 7. A French party of 11 French climbers and an Italian was led by Daniel Petraud and Jean-Jacques Rolland. Leader Petraud and Pierre Blanchard got to the top on October 24, Gilbert Lombard and Mlle Marie Sangnier on the 25th and Eric Bérard and Petraud again on the 27th. American Peter Athans, who led 14 Americans, accompanied the French to the summit on October 24, while Scott Cole, Jason Keith and Todd Burleson got there on November 7. Frenchman Jean-Noël Roche led another Frenchman, 4 Americans, 2 Belgians and 2 Italians. Roche with Americans Timothy Gill and Richard Southwell reached the summit on October 25, followed on October 28 by Roche again and Italians Pierluigi Avataneo and Mauro Gaido. Tragically Belgian Karine van Dooren died in a fall. Nine Spaniards were led by Lluis Giner. On October 26, leader Giner, Tomás Bravo, Sergi Martínez, Manuel de la Motta and Diego Fernández got to the top, followed on November 4 by Carlos Bravo and de la Matta again. Laurent Terray, leader of a four-man French expedition, climbed to the summit on November 12. The only successful group not to climb the normal route, 3 Australians and 2 Canadians led by Richard Howes, ascended the southeast ridge and descended the southwest ridge. On November 1, Australian Richard Howes, Matt Godbold and Ray Vran and Canadian Kobus Bardard reached the top. Three unsuccessful expeditions attempted the northeast ridge. They were 6 Britons, an American and a Norwegian led by Malcolm Duff (high point: 6170 meters on October 10), 2 Italians led by Renzo Turri (high point: 5350 meters on October 13) and 3 Swiss led by Beat Baumann (high point: 6000 meters on October 15).

ELIZABETH HAWLEY

Ama Dablam Winter Ascents. Five expeditions climbed Ama Dablam by its normal southwest ridge in the last month of 1992. Five Swiss were under the leadership of Franco Dellatorre, who reached the summit alone on December 1. Five Belgians and a Swiss led by Alain Hubert completed the 113th ascent of the peak on December 3, when Belgians Hubert, Didier Goetghebuer, Swiss Jacques Richon and Mana Ram Tamang got to the top. The summit was reached by Japanese Hiroshi Aota on December 6, leader Yoshiki Sasahara and Toshio Ono on December 7 and Yasushi Yamanoi also on the 7th, but the latter had climbed to the southwest ridge via the west face. Seven South Koreans were led by Cha Jae-Woo. On December 7, Kim Wi-Yeoung with Sherpas Sonam Tschering and Ang Dawa climbed to the summit, followed on the 9th by Kee Su-Young. Another South Korean group of nine was under the leadership of Chun Byung-Tai. On December 7, Chun, Sim Jung-Shup, Kim Jin-Yong and Dawa Sherpa completed the ascent, followed on December 11 by Jeon Woo-Song, Jeong Duk-Ki, Shim Sung-Bo and again Dawa.

ELIZABETH HAWLEY

Lhotse South Face, More on Tomo Česen's 1990 Ascent. When Scott Fischer and I returned to Kathmandu after climbing Lhotse in May 1990, we were interviewed by Liz Hawley and at that time we verified that Česen had reached the summit of Lhotse. As I recall, we were sure that he had been there based on his description of the summit area, which Liz related to us a few days after she had interviewed him. Among other things, he described seeing an old orange oxygen bottle on a small platform just below the summit, which is a small snow cone. He also told Liz that he had decided against climbing the last eight meters up onto this snow cone because he questioned its stability, evidence that besides being exceptionally skilled, this guy has some good sense. Fischer and I did climb gingerly to the top, but we had the (false) security of being roped together. The interesting thing is what we have been hearing since, about a disputed photo which Česen claims to have taken from the summit showing the view into the Western Cwm. The French, apparently, have claimed you cannot see the Western Cwm from the summit of Lhotse. One of the great regrets of my climbing career so far is that there was almost no visibilty on our summit day. I had been excited about the prospect of checking out the feasibility of a traverse to Lhotse Middle from the summit. As it was, I never saw Lhotse Middle that day, but I did see, faintly, the rock summit on the opposite side of the couloir which we had exited left to reach the true summit. This point is only slightly lower than the true summit and I remember thinking it might block a good view into the Cwm. The confusion about this is unfortunate because, based on his description to Liz Hawley, I have no doubt that Česen, Fischer and I went to the same place in May of 1990, he, of course, by his remarkable solo ascent of the south face. I certainly hope it was the top of Lhotse!

WALLY BERG

Everest, Ascents, Attempts and Tragedies via the Western Cwm in the Pre-Monsoon Season. The scene on Nepal's side of Everest was not one of unmitigated joy despite all the summit successes. Four men died. The Base Camp area was crowded with 268 climbers plus their Base Camp staffs. They belonged to an unprecedented total of 13 expeditions. One team, the British Joint Services Everest Expedition, acted as mediator amongst the others from time to time and early on suggested areas where teams should sleep, where toilets should be and where a path should run between the various expeditions. This last suggestion was made after Spaniards and Netherlanders threw stones at each other for walking through their camps. American and New Zealand expedition leaders complained about Russians pushing ahead of them on a climbing route for which the Russians had no permit, doing so in violation of their repeated promises to wait briefly for those who did have permission to move up first, and in contravention of the Nepalese authorities' instructions to stick to their own more difficult route; the result of this conflict was that eight Russian summiters and their leader have been banned from entering Nepal again for five years. The Russians complained that the American and New Zealand leaders were making large profits conducting incompetent clients whom they charged US $35,000 each, that this was merely business, and that the American leader was no gentleman in the language he used. The British made a formal complaint about a Czechoslovak who "was wandering all over the mountain; he asked if he could climb up our ropes to the west shoulder. When I said, 'No,' he came up anyway." A New Zealander, whose commercial expedition caused much of the long delay for others having to wait their turn to ascend the Hillary Step, complained of "the most frightening time of my life" when he was descending the step. Indians were ascending roped to each other but belayed to nothing else. One of them, who kept slipping, was grabbing him for a handhold "and I could see myself falling down the southwest face tied to four Indians." A Chilean who reached the summit from the Nepalese side complained of the rudeness of other Chileans whom he met on the top. They had come from the Tibetan side and greeted him with epithets instead of a friendly welcome. He had been ready to congratulate his compatriots, the first South Americans to the summit and only the second successful team on their climbing route, the steep east face to the South Col. (See their report in the Tibetan section.) A general complaint by well-organized, well-financed teams was that others climbed on their backs. The wandering Czechoslovak, Russians, French expedition members and a Briton who was not really anyone's team member were mentioned as climbers who would never have made any progress on the mountain, and some of whom would have perished. There were charges that the Russians helped themselves to other people's food and tents. A Netherlander refused entry to his small tent to a Russian who said he couldn't find his tent at that camp; the Netherlander said later that there was no Russian tent at the camp and that he had no idea what became of the Russian. Actually, an American took the Russian into his tent. When a Frenchman became seriously ill from the high altitude, his radio-less team's leader asked the British to send word down to Base Camp on their radio and to supply his oxygen-less team with three very expensive bottles of oxygen, medicines, a stretcher and much of the manpower to carry the sick man down the exceedingly difficult Khumbu Icefall to Base Camp. The British reckoned that only five of the 13 parties on the mountain were truly equipped for the task. All except one of this spring's summiters used artificial oxygen. The exception was Ang Rita Sherpa, who went to the top on May 15 for his record-breaking *seventh* ascent of Everest and who says that he has never used oxygen on the mountain. All but one of the successful teams from Nepal climbed by the way of the standard route up the Lhotse Face and the southeast ridge. The team that did not follow the normal route was a group of Spaniards, mostly army men, who peacefully (they were not the stone throwers) and happily climbed the south pillar alone, joined the southeast ridge above the south corridor to the right of the pillar and sent three Spaniards and two Nepalese to the summit on May 15, when altogether 19 climbers went to the top. There has been considerable comment on the massive number of participants, some of whom, from the Russian and an unsuccessful Indian expedition, were not even on their teams' membership lists approved by the Nepalese authorities. An Italian visitor to Everest Base Camp said it was difficult to move amongst the tents at what looked like a fairground. May 12 saw a grand total of 32 people from five expeditions on the summit of Everest between 10:30 A.M. and one P.M.: six Americans, four Russians, three Indians (including a woman), three New Zealanders, two Netherlanders, the first Belgian woman, the first Israeli, the first Hong Kong Chinese and 11 Nepalese, who were there chiefly to help the foreigners. The largest number of Everest summiters in any previous season was 31 on four different days in October 1990. This season altogether 55 people reached the summit, also on four days, from the Nepalese side, while three more climbed to the top from Tibet. The Everest summit figures assume that all claims were correct. This spring, doubts were expressed on whether four climbers went to the summit on May 14, a day when the weather was not good, but others including Americans are confident that they did. (A claim by the Russians that they had first attempted their assigned route, the southwest face, and had reached 7250 meters on April 6 was, however, greeted with nearly universal disbelief amongst other teams.) And others wondered whether an Indian party of three had really managed to get all the way to the top on May 10, another day of bad weather; they stoutly assert they did. A negative is that four lives were lost, although the toll was small for such a large number. Two members of an unsuccessful and somewhat disorganized Indian expedition, leader Deepak Kulkarni and Raymond Jacob, died of exhaustion and exposure after they had failed to reach the shelter of their highest camp on the South Col. They had been climbing extremely slowly through snow and wind during the day and into the night of May 1. They were discovered the next morning, barely alive. Jacob was lying in the snow some 30 meters from their camp; Kulkarni was hanging on the fixed ropes a bit farther down. For the other Indian team, a well-organized group from the Indo-Tibetan Border Police, all went well, with summit successes on two different days, until the last day when they were descending to Base Camp. Sher

Singh, who had been a cook at Camp II and had helped carry loads although he was really not a climber, slipped on a tilting ladder about 20 meters from the bottom of the Khumbu Icefall. He had a nylon sling tied around his waist that he had attached to the safety rope along the ladder. When he fell, it pulled tight like a noose, ruptured his kidney and broke his back. The fourth man to die with an Everest expedition on the Nepalese side was a 43-year-old Nepalese, Subba Singh Tamang, who was cook at Base Camp for a Spanish team. He never went above Base Camp, but he suffered a fatal heart attack.

A summary of all this activity via the South Col follows. *15 Indians* led by Hukam Singh: summit reached on May 10 by Prem Singh, Sunil Dutt Sharma, Kanhayalal Pokhriyal and on May 12 by Lopsang Sherpa, Miss Santosh Yadev, Mohan Singh Gunjyal, and Nepalese Sange Sherpa and Wangchuk Sherpa; *5 New Zealanders, 5 Americans, 1 Belgian, 1 Israeli, and 2 Hong Kong Chinese* led by Rob Hall: summit reached on May 12 by New Zealanders Rob Hall, Gary Ball, Guy Cotter, Americans Ned Gillette, Douglas Mantle, Randall Danta, Hong Kong Chinese Cham Yick-Kai, Israeli Doron Erel, Belgian Miss Ingrid Baeyens, and Nepalese Sherpas Sonam Tshering, Ang Dorje, Tashi Tshering, Apa and Ang Dawa; *10 Netherlanders* led by Roland Naar: summit reached on May 12 by Roland Naar, Edmond Öfner, Dawa Tashi Sherpa and Nima Temba Sherpa; *19 Russians and 1 Pole* led by Vyacheslav Volkov: summit reached by Aleksandr Gerasimov, Andrei Volkov, Ilia Sabelnikov, Ivan Dusharin on May 12 and by Sergei Penzov, Vladimir Zakharov, Yevgeni Vinogradsky and Fiodor Konyukhov on May 14; *13 Americans, 1 Briton and 1 German* led by Todd Burleson; summit reached by Americans Skip Horner, Louis Bowen, Vernon Tejas, Dawa Temba Sherpa and Ang Gylzen Sherpa on May 12 and by Peter Athans, Todd Burleson, Hugh Morton, Briton Keith Kerr and Nepalese Lhakpa Rita Sherpa, Gopal Man Bahadur Tamang and Dorje Sherpa on May 15; *17 Spaniards* led by Francisco Soria on the South Pillar: summit reached on May 15 by Francisco Gan, Alfonso Juez, Ramón Portilla, Lhakpa Nuru Sherpa and Pemba Norbu Sherpa; *5 Chileans* led by Mauricio Purto: summit reached on May 15 by Mauricio Purto, Ang Rita Sherpa and Ang Phuri Sherpa; *2 Czechoslovaks, 1 British, 1 Russian* led by Miroslav Šmid and Mrs. Dina Šterbova: summit reached on May 15 by Briton Jonathan Pratt; *6 Frenchmen* led by Denis Chatrefou: high point of 7900 meters reached between May 14 and 18; *15 Indians* led by Deepak Kulkarni: high point of 8750 meters reached on May 12; *6 Spaniards and 1 American* led by César Pérez de Tudela and Juan Luis Salcedo: high point of 7400 reached on May 4; *10 Spaniards* led by Albino Quinteiro: high point of 8000 meters reached on May 13.

ELIZABETH HAWLEY

Everest West Ridge Attempt. Our British Services Everest Expedition was composed of Majors Bronco Lane, N.G. Williams, C.D. Spencer, R.C.A. McAllister, Lieutenant Colonel M.G. Bridges, Captain S.P. Lowe, Sergeants C. Barnes, T. Moore, Lance Corporals Angphula Sherpa, Lalitman Limbu, Flight

Lieutenant S. Hunt, Flight Sergeants J, Morning, D. Howie, Chief Technician W. Batson, Corporal G. Stamp, Surgeon Lieutenant Commander A. Hughes, Surgeon Lieutenant P. Davis, Lieutenant S. Bell, Mr. Lincoln Rowe and me as leader. Our objective was to climb Everest via the Khumbu Icefall and the west ridge. After acclimatization on lesser peaks, our team was complete in Base Camp on March 20. We occupied Camps I, II, III, IV, V and VI at 5910 meters, 6400 meters (in the Western Cwm), 6900 meters, 7640 meters (on the west ridge), 8000 meters (at foot of Hornbein Couloir) and 8500 meters (at top of Hornbein Couloir) on March 26, April 2, 11, 21, May 11 and 17. The weather was bad throughout the season. From April 27 to May 6, high winds and cold held up all expeditions. On the night of May 20, the tents at Camp V were destroyed by wind. With the supply line to Camp VI cut and oxygen and gas running out, the decision was taken to withdraw all climbers. We left Base Camp on May 24. Our route from the Western Cwm went straight up the ice wall and through a prominent gully onto the west ridge and did not follow the 1963 American route. On May 20, several of our team were involved in the rescue of a member of the French Ultra Lightweight Expedition, that had no oxygen. The climber was suffering from severe high-altitude sickness and was kept alive only with the aid of three of our 1400-liter oxygen cylinders. It took our team 14 hours to get him down the Western Cwn and the Khumbu Icefall. Throughout the season, we and the Spanish military expedition had considerable difficulties with small, badly equipped parties attempting alpine-style attempts. Had we, in agreement with four other teams, not opened and constructed the route through the icefall, they would not have got near the mountain. They were literally climbing on our backs.

MICHAEL H. KEFFORD, *Colonel, British Army*

Everest Survey. Vernon Tejas and Skip Horner accompanied Louis Bowen to the summit of Everest on May 12 with the assistance of Sherpas Ang Gyalzen and Dawa Temba, who carried up the stand, the housing and the tubing for the laser prisms. Vern assembled these and the 90 inches (2.3 meters) of aluminum tubing sections on which they sat. It had been planned to have the stand and housing erected on the tubing, which would be driven into the snow until it hit bedrock. However, everywhere the snow was too deep to have the aluminum tubing sections reach bedrock on the summit. The stand and housing were anchored by the tube and rested on the surface. When Vern looked for the prisms, he found that they had been left in a stuff sack on the South Summit with the oxygen equipment. They then descended upon what was an Everest record summit day when no less than 32 climbers found success on the rooftop of the world. On May 15, the weather looked dubious but improving. Todd Burleson and I sounded the call to arms and Sherpa leader Lhakpa Rita readied the team for departure. Dorje Sherpa and Gopal Man Bahadur Tamang plus American Hugh Morton and Briton Keith Kerr (who would finish the ascent of the seven summits of the continents that day with his ascent of Everest) also climbed with

Todd, Lhakpa and me. Two hours after departure, the weather cleared beauti-fully and the winds became light. By ten A.M. Lhakpa and I were on the summit, having picked up the prisms, and found the erected stand and housing that Vern had placed. We tried again to put it in different positions along the summit promontory but were unable to find a place where the bottom of the aluminum tubing rested on bedrock. This showed that there was a minimum of 90 inches or 2.3 meters of snow on the summit. With Lhakpa's assistance, I aimed the housing over the Nuptse ridge and slightly right of the Thamserku north face. Lhakpa confirmed it and then we inserted the prisms into the top and bottom of the three mounts. Fortunately it was extremely mild (20°F) and nearly windless. Keith, Todd, Hugh, Gopal and Dorje arrived and we celebrated by taking innumerable photographs. On the day that Brad Washburn and competent geodisists from the Survey of Nepal made the laser sightings of the prisms on the summit from Thangboche, we were all back in Base Camp and unfortunately missed the dramatic moment. These laser sightings give the exact distance from the Thangboche station, but further GPS work is needed to complete the survey.

PETER ATHANS

Everest, 1991, Correction. Inadvertently, on page 204 of *AAJ, 1992,* the name of Spaniard Antonio Ubieto was omitted from the list of those who reached the summit of Everest on October 6, 1991.

Everest, Post-Monsoon South Col Ascents and Attempt. A total of 32 climbers ascended Everest in the post-monsoon season, all via the South Col. On September 25, Spanish Basques Pitxi Eguillor, Patxi Fernández and brothers Alberto and Félix Iñurrategui got to the top, followed on October 1 by Iosu Bereciartúa and on October 3 by leader Pedro Tous, Juan Tomás and Mikel Reparaz. A Franco-Italian group led by Agostino Da Polenza put Italians Giuseppe Petigaz, Lorenzo Mazzoleni, Mario Panzeri, Frenchman Pierre Royer and Lhakpa Nuru Sherpa on the summit on September 28, Frenchman Benoît Chamoux and Italian Oswald Santin on the 29th and Italians Abele Blanc and Giampietro Verza on the 30th. Frenchman Bernard Muller's expedition of two Frenchmen, a Belgian and a Luxembourger placed the latter, Eugène Berger, on the summit on October 1. Six Germans, four Swiss and an Austrian were led by German Ralf Dujmovits. Dujmovits and Sonam Tshering Sherpa climbed to the top on October 4. Frenchman Michel Vincent led three Frenchmen, two Amer-icans, a Canadian, a Mexican, a Spaniard and a Nepalese. Vincent reached the summit alone on October 7, followed on October 9 by American Scott Darsney. Mexican leader Sergio Fitch Watkins left his expedition before the climbing was completed, handing over the leadership to American Wally Berg. There were eleven other Americans, another Mexican and a Peruvian. On October 9, Berg, Mexican Alfonso de la Parra, Peruvian Augusto Ortega and Sherpas Pasang Kami and Apa made the ascent. The last successful expedition was composed of

24 Frenchmen, a Swiss and a Portuguese led by Michel Pellé. On October 9, Frenchmen Pellé, Philippe Grenier, Thierry Defrance, Alain Roussey and Pierre Aubertin got to the summit. Some of the climbers achieved personal "firsts." Berger was the first Luxembourger to stand atop Everest and Ortega the first Peruvian. Other planned firsts were not accomplished. Marc Batard of France did not succeed in becoming the first person to sleep at the top of the world—he didn't actually manage to reach the top. If he had, it would have been his third time there. Nepalese Iman Gurung became ill at 7300 meters on October 7 and did not realize his ambition of setting a new speed record by climbing from Base Camp to the summit in just 20 hours. This left still standing Batard's record of 22 hours and 29 minutes, set four years ago.

ELIZABETH HAWLEY

Everest, Southwest Face Attempt. The huge, steep southwest face of Everest has been successfully scaled by only three expeditions. This autumn, a team led by Ukrainian Mikhail Turkevich, who had already climbed the face in 1982, was composed of ten Ukrainians, three Russians and two Frenchmen, including Christophe Profit. They employed no Sherpas and had no climbing oxygen. They wanted to make a new direct route straight to the summit, but they were somewhat late in getting started and, after two weeks of climbing, reluctantly concluded they could not open a new line in the time and with the resources they had. They decided instead to attempt to repeat the 1975 British route. After two more weeks of team effort, three Ukrainians reached 8500 meters before two of them became frostbitten and had to descend. The remaining man, Igor Svergun, stayed high on the face alone and the day after his teammates had gone down, he made a solo bid for the summit. Just how high he reached he doesn't know. It was a dark night on October 19 and his headlamp batteries were dead when he stopped ascending. Without artificial oxygen, he became confused. He surely got to the south summit. By his description of the area where he had to stop because he was confronted by a steep wall with a lot of fixed ropes, he may well have reached the Hillary Step, not far below the summit. Wherever he was, he waited for the moon to rise to give him light, too confused to remember that it was the time of the new moon. After three or four hours' wait, a very strong wind blew up and he decided to go back down. By the time he had gotten down to the highest camp at 8300 meters, he could scarcely breathe, possibly having developed pulmonary edema. Luckily, slightly above the camp, he had found a bottle of some other expedition's oxygen. Without an oxygen mask, he simply opened the valve and breathed in pure oxygen in gulps. He continued the descent with the bottle on a rope, from time to time taking more gulps from it. In a period of 24 hours through the day and night, he climbed down from the highest camp to the camp at the foot of the face at 6400 meters. Even then, he didn't stop for many hours. He and his bottle, "like a woman with her dog on a leash," went on downward with the bottle sliding before him through the Khumbu Icefall, helping him to avoid crevasses as well as supplying him with occasional bursts

PLATE 62

Photo by Pedro José Tous
KHUMBU ICEFALL.

of oxygen. By the time he got to Base Camp, he was in remarkably good condition considering all he had gone through during three trying days.

ELIZABETH HAWLEY

Everest. Our expedition consisted of Americans Robert Hoffman, Kurt Cox, Bradford Bull, Edward DeLean, Philip Perrin, Robert Elias, Karen Stephens, Sherman Bull, Dean Johnson, Ross Berry and me, Mexicans Sergio Fitch Watkins and Alfonso de la Parra and Peruvian Augusto Ortega. [Fitch Watkins and Hoffman had to leave the expedition early because of serious disputes with members over money matters. —*Editor.*] We arrived at Base Camp on September 2 and by October 3 had Camp IV stocked on the South Col. We decided that October 9 would be our one summit attempt. On October 7, Sherpas Apa, Pasang Kami and Tashi and Bradford Bull, DeLean, Johnson, de la Parra, Ortega and I left Camp II. Our night at Camp III was a long one due to a stove mishap which burned a tent. Bull hastily evacuated the tent in his inner boots and slipped, which left him 30 feet down a crevasse. He was uninjured but his retrieval and rewarming and the adjustments to the camp made for an unproductive night of rest. We arrived on the South Col on the afternoon and early evening of October 8. We left the South Col at 12:30 A.M on the 9th without Johnson, who elected to remain at Camp IV. DeLean turned back at 27,500 feet and Bull and Tashi stopped just below the South Summit. Ortega, de la Parra, Pasang Kami Apa and I, reached the summit at eight A.M. In keeping with the Nepalese Ministry of Tourism's new regulation, we deposited $4000 as security that we would remove all non-burnable rubbish from the mountain and Base Camp and that we would ship our empty oxygen cylinders, used batteries and other such items back to the United States. We did so and our deposit was refunded in full. The empty oxygen bottles had to be shipped via air freight because they are not accepted in overland shipments at the Indian border.

WALLY BERG

Everest. Our members were Patxi Fernández, Mikel Reparaz, Juan Tomás, José Ramón Zubizarreta, Félix Iñurrategui, Juan María Eguillor, Iñaki Ochoa de Olza, Josu Bereciartua, Alberto Iñurrategui and I as leader. We climbed the standard South Col route. We established Base Camp, Camps I, II, III and IV on August 23, September 1, 6, 13 and 24 at 5350, 6000, 6500, 7300 and 7980 meters. Eguillor, Fernández, and the Iñurrategui brothers made the first post-monsoon ascent on September 25, the latter two without artificial oxygen. Ochoa de Olza had to turn back at 8500 meters because of frostbite. Eguillor went snow-blind and he and Fernández had to bivouac at 8700 meters on the descent, suffering frostbitten feet and hands. After they were evacuated from Base Camp by helicopter, Bereciartua climbed to the summit on October 1. On October 3, Tomás, Reparaz and I reached the top.

PEDRO JOSÉ TOUS, *Spain*

Everest. Our international group consisted of Frenchmen Michel Vincent, leader, Jean-Pierre Maurus, Phillipe Arvis, Spanish Basque José Luis Sesma, Mexican Oscar Rodríguez, Canadian John Arnold, Sherpani Pasang Lhamu, and Americans David Powers and me. Arnold and I had originally been with another American team but switched when invited by Vincent. We arrived at Base Camp on September 5. With our Sherpas, we prepared the standard route with the six other expeditions. We put in the route between Camps II and III on the lower Lhotse Face. All nine members reached Camp IV on the South Col on September 24, but no one got above 8200 meters due to wind and stove malfunctions. A second attempt failed in even higher winds. At that time, all but Vincent, Arnold and I gave up. Finally, on October 7, Vincent made a solo ascent from Camp IV. On October 9, I successfully climbed solo to the summit.

SCOTT C. DARSNEY

Skiing Off Mount Everest. In the pre-monsoon season, German Reinhard Patscheider skied down the normal South Col route on Mount Everest from 8400 meters. His record was beaten on September 27 when Frenchman Pierre Tardivel skied from the South Summit (8748 meters, 28,702 feet). He used supplementary oxygen during his descent. Also in the spring, Hans Kammerlander and Norbert Joos skied down from 7800 meters on the north side of Everest.

Everest, Winter Attempt. Ten British climbers and an American under the leadership of Lieutenant Colonel Philip Neame unsuccessfully attempted to climb Everest via the South Col. They reached a high point of 7850 meters on the Lhotse Face on December 22.

ELIZABETH HAWLEY

Everest Solo Winter Attempt and Death of a Sherpa, 1993. Spaniard Fernando Garrido made an unsuccessful solo attempt on the South Col route on Mount Everest. He was helped by a few Nepalese climbers to get safely through the Khumbu Icefall and to stock Advance Base at 6400 meters. On January 15, 1993, Ang Tshering Sherpa was carrying a load into the Cwm when he plunged into a bottomless crevasse. On February 3, Garrido made a bid to reach the South Col, but he was too tired to get above 7750 meters. This was his high point.

ELIZABETH HAWLEY

Pumori Pre-Monsoon Attempt, Ascent and Tragedy. Two Germans and an Austrian led by Christof Drechsel attempted to climb Pumori (7161 meters, 23,494 feet) by the normal route. They reached a high point of 6300 meters on March 24. Some time later, a South Korean expedition of five, led by Seo Seoung-Soo, attempted the peak. On May 12, the leader Seo, Seo Yeong-Deok, Kim Baek-Gyoon and Nepalese Bhakta Bahadur Rai completed the 73rd ascent of the mountain by the seldom climbed southwest ridge. They returned to their high camp and vanished. When a teammate and a Sherpa went up to learn what had become of them, they found that an avalanche had swept the high camp completely away. The only thing remaining at the site was one glove lying on the snow. Their bodies have not been found.

ELIZABETH HAWLEY

Pumori, Post-Monsoon Ascents, Attempts and Tragedy. A number of ascents of Pumori (7161 meters, 23,494 feet) were made in the post-monsoon period, all by the southeast face and east ridge except where noted. An expedition of 8 Swiss and 2 Germans was led by Norbert Joos. Leader Joos, Martin Zingg and Peter Marugg on October 21, Ernst Marti on the 23rd and Daniel Santschi on the 25th reached the summit; all were Swiss. Americans Scott Hartl and Tom Rosencrans of Hartl's seven-member expedition climbed to the summit with the Swiss on October 21. Eight French climbers were led by Michel Richard. Along with Swiss Santschi, Richard and Sarki Nuru Lama Sherpa reached the top on October 25. All of another Swiss expedition led by Olivier Roduit ascended to the summit by the southwest and south ridge up and down the southeast face: Cédric Bersandi, Daniel Compte and Pierre de Mestral on October 27 and Paul-Victor Amoudruz and Roduit on October 29. Unsuccessful were 13 Canadians, an American and a Briton led by Stephen Adamson, who got to 6850 meters on October 16; 7 Netherlanders led by Kick van Koningsbrugge, who reached 6950 meters on October 16; and 4 Germans led by Christian Fütterer, whose high point was 6200 meters on September 19. Seven Koreans led by Lee Jae-Won were unable to get higher than 6100 meters on the southwest ridge, which they reached on September 30. Kim Jun-Ho, 19 years old, fell fatally ill on September 16, apparently a victim of altitude sickness, a day or so short of Base Camp. His Korean teammates went on with the climb, but their hearts were not in it.

ELIZABETH HAWLEY

Pumori, Winter Attempt. South Korean Shinji Sasaoka failed to climb the northeast face of Pumori solo. He reached 6700 meters on December 25.

ELIZABETH HAWLEY

Lobuje East and Kwangde Shar, 1990. Micha Miller and I climbed Lobuje East on the Bibler-Freer route on the east ridge (5.9, A1) on mostly solid rock, before we merged with the normal route. We did the climb alpine-style in five days. We also climbed the classic northeast buttress on Kwangde Shar, the perfect ridge seen from Namche dropping directly from the summit. We took five days to climb some 35 pitches (4 to 5.8). We descended into the remote Lumding valley, which added to the adventure.

MARK GUNLOGSON, *Tippy Turtle Alpine Group*

Kusum Kanguru Tragedies, 1991. Ulric and Cathy Jessop were married in October, 1991 and decided to spend their honeymoon climbing in the Nepalese Himalaya. Their objective was the northwest ridge of Kusum Kanguru (6367 meters, 20,889 feet). They acclimatized carefully, approaching high altitude slowly and resting in their Base Camp. In mid November, they started their alpine-style ascent. On the second day, Ulric became concerned about Cathy, who was weak and lethargic. At their second bivouac, she developed symptoms of pulmonary edema. In the morning, they set off down to get her to lower altitude. Sadly, at the start of the second rappel, she collapsed and died. A second death occurred on the mountain shortly afterward. Japanese climber G. Ohta set out on December 28, 1991 to attempt a solo winter ascent on the north face of Kusum Kanguru. He disappeared after leaving Base Camp and has not been seen since.

Kusum Kanguru, North Face, 1991. In mid May, 1991, I soloed a direct finish to the Curtis-Ball route on the north face of Kusum Kanguru. This was my most aesthetic climb and my most moronic. Leaving the Curtis-Ball at half height, I climbed emerald gullies falling from an azure sky. The gullies often ended and I had to cross terrifying, crystalline, rotten-snow ribs to find more ice. At three-quarters height a cough became debilitating and I bivouacked, hacking up inch-long pieces of yellow phlegm . . . and blood. I wondered if I'd be alive in the morning. Going up the final 1000 feet seemed a safer option than rappelling 4000 feet on a single-length 7mm rope. A blizzard obscured the col atop my descent route to the east. I bivouacked again in a snow cave dug with crampons and helmet. More hacking and more blood. The next morning, I descended 1000 feet of tumbling glaciers, rappelled 1000 feet more on sérac walls and finally rock. In the early afternoon I walked into Base Camp. My sirdar had built a small shrine and was burning juniper for me . . . or for my soul.

BARRY BLANCHARD, *Alpine Club of Canada*

Kongma Tse, P 5886, Kusum Kanguru and Attempt on Kwangde, 1991. Between October 16 and November 14, 1991, I visited the Khumbu area, joined for the first 15 days by Ed Pope and Betty Roberts. We established Base Camp at 4900 meters below the west side of the Kongma La, five days after leaving the Lukla airstrip. On October 23, I walked out of Base Camp at 11:30 A.M., "intending to take a little hike." Beginning at the mouth of the Lingtren Lake (4939 meters) on the east side of the Khumbu Glacier, I climbed the west ridge of Kongma Tse (5792 meters, 19,002 feet), mostly fourth-class with two pitches of 5.7. Some of the rock was very loose. At 2:30 P.M., I reached the summit and descended the east face and crossed the Kongma La to get back to Base Camp at four P.M. On October 26, Ed and I climbed a new route on the west face of P 5886 (19,312 feet). The west face was first climbed by Canadian Barry Blanchard and American Jim Scott in April, 1991. (See *AAJ, 1992*, pages

206-7.) Our route follows the buttress bordering the west face on the left. Although the approach was moderately threatened by séracs, the buttress itself was safe and interesting mixed climbing. Seven moderate pitches (5.6) led to the northwest ridge, which we followed to the summit after 8½ hours of climbing. We descended the north ridge, which connects Kongma Tse to Nuptse. We were back in Base Camp at seven P.M. and in Lukla three days later. I returned up-valley to the village of Monjo to camp at 6370 meters below the north face of Kusum Kanguru on November 2. On November 5, I left Base Camp at 4:30 A.M. and arrived at the foot of the 1500-meter-high wall at seven A.M. I bypassed the bergschrund on rock (5.7) and joined the central couloir, first climbed by John Ball and Tom Curtis in 1985. Four hundred meters up the face, my helmet was shattered by falling ice. Luck and a good ice placement kept me from going to ground. I continued on good ice, which was a sustained 60° to 80° on the upper half. I declined to climb the rotten snow of the final 20 meters and photographed the summit (6367 meters, 20,890 feet) from there at 2:30 P.M. The descent was frightening. After 12 rappels and 1000 meters of down-climbing, I got back to the foot of the wall at 6:30 and to Base Camp at 8:30. I had permission to try the Lowe-Breashears route on the north face of Kwangde (6011 meters, 19,720 feet). Due to a dry and warm post-monsoon season, there was little ice on the lower 300 meters of the wall. Faced with compact slabs and a two-day snowstorm, I abandoned the attempt and flew out to Kathmandu on November 14.

MARC FRANCIS TWIGHT

Cho Oyu from the South in the Pre-Monsoon Season. As in past years, the west side of Cho Oyu has been a very popular objective for many expeditions. A Belgian expedition was led by Bernard Mousny. On May 7, Pascal de Brouwer completed the 100th ascent of the peak along with Swede Göran Kropp, who was with an expedition approaching from the north. On May 8, Mme Linda LeBon and Danu Sherpa also reached the top with climbers who had approached from the north. On the descent, Danu sped ahead, leaving exhausted Linda LeBon far behind. She decided to sleep without bivouac gear at 8000 meters and set off a night-rescue alarm. An expedition of eight Germans and seven Austrians led by Peter Geyer placed Teja Finkbeiner on the top on May 17. An eight-member American expedition led by Donald McIntyre failed, reaching 6100 meters on April 17. (See also expeditions to Cho Oyu from Tibet.)

ELIZABETH HAWLEY

Cho Oyu, Post-Monsoon Spanish Expeditions. Our expedition from Navarra was composed of Dr. José María Artetxe, Alfonso Ballano, Javier Bermejo, Juan Beroiz, Pili Ganuza (f), José Miguel Goñi, Agustín Pagola and me as leader. On September 2, we arrived at Base Camp below the Nangpa La at 5100 meters. We followed the normal route, traversing the west face and installing Camps I, II and III at 6300, 6900 and 7300 meters on September 6, 7 and 18. The route is easy and only the séracs between Camps I and II require much attention.

The route is rather direct and crosses two rock bands by means of an evident couloir. On September 20, Artetxe and Ganuza reached the summit along with Japanese, Sherpas, Italians and Koreans. Not having used her sun glasses on the ascent and having suffered frostbite, Pili Ganuza had to be helped down the mountain and eventually helicoptered to Kathmandu. On September 29, Ballano, accompanied by Juan Jimeno from a Spanish expedition from Aragón, also reached the summit. Basques Iosu Bereciartúa, Amaia Arantzábal (f) and José Urbieta were also included in our permission. On September 17, Bereciartúa and Arantzábal, along with Joan Colet leader of a Catalán group, climbed to the top. Urbieta stopped on the slightly lower central summit. Amaia Arantzábal was also frostbitten and was evacuated with Pili Ganuza. Bereciartúa went from Cho Oyu to Everest and reached the summit of Everest on October 1 by the South Col route.

GREGORIO ARIZ, *Club Anaitasuna, Spain*

Cho Oyu in Winter, 1993. An expedition of six Spaniards, a Swiss woman and an Argentine was led by Manuel González. They made two successful summit climbs from Camp IV on the normal route. They made Base Camp on January 13, 1993 very low, at only 5070 meters, because of much snow. Both Base Camp and Camp I were on the Nepalese side of the border. On January 26, they placed Camp II at the base of the mountain in Tibet. Camp IV was established at 7400 meters on February 7. On February 8, 1993, leader González, Manuel Morales, Manuel Salazar and Fernando Guerra climbed to the top. On the 10th, Spaniard Luis Arbues, Argentine Miguel Angel Sánchez and Swiss Marianne Chapuisat also completed the ascent. They had no climbing Sherpas and used no bottled oxygen. Sánchez was the first Argentine to climb Cho Oyu and the first Latin American to climb an 8000er in winter. Mlle Chapuisat was the first woman of any nationality to climb an 8000er in winter.

ELIZABETH HAWLEY

Cholatse. Cholatse (6440 meters, 21,129 feet) was successfully climbed by all members by the west rib to the southwest ridge. The summit was reached on September 26 by New Zealanders Martin Hunter, leader, Derek Chinn and Can Falkner and on October 3 by Australian Adam Darragh.

ELIZABETH HAWLEY

Dorje Lhakpa, Solo. A full article on Carlos Buhler's solo ascent of Dorje Lhakpa appears earlier in this *Journal.*

Langtang Lirung Winter Ascent and Tragedy. Langtang Lirung (7234 meters, 23,734 feet) received its 13th ascent on December 18 when South Korean Kim Jin-Ryun and Nepalese Dorje Tamang and Bir Bahadur Tamang reached the summit from Camp IV at 6800 meters near the junction of the southwest and southeast ridges. (Their first summit try on December 13 had been defeated by fierce winds.) On the 18th, they left camp at six A.M. and reported by walkie-talkie at one P.M. that they had surmounted a steep face and had just gotten to the summit. They were all right but would be late in getting back to Camp IV. Companions in Camp II said that they saw them in the twilight at about 6900 meters at six P.M. At eight P.M. came their last radio message; they could not find Camp IV and the fixed ropes, which must have been carried away by an avalanche two hours earlier. They wanted to bivouac where they were. They were not seen or heard from again. A member of the expedition in a helicopter on the 26th took a careful look at the Camp IV area, but it was completely changed after being swept by a number of avalanches. They could see no trace of them or the camp. The expedition leader was Lee Jong-Ryang.

ELIZABETH HAWLEY

Ganesh III Attempt. Kim Jong-Min led a group of eight South Koreans who attempted to climb the northeast spur to the north face of Ganesh III (7110 meters, 23,327 feet). On April 20, they reached a high point of 6820 meters.

ELIZABETH HAWLEY

Manaslu Ascent and Tragedy. Our expedition was made up of Italians Marco Bianchi, Giorgio Passino, Christian Kunter, Mario Corradini, Belgian Sven Vermeiren, Bulgarians Yordanka and Borislav Dimitrov, Poles Barbara Stocka, Sylwia Dmowska, Mariusz Sprutta, Krzysztof Pankiewicz and me as leader. Hoping to climb Manaslu by the standard northeast route, we placed Camps I and II at 5500 and 6600 meters on September 16 and 21. On September 28, Bianchi, Kuntner and I climbed directly to the summit (8163 meters, 26,780 feet) from Camp II and descended to Camp I. The next day, the Bulgarian pair hoped to repeat the climb, but they ran out of time and descended from 7700 meters. We realized that for further ascents Camp III was needed at 7300 meters. On October 2, on the way to establish it, Sylwia Dmowska slipped and fell to her death. A night search for her was in vain. The next morning, Vermeiren was descending alone toward Camp II when at 6800 feet he slipped and fell 350 meters. He died in the afternoon because of head injuries. Due to the tragedies, the expedition was abandoned.

KRZYSZTOF WIELICKI, *Klub Wysokogórski Katowice, Poland*

Manaslu, Ascent of Manaslu North I and Attempt on Manaslu North II. An expedition of 11 South Koreans was led by Park Tae-Gyu. On September 25, Lee Yong-Cheol and Ngawang Phurba Sherpa claimed to have completed the ascent of Manaslu (8163 meters, 26,781 feet) via the northeast face, but the Polish-

PLATE 63

Photo by Yukio Niwa

CHEO HIMAL (left) and **HIMLUNG HIMAL** from the north.

Italian-Belgian-Bulgarian party reported that their footprints stopped at a fore-summit. However, a communication from the leader states that the snow was very loose to the foresummit, but from there on, it was so wind-blown and hard that they left no tracks whatsoever. On October 1, Canadians failed at 8050 meters to reach the summit, also by the northeast face, but that same day Geoff Powter and Peter Tucker made the third ascent of Manaslu North I (7157 meters, 23,481 feet) by its south ridge. This summit lies immediately north of Manaslu. The six Canadians were led by Michael Galbraith. Nine Frenchmen led by Claude Rey attempted to climb Manaslu North II (7050 meters, 23,130 feet), which lies north of Manaslu North I. Climbing the north ridge from the east, they reached 5500 meters on October 18.

ELIZABETH HAWLEY

Nepal Alpine Guides Course. The Aleš Kunaver School was established in 1979 in Manang in the Peri Himal by our Planinska zveza Slovenije (Slovene Mountaineering Association). In 1992 between August 20 and September 25, it was directed by Matevž Lenarčič, Aleš Lipnik, Boris Strmšek, Dr. Žare Guzej and Dr. Bogo Ferfila. There were 33 students and two 6000-meter peaks were climbed during the course.

FRANCI SAVENC, *Planinska zveza Slovenije*

Corrections in AAJ, 1992. On page 215, Tomaž Azman and Marko Štremfelj's names were misspelled. A better transliteration from the Russian on page 218 would have been Chorny. Patynowska and Mieczysław were misspelled.

Himlung Himal, Probable First Ascent. Himlung Himal (7126 meters, 23,380 feet) lies northwest of Manaslu near the Tibetan border. This autumn, a 14-member Japanese expedition led by Yukio Niwa was the tenth to go to Himlung. Of their nine predecessors, only one, also Japanese, there in 1983, reported that they had been successful, having climbed the east ridge from the south. But when Niwa returned to Kathmandu this year, he said he was "99%" sure that his own team had made the very first ascent of Himlung, climbing the northwest ridge with no great difficulty. He was convinced that all previous climbs had taken place on another mountain just to the south, Nemjung (7139 meters, 23,422 feet). He pointed out that the map coordinates assigned to Himlung by the Nepalese government correspond on the best Nepalese map of the region to those of the northern of these two mountains, not the southern one, labeled Nemjung.

ELIZABETH HAWLEY

Himlung Himal, Further Details of the Climb. Our expedition was composed of Osamu Hanai, Takeshi Yamaguchi, Minoru Masuda, Akio Koizumi, Norio

Kawai, Hideaki Toda, Osamu Shimuzu, Kazuo Higuchi, Eiji Ishibashi, Kiyokatsu Saito and me as leader. On September 25, we established Base Camp at 4850 meters at the foot of the northwest ridge of Himlung Himal. Camp I was placed at 5450 meters in the icefall of the glacier of the northwest ridge on September 27 and Camps II and III at 6000 and 6250 meters on the ridge on October 1 and 2. On October 3, Hanai, Koizumi and Nima Sherpa climbed steep snow to the summit, followed on the 6th by Shimzu, Higuchi and Danu Sherpa.

YUKIO NIWA, *Academic Alpine Club of Hokkaido, Japan*

Nemjung Attempt. An expedition of six British climbers led by Peter Hudd also had a permit for Himlung and arrived at Base Camp more than two weeks after the Japanese mentioned above had left theirs. Hudd readily agrees that Niwa could well be correct. "The Japanese probably have a fair claim to having been the first atop Himlung, even first anywhere on the mountain," he said. His party unsuccessfully attacked the southern peak by the south ridge, knowing it was called Nemjung on the map. "Previous expeditions' reports were the only information we had and they indicated that we were where they had been. But there is no reason why the map should be wrong." His party reached 6400 meters on November 16.

ELIZABETH HAWLEY

Kang Guru. A five-man Japanese expedition successfully climbed Kang Guru (6981 meters, 22,904 feet) by the southwest face to the west ridge. On September 22, leader Takashi Arai, Hirohisa Matsuyama, Akira Shimizu, Hiroshi Togawa and Sarki Norbu Lama reached the summit.

ELIZABETH HAWLEY

Bhrikuti. Bertrand Doligez led a second expedition of ten French climbers to Bhrikuti (6364 meters, 20,879 feet), which completed the third ascent of the peak again by the southeast ridge. He had led another successful group there in 1991. On November 1, the summit was reached by Daniel Rossetto, Roland Hamel, Mme Martine Moron, Daniel Faveau and Gyalzen Sherpa. They were followed on November 2 by Doligez, Christian Reynaud, Mme Elisabeth Berard, Dominique Moussu, Nima Sange Sherpa and Dawa Sange Sherpa.

ELIZABETH HAWLEY

Annapurna IV. The British Joint Services Expedition consisted of Brian Tilley, Lothar Kuelheim, Mark Samuels, Nick Arding, Dave Evans, Steve Willson, Rod Dunn, Gail Waller, Glyn Sheperd, Vick Barrows, Dr. Helen Robertson and me as leader. We arrived at Base Camp at 3800 meters on March

31 after a week's approach from the roadhead at Besi Sahar. Weather was bad throughout the climb. Advance Base was established on April 3 at 4800 meters after a concerted effort by the team and four porters. We followed the prominent ridge to the dome between Annapurna III and IV. This gained the main shoulder of Annapurna IV. Features on the mountain had changed significantly in the past ten years. Large cliffs and sizable crevasse-fields had formed as large chunks of the mountain had given way. This may account for the high failure rate during the previous decade. Camps I and II were established on April 7 and 10 at 5100 and 5400 meters. Then began the main difficulties of the climb. It took ten days to force the route to Camp III at 6100 meters. A heavy snowfall on April 23 forced the team off the mountain for three days. On April 29, we placed Camp IV at 6450 meters on the main shoulder. On May 3, three pairs set off and established an assault camp at 7000 meters, but they were stormbound for 48 hours. However, a fine spell followed and Tilley, Samuels, Dunn, Willson and Sheperd reached the summit (7525 meters, 24,688 feet) on May 5. Base Camp was evacuated on May 10.

MICHAEL TRUEMAN, *Major, 10th Gurkha Rifles, British Army*

Annapurna IV, Post-Monsoon Ascents and Attempt. There were three successful ascents of Annapurna IV (7525 meters, 24,688 feet) and one unsuccessful one, all by the northwest ridge. An expedition of six South Koreans under the leadership of Goo Hwa-Sub completed the climb when on September 21 Lee Dai-Haeng, Kim Jong-Sub and Bir Bahadur Tamang reached the top. On September 23, the only member of another Korean expedition, Rim Jong- Bum, with Nepalese Dagumbu Sherpa, Jambyang Lama and Nanda Prasad Magar, climbed to the summit. [This was a remarkable ascent, as Rim is a Buddhist monk who was on a special pilgrimage. He wrote the following to the Editor, "Throughout history, the Himalaya has been a source to understand and practice Buddhism. When I reached the summit, I had in my mind a sense of happiness and a deep respect for the noble ideas the monks before me possessed. I hope to find out how strong the human will is through nature. I want to challenge myself through challenging nature."] On September 24, Spanish Basques Asier Eizagirre, leader, Angel Navas, Patxi Navas and José María Sarasola also completed the ascent. A six-member Japanese expedition led by Satoshi Ikenuma reached a high point of 6400 meters on October 3.

ELIZABETH HAWLEY

Annapurna South Face Tragedy. One of France's foremost climbers, Pierre Beghin, and I had hoped to climb a new, difficult route on the south face of Annapurna between the 1970 British route and the 1981 Japanese one. Starting on September 29, we first made an acclimatization climb on our route to 6500 meters and the next day fixed rope 150 meters higher before descending. Pierre was suffering from a bad sore throat. On October 7, we left Base Camp at one

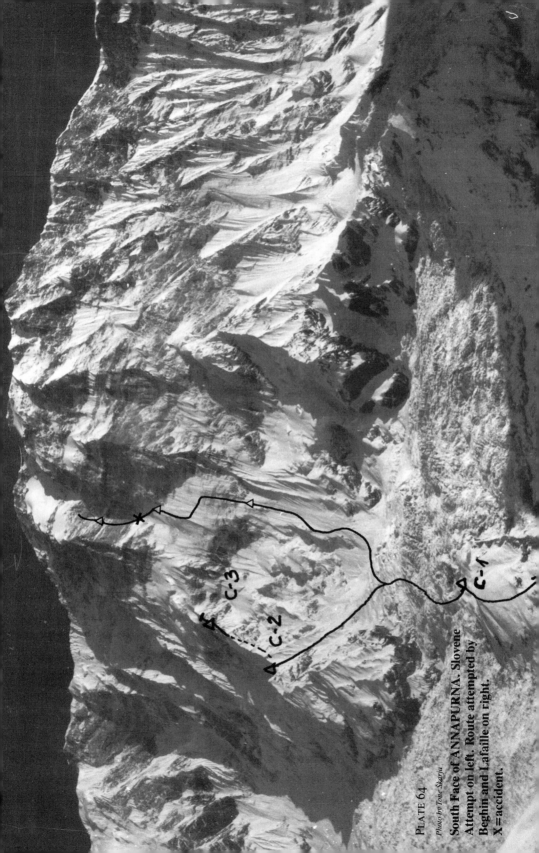

PLATE 64

Photo by Tone Škarja

**South Face of ANNAPURNA. Slovene
Attempt on left. Route attempted by
Béghin and Lafaille on right.
X = accident.**

C-3

C-2

C-1

A.M. for Advance Base at 5300 meters, where we spent the daylight hours. Rockfall forced us to climb primarily in the dark. The next day, we again made a pre-dawn start and climbed the lower part of the wall to bivouac in a safe and comfortable spot at 6500 meters. On October 9, we made a third night start and climbed to bivouac at 7000 meters. It was obvious that the next section was of extreme technical difficulty and so we climbed the next day only in the daylight, reaching 7300 meters, where we had a miserable hanging bivouac carved from the 70° ice. The weather began to be unsettled. However, on October 11, we set out in poor weather and reached 7500 meters at nine A.M. before deciding to descend. At 7200 meters, Beghin rigged a rappel from a Friend and urged me to remove the back-up piton, since we would need them all lower down. We exchanged packs; he took the one with the technical gear and I put on the bulkier one with the tent, stove and a bit of food. He also handed me his ice axe. The pack and the axe doubtless later saved my life. He had descended 25 meters when the anchor pulled out and he plunged to his death. I sat stunned for half an hour, not able to convince myself that he had not been able to catch himself below the overhang. I had to descend terribly difficult 75° to 80° terrain, unable to give myself any protection or to rappel. Not until nine P.M. did I reach the 7000-meter bivouac. The next day I did not move. Finally, on October 13, I started down, having found there 20 meters of 6mm rope. Tent pegs had to serve as anchors. I descended ice slopes and mixed terrain averaging 55° to 60°. Rockfall continued and avalanches of very heavy new snow sloughed off. I dropped one crampon and found it lower down two hours later. At four P.M., as I was approaching the tent luckily on the rope we had fixed, a stone crashed down on me and broke my right arm. (I am right-handed.) On October 14, it took me half an hour to light the stove. I hoped to have help, having shouted to Slovenes on the British route the day before. Having splinted my arm, I finally started on down, rigging 10-meter rappels with my sound arm and my teeth. It was not until early on the morning of October 15 that I got to Advance Base. The tent there was so covered with snow that I could extract nothing. There was no one in the Slovene Advance Base. I staggered down to the Slovene Base Camp, where two Slovene doctors tended to my compound fracture and medicated me. They had a radio and a helicopter was summoned to evacuate me to Kathmandu.

JEAN-CHRISTOPHE LAFAILLE, *Fédération Française de la Montagne et de l'Escalade*

Annapurna, South Face Attempt. Our expedition was composed of Slovenes Viktor Grošelj, Dr. Igor Tekavčič, Filip Bence, Vanja Furlan, Matjaž Jamnik, Miha Kajzelj, Benjamin Ravnik, Slavko Rožič, Uroš Rupar, Robert Supin, Iztok Tomazin, Janez Hrovat and me as leader and Croat Stipe Božić. We established Base Camp and Camps I and II at 4050, 5050 and 5900 meters on the British route on September 29, 30 and October 4, according to plan. We moved along the ridge from October 6 to 10, avoiding a gully threatened by falling ice. We had instead to climb difficult snow-and-ice cauliflowers along the sharp ridge.

Photo by Jiří Novák

TILITSO's North Face. French first-ascent route on right. Swiss variant on left.

Heavy snow fell from the 11th to 14th, trapping Furlan and Supin in Camp II. It was during this storm that Pierre Beghin was killed. We then continued along the ridge and set up Camp III at 6600 meters on October 18. However, Grošelj, Božić, Jamnik and Ravnik gave up their attempt to climb higher because of the snow. On October 20 and 21, Tomazin and Bence forced their way to 6700 meters but decided that reaching the summit was out of the question. We gave up the British route and hoped to reach the long, but easier east ridge via the extreme right wing of the south face. Grošelj and Božić finally found a passage to the foot of the ice slope leading to the ridge, but snow conditions were bad and it began to snow again. We started to clear the route. Because so much snow had fallen up high, there was no chance for the east ridge either. Evacuation of Base Camp went forward in the next days.

TONE ŠKARJA, *Planinska zveza Slovenije*

Tilitso Attempt and Tragedy. Our international expedition under the leadership of Italian Francesco Santon was composed of eleven Italians, two Argentines, me from Czechoslovakia and three Sherpas. Our objective was the north buttress of Tilitso. We reached Base Camp at 5000 meters near the Mesokanto La on September 9. On the 5th, we established Camp I at 5500 meters. After a period of bad weather, Camp II was placed at 5950 meters on September 12. Two Sherpas descended, leaving Italians Gianluigi Visentin and Roberto Malgarotto there. The lower part of the route to Camp II was in part on Grade IV rotten rock, where we fixed rope. We hoped to climb to the summit from Camp II. In the next days, the weather was unsettled with some snowfall. The two Italians waited for an improvement. On the morning of September 15, the weather cleared and let us see that not much snow had built up, but there seemed to be some windslab. After it clouded in again, we had radio contact with them at eleven o'clock. With clear skies on the 16th, we could see that Camp II had been swept by an avalanche. That same day, three members ascended and found that Camp II was covered with some three meters of snow. The bodies could not be recovered. The expedition was given up.

JIŘÍ NOVÁK, *Czechoslovakia*

Tilitso Attempt. Seven South Tiroleans led by Othmar Zingerle attempted to climb Tilitso (7134 meters, 23,406 feet) by the northeast spur and the north ridge. Their high point of 6200 meters was reached on November 5.

ELIZABETH HAWLEY

Dhaulagiri Ascent and Tragedy. An expedition of five Russians and five Germans was officially led jointly by Vladimir Musienko and Erwin Beyerlein. They climbed the northeast ridge of Dhaulagiri. On April 30, Russians Alexei Guliayev, Valeri Kokhanov, Peter Kuznetsov, Nikolai Smetanin and Nikolai

Zakharov reached the summit from Camp V at 7700 meters. Tragically, well-known German climber Hubert Weinzierle died on May 2 of heart failure at Camp III at 7000 meters. Smetanin was not on the official list of climbers and so both he and the official leader Musienko are banned from entering Nepal for the next five years. The strange thing is that Musienko was only the formal leader and was not present in the Himalaya.

ELIZABETH HAWLEY

Dhaulagiri Tragedy. Two Romanian women, Mrs. Taina Coliban and Mrs. Sandita Isaila disappeared on the normal northeast-ridge route of Dhaulagiri. Mrs. Caliban was 48 years old and Mrs. Isaila 42. Perhaps because of their age, they were extremely slow climbers. They had few other climbers on their team and attempted to reach their towering summit without companions, without artificial oxygen, without a means of communication to Base Camp and with a minimum of climbing gear. Mrs. Coliban had climbed in Nepal once, seven years ago, during a brief attempt on Dhaulagiri, and both women had successfully scaled 6995-meter (22,950-foot) Khan Tengri in the Tien Shan. They had not intended to climb alone but had hoped to add themselves to someone else's expedition to an 8000er. Unable to do so, they took a permit for Dhaulagiri, put the names of Wanda Rutkiewicz and the young Pole who was with her on Kangchenjunga on their membership list and added a Chilean, who started with them but was able to climb only a short distance above Base Camp before becoming ill and left Base Camp before they were reported missing. Since their equipment was not of the best, their Sherpa Kazi thinks that perhaps inadequate tent pegs could not hold their small tent securely while they were in it and it may have blown off the ridge. The two women were last seen at midday on May 11. Kazi had been helping them carry supplies to the base of the climb. He was asked to stay at Base Camp while they went as quickly as possible for the summit and to watch them from there with binoculars. The mornings were clear but it clouded and snowed in the afternoons. On May 11, he saw them on a snow ridge at 6500 meters, climbing toward their intended campsite at 7000 meters. The site was visible from Base Camp but Kazi never saw their tent there. He scanned the ridge day after day but never saw any sign of them. There was a big snowstorm on May 23. He finally struck camp on May 29, taking their personal belongings to Kathmandu but leaving food and fuel in case they miraculously got back down to Base.

ELIZABETH HAWLEY

Dhaulagiri, Post-Monsoon Northeast Ridge Attempts. There were five expeditions that attempted to climb the normal northeast ridge of Dhaulagiri, but none succeeded. They were 5 Frenchmen led by Daniel Bianchi (high point: 7500 meters on September 28), 7 Spaniards led by Jorge Egocheaga (high point: 8000 meters on October 3), 2 Japanese led by Ichita Ono (high point: 7000 meters on October 3), 4 Spaniards led by Jon Lazkano (high point: 6000 meters on October 3) and 8 Italians led by Dino Favretto (high point: 6800 meters on October 9).

ELIZABETH HAWLEY

Dhaulagiri II Attempt. A seven-member South Korean expedition led by Ryu Si-Dong hoped to climb Dhaulagiri II (7751 meters, 25,430 feet) by the south face to the east ridge. They had to give up on April 6 at 6300 meters.

ELIZABETH HAWLEY

Putha Hiunchuli Attempt. Two Britons and a Swiss under the leadership of Andrew Kerr attempted to climb Putha Hiunchuli (7246 meters, 23,773 feet) by its south ridge, which they reached from the east. They got to 7050 meters on October 17 before giving up the attempt.

ELIZABETH HAWLEY

Sita Chuchura. Our expedition, composed of Guy Hiron, Guy Mattioni, Jean-Louis Guillet, Claude Hameau, Philippe Lataud, Ang Tarke Sherpa and me as leader, made the second ascent of Sita Chuchura (6611 meters, 21,690 feet). After a ten-day approach, we got to the Dhaulagiri Base Camp at 4700 meters on October 1. We ascended to the east ridge from the south. We placed Camp I at the end of the glacier at 5500 meters on October 4 and Camp II at 6000 meters in the col below the South Dome on the 6th. On October 7, Camp II was established at 6100 meters on the snowy south spur after we had descended 250 meters and crossed the great south basin. On October 8, Hiron, Guillet and I climbed the south spur on 45° good snow to the 6350-meter shoulder. Because the east ridge was heavily corniced, we traversed on the opposite 50° to 60° slope for eight or ten rope-lengths to reach the summit at 1:45 P.M. We descended the same route.

JEAN-PIERRE LAURENT, *Club Alpin Français*

Tukuche Attempt. Four Frenchmen led by Georges Derycke attempted to climb Tukuche (6920 meters, 22,703 feet) by its northwest ridge but had to turn back at 6700 meters on May 27.

ELIZABETH HAWLEY

Tukuche Attempts. Two post-monsoon expeditions on the northwest ridge of Tukuche (6920 meters, 22,703 feet) were unsuccessful. Seven Britons led by Miss Isobel Inglis reached 5950 meters on October 28, while a nine-member French expedition led by Didier Delahaye had to turn back at 6840 meters on October 29.

ELIZABETH HAWLEY

P 6180, Mustang Himal and Source of the Kali Gandaki. Austrian Helmut Burisch and I followed up the Kali Gandaki to where it forks near the Tibetan border. The bigger branch flowed from the northwest from the heart of the Mustang Himal. It obviously flowed from the five glaciers that clothe the slopes of the holy mountain, Dongmar. We followed the stream for two days to where at 5500 meters it emerged in an amphitheater from the glaciers. In 1953, Herbert Tichy had climbed Dongmar (6210 meters, 20,374 feet, now usually called Kangdungmar). We climbed P 6180 (20,276 feet), which lies west of Lo Mantang, the medieval-like capital of Mustang. Local people told us the mountain was called Kang Gongola.

BRUNO BAUMANN, *Deutscher Alpenverein*

Kangdungmar. An Italian expedition visited the Kingdom of Mustang and climbed in the Thingar region. Their objective was the highest mountain in the region, Kangdungmar. [The first ascent had been made in 1953 by Austrian Herbert Tichy.] On August 13, Mauro Dell'Amico and Andrea Zini climbed the mountain via the east ridge despite unsettled weather. Other members of the party were Andrea Cocconi, Giuliana Iott, Mauro Sant and Marco Zuccardi.

JÓZEF NYKA, *Editor, Taternik, Poland*

Saipal Attempt. Our members were Frank Evans, Matthew Heffer, John Holland, Caroline Purkhardt, Julia Wood and I as leader. We had hoped to climb Saipal (7031 meters, 23,068 feet) by a new route, approaching from Surkhet in 18 days up the Karnali River system. We finally reached the Kuwari Khola and established Base Camp below the east face of Saipal at 3650 meters on April 26. We made Advance Base at 3850 meters in the middle of the glacier below two large icefalls separated by a rock buttress. Avalanches and rockfall ruled out any direct assault on the face. We circumvented the right icefall to the north and camped at 4800 meters, but attempts to reach the north ridge via its northeast spur were unfruitful. We descended into Humla and climbed avalanche-prone slopes to camp at 5200 meters. Our final effort was to climb to 5700 meters on the northeast spur. While descending from this camp, Nuru Sherpa fell and broke his ankle. A marathon journey was made over the Chote Lagna (4700 meters) to Simikot to order a helicopter, which evacuated him on May 21. We left our Base Camp on May 26, traveled through upper Humla and completed the loop by trekking from Simikot to Jumla via Rara Lake.

CHUCK EVANS, *England*

Api Attempt. A five-member British expedition led by Robert Brown was unable to complete the climb of the south face of Api (7132 meters, 23,399 feet), reaching only 6000 meters on October 10.

ELIZABETH HAWLEY

India—Kumaon and Garhwal

Panch Chuli II and V, Kumaon. An article about the ascent of these two difficult peaks and the extraordinary rescues appears earlier in this *Journal.*

Bamba Dhura, 1991. On page 229 of *AAJ 1992,* mention was made of the first ascent of Bamba Dhura (6334 meters, 20,780 feet) by an Indo-Tibetan Border Police team led by Mohinder Singh. On September 13, 1991, Ang Phuri Sherpa, Dawa Ringzin, Gajendra Singh, Bhagat Singh, Surender Prakash, Dayal Singh, Mohan Singh and Harish Singh reached the summit.

Uja Tirche Attempt. Bad weather and unseasonably heavy snowfall in July defeated a three-member Bombay expedition led by Vinay Hegde on Uja Tirche (6202 meters, 20,350 feet). They approached via the Sirvanch valley to the west. The mountain was first climbed in 1937 by a Survey of India party.

HARISH KAPADIA, *Editor, Himalayan Journal*

Nandabhannar, Nandakhani, Shallang Dhura. There has been considerable interest in a pass in Kumaon first crossed in 1926 by Hugh Ruttledge's porters. An Indian team explored its existence in 1988. This year a team from Bombay led by Divyesh Muni reached the pass and the plateau about it. They climbed Nandabhannar (6236 meters, 20,450 feet), Nandakhani (6029 meters, 19,780 feet) and Sahallang Dhura (5678 meters, 18,630 feet).

HARISH KAPADIA, *Editor, Himalayan Journal*

Bauljuri. The National Outdoor Leadership School sponsored a mountaineering course which climbed Bauljuri (5922 meters, 19,429 feet). From the roadhead at Song above Almora, we walked three days up the Pindari drainage to Base Camp at 12,000 feet. The summit of Bauljuri was reached on September 24 by instructors Tom Bol and Krishnan Kutty and students Mark Wironowski, Julia Wilmerding, John Patton, Richard Lewis, Rob Holcombe and liaison officer P.K. Ganesh.

LYNNE WOLFE, *NOLS*

Nanda Devi East Correction in AAJ, 1992. On page 230 the name Mstislav is misspelled.

Panwali Dwar Attempt. A Korean expedition to Panwali Dwar (6663 meters, 21,860 feet) was led by Her Tai-Han. They made Camp III at 6150 meters on the southeast ridge in mid July, but bad weather and the failure of their stoves prevented their getting higher.

HARISH KAPADIA, *Editor, Himalayan Journal*

Maiktoli Tragedy. An Indian expedition led by Ram Chandra Bharadwaj was mostly inexperienced and badly equipped. They set up Base Camp on the Sundardunga Glacier on September 7. After a long period of bad weather, Ratan Singh Bisht left Advance Base on September 21, slipped and fell into a deep chasm. Apparently no rescue was attempted. Meanwhile, Jagdish Bisht, Deepak Negi and Tribhuvan Turanga, who were at Advance Base, lost their lives when an avalanche swept the camp. Their bodies were located on September 26.

KAMAL K. GUHA, *Editor, Himavanta, India*

Trisul Attempt. American Arthur B. Ferguson led Griff Smith and Robert Wade to the west face of Trisul (7120 meters, 23,360 feet). They established Base Camp on June 14 and Advance Base on June 20, but the weather in June continued bad and they could not complete the climb.

HARISH KAPADIA, *Editor, Himalayan Journal*

Kamet and Abi Gamin. This massif is the goal each year of a number of Indian expeditions trying the normal route. In 1992, Kamet and Abi Gamin were the objectives of at least five parties. One is described below. A group from Durgapur led by Swapan Kumar Ghosh established Base Camp on August 31 and climbed Kamet (7756 meters, 25,447 feet) on September 2 and Abi Gamin (7355 meters, 24,130 feet) on September 3. Further details are missing.

Abi Gamin Ascent and Tragedy. An expedition of the Indian Corps of Engineers was led by Captain S.B. Vajramati. They set up Base Camp at Vasundahara Lake on September 12 and Camps I and II on the east Kamet Glacier at 6045 and 6450 meters. Camps III and IV were pitched at 6800 and 7100 meters in the third week of September. On September 27, Lance Naik Adiyapan and Captain Vinay Gupta set up a summit camp above Meade's Col and climbed to the summit of Abi Gamin (7355 meters, 24,130 feet) the next day. On September 29, Lance Naiks S.P. Bhatt and Kulwant Singh, Subedar Kangaraj and Lieutenant Sundeep Lumba reached the top. While on the summit, Lumba fell and plunged thousands of feet to his death.

KAMAL K. GUHA, *Editor, Himavanta, India*

Mana and P 5730. A 19-member Indian Army Ordnance Corps expedition was led by Captain S.P. Malik. They approached from the west via the Nagthuni Glacier and the Gupta Khal. The team was involved in an avalanche on June 11 and injured members had to be evacuated. On June 19, Captain M.C. Jaykrishnan, Lance Naik S.K. Rao and Sepoys N.S. Rawal, Surbeer Chand, Rajendra Singh and Kundan Singh reached the summit (7272 meters, 23,860 feet). Earlier, on June 11, Captain Malik, Captain B.P. Singh, Naik Subedar S.K. Dogra, Havaldars A.C.K. Singh, D. Deb, N.S. Tamang, Lance Naik D. Limboo and Sepoy N.S. Negi climbed P 5730 (18,799 feet), which rises above the Gupta Khal. They ascended from Camp IV.

HARISH KAPADIA, *Editor, Himalayan Journal*

Mana Northwest Attempt and Ascent of P 6687. Unclimbed Mana Northwest (7092 meters, 23,270 feet) lies northwest of Mana and south of Kamet on the ridge which connects the two. Our four-member team from Bombay, P.B. Bodhane, Subhas Kharde, Anil Chavan and I as leader, attempted it from the east via the Purbi Kamet Glacier. Bodhane fell ill and had to leave. We placed three camps on the glacier, at 5000, 5300 and 5600 meters. On June 18, we set up Camp IV at 6200 meters on the northeast face of Mana Northwest. On June 21, Kharde and high-altitude porter Jagat Singh climbed a gently rising ridge and then up through séracs toward the summit of Mana Northwest. At 6900 meters, Kharde felt giddy from dehydration and the altitude and they had to return. That same day, Chavan and I established Camp V at 6450 meters. On June 22, we two set out in cold and wind but soon had to retreat to avoid frostbite. The next day, we again started but after three hours of climbing it began to snow hard. Two hours later, we turned back at about 6800 meters. On June 25, Kharde, Jagat Singh and I set out for P 6687 (21,940 feet) which lies between Mana Northwest and Kamet. I was slow and returned to camp, but the other two completed the first ascent of the peak.

ARUN SAMANT, *Holiday Hikers' Club, Bombay*

Mukut Parbat. An Indian expedition from the Border Security Force led by S.C. Negi made the second ascent of Mukut Parbat (7242 meters, 23,759 feet) at the end of September. Further details are awaited.

KAMAL K. GUHA, *Editor, Himavanta, India*

P 6940 ("Saraswati"). This peak lies on the Indo-Tibetan border, rising from the Saraswati valley near Badrinath. It is near Mana Pass and northwest of Kamet. The Indo-Japanese ladies' expedition gave it the name of "Saraswati" after the river valley. They were led by Indian Subedar Santosh Yadev and Japanese Mrs. Reiko Terasawa. They approached from Badrinath along the Saraswati valley and turned northeast up the Balbala Glacier until they were at the top of the Schlagintweit Pass (6236 meters). (The Schlagintweits had crossed here to Tibet to approach Abi Gamin in 1855. No other party is believed to have reached the pass since.) The summit (6940 meters, 22,770 feet) was climbed from the pass along the southeast ridge. The summiters on August 18 were Santosh Yadev, Jyotika Negi, Mamta Thakur and Bhanita Timungpi, the last three Havidars of the Indo-Tibetan Border Police. On August 19, Mrs. Terasawa, Takako Kato, Mayumi Shirasawa, Emiko Yamaguchi, Yoshie Kameda,

Eri Kusuda of the Himalayan Association of Japan and liaison officer Aparna Pangtey reached the summit.

HARISH KAPADIA, *Editor, Himalayan Journal*

Nilkanth Attempt. In October, four of us Scots attempted the long, challenging southeast ridge of Nilkanth (6596 meters, 21,640 feet), previously tried by British and American expeditions. From Advance Base at 5000 meters, south of the ridge, we crossed three major pinnacles during six days of relatively fine weather and got to the snow col between the third and fourth pinnacles. We had much loose rock and snow-covered sections. We retreated because of the objective dangers and the very committing nature of the ridge.

GRAHAM LITTLE, *Scottish Mountaineering Club*

Chaukhamba. Colonel Amit C. Roy of the Corps of Signals, Indian Army, led a successful ascent of Chaukhamba (7138 meters, 23,420 feet) from the northeast. Captains Sanjeev Singh, Nandeem Arshad and Vipin Verma, Lance Naik M. Ayoub Sofi, Nima Norbu, Makalu, Bibhujit Mukhoti and Shyamal Sarkar got to the summit on June 14. On June 17, Captains J.K. Jha, V. Dogra and S.P. Sira, Havaldars Umed Singh and R.S. Yadev, Lance Naik Jarnail Sing and Signalman C.S. Champawat also climbed to the summit.

HARISH KAPADIA, *Editor, Himalayan Journal*

Satopanth. Three Indian expeditions climbed Satopanth (7075 meters, 23,212 feet) in the summer of 1992, all following the northwest ridge, the route pioneered by André Roch in 1947. The summit was reached on June 22 by leader Prasad S. Dhamal, Surendra Chavan and Moreshwar Kulkarni. On July 31, members of the expedition led by Chandra Prabha Aitwal climbed to the top. They were the leader Aitwal, Ms. Vijaya Gadre, Jasbir Singh Bhandari and Ganga Singh Martolia. Leader Dr. Salin Hu was accompanied by Vijay Parikh, Cyrus Shroff, Fulton Nazreth and Christopher D'Souza to the summit on September 1.

HARISH KAPADIA, *Editor, Himalayan Journal*

Bhagirathi III. Micha Miller and I climbed Bhagirathi alpine-style by the Scottish route, using no fixed rope, in nine days with perfect weather. We spent two more days rappelling the route. We had originally hoped to do the Spanish route, but poor weather during the first three weeks of our stay left that route plastered with snow and with ice in the cracks. The Scottish route has a southwest exposure and is thus exposed to more sun. The route consisted of 30

PLATE 67

Photo by Mark Gunlogson

BHAGIRATHI II: 1=Standard Route, 2=North Face (Irish), 3=West Ridge (Italian). P 6193: 4=(unfinished). BHAGIRATHI III: 5=West Face (Spanish), 6=West Face (Slovene), 7=Southwest Buttress (Scottish).

pitches on beautiful granite (5.9, A2) before it joins a 45° to 60°, 1700-foot-high ice slope that led to the summit, which we reached on October 1. Aside from some rockfall and several poor bivouacs, the route is excellent and highly recommended for small, lightweight parties.

MARK GUNLOGSON, *Tippy Turtle Alpine Group*

Bhagirathi III Attempt. Seven Czechs led by Dr. Miroslav Coubal attempted a new route on the rocky west wall of Bhagirathi III (6454 meters, 21,175 feet) but due to inclement weather they failed, reaching 5800 meters on September 5. The team included the accomplished rock climbers, the brothers Miroslav and Michal Coubal.

HARISH KAPADIA, *Editor, Himalayan Journal*

P 6193 Attempt. In late August, a Slovene expedition attempted the west face of shapely P 6193 (20,320 feet), which lies above the Gangotri Glacier southeast of Bhagirathi II. Janez Kešnar, leader, and Marjan Kovač reached 6000 meters but bad weather prevented their reaching the top. They were accompanied by Ivo Ivanc.

FRANCI SAVENC, *Planinska zveza Slovenije*

Bhagirathi II. Spaniards Carlos Dávila and Adolfo García climbed Bhagirathi II by the east face, arriving at the summit (6512 meters, 21,364 feet) on September 13.

Yogeshwar. Our team was composed of Steve Adderley, Malcolm Bass, Julian Clamp and me. On October 2, the latter three made the second ascent of Yogeshwar (6678 meters, 21,910 feet) by a new route on the objectively dangerous south face. We thought we were making the first ascent, not knowing that Indians led by Ramakant Mahadik had climbed the mountain by the southeast ridge in June, 1991. We used the Swetvarn Glacier for our approach. We established Base Camp and Advance Base at 4800 and 5500 meters on September 12 and 20. On September 24, Adderley and Clamp made an attempt on the mountain via the west ridge, which they reached via the col between Yosheshwar and Chaturbhuj. They retreated at 6200 meters in the face of extremely unstable snow on the ridge. All four of us helped with the evacuation of an Indian climber from a Shri Kailas expedition. On September 28, Bass, Clamp and I reoccupied Advance Base. On the 29th, we bivouacked below the horribly loose east col, to which we had not climbed that day because of stonefall. We did get to the col (5950 meters) the next day, where we took a rest day. Just after midnight on October 2, we followed a series of gullies from the col onto the south face. Though threatened by séracs and potential avalanches, we crossed the south face to gain the southeast ridge at 6400 meters. We were on the summit at 11:30 A.M. By 5:30 we had descended the southeast ridge, crossed the Shyamvarn Glacier and reascended to our bivouac on the east col.

SIMON YEARSLEY, *England*

Sudarshan. Sudarshan (6507 meters, 21,350 feet) has become a very popular objective particularly for Indian expeditions. An expedition led by Gautam Mukherjee reached the summit on June 6. A Spanish expedition and three other Indian groups were also given permission to attempt the peak, but their outcome is not yet known.

Kedar Dome. An Indian team climbed Kedar Dome (6831 meters, 22,410 feet) on June 2. Summiters were leader Sachin Karato, Sumanta Talukdar, Samir Krishna Das and Bujay Hazare. Another Indian expedition climbed the mountain when on September 29 Uttam Samanta gained the summit.

HARISH KAPADIA, *Editor, Himalayan Journal*

Bharte Khunte Attempt. An Indian team led by Romesh Bhattacharjee attempted Bharte Kunta (6578 meters, 21,580 feet) from the Gangotri Glacier. They reached a high point of 6450 meters.

HARISH KAPADIA, *Editor, Himalayan Journal*

Shivling. An eight-man commercial French team led by Gilles Buisson and Jean-Pierre Frachon and organized by Atalante completed the first French ascent of Shivling. On September 3, Frachon, Christian Carre, Peter Bruijs and Alain Crocombette reached the summit (6543 meters, 21,467 feet) via the west ridge by which the mountain was first ascended in 1974 by Indians. Base Camp was reached on August 23. They established Camps I, II and III at 5100, 5400 and 5850 meters and fixed 1500 meters of rope.

HARISH KAPADIA, *Editor, Himalayan Journal*

Thalay Sagar Attempt. Japanese Hiroshi Kawasaki and Kimihiro Kumaga attempted the west ridge of Thalay Sagar in July. They placed Camp I at 5500 meters on July 20, but monsoon rains and snow increased the danger of avalanches and they abandoned the climb.

HARISH KAPADIA, *Editor, Himalayan Journal*

Thalay Sagar from the South and Rudugaira. Our expedition made a second, and this time successful, attempt by a new route on Thalay Sagar from the Phatung Glacier to the south. Our previous try was in 1990. Because of deep winter snow, most of the porters could not reach Base Camp at 3700 meters, established on May 9. The lower section of the route above Advance Base at 4600 meters followed a steep glacier to the left (west) of the rock buttress climbed in 1990. A lower-angled glacier and a 60° snow slope led to the foot of the granite headwall, where Camp III was placed at 6300 meters. Equipment had to be carried up specially to attempt the vertical south face. Regular afternoon snowfall and lack of continuous cracks stopped progress. Severe spindrift often buried tents in several minutes. The summit push started on May 23 from Advance Base but was delayed at Camp I at 5700 meters by bad weather. Camp III was established on June 3 and the summit was reached three days later from Camp IV at 6500 meters. Charles French and Julian Fisher descended while Tom Prentice and I carried on and bypassed the granite by climbing to the left up a vertical sérac to reach a big snow cone. After a short foray on the south face, we joined the original route on the steep and rocky west ridge and reached the summit (6904 meters, 22,650 feet) on June 6. The west ridge was mostly snowy rock climbing with a few aid moves and proved quite difficult with some loose rock. Everyone helped clear the mountain. Rudugaira (5364 meters, 17,600 feet) was climbed by Gordon Scott, Prentice and Susan Grimley. [This is not to be confused with the 5819-meter Rudugaira which lies some 15 kilometers to the northwest.] Nearby P c.5100 (c.16,733 feet) was climbed by Fisher and American Jordan Campbell. These may have been first ascents. Ratangrian (5858 meters, 19,220 feet) was attempted by Scott, Grimley and Campbell.

KEITH MILNE, *Mountaineering Club of Scotland*

Thalay Sagar Attempts by Spaniards. Two Spanish expeditions were unable to complete the ascent of Thalay Sagar (6904 meters, 22,650 feet). On the night of August 20, Carlos Suárez and Alfonso Vizán started up the north face. They climbed through much of the day but could find no place to bivouac on the precipitous slopes, which were being swept by avalanches. They descended in 15 rappels from 6450 meters. Another group, principally Basque, attempted the mountain via the col between it and Bhrigupanth. They were Juan Carlos (Txingu) Arreita, the brothers Patxi and Juan Lasarte, Lucio Egiguren and Jaca Chiro Sánchez. From the col they hoped to climb the Polish-Norwegian route on the northeast ridge, but they gave up below the col at 5900 meters because of the great quantity of loose snow, which avalanched and carried Juan Lasarte 400 meters down the couloir. Luckily, he escaped with a broken ankle, but he had to be helicoptered out.

Manda III. Scot Andy Cunningham, Englishman Richard Mansfield and Irishmen Gary Murray and I arrived on the Bhrigupanth Glacier on September 8 but were confined to Base Camp for the next eleven days by very bad weather. When it eventually cleared, we climbed Manda III or P 6529 (21,420 feet) via

Plate 68

Photo by Ian Rea

**BHRIGU PATHAR from the
northeast.**

the southeast flank and southwest ridge. Apart from the snout and icefall of the Bhrigupanth Glacier, which was difficult and dangerous, the ascent was technically easy, although long and arduous on account of poor conditions high on the mountain. There were three to four inches of breakable crust overlying up to a foot of powder snow or more. We took five full days to reach the top alpine-style on September 22 and to descend. We believe this was the first ascent. British climbers attempted the peak from the northwest face and north ridge in 1986 but failed because of deep snow at 6100 meters.

IAN REA, *Dalriada Climbing Club, Ireland*

Bhrigu Pathar, 1991. On page 234 of *AAJ, 1992,* we reported the first ascent of Bhrigu Pathar (6038 meters, 19,810 feet). Less than a month later, Spaniards José María Codina, Víctor Fernández and Cristóbal Díaz repeated the same route. They fixed rope on the first four pitches. They then bivouacked three times on the final ascent and once on the descent. They reached the summit on October 5, 1991.

Draupadi-Ka-Danda and Jaonli Ascents and Tragedy. A 29-member Japanese team to Draupadi-Ka-Danda and Jaonli was led by Yoshiki Yamanaka. There were four instructors and the rest were divided into a basic course and an advanced one. Their original objective had been Satopanth and Chaturangi, but the road to Gangotri was blocked by heavy rains and landslides. They then turned to Draupadi-Ka-Danda and Jaonli, the basic group under the leadership of Kazuyoshi Kondo heading for the former. Eleven members climbed to the summit of Draupadi-Ka-Danda (6038 meters, 19,800 feet) on August 10, 14 and 16. The peak lies at the head of the Dokriani Glacier. Members of the advanced group also climbed the peak on the 15th to observe their route over P 6083 to ascend Jaonli. Some of the group then left. During the trip back to Uttarkashi, the bus was struck by rockfall. Miss Takamoto Nobuko was killed and two others were injured. She had been a member of the editorial staff of *Iwa To Yuki* for ten years and had joined the expedition as an instructor.

TSUNEMICHI IKEDA, *Editor, Iwa To Yuki*

Swargarohini Attempts. Briton Nicholas Banks and a companion failed on the northern approaches of difficult Swargarohini (6252 meters, 20,512 feet). They established three camps during continuous bad weather and made final attempts between May 25 and 28. A three-man Spanish expedition led by Xavier Carrento attempted the east ridge. They were beaten back by bad weather on August 20.

HARISH KAPADIA, *Editor, Himalayan Journal*

India—Himachal Pradesh

Dharamsura Attempt and Ascent. Two Japanese expeditions approached Dharamsura (6446 meters, 21,150 feet) from different directions. Four climbers led by Zenkosuke Sakurazawa approached from Manikaran in Kulu in July. They were stopped by monsoon weather at 5800 meters. A second group, Jum Katori, leader, Hiroshi Yamaoka, Takashi Aoki and Mitsuru Ayoma, approached from the Bara Shigri Glacier in Lahul. They reached the summit via the southeast ridge on August 15.

HARISH KAPADIA, *Editor, Himalayan Journal*

P 6225, above Bara Shigri Glacier, Attempt. Britons Christopher Cheesman, leader, James Andrew Winspear and James Richard Mason attempted this peak which rises south of the Chandra River in Lahul. After a sérac collapsed on their route, the final summit attempt stopped at 6000 meters.

HARISH KAPADIA, *Editor, Himalayan Journal*

Chau Chau Kang Nilda. Indians Amit Chatterjee, leader, Krishnendu Chatterjee, Samaresh Saha and Miss Sutapa Sarkar left the roadhead at Langja and arrived at Base Camp at 5060 meters on August 4. They set up a high camp at 5275 meters on August 6 and the next day all climbed to the summit of Chau Chau Kang Nilda (6303 meters, 20,680 feet).

KAMAL K. GUHA, *Editor, Himavanta, India*

"Neverseen Tower" and Other Peaks, Miyar Valley. Italians Massimo Marcheggiani, Leone Di Vincenzo and Alberto Miele completed the first ascent of a bold needle, "Neverseen Tower" (c. 5950 meters, 19,520 feet). The 900-meter-high route was climbed from September 22 to 24 and graded with pitches of VI+ and VIII UIAA difficulty. The tower had been attempted in 1991 by a team led by Paolo Vitali. Some days earlier, the three climbed a 5725-meter (18,783-foot) virgin tower (UIAA V). The other two members, Silvano Bianchi and Claudio Mastrinicola, ascended P 6050 (19,849 feet), another unclimbed peak, on 45° to 50° snow and ice.

JÓZEF NYKA, *Editor, Taternik, Poland*

M-10 Ascent and Mulkila and M-5 Attempts. A team from Bombay led by Dhiren Pania climbed M-10 (5730 meters, 18,800 feet), which rises above the Milang Glacier. Vinit Rao and Tikam Ram Thakur reached the summit on September 1. Nandu Joshi and Arti Shah had to turn back 150 meters from the top. The team had earlier attempted Mulkila (M-4) and M-5 (6517 and 6370 meters, 21,380 and 20,900 feet). Both attempts were given up at about 5800 meters due to crevasses and cornices.

HARISH KAPADIA, *Editor, Himalayan Journal*

India—Kashmir and Jammu

Mardi Phabrang and Tupendo I Attempt, Eastern Kishtwar. A seven-member British team led by David Mortimer had hoped to climb Mardi Phabrang (6062 meters) and Tupendo I (5700 meters). When Dr. Jonathan Bamber was struck in the leg by rockfall on September 3 on Tupendo, climbing efforts were given up. Eventually on September 9, he was evacuated by helicopter.

HARISH KAPADIA, *Editor, Himalayan Journal*

Hagshu Attempt. Englishman John Barry has made several unsuccessful attempts to climb Hagshu by a new route, the north face. He was back again in September, 1992, accompanied by Bevis Bowden and D.J. "Smiler" Cuthbertson. The 3500-foot-high face has steep, mixed climbing. This year they were able to get up only 400 meters, some 200 meters lower than their 1989 high point.

Nun. A commercial Spanish expedition reached the summit of Nun (7135 meters, 23,410 feet) by the normal route, the northwest ridge. They established Camp I at 5400 meters and then fixed 800 meters of rope between there and Camp II at 6200 meters. Camp III was at 6600 meters. Those reaching the summit were leader Fernando Cobo, Angel Blázquez, Luis Quesada, José Ramón Mesía, Santiago Martín and Joaquín Guridi. A 14-member Japanese team led by Hirotaka Imamura climbed Nun also by the normal route. They established Base Camp and Camps I, II, III and IV at 4100, 4900, 5400, 5900 and 6300 meters. On August 13, leader Imamura, Masaharu Moriya and Ayumi Nozawai reached the summit, followed on August 15 by Kouji Sekine, Keichi Sutoh, Naoyasu Morio, Masao Keseki and Ken Satoh.

Kun. Ten members of a French commercial group led by guides J. Dubrusson, F. Eynac and D. Petraud climbed Kun (7087 meters, 23,285 feet) by its east ridge. Thirteen Spaniards, led by Karmel Leizaola, arrived at Base Camp on August 11. Eleven of them got to Camp III at 5600 meters, but all but two withdrew because of possible avalanche threats. On August 23, Josu Agirretxe and José Antonio Martín climbed to the summit.

HARISH KAPADIA, *Editor, Himalayan Journal*

Z3, Zanskar. Italians led by Sergio Maturi completed the seventh ascent of Z3 (6270 meters, 20,570 feet). From Camp II, on August 15, Tiziano

Cantalamessa, Franco Giansanti, Andrea and Stefano Di Lello climbed to the summit.

LUCIANO GHIGO, *Centro Italiano Studio Documentazione*
Alpinismo Italiano

India—Eastern Karakoram

Mamostong Kangri. This high peak continues to attract climbing teams. An Indian ladies' team, led by Bachendri Pal, climbed the normal route from the Mamostong Glacier, crossing the 5885-meter Mamostong col and up the east ridge. The summit (7516 meters, 24,650 feet) was reached from Camp IV at 6700 meters by 15 climbers, all on August 15, in three groups. The first summit party consisting of Deepu Sharma, Kunga Bhutia, Anita Devi and Harsha Panwar was accompanied by instructor Rajeev Sharma and Sherpas Kushang and Nadre. They reached the top at one P.M. Sarla Negi, Radha Devi, Dickey Dolma, Bimla Negi and instructor Baldev Kanwar got to the summit at two P.M. Suman Kutiyal and Savita Martolia summited at 2:30 P.M. with porter Vijay Singh. A fourth attempt was thwarted by bad weather. The All-Women Pre-Everest Expedition had 17 members and a doctor. This is the second expedition in preparation for the 1993 Indo-Nepalese Women's Expedition to Everest.

HARISH KAPADIA, *Editor, Himalayan Journal*

Teram Kangri. Teram Kangri (7433 meters, 24,485 feet) rises near the junction of the Teram Shehr and the Siachen Glaciers. It was climbed in 1992 by and Indian army team led by Colonel M.S. Gill. More details are awaited.

HARISH KAPADIA, *Editor, Himalayan Journal*

Pakistan

Gasherbrum I Attempt and Tragedy. Our international expedition had as members Americans Barbara Shelonzek, Errol Altay, German Gerhard Schnass, Italians Marco Bianchi, Paolo Bernascone, Giorgio Passino, Kurt Walde, Poles Mariusz Sprutta, Dr. Lech Korniszewski, Ryszard Warecki and me as leader. We set up Base Camp at the foot of the Gasherbrum peaks at 5100 meters on May 26. There was much winter snow and the weather was unstable with snowfall every day. Camps I and II were placed at 6000 and 6550 meters (Gasherbrum La) on May 29 and June 3. Following more or less the Messner route, we fixed rope and made a dump at 7000 meters. A summit attempt on June 26 reached 7200 meters. Due to dangerous conditions, further attempts were given up. On May 30, tragically just below Camp I a snowslab struck two descending Italians. The fixed rope broke and they were swept away. Kurt Walde survived while Paolo Bernascone was killed instantly. The region has terrible environmental problems. In the Base Camp lie hundreds of tins, bottles and containers, but a cleaning operation would be easy. The worst situation is on the Baltoro Glacier, where the litter increases year by year. About 90% of the rubbish is produced by the Pakistani military, who camp up to 6000 meters. Heaps of rusty tins and other garbage lie all around their campsites.

KRZYSZTOF WIELICKI, *Klub Wysokogórski Katowice, Poland*

Gasherbrum I (Hidden Peak) Attempts and Ascent. The international team led by Pole Krzysztof Wielicki, the first expedition to Gasherbrum I in 1992, is described above. A four-man Spanish Basque group led by Mikel Egibar attempted the Messner route but got only to the Gasherbrum La at 6550 meters, which they reached on July 17. Bad weather and inexperience were to blame. It is reported that during the approach one of their porters was drowned in a stream. A Japanese pair, Masatoshi Todaka and Hirofumi Konishi, had hoped to climb the Messner route alpine-style but they abandoned their attempt at the Gasherbrum La on July 25 because of bad snow conditions. Later, they joined the route of a large Japanese expedition on the west ridge and got to 7100 meters. A ten-member Japanese expedition led by Eiho Ohtani had Nazir Sabir as liaison officer. These two had reached the summit of K2 together in 1981. The expedition was attempting the Slovene route on the west ridge. They established Base Camp on July 8, Camp III and IV at 7100 and 7500 meters by the end of July and by mid-August. The weather was generally bad. Their last try failed at 7900 meters after which the Japanese called off the attempt on August 23. While the Japanese were preparing their return, Nazir Sabir and Hunza porters Rajabh Shah and Mehrban Shah started to climb from Base Camp in good weather. Nine hours later, they were at Camp III. The following day, August 25, they reached the summit in exceptionally clear weather and returned by nightfall to Camp III and the next day to Base Camp. Nazir Sabir becomes the first Pakistani to have climbed four 8000ers, all in the Baltoro region. It was the second ascent of Hidden Peak for Rajab Shah, who has also climbed Nanga Parbat.

XAVIER EGUSKITZA, *Pyrenaica, Bilbao, Spain*

Gasherbrum II Ascents and Attempts. As has been the case in past years, many climbers have been attracted to Gasherbrum II (8035 meters, 26,360 feet). Those noted here were on the standard route. From a six-man German expedition led by Rollo Steffens, Günther Schmieder, Jan Pracker and Heinz Wittmann summited on July 18, followed on July 20 by leader Steffens and Sepp Hasholzner, who at 60 years of age is the oldest person to have climbed Gasherbrum II. A six- member Mexican expedition was led by Antonio Cortés. Isabel García suffered from high-altitude edema and had to be helped down to Base Camp. On July 18, the summit was reached by Rogerio González, Lucio Cárdenas, Alejandro Velázquez and Germán Figueroa. A Spanish Catalán expedition was composed of leader Joan Oliva, Agustí Boada, Roger Cortés, Carles González, Carles Sánchez, Emili Durán, Manuel Benavent, Manuel Miranda and José-

Carlos Recio. They were joined for permit reasons by Italians Giulio Beggio and Valentina Lauthiers, but this pair acted independently. On July 18, the two Italians reached the summit; Signora Lauthiers was the 21st woman to have climbed Gasherbrum II. On July 23, Benavent, Miranda and Recio also climbed to the top. An eight-member Bulgarian expedition led by Minko Zankovski included one woman. The summit was reached on July 23 by Gospodin Dinev and Radko Rachev. A Japanese expedition led by Tadakiyo Sakahara had so many difficulties during the approach that they decided to turn elsewhere on arrival at Concordia. [See below.] A Spanish expedition from Valencia composed of Joan Agulló, Vicente García, José-Antonio Alejo and Dr. Carlos Sanchís suffered bad weather and failed at the end of September.

XAVIER EGUSKITZA, *Pyrenaica, Bilbao, Spain*

Gasherbrum II, 1991, Correction. On page 249 of *AAJ, 1992,* the successful ascent by two South Korean expeditions of Gasherbrum II was reported, but the facts given there were inaccurate. One expedition led by Han Sang-Kuk placed four members on top on July 19, 1991 by the standard route: leader Han, Kim Chang-Sun, Kim Su-Hong and You Soek-Jae. The leader of the second expedition which placed five climbers on the summit on July 20, 1991 was Song Jung-Doo and the summiters were Han Young-Jun, Lee Yong-Soon, Park Eul-Gyu, Jang Sang-Gi and Cho Jae-Chul.

KIM KYUNGMI-PAE, *Korean Alpine Federation*

Gasherbrum IV, Northwest Ridge Attempt. Tom Dickey, Charlie Fowler, Alex Lowe and I arrived at the Gasherbrum Base Camp on May 19, hoping to climb a new route, the northwest ridge of Gasherbrum IV. We had established a route through both icefalls on the South Gasherbrum Glacier by May 29. On May 30, we watched members of the international Gasherbrum I expedition descend an icefall that bypassed that icefall. The slope avalanched, carrying two climbers with it. Our team was close and we were at the accident site within minutes. One was not buried and not seriously hurt. The other was completely buried, but a small bit of his pack was visible. We quickly dug him out, but he did not survive. We established a camp at 20,000 feet in the glacial cirque below Gasherbrum IV on June 1. From June 3 to 5, we placed fixed rope on the snow face that led to the ridge crest. We returned on June 10 and placed more rope until bad weather turned us back near the crest of the ridge. On June 17, after a period of bad weather, we went back to our high point for a summit attempt. We were turned around again at 23,000 feet by a severe storm and thin powder snow over rotten rock. Because of more bad weather, another thwarted summit attempt and dangerous snow conditions, we abandoned our climb. On July 1, we left Base Camp and arrived in Hushe three days later after crossing the Ghondokhoro La.

STEVEN J. SWENSON

Broad Peak Ascent and Attempts. As in previous years, a number of expeditions attempted to climb Broad Peak, mostly by the normal route. An international group of eight climbers from seven different countries was organized commercially and guided by Welchman Martin Barnicott and New Zealander Russell Brice. Although their Romanian member joined an American party and made the ascent, they were not successful. Their attempt is described below. A South Korean expedition led by Yoon Hyun-Jong worked hard on the standard route, fixing great lengths of rope and demanding payment from other groups for the use of them. Eventually they had to give up at 7500 meters. A six-member British team led by Roger Payne was the only party that planned a route different from the standard one on the Pakistani flank. They reconnoitered both the southwest face and the south ridge from the Broad Glacier, near Concordia. Having reached 5400 meters, they found both routes feasible but avalanche-prone at that time. In order to acclimatize for a later attempt, they climbed to 7650 meters on the standard route, but persistent bad weather forced them to cancel their originally planned attempt. Another British team led by Tim Williams reached a high point of 6900 meters in mid June. A German expedition led by Helmut Förster also failed. The only ascent of the main summit was made by a mixed group from various expeditions that collaborated in the final attack. On August 6, six climbers started from Camp III at 7350 meters. From an American expedition were leader David Hambly and Scott McKee. Antonio Tapiador and Pedro Rodríguez were members of a Spanish commercial group led by Carlos Soria. Eudald Martínez was a member of a Spanish Catalan party led by Miquel Casas. The sixth was Romanian Constatin Lacatusu, mentioned above. Depite frostbitten toes, he was determined to reach the summit. The main summit (8047 meters, 26,400 feet) was reached at 5:30 P.M. and shortly thereafter. For Hambly, this was his second 8000er. Lacatusu became the first Romanian to climb an 8000er, but he paid a high price for it; with severely frozen feet, he had to be evacuated from Base Camp by helicopter. Two members of a Mexican K2 expedition, Mexican Héctor Ponce de León and Swede Johan Lagne, made an attempt on Broad Peak, reaching the foresummit (8030 meters, 26,346 feet) on August 5 in unsettled weather. A Chilean expedition led by Claudio Gálvez was delayed for three weeks in Islamabad and arrived at Base Camp on August 8. Towards the end of the month, they had to give up their attempt at 7300 meters because of bad weather. The middle summit of Broad Peak was climbed from China as described elsewhere in this *Journal*.

XAVIER EGUSKITZA, Pyrenaica, Bilbao, Spain

Broad Peak. Our team consisted of David and Diana Dailey, Scott McKee, Nels Niemi, Paul Stevenson and me as leader. We arrived at Base Camp on July 1. We had three camps at 18,600, 21,600 and 23,900 feet. The weather was good enough to climb to the lower camps most of the time, but there were only a few days for a summit bid. Snow conditions above 21,000 feet were always bad. We had contact with six other expeditions. On August 1, six climbers from four expeditions [see above], including Scott McKee and me, arrived at High Camp. The Mountain Gods favored us with a clear, windless day on August 2. We all summited at about five P.M. The combined effort of all to overcome the bad snow conditions was largely responsible for our success. After a long 18-hour day we stumbled into High Camp in the dark.

DAVID HAMBLY

Broad Peak Attempt and Ghondokhoro La. An Himalayan Kingdom expedition was led by Welshman Martin Barnicott with climbing leader Russell Brice from New Zealand. The clients were Italian Fulvio Fresia, Canadian Dr. Stuart Hutchinson, Finn Mikko Valanne, Englishman David Craven, Romanian Constantin Lacatusu and I as the lone American. After crossing a broken bridge in Dassu and later, after rebuilding a washed out road, we left the roadhead, Askole, on June 18 and arrived at Base Camp beneath the standard west-spur route of Broad Peak on June 23. We established Camps I, II and III at 5800, 6700 and 7300 meters on June 28, July 2 and 8. After a few days of rest at Base Camp during inclement weather, we returned on July 15 to the site of Camp III, which had disappeared, presumably in an avalanche. We abandoned the climb due to the deep and unstable snow. Lacatusu remained behind, joined an American expedition and reached the summit of Broad Peak in early August. Leaving Base Camp on July 22, we hiked out over the Ghondokhoro La (35°39'0"N, 76°29'30"E) and arrived in Hushe on July 25. In 1911, the Workmans visited the Ghondokhoro Glacier and determined that no pass led to the Baltoro Glacier. The 1955 Harvard expedition came to the same conclusion. However, Sirdar Mohammad Fakhar-ul-Haq led trekkers across it in 1989. Since then a number of expeditions and trekking groups have crossed the pass, which I found to be a simple route. We ascended the western branch of the Vigne Glacier to where my altimeter read 5730 meters. The southern side had some steep loose rock and scree, leading to the northern lateral moraine of the Ghondokhoro Glacier. The porters from Hushe crossed the pass without undue difficulty.

ROBERT J. SECOR

K2. A full article on the Russian-American expedition to K2 with additional details about the Mexican-New Zealander-Swedish expedition and Chantal Mauduit of the Swiss expedition appears earlier in this *Journal*.

K2, Mexican-New Zealander-Swedish Attempt and Tragedy. A ten-member international expedition was composed of Mexicans Ricardo Torres, leader, Héctor Ponce de León, Adrián Benítez and Berta Ramírez, New Zealanders Rob Hall, Gary Ball and Marty Schmidt and Swedes Johan Lagne, Oscar Kihlborg and Mickael Reuterswärd. Base Camp was occupied on June 28 and a long siege of the Abruzzi Ridge took place in cooperation with the Russian-American expedition. As a diversion from the main attack, Ponce de León and Lagne made a foray onto Broad Peak, reaching the foresummit on August 5. On August 13, Torres, Ponce de León, Benítez, Hall, Ball, Lagne and Kihlborg reached Camp IV at 8000 meters. On August 14, Torres and Benítez decided to descend because of deteriorating weather. Just below the shoulder, at 7775 meters, Benítez fell to his death when a ski pole they were using as a rappel anchor pulled out. On August 15, on hearing the news of the accident, Ponce de León, Lagne and Kihlborg gave up the attempt, leaving only Hall and Ball with the three Americans of the Russian-American expedition at Camp IV to make a summit attempt on August 16. While the Americans reached the summit, the two New Zealanders had to quit at the top of the Bottleneck at 8300 meters. Despite their using supplementary oxygen, Gary Ball had fallen ill as a result of pulmonary emboli. They withdrew to Camp IV where his condition became much worse. Rob Hall and the descending Americans managed in three days to bring him back to Base Camp, from where he was evacuated by Helicopter to Skardu. [More details are found in the full article above in this *Journal*.] During the course of the expedition, a human foot was found inside its sock and boot. The old type of crampon and the nailed boot suggest that the foot must have been that of Dudley Wolfe lost in 1939.

XAVIER EGUSKITZA, *Pyrenaica, Bilbao, Spain*

K2, Swiss Attempt. A Swiss expedition consisting of Peter Schwitter, leader, Beat Ruppen, Norbert Huser, Rupert Ruckstuhl and Frenchwoman Chantal Mauduit made an attempt on the Abruzzi Ridge of K2 that ended at 7400 meters in late July due to bad weather. When the expedition left Base Camp, Mauduit joined the Russian-American expedition and reached the summit of K2 on August 3. [See the full article above in this *Journal* for more details.] Mauduit had just previously made an unsuccessful attempt on Everest.

XAVIER EGUSKITZA, *Pyrenaica, Bilbao, Spain*

K2 Attempt. Wojciech Kurtyka and I had hoped to climb a new route on the west side of K2. We got to the normal Base Camp at 5100 meters on May 26. The route to Advance Base at 6200 meters is very long and we had engaged two porters to help carry to it. They quit after two hours, leaving the job to us two. On June 4, we reconnoitered toward the foot of the face to 6400 meters but gave up because of avalanche danger and windslab. The weather was also unfavorable. On June 9, we abandoned the attempt.

ERHARD LORETAN, *Club Alpin Suisse*

P 6940 Attempt and Ascent of Peak Near Skilbrum. A seven-man Japanese team led by Tadakiyo Sakahara had originally been planning to climb Gasherbrum II, but they suffered such delays in Islamabad that when they arrived at the

PLATE 69

Photo by John Middendorf

The GREAT TRANGO TOWER from the east.

Base

Baltoro Glacier, they realized they did not have sufficient time. They established Base Camp at Gore on August 8 and Advance Base at the head of the Biange Glacier at 4740 meters on August 11. The next day, Sakahara, Kouji Matsui, Shinji Chiba and Toshiyuki Kitamura climbed to the 6010-meter col on the ridge west of Skilbrum and continued to the left up another peak, the summit of which they reached at 6:30 that night. They returned to bivouac in the col. The following day, they attempted to climb P 6940 but were too exhausted to complete the climb.

K7 Attempt. Italians F. Arneodo, M. Bozzolan, D. Longata, S. Rossi and D. Sacchetti attempted to climb K7 (6935 meters, 22,753 feet) via a new route, the southwest spur, from the Charakusa Glacier. Bad weather kept them from getting higher than 4700 meters, after climbing 400 meters on excellent granite.

Trango Nameless Tower. There is a full article earlier in this *Journal* on the remarkable ascent of this spire, which came close to being a tragedy when a huge section of the mountain fell to its base.

Trango Nameless Tower. On August 13, Cho Dukkyu, Cho Chonghwan, So Hoyoung and I completed the ascent of the Slovene route on the Nameless Tower. The other two members of our expedition were leader Sunwoo Choongok and Kim Cheol. After driving to Askole thanks to the new bridge, we walked to Base Camp at 4000 meters in three days. The porters made a sit-down strike rather than marching up the Trango Glacier. After several days of heavy rain, we carried to Advance Base at 5200 meters. The steep snow-filled gully made the carrying dicey. On July 29, climbing started in earnest. Because of the wet weather, there was much water and ice. In the next five days, we established Shoulder Camp at 5500 meters, having climbed 19 pitches despite occasional falling ice. On August 4, we moved rapidly on a summit attempt. In the upper section, we experienced icier conditions. On the 22nd pitch, only 200 meters from the summit, a nasty storm forced retreat to the shoulder. Four days later, low on food, we descended to Base Camp. Since the porters were coming back on the 13th, on August 11 we decided on a final summit blitz and climbed to the shoulder. The next day we got back to our high point. On the 24th pitch, icy conditions produced A2 to A4 difficulty. We feared we were without adequate gear, but five bolts were found in a side pocket; we used three on this pitch. On the 25th pitch, I was hit on the shoulder by a falling rock, ruining my down jacket. We retreated to bivouac without sleeping bags on the 24th pitch. On August 13, climbing went smoothly in the Grey Area. After climbing the ice-choked chimney on the 30th pitch, we reached the summit at 1:30 P.M.

CHU YOUNG, *Southern California Korean Alpine Club*

Trango Nameless Tower Spanish Attempts. Spaniards very nearly made ascents of the Nameless Tower but could not quite reach the summit. They fixed

750 meters of rope on the lower part of the Kurtyka-Loretan route for seven days. On July 7, José Chaverri, Lorenzo Ortiz and Santiago Palacios made their final attempt, which ended ten meters below the summit because of perpendicular unconsolidated snow. Chaverri then joined Basques Kike de Pablos and Jon Lazkano on the Slovene Route, where they had already fixed half the route. On July 19, Chaverri and de Pablos were overtaken by nightfall when they were not far from the summit, but they gave up and rappelled off in the dark.

Great Trango Tower, East Face, Swiss-American Expedition, Second Ascent to the East Summit. Our expedition, consisting of Swiss Xaver Bongard, Ueli Bühler and François Studiman and American photographer Ace Kvale and me, arrived in Pakistan on June 10. On June 24, after a three-day trek from Askole, we made our Base Camp near the mouth of the Dunge Glacier where it runs into the Baltoro on June 24. Bongard and I immediately began preparations for a new route on the east face of the Great Trango Tower. We scoped the line, established Camps I and II on the very dangerous approach, much of which was possible only at night, and fixed the first pitches. On July 13, after some periods of unsettled weather, we spent the first night on the wall in our hanging 2-man A5 portaledge. We climbed capsule-style, with only six ropes total, and established five camps on the wall, four hanging and one at the snow ledge halfway up, fixing our ropes above each camp until we decided it was safe and timely to move the camp up. Many of the belays were in suicidal positions, due to ice-, snow- and rockfall from above, but camps were generally in safe havens. On July 28, we summited, after being trapped 400 feet below the rim for three days in a fierce Karakoram storm. The climbing involved many pitches of technical aid climbing, some pitches of free, difficult ice and mixed climbing. The last five pitches below the snow ledge involved vertical ice climbing and rotten aid and free climbing up a dangerous steep corner system which we named "Gollum's Gully"; this turned out to be a major drainage for the snow ledge. It was possible to climb these pitches only at night, due to incessant ice and snow pummeling down during the day. The rest of the route also had severe objective hazards because of ice, rock and snow avalanching from the snow ledge system and the summit séracs. Occasionally, huge sections would exfoliate off the wall and pound down around us. The upper headwall above the snow ledge was superb, though chimneys in the final section required multiple "Harding Slot" maneuvers in inclement weather at 20,000 feet. The final six pitches from the rim to the summit involved technical ice and tenuous mixed climbing, as well as a tough final slug through deep unconsolidated snow to the summit ridge and onto the east summit. It took us three days to rappel the route. From the base of the actual climb, we had to rappel a buttress to the east of the approach gully because of dangerous all-day and all-night avalanches caused by the warming summer conditions. We made 44 rappels in all. In general, the weather was fine, though we spent many days and nights in freezing storms in our hanging bivouacs. We named the route "The Grand Voyage." It was Grade VII, 5.10, A4+, WI3. We climbed 4400 feet from the actual base to the summit in 33 pitches with a

COLOR PLATE 9

Photo by John Middendorf

GREAT TRANGO TOWER's East Face.

PLATE 70

Photo by John Middendorf

Xavier Bongard on the GREAT TRANGO TOWER.

200-foot lead rope. Our route began well to the left of the Norwegian route. It joined it at the top of the snow ledge, continued along it for three rope-lengths and then branched to the right of it to reach the summit. We sighted fixed pitons and slings on rock outcroppings left by the Norwegians on the final pitches to the summit, verifying the likelihood of their complete ascent. (They doubtless met their accident on the descent.) Our ascent, then, was the second to the east summit (6231 meters, 20,443 feet), as both the Japanese and Spanish teams who repeated the Norwegian route did not venture past the rim. It should be noted that Great Trango Tower has three principal summits: the main (central) summit (6286 meters, 20,624 feet); the west summit (6237 meters, 20,463 feet); and the east summit, to which we climbed. Bühler and Studiman had hoped to climb the Nameless Tower, but Bühler broke his ankle halfway up the Kurtyka-Loretan route when he fell some ten meters. Studiman did a splendid job with the evacuation and they were back in Base Camp in a day and a half.

JOHN MIDDENDORF

Great Trango Tower, Basejump. Our multinational team consisted of Australians Nic Feteris and me, Britons Leo and Mandy Dickinson, New Zealanders Wade Fairley and Geoff Gabites and Russians Vladislav Moroz and Irina Singleman. We arrived in Pakistan on July 17. The road from Skardu now reaches Askole. The journey was an eventful one. A four-wheel drive vehicle carrying 20 porters crashed 150 feet down a rock slide, seriously injuring three people. As the only doctor for miles, I had to treat and transfer the injured to the nearest hospital at Skardu. Despite the delay, we arrived at Base Camp at 4200 meters on the Trango Glacier on August 3. On the Great Trango Tower, we followed the 1984 American route up the gully between the Nameless and Great Trango Towers and then onto the west ridge. We established Camp I at 5000 meters on August 5 in the shelter of a gigantic boulder. Camp II was placed on August 12 at 5500 meters in the lee of a rock finger standing 200 feet above a gully running east from the main gully. A single 20-meter ice wall rose just below camp. From Camp II, the climbing was over steep ice up to 6000 meters. A two-pitch traverse followed to access the narrow tongue between ice cliffs spilling off either side of the mountain. Three more moderate pitches led to a plateau beneath the north summit. We fixed the route to here. Feteris, Vlad Moroz, Gabites and I visited the summit multiple times between August 18 and 24 while investigating many sites on the edge of the northwest face for a rock ledge from which to launch our basejump. We needed a site above a vertical or overhanging section of wall with no protruding ledges for 300 meters. Access to the edge of the rock wall was made difficult by the 70-meter-high séracs lining the face. The site we picked was at 5955 meters. A two-pitch abseil over a sérac gave access to a small rock ledge in the center of the face. We spent a day carving ice off the ledge to widen it. On August 26, Feteris and I strapped on six kilograms of camera gear to our helmets and mounted cameras to chest and leg. Vlad Moroz filmed and Gabites had a motor-drive Nikon next to us. Leo

PLATE 71

Photo by John Middendorf

**Bongard melting snow at the
Snowledge Bivouac on the Great
Trango Tower.**

Dickinson had a long lens just above Camp II and Mandy Dickinson and Irina Singleman had long lenses in the landing area on the northern side of the Dunge Glacier. I was to jump slightly ahead and to the side of Feteris. His helmet cameras faced forward to film me and mine faced backward to film him. We had purpose-built canopies, basejumping rigs and "flight suits." At midday, we unclipped from the ropes, commenced our countdown and launched into space. Almost immediately, Feteris began somersaulting out of control. After three seconds, I also began to somersault. Both of us tumbled until the 6th second and then regained control. At the 8th second, I gave Feteris the open signal and he dumped his pilot chute a half second before me. The canopies took another two seconds to open, by which time we had fallen 500 meters. The film shows that we were 80 meters off the floor of a steep gully. Later, we blamed the rarefied atmosphere and the weight of the helmet cameras which changed our center of gravity and sent us head down into somersaults. The landing at 4200 meters was a hard one due to the rarefied atmosphere. A video copy of the film may be purchased from the author for US $50 c/o 1/1A Greycliffe Street, Queenscliff, NSW 2096 Australia.

GLENN SINGLEMAN, *Australia*

Summary of Trango Ascents. Eight routes have been climbed on the *Trango Nameless Tower* (6239 meters, 20,470 feet). There have been 13 ascents to the summit. 1. June 8, 1976, Britons Anthoine, Boysen, Brown, Howells, south-west face (new). 2. June 15, 1987, Slovenes Cankar, Knez, Šrot, south-southeast face (new). 3. June 23, 1987, Swiss Piola, Schaffter, Frenchmen Fouquet, Delale, west buttress (new). Fouquet descended by paraglider. 4. July 13, 1988, Pole Kurtyka, Swiss Loretan, east face (new). 5. September 3, 1988, Germans Kraus, Lipinski, Schneider and Wilz, Kurtyka-Loretan route to snow band and then Slovene route. 6. September 5, 1988, Germans Albert, Arnold, Güllich, Leinauer, Münchenbach, Schwierisch, same route as 5; Albert, Güllich and Münchenbach climbed free. 7. August 9, 1989 Spaniards Gallego, Ros, Clavel, Seiquer, between west buttress and southwest face (new). 8. September 20, 1989, Germans Albert, Güllich, Kurtyka-Loretan start and then between the British and Slovene routes, "Eternal Flame Route" (new). (On September 18, Albert and Stiegler had climbed to within 300 meters of the summit on the new route and then climbed to the summit on the Slovene route.) 9. September 5, 1990, Frenchwoman Destivelle, Americans Breashears, Lowe, Slovene route. 10. September 9, 1990, Japanese Minamiura, Solo to right of Kurtyka-Loretan route (new). 11. September 15, 1990, Japanese Hoshino, Kimoto, British route to rescue Minamiura. 12. August 13, 1992, Korean-Americans Cho Kukkya, Cho Chonghwan, So Hoyoung, Chu Young, Slovene route. 13. August 23, 1992, American Wilford, Australian-American Child, east side of south face (new). *A drawing of the Trango Nameless Tower with most of the routes appears on page 286 of AAJ, 1990.*

There have been four ascents of the *Main* (central) *Summit of the Great Trango Tower* (6286 meters, 20,624 feet). 1. July 21, 1977, Americans Rowell, Schmitz, Hennek, Roskelley, Morrissey, from the Trango Glacier over the Pulpit (new). 2. August 19, 1984, Americans Selters, Woolums, from Trango Glacier to northwest ridge (new). 3. July 25, 1988, Italian Giordani, probably by northwest ridge 4. Several ascents between August 18 and 24, 1992, Australians Singleman, Feteris, Russian Moroz, New Zealander Gabites, northwest ridge.

There have been two complete ascents of the *East Summit of the Great Trango Tower (6231 meters, 20,443 feet)*. The Norwegian Buttress was climbed with a big variant to the rim but not to the summit by Japanese in 1990 and by Spaniards in 1991. 1. August 5, 1984, Norwegians Doseth, Daehli, east face (new). 2. July 28, 1992, American Middendorf, Swiss Bongard, east face starting left of the Norwegian route and to its right above the snow ledge (new).

"Shipton Spire" Attempt. On July 24, Andy Selters, Chuck Boyd, Mark Bebie and I set up Base Camp at 14,400 feet on the upper Trango Glacier. Our objective was the first ascent of an impressive rock peak, photographed by Eric Shipton. It is about 19,200 feet (5852 meters) high. It lies north of Uli Biaho and west of the Trango Nameless Tower. On July 30, we placed Advance Base at 14,800 feet at the west base of the spire. Over the next four weeks, we fixed ropes on the "wall" section of our route. The climbing was steep and difficult (5.10, A4), protected by hooks, rivets, copperheads and lots of tied-off pins. On several days, progress was 50 meters or less. On August 27, Mark and Andy fixed the last of our 2400 feet of static rope. Three days later, we jümared our ropes, climbed more pitches and bivouacked on the ramp, the first suitable ledge in almost 2000 feet. Three pitches up the ramp brought us to 18,000 feet and a good bivouac. Andy and Mark spent September 1 resting, while Chuck and I fixed several of our lead ropes on the two final rock pitches. The next day, in deteriorating weather, we made our summit attempt. After jümaring the ropes, we traversed on 50° to 60° snow and ice for three pitches. Two long, steep ice pitches and a final snow pitch, our 35th, brought us to 18,600 feet on the summit ridge. At five P.M., we had a difficult decision, whether to spend the night out without stove or sleeping bags in a storm. Disappointed, we began the descent. Rappelling and down-climbing until midnight, we regained our bivouac and spent a wet, unpleasant night. We passed most of the next day in storm descending and cleaning the route. We left Base Camp on September 5. Herds of ibex summer in the Base Camp area. Unfortunately, word filtered down to the army camp at Payu. Soon, with automatic weapons, several soldiers showed up and killed three animals. Although ibex are officially protected, the army is a law unto itself. We informed the Ministry of Tourism at our debriefing. The Minister urged us to publish an account of the killing, presumably to help restrain the army.

GREGORY COLLUM, *R.L.M.C.*

Ascent of P 5495 and Attempt on P 5956, Sokha Glacier, Baltistan. Our expedition was made up by Chris Howarth, Mick Wringley and me. We traveled

PLATE 72

Photo by Gregory Collum

Chuck Boyd on Pitch 17 of "Shipton Spire."

by jeep from Skardu to the roadhead at Doko and walked for 3½ days via Bisil to the junction of the Solu and Sokha Glaciers and up the Sokha Glacier to Base Camp at 4030 meters. We were west of Sosbun Brakk and the Biafo Glacier. This was an ideal position flanked by numerous peaks of about 6000 meters. From August 3 to 5, we all three climbed for acclimatization P 5495 (18,038 feet) by rock and ice on the south face (UIAA IV+). We bivouacked at 4830 and 5010 meters. We made our first attempt on P 5956 (19,541 feet) via the northwest face on August 13 and 14. We reached a bivouac ledge at 4780 meters below the second snowfield. We retreated as Wrigley had injured his knee. Howarth and I made a second attempt from August 23 to 26 via the same route. We bivouacked below the rockband at 5100 meters. Our high point was 5250 meters but we retreated because of technical difficulty and the risk of accident.

IAN ARNOLD, *England*

Mango Brakk and Gama Sokha Lumbu. A lightweight British expedition composed of Paul Drew, Jim Hart and Dominic Leggett climbed in the mountains west of the lower Biafo Glacier. After a two-day approach from Askole, they placed Base Camp at Mango beside the glacier on July 31 and Advance Base 2000 feet higher on August 2. The next day all three set out to climb Mango Brakk (5355 meters, 17,570 feet), but only Hart continued the final bit to the summit, via either the exposed southeast ridge or on loose rock on the right side to the summit block—100 feet of easy and exposed slab and rib climbing. He declined to climb a 30-foot pile of perched blocks which made up the actual summit. After a long period of bad weather, Hart and Leggett reoccupied a bivouac site some 3000 feet above Advance Base at the foot of the southeast face of Gama Sokha Lumbu on August 12. Starting at one A.M. on August 13, the pair climbed to the top of the 50° snow slope by dawn and climbed along the ridge to the summit (6282 meters, 20,610 feet). [We are grateful to Paul Drew for this information.]

Latok Attempt. Jeff Lowe and Frenchwoman Catherine Destivelle spent a month and a half attempting to climb the north face of Latok. After suffering from miserable weather and dangerous snow conditions, they were trapped high on the wall for six days of storm in mid August and gave up the attempt.

Latok II Attempt. A British expedition led by Edward Howard tried to climb the northwest ridge of Latok II (7145 meters, 23,442 feet). They reached Latok Col but bad weather beat back two attempts on the ridge. This ridge has unsuccessfully been tried by a number of previous expeditions.

Latok III Attempt. After losing ten days to lost luggage, Phil Powers and I attempted the unclimbed west face of Latok III (6950 meters, 22,802 feet). On July 30 and again on July 31, we climbed the 500-meter-high snow gully on the left side of the face and traversed 300 meters to the right, carrying fuel and equipment. On August 2, we retrieved our cache and continued up steepening ice sheets to a small bivouac on the left side of the large gully or funnel system. On August 3, we climbed mixed ground to a good bivouac atop a snow-covered spur at 20,500 feet. August 4 was stormy and we could only fix our three ropes over difficult rock and water ice to a pistol-shaped snowfield. The storm increased during the next three days and with the porters coming on August 9, we spent the 8th cleaning and descending the route via 29 rappels.

GREG COLLINS, *National Outdoor Leadership School*

Baintha Brakk Attempt. Baintha Brakk (The Ogre) was attempted by Spanish Catalans Toni Casas, Joan Amils, Elias Coll and Jordi Sunyer. They had hoped to make the first ascent of the southeast face. They established Base Camp at 4400 meters on July 15 and Advance Base at 4700 meters at the base of the climb. After climbing a 350-meter-high icefall and a couloir of 400 meters, they reached a col at 5500 meters, where the very difficult rock and mixed climbing began. They climbed capsule-style, fixing five ropes before moving the lowest higher. They found rock of UIAA V+ average difficulty and ice of 80° to 85°. Their final attempt lasted for 13 days. During the end of this try, they were trapped at 6500 meters by bad weather for three days, during which time they were unable to cook or melt water. They gave up late in September.

Yazghil Dome South Attempt and Tragedy. The members of our expedition were Takeshi Hamamoto, Hiroshi Komura, Fumitake Nakamura, Kazuhiko Yagisawa and I as leader. We started our trek from Huro, beyond Nagar, on July 29 and took five days to reach Base Camp at 4350 meters on a side moraine of the Kunyan Glacier. We placed Advance Base and Camp I at 4500 and 5100 meters on the Kunyan Glacier on August 5 and 8. Between Advance Base and Camp I, the glacier was badly crevassed. On August 15, we established Camp II at 5900 meters near the head of the Kunyan Glacier. We waited out bad weather in Base Camp and began again on August 19. On the 20th, Yagisawa was killed by falling into a crevasse near Camp II. We abandoned the attempt.

MASAHIDE MATSUMOTO, *Denkidaigaku, Tokyo*

Lupgar Sar Tragedy. A six-man South Korean expedition to Lupgar Sar was led by Kim Ho-Young. They lost two of their members, Jung Su-Ken and Kim Young- Jae, who were swept away by an avalanche at Camp III on July 26.

Diran, 1991. On page 252 of *AAJ, 1992,* mention was made of a Spanish expedition to Diran, but details were lacking. The expedition was composed of Lluis Bancells, Pere Gelis and Alex Serra. They reached Base Camp at Tagaferi at 3625 meters on August 5, 1991. They established Camp I at 4800 meters on the north face on August 12 and Camp II on the west ridge at 5900 meters the next day. They climbed to the summit on August 14, 1991.

P 5550 and Badshani, above Pasu Glacier. Jonathan Preston and I arrived at the Pasu Glacier on August 9, hoping for a month's climbing on worthwhile alpine objectives below 6000 meters to make full use of Pakistan's trekking regulations. One week into the expedition, we had to retreat to the valley since I was suffering from a severe bout of Acute Mountain Sickness. Preston returned to Base Camp soon after and soloed both of our main objectives. One was a 700-meter gully line on the south face of P 5550 (18,209 feet), just to the east of Darmyani (6090 meters) on the northern side of the glacier. The line climbed directly to the summit. Descent was via the east face. The second route was the beautiful 1400-meter-high north face of Badshani (5640 meters, 18,504 feet) on the south side of the glacier. The climb took two days on sustained ice with some mixed ground on the northwest ridge near the top (Alpine Grade TD, Scottish IV crux pitches). In the local Wakhi language, the peak is known as Fiyag. Both are probably first ascents.

ROY RUDDLE, *Alpine Climbing Group*

Bublimotin Attempts. Frenchmen Michel Fauquet, Robert Balestra, Marc Guiot and Henri Vincens had hoped to climb the fantastically steep southeast face of Bublimotin, which soars to about 6000 meters on the southern edge of the Batura-Pasu massif. They had barely established Base Camp when the whole face seemed to explode, showering them with rock and ice. Luckily, they were able to take shelter from the falling debris, but they lost much of their gear and had to abandon the expedition. Slovenes Marko Lukič and Miha Praprotnik also had hoped to climb the same face but they backed off because of snow avalanches.

Sani Pakkush, 1991. Our expedition was composed of Arnfried Braun, Hans Jud, Daniel Ketterer, Leo Klimmer and me as leader. On July 13, 1991, we reached Bar at the end of the dirt road from Chalt in the Hunza Valley. We followed the East Kukuar Glacier for five days to Base Camp at 4200 meters below the west face of Sani Pakkush. After a reconnaissance, we left Base Camp on July 25 without Jud, who was ill. On the second day, we set up Camp II at 5700 meters. On the third day, Braun and I climbed the 400-meter-high ice face, which rose up to 65° with powder snow on the surface, while Ketterer and Klimmer returned to Camp I for ice screws and rope. On the fourth day, we four climbed the ice face and secured 200 meters on the very steep ridge between the west and north faces. At 6300 meters, we managed to find room for both tents on the edge of a crevasse. Because the weather seemed stable and after the exertions of the previous days, we took a rest day. On July 29, 1991, we had no difficulty in reaching the summit (6952 meters, 22,808 feet) in spite of deep powder snow on the north face. We reached Base Camp in nine hours on the 30th in steadily worsening conditions.

HUBERT BLEICHER, *Deutscher Alpenverein*

Kohe Shkhawr. Our expedition was composed of Giacomo Bornancini, Francesco Cappellari, Elena Guabello, Luca Proto, Gabriele Masiero, Fiorenza Testa, Dr. Donatella Noventa, Franco Paccagnella, Francesco Pavanini, Paolo Targhetta, Pierluigi Penon, Dr. Andrea Ponchia and me as leader. We hired small buses to Chitral and jeeps to the roadhead at Shagrom. With 40 porters we traveled three days up the Atrak Glacier to Base Camp at 4370 meters, which we reached on August 7. It lay below 6814-meter Kohe Nadir Shah. On August 10, we placed Camp I at 5000 meters on a rock ridge and then made a supply dump at 5600 meters. This was moved up and on August 16, ten members established Camp II at 6050 meters on a snow plateau near the foot of the northwest face of Kohe Shkhawr. Because of unsettled weather and food shortage, six climbers descended. On August 19, Bornancini, Cappellari, Paccagnella and I left Camp II in doubtful weather and reached the summit (7116 meters, 23,347 feet) at ten A.M. after eight hours of hard climbing. We were back in Base Camp on the 20th. Base Camp was evacuated on August 23.

LUCIO DE FRANCESCHI, *Club Alpino Italiano*

Istor-O-Nal North Attempt. We had hoped to climb Istor-O-Nal North (7373 meters, 24,190 feet) by the Lapuch route. The members were Germans Kurt Bartenschlager, Gerhard Grassl, Eckard Kunze, Norbert Pfab, Austrians Erich Bosina, Adolf Deichstetter, Icelander Ari Gudmudsson and I as leader. We were in the region from August 18 to September 4. It took us three days up the Tirich valley and the Tirich Glacier to reach Babu Base Camp at 4900 meters on the left side of the Upper Tirich Glacier. The route ascended the Nobaison Glacier to Camp I at 5700 meters. Camp I was on a rock spur which bordered the northern arm of the Nobaison Glacier on the right. We took a route different from the previous two ascents in the first icefall. Camp II was in a basin at 6050 meters and Camp III at the upper edge of the second sérac zone at 6800 meters. A case of pulmonary edema and other sickness reduced our strength. Not until August 31 could we make a final summit attempt. Just then the weather, which had been perfect, broke. Nevertheless, a summit push reached 7200 meters in bad weather. We left Base Camp on September 4.

ERNST SCHWARZENLANDER, *Österreichischer Alpenverein*

Nanga Parbat Attempt via the Mazeno Ridge. The west ridge of Nanga Parbat is about eight miles long from the Mazeno Pass. It is the longest ridge of any of the 8000ers and remains unclimbed. Although Nanga Parbat is very popular, there has been surprisingly little activity on this major feature. From July 20 to

22, there arrived in Islamabad Serge Effimov and Valeri Perchine from Russia, Ang Phurba and Nga Temba from Nepal and Alan Hinkes, Sean Smith and I from the U.K. We planned to climb the Mazeno Ridge in three stages. After getting to Base Camp at 3500 meters on July 26, we climbed a minor summit opposite Nanga Parbat on the 28th and then the more difficult P 5750 of Lilley Peak (5971 meters) via a new route on the northwest side in a four-day round-trip from Base Camp. Phase two involved climbing the Hanns Schell route on the south side of Nanga Parbat to 6900 meters (Camp IV). Then Effimov, Perchine and I traversed to place a fuel-and-food cache on the west ridge at 7300 meters, about 400 meters above the Mazeno Gap. Hinkes, Ang Phurba and Nga Temba placed a dump at 7000 meters, all on the stormy August 16. Smith was plagued by headaches and had already descended to Camp III. Hinkes and the Sherpas went down all the way to Camp I. On the 17th, whilst descending steep, loose rock between Camps II and I on the Schell route, a massive rock avalanche roared down. Effimov and I found shelter. Smith was turned upside down on the belay 150 feet higher. Perchine, who was about to abseil, was swept down when a rock hit him in the chest. Smith sustained bruised ribs, a crushed toe and a smashed helmet but was otherwise all right. He climbed down with what was left of the abseil rope. Perchine halted his fall 100 meters lower in a shallow depression and was lucky not to fall another 1500 meters. He suffered broken ribs, a cracked pelvis and lacerations on hands and face. It took two days to get him down to Base Camp. Hinkes and the Sherpas had survived another huge rockfall the day before. Hinkes decided to go home. Smith went to Gilgit for a medical check and Perchine remained at Base Camp to recover for the next few weeks. The remaining four members went around towards the Mazeno Pass. After two days of walking from Base Camp, we arrived to camp at 4800 meters on the moraine of the Mazeno Glacier, some three kilometers south-southeast of the Mazeno Gap. The next morning, Effimov, Ang Phurba, Nga Temba and I set off to climb the ridge which goes north to P 6880, the first of the seven Mazeno summits. In our 25-kilo rucksacks, we had food and gear for an estimated eight days up and down along the Mazeno Ridge, to the summit of Nanga Parbat and a descent down the Schell route. We moved together over the glacier and climbed roped on 45° to 50° ice slopes. After 12 hours, we found a suitable campsite on the crest of the ridge at 5850 meters. We spent August 26 climbing around and over the pinnacles of the ridge to camp at 6400 meters. On August 27, we climbed up ice and snow to P 6650 and then over the first of the Mazeno summits, P 6880. We continued east along the ridge, over P 6650, to camp on a wind-swept saddle to the east. On August 28, we climbed P 6970, which is as far as we got. Ang Phurba was definitely worried about the descent. There was no way we could split the party and so we retreated. We were back in Base Camp on August 29 after a good seven-day outing on new ground. After collecting, burning and burying 45 sacks of rubbish from around Base Camp with the help of local children, we packed up. On September 1, we walked out to the roadhead with our 18 loads on the backs of donkeys.

DOUG SCOTT, *Alpine Climbing Group*

PLATE 73

Photo by Doug Scott

**Mazeno Ridge and NANGA PARBAT.
Schell Route used to place supply
cache at 7300 meters on right.
Mazeno Ridge Attempt on left.**

Nanga Parbat Attempt, 1991. In *AAJ, 1992,* we made a brief mention of an unsuccessful Japanese expedition to Nanga Parbat. The *Iwa To Yuki Annual* on page 218 gives details, which we summarize here. The 8-member team, led by Seishi Wada, attempted to make the second ascent of the route on the southest Rupal Buttress first climbed by Poles in 1985. They placed Base Camp and Camp I on the Bazhin Glacier at 3650 and 4500 meters. They then entered the great couloir in which they placed Camp II at 5100 meters on June 24, 1991. Rockfall struck Yasushi Takatsuka on July 2, requiring evacuation. Camp III was established above the couloir on July 18 at 6020 meters. Camps IV and V were placed at 6690 and 7240 meters on August 1 and 6. On August 7, Wada, Tadashi Kajiyama and Tatsuya Ogata made a summit bid but were forced back. They had to wait out a storm for three days in Camp IV on the descent. On August 19, 1991, Kajiyama and Tadashi Tsunoda made a final attempt and climbed 14 pitches to 7950 meters, three short of the ridge, but had to retreat. Thus ended 75 days of effort.

Nanga Parbat Attempt on Rupal Face. A strong South Korean expedition led by Hong Seon-Yoon set up Camps I and II at 5000 and 6100 meters on June 9 and 18. They could get no higher, having only four days of good weather out of the forty they were there.

KIM KYUNGMI-PAE, *Korean Alpine Federation*

Nanga Parbat Attempt from the Rupal Flank via Rakhiot Peak. A ten-member British commercial expedition was guided by Jonathan Tinker and Mark Miller and included five other Britons and three Americans. Their plan was to attempt a new route from the eastern side of the mountain via Rakhiot Peak (7070 meters) and then to follow Buhl's 1953 route. They set up Base Camp at 3400 meters in the Rupal meadows and Camps I and II at 4600 and 5200 meters. A high point of 5600 meters en route to Rakhiot Peak was reached on September 4. Then, huge snowfalls in the next days forced them to abandon the attempt. Once the expedition was over, Miller went on to Nepal from Karachi but died in the plane crash in the hills south of Kathmandu on September 28.

XAVIER EGUSKITZA, *Pyrenaica, Bilbao, Spain*

Nanga Parbat, Diamir Face. Czechs Josef Rakoncaj, leader, Josef Nežerka, Michal Bruner, Martin Kejř, Miroslav Mžourek and German Günter Koch established Base Camp below the Diamir Face on June 12. Camps were placed on the Kinshofer route. After a five-day ascent, Rakoncaj and Nežerka reached the summit of Nanga Parbat at three P.M. on July 4. For Rakoncaj, this was the sixth 8000er and for Nežerka the second. Mžourek fell ill and had to leave early.

Nanga Parbat, Diamir Face, Polish-American Expedition. Our team was made up of Poles Piotr Pustelnik, leader, Józef Goździk, Marek Grochowski,

Leszek Sikora, Dr. Piotr Jedlikowski and me from the United States. After difficult and sometimes unpleasant negotiations with the Ministry of Tourism officials in Islamabad on June 5 to 7, we arrived at Chilas and Bunar Bridge on June 8. At Bunar Bridge we hired our cook, Sadder Khan, and completed our porter arrangements with the Khan family, which assisted each and every expedition going to the Diamir Base Camp. We arrived at Bunar Bridge and left for Diamir, the first camp, in three hours, with no prior arrangements. The Khans are well organized! We arrived at Base Camp at 4150 meters on June 10, along with a 15-member Korean expedition from Seoul, a Scottish team of five and a Swiss group of five. At Base Camp we found three Korean expeditions that had been there for several weeks. Before the trip, I had been concerned about queuing and tent space problems on the Kinshofer route, but these fears were unfounded. After being in Base Camp for a week, a Czech team of five and later a Basque team of five and then another Korean team of six turned up. That meant we needed to share ropes and tent space in the high camps. It also worked out to share food and route information to everyone's benefit. I was also concerned about getting sick from unsanitary conditions. This turned out to be a very real problem. I was plagued by diarrhea during most of the expedition. Weather conditions from June 10 to the end of June were sunny, with mild temperatures, and were generally excellent for climbing. Then the weather became unsettled, with high winds and afternoon storms. By the time we went for the summit and until we left Base Camp in mid July, it rained or snowed much of each day. Temperatures in the high camps were $-30°$ C at dawn. We reached Camps I, II, III and IV at 4800, 5800, 6700 and 7250 meters on June 12, 17, 24 and July 11. Our first summit attempt ended at Camp III on July 4 when one of my companions dropped his pack. Pustelnik and Goździk made the summit on July 12, along with four Basques. They left Camp IV at four A.M. and were on the summit at 12:35, having climbed the central couloir. On July 14, we left Base Camp. We found the route consistently steep, a physical struggle, but safe. The hardest days were climbing the 1000 meters from Camp I to II and the final push, which is 850 meters or so. Some of the liaison officers assigned to the teams in Base Camp were inexperienced, uninformed about local conditions, demanding and often absent. Out of the 41 days spent at or above Base Camp, Pustelnik and Goździk spent 20 nights in a high camp. Grochowski and I spent 17 nights in a high camp. Sikora contributed much but became ill and was forced to leave early.

R.D. CAUGHRON

Nanga Parbat, Kinshofer Route, Diamir Flank. Two South Korean expeditions combined their efforts. The four-man Gwangju Wooam expedition led by Park Chan-Gi arrived on May 14 and began preparing the route. The 14-man Kyung Nam Alpine Club expedition led by Cho Hyung-Gyu arrived at Base Camp at 4200 meters on May 27. Both groups worked on the route, fixing much rope up to 7300 meters and establishing Camps I, II, III and IV at 5200, 6200,

7000 and 7600 meters on May 20, June 11, 27 and 28. At 5:30 A.M. on June 29, Park Hee-Taek and Song Jea-Deuk of the Kyung Nam group and Kim Ju-Hyun and Cho Young-Jung of the Gwangju party set out for the summit, but soon Cho fell behind and quit. Park and Kim reached the summit at 3:15 P.M. Park descended 100 meters for protection from the wind and cold to wait for Song, while Kim continued on down. After Song passed Park, it took him 45 minutes more to reach the top, where he arrived at five P.M. Song was exhausted and Kim was very tired. It was a difficult descent to Camp IV as Song needed much help and encouragement. No further summit attempt was made since the other climbers had to help the summit climbers down. [Cho Hyung-Gyu and Kim Ju-Hyun have been kind enough to supply us with this information.]

Nanga Parbat, Kinshofer Route, Diamir Face. A Swiss group from Bern led by Martin Fischer managed to climb the Kinshofer Route on the Diamir Face. Three men reached 7700 meters and one of them, Christoph Häuter gained the summit on July 8. A Basque expedition led by Mikel Ruiz de Apodaka had originally hoped to ascend the Mummery Rib of the Diamir Face, but after seeing the difficulties and dangers involved, they turned to the standard Kinshofer Route. All four of the team, Ruiz de Apodaka, Juan Oyarzábal, Axto Apellániz and Mari Abrego, reached the summit on July 12 in collaboration with the Polish climbers. This was the third 8000er for the latter three and the second for Ruiz de Apodaka.

XAVIER EGUSKITZA, *Pyrenaica, Bilbao, Spain*

Nanga Parbat Attempts on the Kinshofer Route, Diamir Flank. Aside from the expeditions noted above, there were four expeditions that failed to reach the summit. Peter Long led a group of six Scots who did not get to the top. There were two unsuccessful South Korean expeditions, the leaders of which were Moon Ho-Sang and Kim Byung-Joon. The first group got to Camp IV at 7250 meters but had to quit because of bad weather. The other Korean party got to Camp IV on June 30 but three summit attempts were turned back by bad weather. The last expedition was a five-member Spanish expedition led by Manuel Amat, which had to give up at 7000 meters because of very bad weather in early September.

Nanga Parbat Winter Attempt, 1992-3. Our team was composed of climbers Mlle Monique Loscos and me, four trekkers and liaison officer Ashraf Aman. We hoped to climb Nanga Parbat for the first time in winter by the Schell route on the Rupal Face. We placed Base Camp and Advance Base at 3600 and 4400 meters on December 20 and 23. In bad weather, we two climbers climbed to 5200 meters with supplies on December 27 and bivouacked at 5500 meters the next day. On January 1 and 2, 1993, I climbed solo to 6100 meters, where I bivouacked. That night the wind was so strong that I had to take the tent down.

I returned to Base Camp on January 4. On January 8, I again set out and bivouacked at 5400 meters. On the 9th, I climbed to 6500 meters in bad weather with very strong winds. I could find no proper place for a bivouac. I returned to Base Camp on the 10th. We gave up the expedition on January 13.

ERIC MONIER, *Club Alpin Français*

Southeastern China

Kang Karpo and Meili Ranges. In October, Nicholas Clinch, Peter Davis, Gary Driggs, Brian and Diane Okonek, Peter Schoening and I, supported by Professor Zhou Zheng, Sun Po, Zhou Rong, Lin Cong and Cai Shun-Bo, visited the Kang Karpo and Meili ranges in northwestern Yünnan. [It is interesting that Zhou Zheng has learned that the use of Meili for the Kang Karpo range was a mistake. The mountains south of the Shu La are called the Kang Karpo range (Snow White Mountains) and those north of the pass are called the Meili range. Meili may mean "Chinese Medical Mountains" because of the herbs found there. — *Nicholas Clinch.*] We established Base Camp at Dotun at 14,000 feet on the Shu La trail, an old trade route leading into Tibet. We had good weather at the beginning of the trip and reconnoitered south both on the Yünnan and Tibetan sides of the Kang Karpo range. We found few acceptable routes. One we considered feasible was up the second highest of the Kang Karpo range, P 6509, from the Tibetan side. We decided to try this route, but a sudden storm closed the Shu La to animals. Meanwhile, Schoening and Driggs made the first ascent of Shulajaingoimarbo (5292 meters, 17,362 feet), the highest peak in the Meili range, north of the Shu La. It was mostly scrambling followed by a snow gully. After the storm, when we realized we could not move camp to our real objective, we crossed the Shu La to the Salween River over and back.

EDWARD LEAS

Siguniang, Sichuan. Japanese led by Chiharu Yoshimura climbed Siguniang (6250 meters, 20,506 feet) by its south face. They established Base Camp at 3500 meters on June 29 and Advance Base in the cirque below the face at 4600 meters on July 1. The route ascended the right-hand buttress on the left side of the cirque. They fixed 600 meters of rope on rock of 5.10, A2 difficulty. Camps I, II and III were placed on the buttress at 4900, 5200 and 5500 meters on July 6, 15 and 22. Above Camp III, the route joined the west ridge. A first summit attempt was turned back on July 23 at the second pinnacle on the west ridge. On July 24, Keiji Kodera, Isao Saita at 9:45 A.M. and Terumasa Ryokume and Shigeki Yamamoto at 12:30 P.M. reached the summit. On July 25, leader Chiharu Yoshimura, Ryuji Uchiyama and Ryo Moriyama also got to the top. Fuller accounts and impressive photographs appear in *Iwa To Yuki*, December, 1992 and February, 1993.

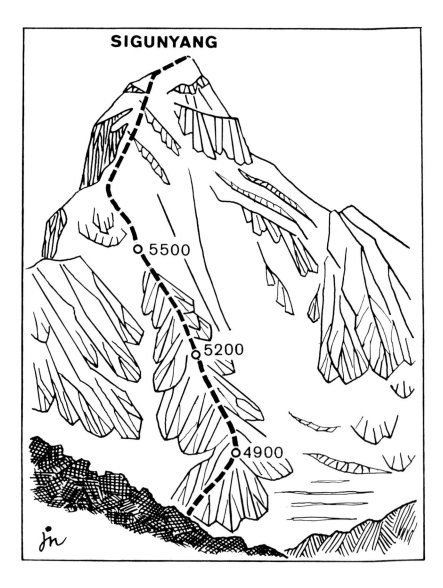

Roh-Weht Attempt, Konka Lehsumgongba Range, Sichuan. On May 6, Steve Thomson and I came within three rope-lengths of the summit of Roh-Weht (5464 meters, 17,927 feet) in the Konka Lehsumgangba Range in Dao Chun County, Sichuan. Our attempt by the northwest face failed due to a late start and bad weather. This mountain was called Tuparu by Dr. Joseph Rock in his July 1931 *National Geographic* article on the range ("Konka Risumgongba, Holy Mountain of the Outlaws"). We believe this to be the first attempted ascent from the Duron valley, which is in the heart of these mountains.

R. DABNEY EASTHAM

Anyemaqin Attempt. Our expedition was composed of Nobumi Nakazawa, Nobuo Matsumoto, Kuniharu Okawa, Akihito Tujino, Tatsushi Aono and me as leader. On July 28, we set up Base Camp at 4500 meters east of Anyemaqin. Camp I was established on July 30 on the badly crevassed glacier. There was very little snow on the lower part of the east ridge and so we approached it from the north. It was not steep but there was much rockfall. After fixing 700 meters of rope, on August 3 we gave up at 5500 meters because our party was too inexperienced.

KAZUHIRO KUMASAKI, *Japanese Alpine Club Youth Section*

Xao Xuebao Ding, 1991. On page 270 of *AAJ, 1992,* we reported on the first ascent of Xuebao Ding in Sichuan but failed to record the ascent by another Japanese expedition of Xao Xuebao Ding (5540 meters, 18,176 feet), which lies just to the southeast. The 12-member expedition climbed the southwest face. On July 30, 1991, leader Kazuo Yamagishi, Ken Wakamatsu, Itsuku Wagatsuma, Kiyo Yamagushi (f), Yasuyuki Yamafuji, Akio Tamai and Tomako Kawamura (f) reached the summit.

Tibet

Namcha Barwa. Japanese and Chinese climbers reconnoitered Namcha Barwa, the world's highest unclimbed peak, in November and December, 1990 and reached 6900 meters on Naipun. A Sino-Japanese attempt in the autumn of 1991 reached 7460 meters, but unfortunately Hiroshi Onishi died in an avalanche while attempting to reach the site for Camp IV. A third joint expedition was successful. The Japanese members were Kazuo Yamamoto, Toichi Mitani, Hiroshi Aota, Atsushi Yamamoto, Masunori Satoh and I as co-leader. The Chinese members were Sanju, co-leader, Jiabu, Tsering Dorje, Bianba Zhashi, Da Chimi and Da Chiong. We climbed the south ridge over Naipun Peak. We established Base Camp and Camps I, II, III, IV and V at 3520, 4350, 4800, 5600, 6200 and 6900 meters on September 14, 15, 16, 23, 30 and October 11. Summit attempts were made between October 13 and 21 but were beaten back by bad weather. The attack party set out again from Base Camp on October 24,

COLOR PLATE 10

Photo by Tsuneo Shigehiro

NAMCHA BARWA. The route angled up from Camp III at the bottom left along the ridge to the summit at the right.

climbing to Camp III. They occupied Camps IV and V on the next two nights. On October 27, they established Camp VI at 6700 meters beyond the intermediate peak, Naipun. On the 28th, they traced the route to 7200 meters. The next day, six climbed beyond the rock band to 7600 meters and bivouacked there because of bad weather. The other six of us set out from Camp VI early the next morning, the 30th. On October 30, a total of eleven climbers climbed to the summit of Namcha Barwa (7782 meters, 25,520 feet). I turned back at the rock band. We left Base Camp on November 7.

TSUNEO SHIGEHIRO, *Japanese Alpine Club*

Ningchin Kangsha. This 7223-meter (23,698-foot) peak lies southwest of Lhasa. It was attempted via its southwest ridge by Japanese in September, 1985, who reached 6800 meters, and was climbed by Tibetans in April 1986. Our expedition was composed of Japanese Mikio Hosada, Isamu Magami, Katuhiko Chiba, Seiko Mantoku, Jungi Oba and me as leader and two Tibetans and five Sherpas. We reached Base Camp at 5000 meters on May 18. We established Camps I and II at 5600 and 6200 meters on the southern snowfields. The first summit attempt was made on May 3 by Hosada, Chiba and Tibetan Ngatey. The summit was reached on May 4 by Chiba and Ngatey.

NAOHIKO OSAKI, *Japanese Defense Forces*

Changsanglamu. Changsanglamu (6324 meters, 20,748 feet) rises south of the Shigatse-Lhasa road between Kado La and Langkarzu. A beautiful lake lies 40 minutes above Base Camp. Legend tells us that formerly the lake was very muddy, but the goddess Changsanglamu cleaned it in only one night. The mountain was named for the goddess. The Tibetan leader was Dorje Phu and I was the overall leader. We established Base Camp, Camp I and II at 4700, 5500 and 5700 meters on April 25, 30 and May 1. We climbed the northeast ridge. From 5900 meters, the mixed climbing was from 50° to 60° until the final part, which was steeper. We fixed rope from 5900 meters to the summit. The summit was reached on May 2 by Japanese Motohiro Iizawa, Akira Nishizawa and Yoshihito Komatsu and Tibetans Danzan Dorje, Zhung Shishfing, Kaizong, Miss Jiji and Miss Zhuoxia. Because Changsanglamu is a holy mountain to the Tibetans, we stopped just below the very top.

AYATOSHI MOMOSE, *Mountain Association of Nagano, Japan*

Everest, Northeast Ridge Attempt and Discovery of the Body of Peter Boardman. There is a full article earlier in this *Journal* on the Kazakh-Japanese expedition which made an attempt to complete the ascent of Everest's northeast ridge and discovered the body of Peter Boardman and other objects from the tragic 1982 expedition.

Everest, Kangshung Face, Second Ascent of Neverest Buttress. On May 15, three members of our Chilean expedition summited on Mount Everest, after completing the second ascent of the east face of Everest directly to the South Col. (See *AAJ, 1989*, pages 1-16 for first ascent.) We were the first Chileans and the first South Americans to reach the top. After a nine-day march from Kharta with 84 porters, rather than yaks, hired after unjustifiable excuses from the Chinese authorities, we established Base Camp at 5400 meters on the Kangshung Glacier on April 7. Following the 1988 route, we placed Camp I at 6400 meters on April 20. This was above the Cauliflower Ridge, where we encountered UIAA V+ difficulties on rock with verglas and overhanging ice, all threatened by avalanches. On May 6, we established Camp II at 7400 meters. Packing loads in waist-deep snow over a badly crevassed glacier was difficult. After a rest at Base Camp, the entire team climbed to the South Col, starting on May 10 and getting there four days later. We rested one day because of high winds. On May 15, Cristián García-Huidobro, Juan Sebastián Montes and I reached the summit at 10:25 A.M. There we met 14 climbers who had ascended the normal route from Nepal. Even more shocking was the contrast of styles, seeing how the Sherpas had broken trail for their clients and carried their rucksacks, spare oxygen bottles and thermos bottles with hot tea. Has the adventure of climbing Everest been lost? Our expedition recovered almost all of the 2000 meters of fixed rope, all hardware, tents and empty oxygen bottles. Other members of our expedition were Dr. Alfonso Díaz, Christián Buracchio, Claudio Lucero, Dagoberto Delgado and Sherpas Chuldim Dorje, Nima and Karma Lama.

RODRIGO JORDÁN, *Club Deportivo Universidad Católica, Chile*

Everest Attempt. Our 17-member team consisted of Germans, Austrians, Swiss Norbert Joos and South Tirolean Hans Kammerlander. The latter two hoped for an ascent without artificial oxygen. There were four women in our number. We had five Sherpa and five Tibetan porters. We reached Base Camp on April 25. Americans led by Dan Larson had already fixed rope to the North Col and above; we paid them to offset the cost and they let us use them. We established Advance Base at 6400 meters and Camp I on the North Col on May 5 and 8. On May 10, Kammerlander and Joos reached the site of Camp II at 7800 meters. On May 11, despite gale winds, a few climbers went for acclimatization to between 7300 and 7500 meters. The Sherpas set up Camp II, which was promptly destroyed by wind. On the 17th the Sherpas were caught in an avalanche and suffered injuries; one had to be evacuated to the hospital in Kathmandu. On May 24, Sherpas got to Camp II and retrieved part of the gear. That same day, Herr and Frau Hölzl climbed with an American to Camp II, but the next day they had to help with the rescue of a Japanese from the Japanese-Kazakh expedition. Since there was no chance for success in the short time remaining, most left Base Camp on May 29. I stayed on a few days longer to clean Advance Base and Base Camp.

SIGI HUPFAUER, *Deutscher Alpenverein*

PLATE 74

Photo by Rodrigo Jordán

Load Carrying at 5760 meters on the KANGSHUNG FACE of EVEREST.

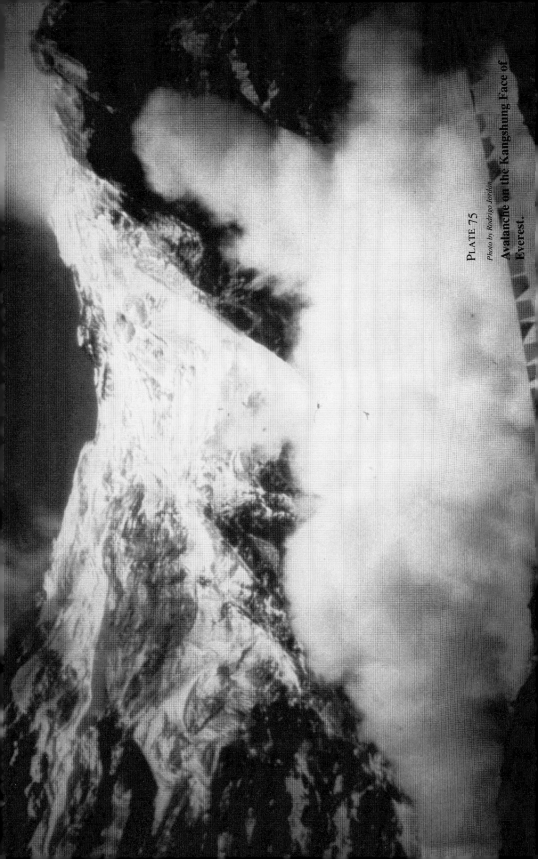

PLATE 75

Photo by Rodrigo Jordán

Avalanche on the Kangshung Face of Everest.

Everest Attempt. An expedition of nine Americans and a Canadian led by Daniel Larson attempted the North Col route on Everest but were turned back at 8200 meters on May 28.

ELIZABETH HAWLEY

Everest Clean-Up. Our 1992 team consisted of Tom Leech, Pierre Braunschwig, Steve Kin, Chris Naumann, Kyle Schmierer, Peter Nichol and me. We arrived in Kathmandu on July 1 after two years of careful planning, expecting a warm welcome from the Chinese authorities in Tibet, only to learn that they had denied our permit to enter Tibet. Eventually, we were allowed to enter that country, but we were only pemitted to spend five days at Everest Base Camp rather than the month we had planned and were ordered not to pick up any rubbish in Tibet. The day after we arrived in Tibet, we were told by a Chinese official that there was no rubbish in the mountains of Tibet and therefore there was no need for any clean-up work. We were, however, allowed to travel to the remote east side of Everest, a several-day trek up the Karta and Kama valleys to the Kangshung Base Camp. Accompanied by Sherku Sherpa from Kathmandu, two liaison officers from Lhasa, four yak herders and ten yaks, we traveled over the Shao La to Base Camp and back over the Langma La. Along the Shao La, used mainly by local villagers and trekking groups, we saw virtually no litter. The Langma La route, used by expeditions to the Kangshung face, contained moderate amounts of trash, particularly at campsites. Although we were forbidden to pick up rubbish, our liaison officers picked it up themselves when we pointed out how it spoiled the beauty of this remote area. A week after we arrived, we were told we must not take photos of rubbish. One liaison officer confiscated two rolls of film and warned of probable trouble when we left Tibet (which fortunately went without incident). We did conduct water quality tests along the way and took stool samples from team members for later analysis by an American Army lab in Bangkok. We also experimented with carrying out all human waste in a spill-proof, five-gallon bucket. Near the end of the trek, the bucket mysteriously disappeared when yak herders passed through camp! We also observed that the forests of the Karta and Kama valleys were being logged, despite a prohibition on cutting timber. We saw villagers, mainly women, carrying heavy loads of hand-hewn timbers to the trailhead near Uba, where the wood was loaded on trucks, destined perhaps for Lhasa and points east. Though not large in scale, this logging threatens some of Tibet's few remaining forests. After the trip to the Kangshung Base Camp, we traveled to the Rongbuk valley, the site of our clean-up efforts in 1990. The number of visitors is increasing. Several foreign travelers without Chinese "hosts" arrived at the monastery while we were there. Some trash was evident in the camping area near the monastery, but Base Camp and Advance Base looked great with little trash. We were delighted to see that the Tibetan Mountaineering Association had constructed two large rubbish-holding areas and two toilet buildings in Base Camp. The stone holding-areas we had built at Advance Base in 1990 are definitely being used, one being nearly full of garbage. We also verified that trash is periodically being transported out of Base Camp in the truck we donated in 1990. Much progress has been made on the Tibetan side of Everest. We shall continue our work in the Himalaya, which needs financial support. We shall be glad to receive donations sent to the Everest Enviromental Project, 3730 Wind Dance Lane, Colorado Springs, Colorado 80906.

ROBERT MCCONNELL

Everest, Post-Monsoon Attempts from the North. None of the expeditions that attempted Everest via the North Col in the post-monsoon was successful. Six Italians and four Swiss, led by Aldo Verzaroli, got to 7600 meters on September 30. From an expedition of thirteen Lithuanians, a Latvian and an American, led by Lithuanian-American Alex Bertulis, climbers stayed at Camp V at 7800 meters a number of times and reached 8000 meters on October 2. The weather was too ferocious to go higher. Three Taiwanese, under the leadership of Gau Ming-Ho, had to turn back at 8200 meters on October 10. Nor were those attempting the north face to the north ridge more successful. Twelve Italians, led by Augusto Zanotti, climbed to 7600 meters on September 17. American leader Douglas Hansen left Base Camp soon after arriving. Stanton Smith reached a high point of 7600 meters in the Great Couloir on September 30.

ELIZABETH HAWLEY

Everest Post-Monsoon Attempt. Our members were Dr. Howard Chuntz, Stanton Smith, Craig Bishop, Dr. Keith Hooker and I as leader. We had been scheduled to fly on the Thai Airbus that crashed and killed all 99 passengers, but we luckily had changed our flight. Once on the north face, we chose to swing over close to the North Col and then traversed back towards the Great Couloir. As is usual on the north face, avalanches were a main concern. Bishop and I suffered from a debilitating cough. I ended up trying out the Gammow bag and was put on the side line. Climbing unroped on the glacier, as most did, nearly proved fatal for Lhakpa Sherpa, who broke through into a hidden crevasse and was barely able to keep from going in all the way. Chuntz ultimately fell victim to dysentery. Smith and Tshering Sherpa made a summit bid. When, on September 30, they arrived at Camp IV at 7610 meters, they found the tent door had been destroyed by high winds and the tent was almost full of snow. They spent a long, miserable night unable to get the stove going. When morning arrived, the only reasonable decision was to descend.

DOUGLAS HANSEN, *Hansen Mountaineering, Utah*

Everest Correction. In *AAJ 1992* on page 263, it states that an Austrian soloist lost his life. The solo climber, Rüdiger Lang, was in fact a German, though a member of an Austrian expedition.

PLATE 76

Photo by Marko Prezelj

Southeast Face of MENLUNGTSE.
Bivouac at 6150 meters is marked.

Menlungtse, Rolwaling Himal. Described by Chris Bonington as "one of the most beautiful and difficult peaks in the Himalaya," Menlungtse has an east and a west summit separated by a 2-kilometer-long ridge. The lower west summit (7023 meters) was climbed by Britons Andy Fanshawe and Alan Hinkes in 1987. Marko Prezelj and I completed the first ascent of the higher summit (7181 meters, 23,560 feet) on October 23, alpine-style, on the southeast face, left from the 1990 American attempt. The 2000-meter-high ice face was not extremely difficult, but in the lower third, very dangerous. With Dr. Žarko Guzej, we got to Base Camp at 4600 meters on October 8. Prezelj and I reconnoitered the slopes below the southeast face and climbed a 6301-meter peak from October 11 to 13, but could not see our objective because of bad weather. We established Advance Base on the 15th at 5150 meters. During the first attempt on October 18, we set out at 12:40 A.M, got to 6150 meters at 5:40 and rested until ten A.M. because of bad weather. At two P.M. we reached 6400 meters where deteriorating weather and avalanche conditions forced a retreat. The final assault began on October 22, but we were able to climb only for 5½ hours before having to take shelter from falling stones and ice in a ice cave at 6150 meters. Starting at eight A.M. the following day, we worked hard and made rapid progress up the 55° ice face. We gained a big plateau at 3:30 P.M. and at 6:30 P.M. climbed to the virgin summit. We descended the same line with a mixture of rappels and down-climbing and got back to the bivouac at two A.M. on the 24th and descended to Base Camp later that day.

ANDREJ ŠTREMFELJ, *Planinska zveza Slovenije*

Cho Oyu Ascents from the North and Tragedy in the Pre-Monsoon Season. Climbing Cho Oyu from the west continues to be done frequently, with approaches both from Tibet and Nepal. (See the Nepalese section for those who approached from the south.) Four Swedes and a Briton led by Göran Kropp approached from Tibet. The leader teamed with Belgian Pascal de Brouwer, who came from Nepal, to complete the 100th ascent of the peak on May 7. On May 8, a group of 19 Italians sent leader Giuseppe Vigani, Bruno Ongis and Nauro Soregaroli to the summit. They were accompanied by Martin Lutterjohann, a member of a seven-member German expedition led by Eckehard Plättner, Belgian Mme Linda LeBon and Danu Sherpa, the latter two also coming from Nepal. Plättner's expedition unsuccessfully attempted the northwest ridge, reaching 7300 meters on May 9. On May 14, nine Swiss and six Germans, led by Hans Eitel, placed German Peter Kowalzik and Musul Kazi Tamang on the summit. Tragically, Swiss Philippe Monnerat was killed in a fall on May 22. Thirteen Germans and two Austrians were led by Reinhard Schmitz. Germans Manuel Schneider on May 22 and Peter Guggemos and Martin Schuhmacher on June 4 reached the summit.

ELIZABETH HAWLEY

Cho Oyu, Post-Monsoon Ascents and Attempt from the North. There were four successful expeditions that climbed Cho Oyu (8201 meters, 26,904 feet) by the normal west-face route. Eight Koreans led by Kim Kwan-Jun put Koreans Nam Sun- Woo, Kim Young-Tae and Sherpas Mingma Nuru and Nima Dorje on the summit on September 20. They continued on to Shisha Pangma and put same two climbers on the summit on October 2. A large expedition of 14 Japanese and a North Korean was led by Hideki Yatsuhashi. On September 20, Akira Hayasimoto, Mamoru Taniguchi, Sigeto Tsukamoto, Kazuyoshi Kondo, Hiroyuki Baba, Takao Suzuki, North Korean An Yong-Jong and Sherpas Nima and Mingma Tenzing reached the summit, followed on September 21 by leader Yatsuhashi, Ken Kanazawa, Yuki Sato, Tanehiko Yanagihara, Sigeto Kimoto and Sherpas Ang Phurba and Dawa Noru. From an Italian expedition of eight led by Giovanni Santambrogio, Fausto Airoldi and Paolo Gugliermina got to the top on September 10. On September 21, Slovenes Franc Urh, leader, his son Matija Urh, Aleš Cvahte, Štefan Lagoja and Marjan Gregorčič climbed to the summit. Six Frenchmen, led by Laurent Davenas, reached a high point of 7400 meters on October 3.

ELIZABETH HAWLEY

Cho Oyu, 1991, Correction. On page 265 of *AAJ 1992*, The name of South Tirolean Fräulein Gabriella Hofer was unfortunately omitted from the list of those in Hermann Tauber's party who got to the summit of Chou Oyu on May 27, 1991.

Cho Oyu, 1991. In addition to the ascents given in *AAJ, 1992*, an Italian ascent should be noted. On September 28, 1991, Sergio De Leo reached the summit by the normal route on the western side from the north.

LUCIANO GHIGO, *Club Alpino Italiano*

Shisha Pangma from the North, Tragedy, Ascent and Attempts, Autumn 1991. At least seven expeditions attempted Shisha Pangma from the northern flank of the mountain in the autumn of 1991. Members of a Japanese expedition, led by Kiyoshi Shimizu, and a Taiwanese one, led by Lian Ming-Ben, collaborated in their attempt to repeat the 1964 Chinese route. On September 19, 1991, five Japanese and four Taiwanese climbers reached 7900 meters at the point where the route deviates to the left to the main summit where they hoped to begin the Chinese traverse. Being late in the day, the Taiwanese retreated to a lower camp, but the five Japanese dug a snow hole on the face and spent the night inside. The following morning, three of them were about to set off for the summit while Hidekazu Gomi and Tetsuichi Miyashita were getting ready, still inside the snow hole. Suddenly, an avalanche swept the face, dragging the three several hundred meters down and burying the two in the hole. Horikawa

Matsugawa of the first group was badly injured and another suffered frostbitten hands trying to locate the pair in the snow hole. Japanese from this and another expedition, Taiwanese and Sherpas evacuated the three surviving climbers but had to give up any attempt to locate the bodies of the other two. A group, led by Chilean Mauricio Purto, included four Chileans, an Italian and a Sherpa. They arrived at Camp III at 7200 meters on September 26, 1991 and the next day climbed the northern ridge to the central summit and then proceeded along the connecting ridge to the main summit (8027 meters, 26,336 feet). They were Chileans Purto, Italo Valle, Fernando Luchsinger, Luis García, Italian Giovanni Mazzoleni and Ang Phuri Sherpa. This was the third 8000er for Purto and Valle and the second for Luchsinger, García and Ang Phuri. A six-member Basque expedition from Azpeitia arrived at Base Camp on August 28, 1991. Félix Azcárate, Miguel-Angel Aizpurua and Alex Zubía pitched Camp IV at 7200 meters on September 21. The following day, Mikel Larruñaga, Julián Soraluze and María-Jesús Larruñaga (f) left Base Camp, accompanied by members of the Chilean expedition, who went ahead. When the Basques arrived at the site of Camp IV on September 27, they found a tent partially destroyed and filled with snow. After some repairs, they spent the night there but the following morning gave up the attempt due to peristent high winds. A Spanish group comprising three from Santander and three Basques, including Belén Eguskitza, had to give up at Camp IV on September 29 due to high winds. Japanese, led by Fumimori Furukawa, had assisted in the rescue of the other Japanese. On October 4, 1991, Tetsuya Takahashi, Seiichi Kodama and Pasang Sherpa reached the central summit (8008 meters, 26,274 feet). Spaniards Bartolomé Quetglas and Ramón Alfredo from Mallorca failed at 7400 meters on October 9, 1991.

XAVIER EGUSKITZA, *Pyrenaica, Bilbao, Spain*

Shisha Pangma, Southwest Face, 1991. A South Korean expedition led by Oh In-Hwan repeated the British line on the southwest face of Shisha Pangma. The main summit was reached on October 8, 1991 by Kim Chang-Seon (his fourth 8000er) and Kim Jae-Soo (his second 8000er).

XAVIER EGUSKITZA, *Pyrenaica, Bilboa, Spain*

Shisha Pangma, Central Summit. Our expedition was composed of Eturou Hino, Toyofumi Miyazaki, Masanori Hasimoto and me as leader. Before entering Tibet, we acclimatized in Nepal. This prevented difficulties with high altitude. We set up Base Camp at 4900 meters on April 14. We placed Advance Base and Camps I, II and III at 5600, 6400, 6900 and 7100 meters. On May 6, Hino and Miyazaki reached the slightly lower central summit.

YOSUKE NARISUE, *Japanese Alpine Club*

Shisha Pangma Central from the North, Post-Monsoon. Several Spanish groups under the overall leadership of Toni Vives, but acting more or less

PLATE 77
Photo by Alfred Grueber
**Southwest Face SHISHA
PANGMA**

independently, climbed Shisha Pangma Central by the normal route. On September 27, Magda Nos climbed to the central summit with Ang Phuri Sherpa. Later that day, Rafael Fuentes, Toni Bericat and Saila Tamang got there, followed at a very late hour by Vives with two women, Amparo Ortega and Inmaculada Fernández. That same day, Nepalese Iman Gurung left Camp III at 7600 meters, climbed to the summit in only three hours and descended to Base Camp. From there he hurried by truck to Everest, hoping to make the speed record on the world's highest peak. He did not succeed in his second goal.

Shisha Pangma Central, Southwest Side. On September 29, Spaniards Ernest Bladé, Albert Castellet, Araceli Segarra and Ferrán Latorre repeated the route climbed on the southwest side of Shisha Pangma by Loretan, Troillet and Kurtyka in 1990. Like the first-ascent team, they got to the central summit. They had camped at 5800 meters below the route and climbed alpine-style with a bivouac at 6700 meters.

Shisha Pangma, Post-Monsoon. As more and more expeditions are attracted to Shisha Pangma, it seems, strangely enough, to be more difficult to get details on all of them. We are grateful to South Tirolean Hermann Tauber for information of his expedition, which was stopped at 7300 meters by deep snow. They had hoped to make a ski ascent. An incomplete report has been received about a ten-member Russian team led by Cherni Statayev. The group, including two women, reached a summit, but it is not clear if it was the main or the slightly lower central summit. There also apparently were two German expeditions and a Swiss one. We have not yet heard about the outcome of these.

Southwestern China

Syn Qing Feng or Buka Daban. The members of our expedition were Toshiaki Sakaue, Takashi Masuda, Kazuyoshi Nakata, Akira Hayashimoto, Yoichiro Shirota and I as leader. On May 4, we placed Base Camp at 4900 meters and on May 7, Advance Base at 5600 meters on the plateau below Syn Qing XVIII, avoiding séracs and crevasses along the glacier. After a snowstorm, on May 12 we traversed the eastern slope of Syn Qing XVIII and set up Camp I at 6000 meters at the head of the glacier before being forced back to Base by another snowstorm. On May 17, Masuda, Hayashimoto and Shirota finally placed Camp II at 6350 meters, and placed fixed ropes to 6500 meters on Syn Qing II's west ridge. Shirota had to drop out because of frostbite. On May 18, Masuda and Hayashimoto climbed a knife-edge which rose up to 60° and reached the summit (6860 meters, 22,507 feet). The mountain lies on the border of Qinghai and Xinjiang provinces. It is a compact group of some 20 peaks. It was attempted by Japanese in 1988 and Syn Xing II was tried by Americans. (*AAJ, 1989*, pages 289-290.) The name is also transliterated as Xin Qing Feng. Its name in Mongolian is Buka Daban.

TADASHI FUKUYAMA, *Himalayan Association of Japan*

Chinese Karakoram

K2 attempt, 1991. After a long approach from Pakistan via Kashgar and Sughet Jangal, we eventually reached the tongue of the K2 Glacier on May 22, 1991. The camels withdrew and we established Depot Camp. We were Romano Benet, Alberto Busattini, Filippo Sala, Osvaldo Stoffie, Luciano Vuerich and I as leader. We carried loads the 20 kilometers up the K2 Glacier to Base Camp at 4900 meters. It took five round-trips for each member. For two days we were helped by six camel drivers to an intermediate camp halfway up the glacier. On July 3, we set up Base Camp. From then on, we never had more than three days of continuous stable weather. Despite this, we started the climb on July 4. On July 9, we set up Camp I at 5650 meters beneath a sérac in the middle of the slope, placing 400 meters of fixed rope. On July 17, we established Camp II at 6500 meters, fixing 300 meters of rope, some of it old rope, on slopes up to 70°. On July 18, we pushed to 7100 meters, but the umteenth storm forced us back to Base Camp. We decided to continue alpine-style. Benet, Busattini and Sala left Base Camp on July 30 and reached Camp II the following day, where the weather held them up for a day. On August 2, they climbed to 7250 meters and the next day to 7800 meters. On August 4, they continued up the ridge to an uncomfortable bivouac at 8200 meters, but they were forced back by a snow-storm. On August 8, Stoffie and I departed for another summit bid, but we were held up by the weather at Camp I and were forced into a final retreat.

FABIO AGOSTINIS, *Club Alpino Italiano*

Broad Peak Central from China. An article on the ascent of Broad Peak's central summit by a Spanish Catalan expedition appears earlier in this *Journal.*

The Crown (Huan Guan Shan) Attempt and Tragedy. The 11-member Himalayan Association of Japan to Huan Guan Shan (7295 meters, 23,934 feet) was led by Kinichi Yamamori. For acclimatization, the expedition first traveled to Mustagh Ata where they made three summit bids, the highest reaching 6900 meters. They left there on August 22 and got to the Huan Guan Base Camp at 4000 meters on the 28th. They attacked the southeast face. Camps I, II, III, IV and VI were placed at 4200, 4400, 5100, 5800 and 6500 meters on September 1, 2, 7, 15 and 22. On September 28, Yuji Futamata and Hiroshi Nakagawa reconnoitered the route to 7000 meters and descended to Camp III. On October 2, they started back up. Between Camp III and IV, 25 pitches were fixed with rope. At about 4:45 P.M., Nakagawa was jümaring the 25th pitch and Futmata was on the pitch behind him. An avalanche swept over them. The rope held Nakagawa, but the rope on the 24th pitch broke at the point where Futamata's Jümar clasped it. Bits and pieces of his equipment were found in the debris, but his body was not recovered. This was the fourth unsuccessful attempt on the mountain and the second that ended in tragedy. (See *AAJ, 1988,* page 286 and *AAJ 1991,* page 301.)

CIS—Kirgizia

Khan Tengri, Tien Shan, First Winter Ascent. The most notable event of the 1991-2 winter season in the high Asian mountains was the first winter ascent of the marble pyramid Khan Tengri (6995 or 7010 meters, 22,950 or 22,999 feet). One of the world's most beautiful mountains, it is the most northerly 7000er. A strong Kazakh party led by Valeri Khrishchaty was further composed of Viktor Dedi, Yuri Moiseyev, Valdimir Suviga, Aleksandr Savin, Igor Putintsev and Malik Ismetov. After leaving Alma Ata on January 25, they acclimatized by climbing to the col between Khan Tengri and Pik Chapayeva, where at 5800 meters they made snow caves for a bivouac. Khrishchaty said that of the five CIS highest summits, Khan Tengri is the most difficult in winter because its rocky pyramid is completely exposed to stormy winds. The final attack began on February 7 with low temperatures and fierce winds. After spending the night in the snow caves, they continued along the ridge, which had been swept by the wind down to bare ice. Here and there, old fixed ropes could be used. Near the top, they found the body of a climber who had died in the summer season. It took some time to extract him from the ice and bury him. Above 6300 meters, the storm could hardly be borne. At two P.M., all seven climbers reached the summit. On February 9, all were back at Base Camp. Khan Tengri is now considered a 7000-meter peak because of a new survey. Khrishchaty has now climbed all five of the CIS 7000ers in winter.

JÓZEF NYKA, *Editor, Taternik, Poland*

Tien Shan and Pik Pobedy Attempt. Our trekking group was allowed to travel from Kirgizstan over the Turugart Pass to Kashgar and the Mustagh Ata Base Camp, a route which has been cut off for decades. We were struck by the contrast between the green, flowery Kirgiz Ala-Too, the white peaks and the desert on the Sinkiang steppes. Our travel on the Kirgiz side was facilitated by helicopter and overland vehicles. On the Sinkiang side, a camel train undertook our baggage transport. While we were there, a German Alpine Club (DAV) expedition led by Ludwig Hösle from the Allgäu attempted the difficult north rib of Pik Pobedy in the central Tien Shan. Because of bad weather and snow conditions, they were unable to get higher than 6000 meters.

KARL F. SCHOTT, *Deutscher Alpenverein*

P 4810, 1000 Years of Russian Christianity, Piramidalny and Other Peaks, Pamir Alai, Kirgizia. Tierry Schmitter, Matthijs van Hasselt, Hans Lanters and I climbed many peaks during our five-week stay in the Asan region. Together with our hosts from Minsk, we arrived at Base Camp at 2800 meters in the Kara Su valley on July 1. After an easy acclimatization climb on Duchtar-Cha (3800 meters, 12,467 feet), we climbed the east buttress (5.10a) of Usan (4329 meters, 14,203 feet) on July 4. On July 8, we climbed the probably virgin, 1000-meter-high, east face of Kara Su Peak (5309 meters, 17,419 feet) in five hours. On the summit ridge lay soft snow on unfavorably layered rotten rock. The first 300 meters of the descent along the north ridge were also tricky. We next turned our attention to the fantastic granite spires. On July 11 and 12, we tried unsuccessfully to make the second ascent of the French route on the east face of P 3850 (12,631 feet) in the Ak Su valley, but we could not find the passage over the big roof halfway up the wall. After a period of rain, we turned to the east-southeast pillar (Kritsuk route, 1300-meters, 5.11, third ascent) of 1000 Years of Russian Christianity (4520 meters, 14,830 feet). On July 17, we bivouacked after 800 meters of mainly 5.7 with two pitches of 5.10c. The next day, the sustained most difficult section awaited us. We mastered 14 pitches before bivouacking. We reached the summit the next morning at 10:30 A.M. after six 5.8 pitches. The descent was long and difficult, with 15 diagonal abseils along the south ridge, followed by 600 meters of abseiling and down-climbing the couloir between our peak and P 4810. We arrived at Base Camp at 11:30 P.M. On July 22, we made what was probably the first one-day round-trip on Asan Peak (4204 meters, 13,793 feet), following the popular Alperin route on the southwest buttress (700 meters, 5.10b). On July 25, we completed the climb of Piramidalny (5509 meters, 18,075 feet) in 5½ hours from an intermediate camp at 4200 meters. Only one pitch under a sérac proved difficult. After bad weather, Smitter and I made the second ascent of the Dutch variant, "Slippery People" (5.10c), on the Yellow Wall. The next day, August 1, we joined van Hasselt and Lanters at the foot of the southwest buttress of the Fitz Roy-like peak, P 4810 (15,781 feet). They had already prepared the first two pitches. In a very long day we climbed to reach a good ledge, 20 meters from the summit in the last rays of the sun. Our 800-meter-high ascent was mainly of 5.7 to 5.9 difficulty with a few harder pitches up to 5.10d. The next day we enjoyed the view from the summit and made 30 rappels down the ascent route. The trip was very well organized by our Belorussian friends.

ROLAND BEKENDAM, *Koninklijke Nederlandse Alpen Vereniging*

Peaks Twelve Kilometers West of Pik Pobedy, Tien Shan. Our expedition was composed of Austrians Leo Baumgartner, leader, Dr. Andreas Paul, Gernot Madritsch, Hubert Engl, Heli Ortner, Netherlander Ton Biesemaan and Germans Tom Stöger and me. On September 15, we were flown by helicopter from Alma Ata in 2½ hours to the Khan Tengri Base Camp. From there, Stöger, Engl, Ortner and I were flown further to a glacial valley twelve kilometers to the west of Pik Pobedy, where we set up our Base Camp at 4000 meters on the Proletariatski Turist Glacier. We were the first climbers in the area. (The others stayed in the Khan Tengri area.) On the eastern side of our valley there were five pinnacles shaped like shark's teeth. On September 16, Stöger and I climbed the First Shark's Tooth (c.5100 meters, c.16,733 feet) by its west face and north ridge. The rock was rotten and of UIAA II and III difficulty. The ice was up to 60°. The upper section, where we roped, had loose snow and cornices. Only one of us could stand on the summit at a time. On the 18th, Stöger and I climbed on its east face to a 5200-meter foresummit of what we called "Half Moon." This lies on the ridge between the Komsomolez and Proletariatski Turist Glaciers. The lower part was of UIAA III+ and 45° ice. We did not attempt the north ridge between the foresummit and the main peak as it was too dangerous because of deep snow, cornices and séracs. On both September 16 and 18, Engl and Ortner also attempted the same peak by its south ridge but they gave up because of bad conditions and technical difficulties.

EDI BIRNBACHER, *Deutscher Alpenverein*

CIS—Caucasus and Pamirs

Elbrus and Pik Korzhenevskoy. On June 12 and 18, I climbed to the summits of Elbrus East (5621 meters, 18,442 feet) and Elbrus West (5642 meters, 18,510 feet) in the Caucasus. I was informed that I was the first American woman to ski from the summit of Elbrus East to Kara Bashi at 3700 meters. In the Pamirs, because of high avalanche danger on Pik Kommunizma, we turned to Pik Korzhenevskoy. Russians Evgeni Prilepa, Sergei Efimov and Sergei Arsentiev, German Karl Heinz and I climbed alpine-style, making three camps, and on July 25 reached the summit (7105 meters, 23,310 feet).

FRAN DISTEFANO, *Trek Around the World*

Diklos-mta, Addala and Addala East, Dagestan, Caucasus. This British-Ukrainian expedition climbed in the Snegovoy and Bogosski ranges in the remote western part of Dagestan in the Eastern Caucasus from August 11 to September 8. We made three first British ascents and two new routes. German Gottfried Merzbacher first climbed here exactly 100 years ago. After him and Hungarian Mór Déchy in 1897, there had been no further climbers from outside the Soviet block. Alpinists from Dagestan and other parts of the Soviet Union added to Merzbacher's nine routes, but the area had really seen little climbing. On August 19, Mike Doyle and I made a new route variant on Diklos-mta (4285 meters, 13,730 feet), a new couloir and a new direction of traverse. Most of the team opted for the established route on the east ridge. They were forced by white-out to turn back just below the summit. Doyle and I, having climbed a couloir to the south ridge, were committed to traversing the mountain via a long and highly dubious crenellated ridge of crumbling shale. On August 27 Doyle, Ewan French, Adam White and I, and Ukrainians Mikhail Bogomapov and Yuri Cherevko climbed the normal northwest ridge of Addala (4151 meters, 13,619 feet), mostly rock. The shale was mainly frozen for the climb but thawed, allowing a rapid sliding descent. Moving to the northeast side of Addala, we found an impressive cirque of peaks. A snow-and-ice line on Addala East (4025 meters, 13,205 feet) looked inviting. It had the advantage of avoiding the shale. On August 30, Doyle, Bogomapov, Nikolai Drobotenko and I completed this new route. The summit message showed the only previous ascent had been in 1986, by the north ridge.

PAUL KNOTT, *Alpine Club*

Mongolia

Taban Bogdo Mountains. A full article on climbing in Mongolia appears earlier in this *Journal.*

Massif of Tsast Uul-Tsambagarev. Italians Gianni Pais Becher, Gastone Lorenzini and Elziro Molin climbed in western Mongolia in June and July. In late June, they first climbed Tsast Uul (4250 meters, 13,944 feet), the second highest peak in Mongolia, by the normal route. On June 27, they established Base Camp at 2520 meters north of the massif and the next day placed a camp in an alpine meadow. On June 29 the three Italians with Mongolians Jndonpuncav, Gotov, Samubun and Battulga climbed a 55° ice slope to the summit of unclimbed P 4030 (13,222 feet). On June 30, they moved camp to Tavan Betchir. On July 2, they started for a peak they had seen from Tsast Uul. They had to climb over a ridge to 3800 meters, down the far side, across a glacier and finally up the icy, 60° northwest face of P 4150 (13,616 feet). The summit was reached by Pais Becher, Molin, Mongolians Dorjpalam, Tumentogootch, Damba, Rentsenbyamba, Gaadamba and Vantchig. [This information was kindly supplied by Signor Gianni Pais Becher.]

Book Reviews

EDITED BY JOHN THACKRAY

K-2, The 1939 Tragedy. Andrew J. Kauffman and William L. Putnam. The Mountaineers. Seattle, 1992. 224 pages, 15 pages of black-and-white photographs. $19.95.

The story of the 1939 American K-2 expedition aroused such controversy for years that many urged that it not be revisited. But one hopes that the lessons of the past, if they are understood, may illuminate the future and prevent similar tragedies. In their search for truth, the authors decided to lay out all the material they could obtain and let readers judge the responsibility for four lost lives.

The two authors originally planned a definitive biography of their close friend, Fritz Wiessner, arguably the leading American climber for thirty years. As their research expanded, however, their attention focussed on this tragic episode in Wiessner's career. As previously unavailable documents were obtained, their unabashed praise of him changed to harsh criticism. Finally, after many revisions, Kauffman (the principal author) achieved a fine balance between conflicting interpretations.

Much of this story is known. The expedition began well: several expert climbers signed on, and ample funds were assured by recruiting wealthy participants. Photos and records from the earlier 1938 U.S. expedition—but none of its members—were available. Insofar as any great mountain can be counted a sure thing, Wiessner's expedition seemed destined to summit the second highest mountain in the world.

It did not work out. The strongest climbers dropped out, another was injured, leaving a weak group with little expedition experience. A brilliant young climber (Durrance) was added at the last moment, to Wiessner's dismay.

The first four weeks were happy and harmonious as they marched to Base Camp and came to know one another. Then one member (Cranmer) became hypothermic in a deep crevasse and during the next week was near death. Durrance (a pre-medical student) was exhausted by five desperate days and nights caring for him, but Cranmer was out of the game. Next Sheldon was grounded with frozen toes. The attack party, weak to begin with, was down to four: a dedicated and able climber (Durrance) who did not acclimatize well, a powerful, determined but inept amateur (Wolfe), the strong leader, and Cromwell, his older deputy, who soon lost heart.

Wiessner was an arrogant and dogmatic leader, the only one with Himalayan experience and obsessed with reaching the top. "If we make this, we're set for life" he had told a friend before leaving. For the entire assault, Wiessner was out in front, leading every foot of the climb, making all the decisions, trying to pull others behind him by example, despite their growing reluctance. Communications broke down completely and confrontations began.

Wiessner drove hard and those without his extraordinary strength and endurance began to wear out. Lacking a radio and with their leader always up ahead, the team, except for Durrance, became inactive, waiting for orders. Most of the Sherpas performed very well but with little direction.

After four weeks Wiessner and his least able companion (Wolfe), and Pasang Lama were near the summit, with adequate supplies and astonishingly good weather. The first attempt turned back when Lama refused to climb through the night. They sunbathed for a day, made a second attempt, but failed because a pair of crampons had been lost the previous day. Wiessner decided to split the party, and, leaving Wolfe alone, went with Lama down to the next lower camp for reenforcements.

Thus the trouble began. Wolfe had been unable to make the first two attempts and chose to stay in the next-to-highest camp awaiting Wiessner's return. (Whether he was sick or well is disputed.) There had been no communication with those below for ten days, and all the camps had been stripped for reasons that are also disputed. Wiessner continued down, dismayed and furious.

At Base Camp he was too exhausted to return for Wolfe. Durrance made a brave effort, reaching 21,500 feet, but he had not acclimatized well, and weeks of ferrying loads had dangerously weakened him. He may have been further impaired by some high altitude cerebral edema. The only ones fit were four Sherpas who volunteered to go to Wolfe.

Pasang Kikuli and Sherpa Phinsoo incredibly climbed from 16,500 to 23,400 feet in one day, joining Pasang Kitar and Tsering Norbu at one of the higher camps. Four days later, Tsering returned reporting that the others had reached Wolfe who refused to come down. After a day of storm, said Tsering, they had tried again. These three brave men and Wolfe were never seen again. The expedition had already fallen apart and straggled homeward.

As the story unfolds, Wiessner emerges as a strong, obsessed dictator. Durrance, who respected Wiessner's climbing ability, though not his personality, had labored desperately to supply the siege camps and carried medical responsibilities far beyond his ability. With no word from Wiessner far up ahead, Cromwell, his deputy, was indecisive. Just why the camps were emptied while three men were high on the mountain would long be bitterly argued. With alleged messages absent, Wiessner laid the blame on Durrance and Cromwell savaged Wiessner.

The story became uglier. After many weeks the divided party reached New York and interviews by their colleagues and the press. Despite Cromwell's furious denunciation, Wiessner's story was accepted: he became the tragic hero and Durrance the culprit in the disaster. But details were missing, contradictions appeared. An *ad hoc* American Alpine Club committee held an inquiry and issued a report—which today seems fair but incomplete. Some called it a whitewash. Charges that Wiessner was wrongly blamed because America was then at war with his native Germany were met by countercharges that his reputation led the committee to suppress his mistakes. Important papers were lost. The party disputed among itself and gave no support to Wiessner. Durrance refused to talk for fifty years. Cromwell was largely ignored. Wiessner resigned from the American Alpine Club, published a defense in a German publication, and resumed a brilliant climbing career in the United States. The dispute simmered down.

To the accepted record the authors have added important new material from Durrance and Sheldon, and from an edited Wiessner diary. Both Durrance and Sheldon talked freely. Extensive quotes, including copies of pages from Durrance's diary add reality to the past.

What's unfortunately lacking is any material from Cromwell. He and Wiessner are now dead. Wiessner's family refused the authors access to photos, original diaries and letters. The final AAC report and a diagram explaining who was where and when are included. The chapters recapitulate hard facts and speculation. A medical section discusses acclimatization and deterioration, but uses the unfortunate and misleading term "Death Zone" too often.

This is a gripping and moving story. It is unlikely that a more complete or accurate account will be written. In the final analysis, Wiessner might be admired for his obsessive perseverance, but he must be faulted for bad judgment and leadership. Despite Wiessner's later denial, he was, like others at extreme altitude, "a sick man walking in a dream," incapable of making decisions which conflicted with his desire—a failing repeated during many subsequent tragedies on this beautiful and terrible mountain.

Excellent photos from Durrance and a map and drawings by Molenaar, plus references, make this book a major contribution to mountaineering history.

CHARLES S. HOUSTON, M.D.

My Vertical World. Jerzy Kukuczka. The Mountaineers, Seattle, 1992. 192 pages. $29.95.

On a sunny afternoon in the fall of 1989, I was coming off a modest expedition in the Khumbu when I heard that the extraordinary Polish mountaineer Jerzy Kukuczka had just died in a fall on the south face of Lhotse. Later in Lukla, I boarded the STOL jet to Kathmandu. In my company were that ill-fated Polish team's remaining members who had gotten and remained good and drunk while waiting to continue their long journey home. They mourned the death of their friend, a quiet, robust working man. He was the second climber, after media star Reinhold Messner, to climb all 14 mountains in the Himalayan rosary of 8000-meter peaks. Unlike Messner's great accomplishment, the routes Kukuczka chose on the Himalayan giants were usually original, many of them first ascents and often done in the grip of winter wind and cold. In *My Vertical World,* Jerzy Kukuczka reveals that he was indeed a very lucky climber, but also that he made his own luck through hard work, dogged determination, and inspired optimism. He was at once a singular, innovative, and unique adventurer.

He considered himself a regular guy and said that it was only when he failed on Nanga Parbat that he realized the Himalaya are for "the normal people," not necessarily elite mountaineer superstars. He knew he could succeed. His ascents of the world's highest mountains stand as some of the most daring in mountaineering history.

He was an "Everyman" to the worldwide community of mountaineers. He grew out of modest means; he was unpretentious, at times diffident, quietly intense. He loved to eat and drink. When a rakish Swiss guide greeted him at the K2 Base Camp with a sarcastic reference to his generous waistline, he held his tongue. Later, Kukuczka muttered to himself, "We can have a chat at 8000 meters." He left the Swiss behind as he and his partner led a difficult new route up the south face of K2 in the infamous summer of 1986. That year 13 climbers tragically died, including Tadek Piotrowski, Kukuczka's partner, when his crampon somehow worked loose and he fell.

In an era in Poland where even the most basic foods were scarce, Kukuczka was able successfully to mount and equip numerous ventures to the far-flung reaches of the world. Usually pressed for cash and equipment, he painted factory chimneys to earn precious złotys to finance his mountaineering dreams. Although not always successful (he was "brought to his knees" by altitude illness on Denali), Kukuczka pursued his dreams on a budget a fraction of what most Western climbers enjoy. His source of drive was not the flash and fame that many highly regarded climbers today thrive on but rather the challenge of climbing the great mountains. Although a devoted husband and father, he was most at home in the big mountains, many times alone.

This book is more a chronicle of remarkable mountaineering achievements that provides clues to Jerzy Kukuczka's personal side, than a revealing autobiography. The text suffers somewhat, perhaps in its translation to English. The photographs generally lack imagination and drama. Yet, what shines through is the indominatable spirit of a man who realized his highest dreams despite a hostile, oppressive government and a harsh, sometimes dangerous environment. *My Vertical World* is an important work in the library of modern achievement and classical mountaineering.

In Jerzy Kukuczka's own words, "I went to the mountains and climbed them. That is all."

GARY RUGGERA, M.D.

Himalayan Climber: A Lifetime's Quest to the World's Greater Ranges. Doug Scott. San Francisco: Sierra Club Books, 1992. 192 pages. $35.00.

Scott is surely one of the most well-rounded climbers of our sport's history. He has climbed the Salathé Wall on El Capitan and nervy routes on Everest, Shivling, and the Ogre. He has visited Chad, Iceland, and Tasmania. He has struggled on Kenya and Waddington and Denali—and on minor crags in Jordan, of all places. Equally at home on rock and ice, the man seemingly lives only for climbing. This is splendid and admirable when seen from a distant perspective, but viewed up close his one-track passion is also perhaps sad, even bordering on irresponsible. His family suffered from his never-ending quest; he was divorced recently, an event he says humbled him more than any mountain ever did.

Each time frequent-flyer Scott leaves England, his Pentax accompanies him, and this book shows his photographic talents to spectacular effect: *Himalayan Climber* is basically a coffee-table picture book. About 300 photos, virtually all in breathtaking color, grace this volume, though this profusion leads to one of the problems with the book: repetition. How many shots do we need of a figure struggling up an icy couloir?

But photographic repetition is nothing compared to the textual. Each of the twelve chapters opens with a block of text covering Scott's climbs of a certain year, or in a certain area. This several-page section is followed by short accounts of the identical climbs, in the form of extended captions. I found it insulting to have to read the same stories twice, as if I were a child made to learn Tennyson by rote. Here's an example from the main text of a Makalu attempt: ". . . [the wind] pinned us down in a swirling holocaust of snow for the whole of the next day. At this point Georges [Bettembourg] began to develop what proved to be a pulmonary embolism." And from the extended caption, six pages later: ". . . the winds pinned us down in our tent next day during which Georges had stabs of pain around his liver—symptoms of pulmonary embolism." This sort of duplication occurs throughout the book and could have been dealt with easily.

Another minor flaw is the difficulty in matching captions to photos. Some captions sleep subtly in the main text, where a parenthetical "right" or "left" indicates that you've just read a caption. Other captions, though more traditional, are often placed in such a way that you have to work hard to match them with their photos. Since seven photos sometimes appear on a double-page spread, your eyeballs get a real workout.

Lackluster writing also mars the book, but even though I usually rant and rave about this shortcoming, I was not bothered this time, for *Himalayan Climber* is one of the finest picture books about mountaineering I have ever seen. The photos are ravishing, full of life and color and action. You can feel the wind in some of them. Even the group portraits, potentially so boring, are worth studying closely when you have people like Messner and Rouse and Anthoine and Whillans and Haston and Kukuczka in them. That many of these lads are now dead serves as a poignant reminder that high-level climbers rarely attain old age.

Scott has been called "the great survivor." I hope for his continued survival, partly for a selfish reason. Given his intelligence, his fascination with Eastern philosophies, his sterling record, and his basic humility, he should be able to write a spirited and thoughtful autobiography, something we see all too little of nowadays.

Leave the camera behind in the next book, Doug, and tell us what it's really like to struggle with your mortality up at 7500 meters. We need to hear more about the Real Quest.

STEVE ROPER

Lost Lhasa: Heinrich Harrer's Tibet. Heinrich Harrer. Abrams, New York, 1992. 200 pages, 200 black-and-white illustrations. $39.95.

Heinrich Harrer was an impatient young man. As he put it: "I was highly ambitious; I often thought that if you can be first, it doesn't particularly matter what you are first at. In mountaineering, you have a lot of chances to be first—at least you did during the 1930s when I grew up." Harrer's ambition led him in 1937 to the north face of the Eiger where with Fritz Kasparek, Anderl Heckmair and Ludwig Vorg he climbed what was then thought impossible. Harrer's ascent of the Eiger's north face was at least in part motivated by an attempt to gain the recognition necessary to be invited on a Himalayan expedition. This goal was fulfilled when an invitation arrived to be a member of the German-and-Austrian reconnaissance of Nanga Parbat in 1939.

Harrer's mountaineering ambitions were dramatically cut short when he was imprisoned in India by British forces with the outbreak of World War II. After several unsuccessful attempts, Harrer was able to escape and make his way to Tibet which, although it was neutral in World War II, was forbidden to foreigners. The outlying districts of Tibet effectively denied penetration by foreigners by simply refusing to supply the provisions which were necessary for travelers to survive. It was here that a Tibetan gave some advice which was to serve Harrer in good stead. His European haste and ambition simply had no place in Tibet. Harrer was told he must learn patience if he wished to arrive at his goal, the forbidden city of Lhasa.

Although it took two years during which he suffered extreme cold and near starvation on the high Tibetan plateau, Harrer and his companion, Peter Aufschnaiter finally reached Lhasa. Ironically, they learned that the closer they came to the forbidden city, the less suspect they became. It was generally assumed that anyone who had make it that close to Lhasa had authority to be there. And rather than being immediately expelled, Harrer and Aufschnaiter were treated with great kindness. In Harrer's words: "I would say that there is no other country in the world where two fugitives would be as welcomed as we were in Lhasa." After the extreme deprivation of their travels, the two Austrians found a life of comfort with "no rush and no stress." Eventually Harrer was befriended by the older brother of the Dalai Lama who was then a teenager. This led to Harrer becoming the tutor to the young ruler. Harrer's tutelage of the Dalai Lama which he describes as being the best years of his life, was cut short by the Chinese communist invasion of Tibet. Both Harrer and the Dalai Lama were forced to flee.

Harrer's classic adventure was the subject of his book *Seven Years in Tibet,* which was published in 1953. Harrer's inspiration to write *Lost Lhasa* nearly four decades later, came after the Dalai Lama was awarded the Nobel Peace Prize in 1989 and declared 1991 to be "The Year of Tibet." *Lost Lhasa* is Harrer's response to the Dalai Lama's effort to rouse the world's attention to the Tibetan cause. Harrer selected 200 black-and-white photos from thousands of previously unpublished photographic negatives to give a view of the forbidden city before the invasion.

Lost Lhasa begins with a message from the Dalai Lama, an introduction by Galen Rowell and some concise introductory chapters. The body of the work is centered around thematic essays on Tibetan customs, personalities, projects, sports and festivals. In Lhasa, Harrer and his camera saw a theocracy where daily life was ordered by religious belief and there was a complete tolerance of other people and creeds. No one was made to lose "face" and aggressiveness was unknown. The photos and essays of *Lost Lhasa* are, in short, a remarkable glimpse of a now suppressed culture and people.

Harrer has dedicated *Lost Lhasa* to the "children of Tibet, with the hope that they never forget their origins." One can only hope that the Tibetan children will have the staying power that Harrer learned from their countrymen—and that one day their patience will be rewarded.

ROBERT F. ROSEBROUGH

The Climbers—A History of Mountaineering. Chris Bonington. BBC Books and Hodder & Stoughton, London, 1992. 288 pages, 40 color photographs, 102 black-and-white photographs, maps and diagrams. £16.95.

Chris Bonington is well acquainted with the history of mountaineering and he is an excellent writer. This is certainly the right combination to make this a very worth-while addition to climbing literature.

My attention was caught immediately by the first chapter, a description of Albert Frederick Mummery's first ascent of the Grépon with the Swiss guides, Alexander Burgener and Benedict Venetz. That outstanding pioneer and developer of the art of climbing was indeed modern in the way he went about it and seems to tie the Victorian age perfectly to present-day climbing. Bonington strengthened that tie even more by repeating Mummery's climb with two French guides, using tweed clothing, nailed boots and equipment of the earlier epoch, albeit substituting nylon rope for the much less safe manila hemp. From there on, Chris does include himself from time to time, as befits one who has been for thirty years on the cutting edge of modern mountaineering.

The beginnings of climbing in the Alps, with particular emphasis on the struggle to ascend Mont Blanc, and in the Himalaya follow. I was particularly interested in his descriptions of the climbing between the two World Wars, having been at an impressionable age when I avidly studied everything that came out in print in either German or English. There was not a single name unfamiliar to me. This was the era of the great North Faces, particulary of the Eiger and of the attempts on Everest and Nanga Parbat. Naturally I was also happy to read about our ascent of Nanda Devi and the American attempts on K2.

After World War II, Bonington's task becomes much more complicated. As he states, "It starts as a clear tumbling stream that is easy to follow but, as we get closer to the present time, it spreads out into a wide delta as opaque as the mouth of the Ganges. It is less easy to pick the main stream, and inevitably I will have left out some ascents or climbers whom my readers feel should have been included." The next hundred pages attempt to describe all that has happened in the mountain world in the last half century. It is well done within the limits of that space, but mountaineering has proliferated to an amazing extent. This possible defect is somewhat remedied by Audrey Salkeld's useful *Brief History of Mountaineering,* which appears as a ten-page appendix. I feel very strongly that he erred in making no more than passing references to climbing in Alaska, the Peruvian Andes and Patagonia, where much fascinating mountaineering history has taken place.

The final chapter, *Always a Little Further—As it is now and as it might be in the future,* is an excellent summary of Bonington's assessment of present-day mountain climbing. Although I am in hearty agreement with the points he makes, I am sure that there will be those who will take exception to his ideas. It is an excellent study on which to base constructive discussion.

I am pleased with the accuracy. There was bound to be an occasional slip. For instance, the Poles mentioned on page 155 climbed Nanda Devi East and not Dunagiri East. On page 203, it states that the Americans lowering stricken Art Gilkey on K2 were all roped together, belayed by Schoening and held by him after a slip. In actual fact, it was much more amazing. Schoening was holding Gilkey at the end of his rope. The others, slightly above, were on two separate ropes. Bell fell and crashed into the climbers on the second rope, knocking them off. Miraculously, all the ropes snagged and Schoening held all the five climbers on his ice-axe belay. But such very few minor errors do not detract from the high standard.

The volume is profusely illustrated both with black-and-white shots from the past as well as more recent ones and a large number of beautiful color photographs. This is a volume well worth owning.

H. ADAMS CARTER

The Merry-Go-Round of My Life: An Adventurer's Diary. Richard Hechtel. Vantage Press, New York, 1991. 219 pages, 10 black-and-white photographs. Hard cover. $13.95.

Richard Hechtel's climbing memoirs were first published in 1989 by Bruckmann Press in Munich, Germany, under the title: *Lebenserinnerungen: Vom Klettergarten zu den Bergen der Welt.* When Hechtel decided on an American edition, he translated his German manuscript into English at the same time adding and deleting material according to his perception of what an American reader might prefer.

In *The Merry-Go-Round of My Life,* we find that Hechtel was born in Germany in 1913. At age twenty he becomes an active climber. By 1935 he is skilled enough to complete an early ascent of one of the great prizes of the day: the difficult south face of the *Schüsselkarspitze.* In 1937 he startles the mountaineering community by completing the first solo ascent of the Peuterey Ridge in 36 hours from *Entrèves.* The war years now intrude: there is a brief tour of duty in a fighter pilots school; then Hechtel becomes a research assistant at a wireless station in Bavaria. Finally, in 1941, he is sent to the German Aeronautical Institute in Berlin. Even during these trying years, he manages some climbs in the *Wilde Kaiser* and the *Elbsandsteingebirge;* then, as the air raids increase and Russian artillery units eventually reach the outskirts of Berlin in March of 1945, Hechtel convinces his superior at the Institute to ship Hechtel's unit, all the equipment and some 25 workers, to a safer place in the Austrian Alps. And so, he is captured by Americans rather than Russians and has a brief vacation at a POW camp in Innsbruck before returning home in June of 1945.

These war years and events in his life leading up to his coming to the United States in 1958 are fascinating reading. Two important climbs are made in the early 1950s: the first one-day ascent of the northeast face of Piz Badile and the first ascent of the Integral Peuterey Ridge, starting with the daunting south ridge of the *Aiguille Noire.* On this latter climb, as the group approaches the summit of Mont Blanc in a fearsome blizzard, Hechtel asks: "How did we find our way to the summit of Mont Blanc and the Vallot Hut?" "I do not know," he replies, "but I was sure of my way, not one second in doubt, never asking my compass or the map, like the migrant bird that finds its way with unfailing certainty." This is a nice sentence, but unfortunately Hechtel's writing in the bulk of the book is not nearly as evocative. (His first language, of course, is German.) But his prose is actually quite readable, once you become acclimated. It is modest and undistinguished, with few images, but very honest. And his humor (wry and only occasionally sophomoric) comes across very well.

The balance of the book, after he comes to America as a research scientist, covers various expeditions to South America, Africa, the Hindu Kush, and the Himalaya (he is a member of a 1964 expedition that makes the first ascent of Talung Peak (near Kangchenjunga) plus numerous smaller trips.

Unfortunately, *The Merry-Go-Round of My Life* (unlike its German counterpart) is a cheaply crafted book. The few photographs are substandard and the silly title somehow warns us of bizarre translations and word-usage that often intrude in the text, a text which occasionally seems to have escaped the editing (and fact-checking) process at Vantage Press. I have never read of clouds tearing across the sky referred to as "cloud-rags" (*Wolkenfetzen*), nor was I certain what had transpired when I read the sentence: "Within the following quarter of a century the Dachl north face had lost some of its nimbus." (A literal translation of a perfectly normal German expression.) But all this is rather unimportant and we might even credit Hechtel for inventing some quaint neologisms. But I detest the habit of always showing the height of a peak in meters followed by the equivalent in feet, both in parentheses. Use either meters or feet, but not both. And why couldn't anyone discover the following errors before going to print? Quito, Ecuador, is not 10,000 feet in elevation, but lies at 9350 feet; and Lionel Terray was not killed on an insignificant route in the "French Verdon," but on a rather severe route in the Vercors near Grenosble.

At the end of the book, around 1986 at the age of 73, Hechtel is still climbing 5.10s and 11s at the local rocks, suffering perhaps (as he suggests) from an uncommon German ailment called *Torschlusspanik*, a panic occurring at the thought of spending the rest of one's life in a rocking chair in Warren Harding's Rock of Ages Home for Old Climbers.

ALLEN STECK

A Lifelong Love Affair with the Mountains. John Filsinger. A. G. Halldin Publishing Co., Inc., Indiana, PA 15701, 1991. 380 pages, 944 photos (301 in color). $29.95.

This profusely illustrated book is a personal document covering a half-century of climbing and mountain treks among the ranges of the U.S., Canada, Mexico, the Alps, Spain, Peru, Japan, and Nepal. The author's first-described climbs are during World War II, in Mexico's Sierra Madre Oriental and Jamaica's Blue Mountains, where he served as cryptographer in the U.S. Army. During a subsequent career as teacher of English and Spanish language and literature, Filsinger's summers off allowed him to pursue his mountain odysseys across the globe. Many of his climbs and trek leaderships have been with groups from the Colorado Mountain Club, Iowa Mountaineers, and Mountain Travel USA. Readers acquainted with members of these organizations will enjoy meeting them again through Filsinger's accounts. The book provides both active and retrospective accounts of his travels, and includes his mountain poems, many of them previously published in climbing periodicals.

Filsinger's informative and sensitive writing rings a bell in this reviewer's own retrospections during mountain travels in some of the same areas. Filsinger's initial love of nature and the mountain world similarly came from Thoreau's *Walden* and the writings of John Muir. The book will be particularly enjoyed by those whose prime climbing was during the 1930s through 1960s, a generation whose perspective was tempered—and probably enriched—by a greater familiarity with mountaineering history and literature.

The book is rich in descriptions of personalities, including meetings with several world-class climbers in their own mountain domains. The author emphasizes the rewarding aspects of friendships gained in the mountains, often among peoples from other cultures and with different professional backgrounds.

Among the most significant of the author's experiences are those which occurred while leading five expeditions into the Andes hinterland. He describes—with saving humor—the frustrating exigencies confronted by him and César Morales, a Peruvian official, while pioneering the complex procedures of launching large-scale expeditions in that country—on the eve of the subsequent voluminous rush of mountaineers from all over the world to Peru's magnificent cordilleras. In 1971 and 1972, he and Morales led Mountain Travel's initial climbing treks through the Cordillera Blanca and Cordillera Vilcabamba, the former on the heels of the great 1970 earthquake in northern Peru, which killed 67,000 and left 600,000 homeless. He describes trekking through the rearranged mountain terrain there and portrays the physical and human devastation of the great avalanche that fell from the upper west face of

21,837-foot North Huascarán, which completely buried the town of Yungay and most of its citizens.

At the back of the book are a glossary of mountaineering terms, detailed supplementary notes amplifying references in the text (including some covering the achievements of distinguished mountaineers he's met in his travels), and photo credits and detailed photo captions.

The book may be ordered directly from the author at RFD #3, Box 262, Clearfield, PA 16830, for $32.00 postpaid.

DEE MOLENAAR

The Ascent. Jeff Long. William Morrow, New York, NY, 1992. 284 pages. $20.00.

Jeff Long's second novel describes an attempt on the north side of Everest. The route, the "Kore Wall," is "an imaginary monster," but it often feels very real indeed. One of Long's strengths is his ability to make the mountain a ferocious mass of rock and ice, hurling debris upon its puny challengers. The cold, the wind, the whole hostile environment are rendered with vividness and force.

The expedition is called the U.S.U.S. (us, us!), and some of its members seek only material advancement. The worst of the lot, alas, is its leader, "an accountant who had somehow ascended to the presidency of the American Alpine Club" and whose true objective is a cabinet post in Washington. At the other extreme are the central figures, Daniel and Abe, with their deeply personal goals. Their relation begins with one of the finest sections of the book, a harrowing overture in which Daniel's young climbing partner, Diana, dies in a crevasse, while the badly injured Daniel is saved. Diana's death is prolonged; toward the end she eerily breaks into song. And all the while Abe, age 17, is keeping futile watch over her. Nearly twenty years later Abe has almost forgotten Daniel, but Daniel has secretly maintained the connection (his name is Corder: cord-er) and recruits Abe for the expedition. He wants—he needs—to reach the top with him: "Same day. Same rope." Abe, who has had trouble making connections of his own, accepts this one.

The Ascent is nothing if not ambitious. It links the expedition with the tragedy of Tibet itself: "a graveyard and gulag garrisoned by Chinese troops and overrun by 7.5 million Chinese colonists." Thus Long brings to Base Camp a Tibetan monk, Wangdu, savagely tortured by the Chinese, who are determined to keep him in the country, alive or dead. Wangdu becomes a touchstone for the moral qualities of the climbers; some take risks to defend his ebbing life, while others betray him with little conscience. Long implicitly associates the ravaging of Tibet with the worst aspects of this American attempt on Everest, which is pointedly described in the language of sexual and military assault. While the expedition has a spiritual meaning for Abe and Daniel, for others it is driven by the most worldly considerations. "We're in the latest Rolex commercial," the leader proclaims at one point. One of the two women in the group has garnered hundreds of thousands in funding for the expedition by her looks—"a pantyhose company has kicked in $80,000 for rights to her legs." The fury that Everest unleashes seems only too well deserved.

For all its strengths, the book has a crucial weakness: its characters lack strong definition. They are less interesting than their actions imply. I found it easier to remember some of the minor players, like the unsympathetic AAC president or the devious Chinese liaison officer, then I did its central ones. Thus the Abe-Daniel nexus, which should dominate the narrative, feels merely peripheral. Unlike Long's first novel, *Angels of Light*, this one is without really strong figures to match—or enhance—the power of its action or the clarity of its physical description. This major defect undercuts many of the book's intentions.

Although *The Ascent* may disappoint admirers of the very promising *Angels of Light*, its achievement remains considerable. Long is a bold writer, ready to address major subjects and expert at describing the harsh environment of the big mountains. As in the earlier novel, he has perhaps more material than the narrative can bear, but in the end, he draws the threads of his story together: Wangdu, Diana, the bond between Daniel and Abe. He fashions a fitting conclusion to his violent and sobering tale.

Steven Jervis

Flammes de Pierre. Anne Sauvy. Diadem Books. London/USA, 1992, distribution by Trafalgar Square, North Pomfret, VT, 05053. $22.95.

The name of this book of sixteen short stories—which literally means Flames of Rock—refers to the ridge of pinnacles which radiate from Les Drus, in Chamonix. The author has climbed around Chamonix for many years and has absorbed the spirit and the quirks of the climbing scene there—at least the French side of it.

The tales in Flammes de Pierre revolve around those who frequent the mountains of Chamonix: the climbers, both aces and hacks, guides and their clients, and some phantasmagoric characters too. Twists of fate, ego and ambition, the fantastic and the supernatural, all are her subject matter.

The style of Sauvy's writing is markedly different to the fast-paced, action-oriented journalism about world-class climbing epics we have grown used to in today's climbing magazines. Her tales build slowly, patiently. Just when you think the story isn't really heading anywhere, she delivers a strange or dramatic element that hooks the reader till the end. Sauvy's is a formal and precise style of writing.

Among the most evocative stories in this collection are *The Collector*, in which a solo climber devises an elaborate scheme to achieve greatness, posthumously, and *The Abseil*, a nightmarish tale literally about the eternal rappel. Others stand out as being well-crafted too: In The *The Bishorn Ghost* a malevolent spirit who haunts the Alps and delights in causing mayhem to unsuspecting climbers finds love; and, as in *La Fourche*, what climber has not wondered whether he or she would sign that Faustian pact if Satan offered a career of stunning success on the heights?

Not every tale works well though. Sauvy plumbs the realm of silliness with satires like *The Star*, which tells the story of a climbing star manufactured by Hollywood-like image makers, and, in *Intrusion*, we meet a blob from outer space that consumes climbers to absorb their knowledge—predictably the blob doesn't think much of climbing.

But other of her satires are cunning parables that made me read closely, as in *Liberation*, in which the mountains of the Alps are given personalities and a yen for political organization, which ultimately ends up being about as organized as today's Yugoslavia.

The book first appeared in 1982 in France and won climbing-writing awards there and in Germany. Her most recent collection, *La ténèbre et l'azur*, from 1991, also won an award in French climbing-literary circles.

GREG CHILD

The Grand Controversy. Orrin and Lorraine Bonney. The AAC Press, New York, 1992. 457 pages. $28.50.

This book is a pleasant surprise. One might expect 457 pages of elaborately documented research into a minor historical issue to be dull, to say the least; but Lorraine Bonney, finishing (after nearly twenty years) the work begun by her late husband Orrin, manages to pull the story together in eminently readable form.

Admittedly, there are those for whom the question "Who first climbed the Grand Teton?" is not a "minor historical issue"; were it not for such people we might be lacking in entertainment. One such individual was William Owen himself, the main protagonist of this book, whose efforts to establish his own claim to the first ascent are at the heart of *The Grand Controversy*.

I, for one, am impressed and convinced. Endowed with the historical sense of a two-by-four (I have to be reminded by others of routes I had forgotten I had climbed), I have always assumed that many of my ascents on the Grand were on the Owen-Spalding route; now I may have to begin calling it the Langford-Stevenson. Of course, when the Owen-Spalding partisans come out of the woodwork (or the grave, as the case may be) I may have to change my mind again; so it goes with historical debates. Once we have passed beyond the possibility of hard physical evidence, the dialectic of inference, presumption, and *ad hominem* arguments takes over. Only our stubborn insistence that there is such a thing as objective truth keeps these arguments alive.

For the Teton enthusiast, there is more to recommend this book: accounts of much of the rest of the early history of the range and Jackson Hole itself. Sections of historical black-and-white photographs are interspersed with tales of the pioneer climbers, often first-person accounts. Some inaccuracies in the photo captions can be discerned by the discriminating reader, and indeed lead to the reflection that this is precisely how such controversies maintain themselves; but in general the volume is well edited.

If there is a weakness in *The Grand Controversy*, it comes in the form of occasional lapses from a tone of objectivity into a more impassioned advocacy. Clearly the emotional nature of the Owen-Langford debate has carried on even to the present. To my mind Owen hoists himself on his own petard when his argument with Langford turns vitriolic; the Bonneys on occasion adopt the same demeaning manner towards William Owen, thus weakening what seems like a good case otherwise.

I would be very surprised if this book turned out to be the last we shall hear on its subject matter, but its thesis will not easily be overturned. Meanwhile those of us with less historic sense will continue to use the same hand- and foot-holds on this magnificent peak, regardless of who might have touched them first; it is some measure of what an exceptional place this is that it both engenders and trivializes this sort of debate.

RON MATOUS

Zen in the Art of Climbing Mountains. Neville Shulman. Charles E. Tuttle Co., Boston, Rutland, Tokyo, 1992. 117 pages, black-and-white photographs, foreword by Chris Bonington. $12.95.

Zen in the Art of Climbing Mountains is the account of Neville Shulman's inner struggles in climbing Mont Blanc—the obstacles of ignorance, fear, weakness, doubt, and despair that he had to overcome to reach the summit and, more importantly, to attain the spiritual realization it brought him. Middle-aged, out of shape, and a total novice to mountaineering, Shulman felt something lacking in his life and on impulse responded to an ad to join a guided trip up Mont Blanc. In his mind the climb assumed the proportions of a major Himalayan expedition —as well it might to a beginner—and he prepared himself for it according to the principles of the Japanese Zen he had been studying and practicing.

Shulman joins his group near Chamonix and describes the training ice climbs they make on lower glaciers before setting out on an ill-fated bivouac that ends in a storm. Despite that inauspicious beginning and numerous mishaps due to his own inexperience, Shulman manages to reach the summit of Mont Blanc, where he has the following experience:

Through the climb I have gained enlightenment. It is true *satori* Zen. Even if it is only temporary, I feel uplifted, my heart swelling to fill my body . . . I am experiencing the high of sheer spiritual joy. It is a feeling of ecstasy that spreads rapidly throughout my body; I feel myself lift skywards and start to float over the summit itself.

Throughout the preparations, the ascent, and the descent, Shulman reflects on Zen philosophy and quotes from various Japanese masters. Curiously, he does not quote from the master best known for his thoughts on mountains —Dogen, author of *The Mountains and Rivers Sutra*. This may be because Shulman apparently adopts the approach of the Rinzai School of Zen Buddhism and views the ascent of Mont Blanc—and the path to enlightenment—primarily as a dramatic struggle, a contest between himself and the mountain which he is determined not to lose; Dogen, on the other hand, is a chief expositor of the Soto school that sees the process of enlightenment more as the quiet cultivation of insight and awareness leading to a sense of oneness with mountains and the realization of emptiness, the ultimate nature of reality.

Shulman's single-minded focus on reaching the summit and attaining *satori* results in an intriguing, but rather self-centered, account of his climb. He tells us very little about his companions—we never learn their names or hear them speak—and most of the photographs are of Shulman. This is strangely at odds with the goals of Zen, which are to take a person beyond the individual self or ego. In fact, the author's writing about Zen tends to be somewhat self-conscious. On the other hand, this very quality of the book serves a useful purpose, frankly exposing the inner doubt and turmoil, hope and ecstasy, that more experienced climbers often experience but are reluctant to express.

EDWIN BERNBAUM

Medicine for Mountaineering. Edited by James A. Wilkerson, M.D. The Mountaineers, Seattle, Washington, 1992. 416 pages, line drawings. $16.95.

It is unusual for the layman to find books on how to recognize and manage medical problems, let alone books that instruct people about how to handle esoteric medical problems in a remote setting with little or no access to modern-day medical infrastructure. A book with such an objective is an onerous task, since the author must navigate the book between the Scylla and Charybdis of providing too little information versus deluging the reader with medical minutæ. *Medicine for Mountaineering* exemplifies a fine job of editing by Dr. Wilkerson, who has managed the offerings of numerous contributors on diverse subjects in a remarkably cohesive fashion.

The book is divided into three sections, in addition to a very readable introduction and informative appendices. The first section is devoted to the principles of medical diagnosis and management and serves as a well written primer for the uninitiated. It includes a detailed discussion on the all important aspects of sanitation and water purification. However, by suggesting that in underdeveloped countries, bottled, carbonated drinks are safe to drink, it fails to recognize a source of gastrointestinal misery for many a mountaineer: In many remote regions these "bottled" drinks are in fact clandestinely recapped by shopkeepers and therefore no safer than drinking the local water!

The second section is a short text upon the management of numerous traumatic and non-traumatic ailments. This section covers a lot of ground "from ophthalmology to orthopædics" and is quite informative about the conditions it deals with. The line drawings accompanying the text are very useful. The authors have resisted the temptation of using medical jargon and instead they have painstakingly explained signs and symptoms with the layman in mind. This otherwise well-written section, however, did have its share of blemishes. It does not recognize that differences of opinion do exist about some of its statements and recommendations. For example, on page 151 the authors state that "The most important part of asthma treatment is adequate fluid intake;" surely relieving the widespread narrowing of air passages is considered just as, if not more important. Another example exists on the treatment of *Giardia* with Tinidazole where the authors state (page 173) ". . . in view of the similarity of this agent to Metranidazole, both advantages must be regarded with skepticism." However, numerous studies and most authorities consider Tinidazole rather than Metranidazole to be the drug of choice against *Giardia*. Additionally, it was surprising that this section does not include guidelines to distinguish bacillary from amœbic dysentery, since these disorders are not uncommon in many mountainous regions of the world.

The final section is one that the wilderness enthusiast and mountaineer will find especially interesting and pertinent. This section has been developed by top-notch contributors to the field and reading it before going off on an expedition should be *de rigueur*. The chapter on altitude sickness does a good job by including both the patho-physiological considerations of high altitude disorders and some case studies from lower elevations. This section is quite comprehensive and includes some recent advances in the management of altitude sickness such as Nifedipine and portable hyperbaric chambers. Hopefully the next edition will include a discussion of the recently described syndrome of subacute mountain sickness, which is a surprising omission. Taken together, this section should adequately drive home the need to acclimatize and thus avoid many of these problems. As the authors put it rather succinctly in context of altitude sickness, "Individuals who get more than slightly sick have only themselves to blame."

To all mountaineers, I'd say: "Don't begrudge the excess 580 gms." If you are travelling without a doctor you will find *Medicine for Mountaineering* a welcome addition to the medical kit.

TEJVIR SINGH KHURANA, M.D., PH.D.

The Mont Blanc Range Topo Guide. Volume 1. Michel Piola. Editions Equinoxe, Vernier, Switzerland, 1988. 207 pages. Maps, 30 black-and-white photographs. Softcover. Translated from the French by Jules Mills. French francs 111 (approx. $20).

This excellent guidebook, which includes 201 routes and 83 topos, is the first in a proposed series that presumably will include all the rock climbs (no ice or mixed routes) in the Mont Blanc Range. I say this advisedly, since I do not know for sure what Piola actually has in mind. Volume 1 features the following sections: *Aiguille du Midi, Rognon du Plan/Dent du Requin, Envers des Aiguilles* (upper and lower sections), *Aiguilles de Chamonix* (northwest side), and the *Aiguilles Rouges*.

The booklet, at 4¾ x 6¾ inches and weighing about 10 ounces, is small enough to fit in a rucksack pocket. Topos and photographs are full page and excellently reproduced on quality paper. The topos, drawn by Piola himself I was told, deserve particular attention for they are the best pen and ink drawings I have seen anywhere. First, the basic structure of the formation in question is drawn, utilizing some 30 icons to provide a wide variety of rock detail. If there are 12 routes, say, on a formation, he will use 3 separate pages (same drawing) each showing 4 routes with heavy dotted lines, with a rating for each pitch. The missing routes on each page are shown with a faint, tiny dotted line, so the reader always has an idea how all 12 routes relate to each other. This method results in much less confusion, at the expense, of course, of more pages in the guidebook.

Route description text is minimal. After a brief introduction to a particular drawing, the route names are listed, including grade, length, rating for the most difficult compulsory move, first-ascent names, descent information. Rarely is gear information provided.

The majority of the routes in this book were done in the 1980s, many by Piola and his friends. They are of a very high standard, usually well-equipped (bolts and rappel stations) and extremely popular. During the 6 weeks I was there I climbed 9 Piola routes; one of them, *L'Eau Rance d'Arabie,* I thought was the most magnificent, consistently difficult, 7-pitch rock climb I'd ever done.

ALLEN STECK

Classic Climbs in the Caucasus. Friedrich Bender, translated by Jill Neate. Diadem Books, London, Menasha Ridge Press, Birmingham, Alabama, 1992. 316 pages. Photographs, maps. $24.95.

This beautiful pocket-sized volume is sure dramatically to increase outsider climber traffic and route development in the Caucasus, which has been in a geopolitical time warp for half a century. Thanks to the collapse of the Soviet state, and its defunct bureaucracy of climbing and travel restrictions, large numbers of Western climbers will now be drawn to "this mysterious and as yet not overrun mountain world of glaciated four- and five-thousand metre peaks," to quote from Bender's introduction. He's culled 80 selected climbs in the Elbrus and Bezingi regions of the Svanetian Range from his large German guides to the region. These are presented with magnificent photographs, sketches, maps and short route descriptions, plus advice about travel and accommodations en route to the peaks.

JOHN THACKRAY

The Columbia Mountains of Canada—Central. John Kevin Fox, Roger W. Laurilla, William L. Putnam, Earle R. Whipple. American Alpine Club Press, 1992. 540 pages, maps and photographs. $28.50.

The Columbia Mountains of Canada—West and South. Earle R. Whipple, Roger W. Laurilla, William L. Putnam. American Alpine Club Press, 1992. 230 pages, maps and photographs. $25.00.

The long overdue seventh edition of the climber's guide to the Interior Ranges of British Columbia has finally arrived. The wait has been worth it. We finally have a climber's guide, as distinct from a compilation of routes that have been climbed.

The Interior Ranges of British Columbia have now been designated the Columbia Mountains, so the title of the guide has been changed to reflect this. While the previous edition ran to two volumes, the latest edition runs to three, reflecting more descriptive climbing activity in the region during the last 15 years or so, and expanded treatment. The "Central" edition covers most of the Selkirk Mountains, from the Big Bend of the Columbia River south to the Lardeau River. The "West and South" edition covers to Cariboo, Monashee, and southern Selkirk Mountains, while the "East" edition covers the Purcells.

The editors must be given credit for an exhaustive search for information (over 200 people are given credit for assisting with research for the guide). The result is the inclusion of many ascents missing from the previous edition, together with numerous more recent climbs. Virtually all routes are now given ratings—a basic feature of any climbing guide, since most users are not the elite capable of climbing any route, but rather are lesser mortals who like to choose appropriately difficult climbs. The rating system used is interesting in that it includes a grade (overall scope and magnitude of the climb), a class (technical difficulty of the hardest move on a rock pitch), an artificial aid indicator (ease of any aid climbing), and a subjective estimate of the overall quality of a route. The presence of snow, glaciers, and/or ice on a route is also indicated. Thus, one can prepare oneself well for a climb. However, one can still experience the thrill of adventure as the editors have tried, usually—but not always—with success, to adhere to Thorington's dictum that route descriptions should not be as detailed as "handhold by handhold."

The assessment of route quality will be controversial, as this is such a subjective thing. Not all of the routes have been rated for quality. That so many have been so rated, however, is due to the editors' admirable and enviable, but ultimately impossible, goal of climbing all the routes. The usefulness of such ratings is itself subjective. While few may disagree with the northwest ridge of Sir Donald in the Rogers Pass area being given the highest quality rating, the accuracy of many other ratings can be challenged.

The guide uses only metric units, which are consistent with those of the new Canadian maps. The editors must again be commended for helping climbers familiarize themselves with the units of the future, and for facilitating use by international climbers.

Blemishes are few. Occasional typos can be found and one paragraph seems inappropriate. This is the only double-page photograph in the "West and South" volume—a grainy one of Mount Sir John Thompson. This is a magnificent mountain which, seen from the west, bears a striking resemblance to New Zealand's premier ice peak, Mount Tasman. The photo does not really do justice to this and is not very informative. The many other photos, however, are generally of high quality, informative and of the panorama variety.

Perhaps the greatest deficiency of the guide is its treatment of access and human intrusion into the mountains. Of all mountain ranges in British Columbia, the Columbia Mountains have become the most commercialized and privatized. From the U.S. border to the northernmost Cariboos, most of the mountain areas covered by the guide have been licensed to various commercial heli-skiing companies. The heli-skiing often becomes heli-hiking and heli-everything in summer. Large commercial lodges, small commercial lodges, and small private ones have proliferated. From the town of Golden, a helicopter can access approximately 20 private/commercial lodges in the Columbia Mountains. It is impossible to climb in the Premier Range during the summer without hearing helicopters most days. The Monashees, "the most inaccessible" of all the Columbia Mountains, boast a number of private lodges. None of this is described or mentioned in the guide. Climbers seeking a wilderness climbing experience could suffer a rude awakening.

Human intrusion is not only in the form of lodges but also by logging. Access is changing rapidly in the Columbia Mountains, more rapidly than the guide indicates. For example, the guide describes a logging road into the Hellroar Group in the Monashees. This road now has 2 major forks and the valley "8km from the end of the logging road" is now considerably closer. Also, the Scrip Range is described as having the most difficult access of all the Monashees. New logging roads up the valleys of the Adams River and its tributaries have rendered this statement questionable. Users of the guide should contact the appropriate Forest District office of the British Columbia Ministry of Forests. It would have been helpful if the guide had indicated at least the Forest District, if not the address of its office, in which each range or groups of mountains lies.

These comments notwithstanding, the guide is truly a vast improvement over earlier editions and will remain a valuable companion to the Columbia Ranges for many years to come.

MICHAEL FELLER

Selected Alpine Climbs in the Canadian Rockies. Sean Dougherty. Rocky Mountain Books, Calgary, Alberta. 1991. 320 pages. 129 marked photos. Several sketch maps. Soft cover. $19.95.

It is a truism that the younger crowd always believes that its predecessors didn't know much of anything and didn't do anything really of note. Thus the condescending tone of this book. In evaluating it, it is difficult to be impartial and objective when one reads in the foreword that previous works of this sort were done "primarily by poorly-informed nonresidents." Thus are gratuitously dismissed 70 years of efforts by Howard Palmer, J.M. Thorington, Bill Putnam,

Chris Jones and the present reviewer. Nonresidents all, who participated in exploration and first ascents in the Canadian mountains, and the chronicling thereof, before very many Canadian climbers had emerged from the primeval slime. (Is "nonresident" used because many of the people associated with this book are themselves not native-born Canadians?) Certainly Schliemann knew a lot more about Troy than the Turks who farmed amongst its stones. Why is it necessary to put others down in order to elevate oneself?

To be fair, I *am* poorly-informed about many of the recent, highly-technical routes put up in the past 10 or 20 years by climbers several generations younger than myself. And it is on these routes that the author has done a useful piece of work, judging from those with which I am familiar. Indeed, he would have been well-advised to concentrate solely on these modern routes, relegating the normal routes to the descent. He is not sufficiently selective. 200 routes is too many, but of course he and his publisher are seeking as large a market as possible. Even Rébuffat in his classic selection of routes in the Mont Blanc massif—an infinitely richer venue—keeps it to 100.

Speaking of selection, except for the remote "musts" like Assiniboine or Clemenceau, the orientation is toward climbs easily accessible from the road, especially rock routes in the Kananaskis or in the vicinity of Banff. Why no mention of routes in the Royal or Mummery or Freshfield or Alexandra or Chess or Sir Alexander Groups? Ah, because they require a long bash or they are in British Columbia, or both—and this book was subsidized by an agency of the Alberta government. There are a number of routes that I would inject in preference to some that are included: Mount King George by the east face of Val Fynn (he wasn't a Canadian either, simply the best climber of his time in Canada!); the traverse of Mount Balfour; Mount Mummery; the traverse of the three central peaks of the Lyells (if not all five); the north face of Mount Brazeau (oh, so many days from the road); Mount Hooker (again many days from the road); the traverse of Mounts Shipton, Chettan, and Irvine; and little old Mount Parnassus in the Fryatt.

The author is inconsistent too. He talks about avoiding shit piles and then selects Pinnacle and Mitre, both of which I remember as classic examples of the genre. Nor do I remember any 5.5 pitch on the latter; had there been any such difficulty on that loose crap, I would have not dared to try it. And except for Mount Fay and Deltaform, why mention the rest of the ten peaks except as part of the complete traverse? In fact, the route on Mount Fay to which my name is attached fits the crappy description as well. The author is altogether too casual about the generally dreadful rock in the Lake Louise district, which can provide a frightening experience for the climber who comes from afar.

As part of his castigation of the pre-existing AAC guidebooks, which his book presumes to replace, the author writes "often the information about the way up is incorrect!" Mr. Dougherty will find that errors are an occupational hazard in guidebook writing. To wit: after climbing the north face of Mount Belanger, any reasonable person will descend on the south side rather than go back down his up route. (2) After surviving the east face of Mount Babel (IV, 5.10, A1), the climber is advised to descend by the north ridge (III, 5.5) when it is a walk-off via the south ridge and an hour or so to the Colgan hut. (3) Mount Bryce is big, remote, and difficult by any route, yet no mention is made of the easiest route off, which goes down the south glacier and traverses easy ledges in the direction of Thompson Pass. It's all in the old book. (4) No rappels are necessary to descend the west face of Mount Columbia, nor are there any descent anchors in any case. (5) For those intrepid souls who complete the grand central couloir on Mount Kitchener's north face, it is suggested that they descend by the east ridge (a route I recommend in the upward direction), rather than walk off the back on the normal route. Maybe these heroes never loose their composure and never get tired? And it would be nice if my name were spelled correctly, but doubtless that's part of the put-down.

The most positive feature of this book is the profusion of well-marked photographs, which will be helpful to even those who are not hard men. Some other good things: the somewhat complicated and worthwhile, descent of Mount Victoria to Lake O'Hara via the Huber Glacier is well described. Mount Hector, a real "dog" in summer, is described, and suggested, as a ski ascent, as are several of the Columbia Icefields summits. The author has done a service in ferreting out information, which doesn't appear in the journals, about recent difficult climbs from those who have done them. For those modern climbers who like to drive from place to place, bagging those climbs which build a reputation, this is probably a useful book. But for the traditional recreational mountaineer, who simply enjoys the outdoors rather than being an athlete, it is not a substitute for the comprehensive old guidebooks.

ROBERT KRUSZYNA

Yankee Rock and Ice. Laura and Guy Waterman. Stackpole Books, Harrisburg, PA, 1992. 354 pages, 125 black-and-white illustrations. $24.95 (paper).

You needn't be a Yankee to relish this companion to the Waterman's rich, *Forest and Crag*. You don't even need to be a climber: the authors teach you as you read along. The stories start with Herschel Parker training on Mount Washington for his attempt on Mount McKinley and describe how every route on Washington has been put in since then.

We're told how two Yale undergraduates, Whittlesey and Scoville, climbed Washington's Pinnacle Gully, which had defeated the best in the east. Guy and Laura asked one of the two how he learned to climb: "Can't say I really got started." What other climbs did they do: "That was the only one." In one of their many puckish adventures the Watermans repeated that classic climb 60 years later, wearing similar clothes and carrying Whittlesey's old pack. Dividing their account roughly into decades, and describing the major eastern climbing areas in loving detail, Guy and Laura weave a rich tapestry with vivid scenes in which they portray the leading players. Some flashed briefly through the climbing world, others seem immortal.

We're told how nylon rope opened a whole new scene when Bob Bates rappelled out of a Washington office building. Nylon stretched rather than broke, encouraging more daring moves. Ice climbing reached new heights when Yvon Chouinard introduced the short ice tool, and together with front-pointing made accessible an exciting new playground: vertical ice.

The Waterman's reflect gently on commercialism, vandals, competition, and the lust for notoriety. One hopes their modest essays will be widely read and pondered. Their thoughtful visit to Geoffrey Winthrop Young's theme "The leader does not fall" applies not only to rock and ice acrobatics, but also, in a broader sense, to assaults on great distant summits.

Specially refreshing are seven short "Interludes" in which the authors muse about the siege tactics which preceded success on the most difficult new routes. About style they believe: "The cat is a better model than the goat." From a period when style dictated that artificial aids were unacceptable, then through the frenzy of bolting and nailing and top-roping, they take us to free climbing, to the principles of environmental awareness and conscience—and finally, back to bolting!

We watch as each new area is discovered, described, and over-run by aspirants. We marvel as a new star climbs the impossible "on sight." Pushing the envelope is a major theme of the last few chapters, deserving serious attention from tomorrow's climbers.

The details of new routes are breath-taking, many taken from interviews with the pioneers. The extent of the authors' ten years of research is staggering: they talked with hundreds of people, read countless old letters, essays and unpublished diaries, and repeated many of the climbs.

Guy and Laura seem unlikely adventurers: small, shy, unassuming, wonderful listeners, and rich with humor. They built their home on homesteaded land, half a mile from the road, without electricity or what most people consider material necessities, and pecked out this marvelous book on an old manual typewriter.

The 154 photographs are an extraordinary collection of people and places, and that alone makes the book invaluable. Little escaped the authors. Indeed if the book has a flaw, there is sometimes too much detail. One might also fault them for the charity with which they treat some of the flawed personalities. If they can think of nothing nice, they say nothing at all.

Rush out and buy—and relish this remarkable book. It's a fun read and an inexhaustible reservoir of history, and certain to be a classic.

CHARLES S. HOUSTON, *M.D.*

Summit Guide to the Cascade Volcanoes. Jeff Smoot. Chockstone Press, Evergreen, Colorado, 80439, 1992. 182 pages. 62 black-and-white photos, 14 peak sketches. 46 line maps. $12.95.

This volume is a handy guide for all who aspire to scrambling up these fire-and-ice mountains of the Northwest. Concise descriptions are provided of routes up a total of 19 volcanoes: running from Mount Garibaldi (B.C.) in the north to Mount Shasta and Lassen Peak in California.

Also described are the problems inherent with these ice-clad and loose-rock volcanoes. The climbs are classified according to the various types of difficulty and related hazards, and special techniques often utilized for scaling these peaks. Discussed are (1) generalized geologic settings, (2) local weather conditions, (3) climbing seasons and regulations, and where permits/reservations can be obtained if required, (4) clothing and equipment, (5) altitude-related illnesses and hypothermia, (6) avalanche survival and rescue, and (7) ski mountaineering, with recommended areas and trails. Symbols on peaks sketches show areas prone to hazards of avalanches, rockfall and icefall. Emphasis is placed on the "No Trace" ethics—the climber should leave the area as clean or cleaner than when visited.

The simple line maps show roads, trails, and climbing routes, but ridge lines are the only indications of typography. However, aerial photos of the peaks do show the routes—with a few minor discrepancies. Also, several photos of Mount Shasta fail to include one clearly showing the popular "dog route" up the south side. Routes are described by an informal classification system designed for glacier-clad volcanoes, and their lengths are given in approximate hours.

A bibliography reveals substantive research, with citations of 74 books, newspapers, and maps, and personal interviews and correspondence with 30 local climbing authorities.

DEE MOLENAAR

Adventure Guide to Mount Rainier: Hiking, Climbing and Skiing in Mount Rainier National Park. Jeff Smoot. Chockstone Press, Evergreen, Colorado 80439, 1991. 172 pages. 38 photos, 54 line maps, 27 oblique-perspective (and profile) peak sketches. $12.95.

This information-loaded reference provides concise descriptions of the Mount Rainier volcano and glaciers, the geologic and climatic settings, a brief history of explorations, the park's flora and fauna, and climate and weather. Described are 29 summit routes, and these are delineated on aerial photos, with some local details given in sketches. Information on round-trip times and elevation gains is provided for 41 hiking trails (with a category of "trail types"), including the round-the-mountain Wonderland Trail. 25 off-trail routes are also included. Also described are recommended auto and bicycle touring routes—both paved and dirt roads. A section on winter recreation describes 35 recommended cross-country skiing routes around the mountain. Also included are backcountry camping regulations and permit requirements, and problems of human-wastes disposal, with emphasis on the "No Trace" ethics.

A bibliography includes references to 42 books and 8 maps, and 32 personal interviews/correspondences.

DEE MOLENAAR

Climbers Guide to Smith Rock. Alan Watts. Chockstone Press, Evergreen, CO, 1992. 341 pages. $19.95.

This long-awaited guide goes way beyond serving as a roadmap for the more than 1000 routes at the park: it's a riveting read, a fascinating glimpse into Smith Rock history, and at least for me (a Smith devotee), a worthy book of worship. If you climb at Smith regularly, it's a must-buy; if you're just visiting, you'll find yourself borrowing a copy from the nearest climber every time you put down your pack.

Watts' guide provides several crucial pieces of information that will help you enjoy Smith to the utmost: star ratings, which are impossible to guess at from the ground when you're looking at blank walls of tuff ("is it loose?" is always the big question); good topos for the lesser travelled basalt gorge columns and outlying spires; and insightful tips that sometimes go beyond conventional route descriptions (I for one would have saved some rope wear on a route if I had read his comment that "you can avoid the lunge if you use holds to the left"). His comments about the amount of rotten rock on routes is particularly useful, since at Smith you have to expect the possibility of a portable hold on any but the most solid lines. His area topos and descriptions are also very helpful for the newcomer; since some Smith walls are more than a few minute's hike from the parking lot, and the hairpin topography of the crags can easily cause any first-timer to use a longer than necessary approach. Watts lends a helping hand with a brief comment on the most direct approach to these crags, and a time estimate for hiking to the farthest formations.

It's hard to find fault with Watts' magnum opus. A few climbers may feel unjustly humbled by rating downgrades from the previous "Route Finder," published by Redpoint Climber, a low-cost cluster of stapled photocopies, (for example, *Light In The Path* has changed from 5.10a to 5.9), but that would miss the point of Watts' attention to changed ratings. The petrified mud of Smith mutates over time, so the topography really does alter—occasionally down but almost always up (as a very popular route, *Gumby*, has gone from 10a to 10b).

There are a few goals and slipshod copy-editing in the book. But I found the typos none too irritating. The upside-down photo of a climber on *Take a Powder* is easily forgiven when the overall quality is so good.

The historical introduction and first-ascent information are first rate. So too the bouldering guide complete with a name and topo for most boulders. At the back of the book there's a checkoff list of all Smith routes—boulders excepted. No matter what you're looking for, Smith is so packed with routes worth climbing that you need to plan your days, like deciding which parts of the Metropolitan Museum to visit first, since you know you'll never get to everything. A few hours with this guide and a pencil and you can't go wrong. And when you're ready to refuel and recount the day's exploits, flip to Watts' thoughtful overview of local eateries.

JOHN FINE

The High Sierra: Peaks, Passes, and Trails. R.J. Secor. The Mountaineers, Seattle, WA, 1992. 368 pages. Black-and-white photos and maps. $19.95.

R.J. Secor contributes, with this latest guide to the Sierra Nevada, new climbing routes gleaned from various publications. But the bulk of route descriptions and ratings are the same as are found in Steve Roper's *Climber's Guide to the High Sierra,* published in 1976. This inevitably perpetuates past errors. In addition, consensus amongst Sierra climbers is that Secor's research was incomplete or non-existent, leading to the creation of many new errors. For example, Secor states, "Mono to Morgan Traverse. This multi-day traverse rivals and in some places exceeds the Palisade traverse. . . ." The statement is inane. Secor failed to contact anyone who might have made an informed comparison or comment. Other examples include the wrong photo for the North Rib of Mount William-son, the incorrect numbering of the Ericsson's Crags, the wrong description for the east face of Devil's Crag Number Two, and others.

The book's introduction also serves as a source of misinformation and confusion. For example, in the "Conservation" section of the introduction, the reader is told that fire wood is a "finite resource and must be used sparingly," followed by "instead of a wood fire, cook on a stove," followed by advice on how to build a fire, followed by ". . . but consider using a stove." Or advice is given, such as "Despite having discouraged hikers from using Kearsarge Pass, I do encourage them to use Kearsarge. . . ."

In the "Avalanche" section, Secor makes the general statement, "Avalanches occur most frequently after a snowfall of four inches or more." The advice to "stay off steep terrain for at least one day after said snowfall" is laughable in the context in which it is presented.

The examples could continue but are too many for the space available. Consensus amongst Sierra climbers and others is that although Roper's guide is in need of update and correction, that eloquently written book still serves the reading public quite well, and much better than this latest arrival.

CLAUDE FIDDLER

Rock Climbs of Tuolumne Meadows. Third Edition. Don Reid and Chris Falk-enstein. Chockstone Press, Evergreen, CO, 1992. 180 pages, topos and black-and-white photos. $18.00.

If Yosemite Valley is the St. Peter's of rock climbing, Tuolumne Meadows must be the Sistine Chapel—exquisite faces and ethereal views in a spiritually uplifting atmosphere. As the faithful know (and the guidebook illustrates), not much has changed in the Meadows; a few routes have been retrobolted, but many of the old, questionable quarter-inch bolts, along with R and X ratings, remain.

In the past, falling while leading has not been an option in Tuolumne. But that is changed with this guide which has a list of recommended sport climbs, with over 100 routes in the 5.11-5.13 range. The pilgrims who do not climb at these rarified grades will vie for the 10 sport climbs rated less than 5.10b or be humbled on the knobby, runout faces that characterize the Tuolumne experience.

Predicting your chances of meeting your maker is made easier by the authors' use of question marks that tell the reader what they do and do not know about a route. After nearly every route's name and rating are parentheses which enclose a protection grade (PG, R, X) and a quality rating (one to three stars). When the authors have not done the climb or have received less than reliable information, they've informed the reader by using (?, ?). Be prepared to pray if you embark on a route followed by these symbols.

Whether you're a slab-mongering devotee, a recent convert or waiting to take your vows, this book will show you The Way. See you in the Meadows!

SALLY MOSER

Best of Boulder Climbs. Richard Rossiter. Chockstone Press, Evergreen, CO, 1992. 180 pages, topos and black-and-white photos. $14.95.

Who decided which are the best of Boulder climbs? Why, the best Boulder climbers, of course. Knowing that any list compiled would receive intense scrutiny, Richard Rossiter recruited 50 of "the area's most experienced climbers" to vote on the best Boulder routes. While the results definitely emphasize bolted climbs 5.11 and up, Rossiter notes that the highest-rated route was Yellow Spur, a classic 5.9, with 32 votes.

Though the majority are face routes, the sandstone and granite climbs also feature liebacks, small pebble pulling, and cracks of varying sizes. However, a final list of the routes' scores should have been included; it's hard to tell which lines are considered the best as each topo and photo illustrates a group of climbs, with no stars or other notation to show which is the more recommended.

Still, this guide is a boon for those who don't wish to invest $50 in Rossiter's two tomes, *Boulder Climbs North* and *Boulder Climbs South,* which total 717 pages. Featuring Rossiter's Oriental-styled topos and maps along with plenty of black-and-white photos, *Best of Boulder Climbs* contains enough information to keep a climber busy on a lengthy stay.

SALLY MOSER

Climber's Guide to Tahoe Rock. Mike Carville. Chockstone Press, Evergreen, CO, 1991. 294 pages, photos, maps and topos. Soft cover. $18.00.

This is a welcome and much-needed addition to the rapidly-expanding California (and Nevada) guidebook repertoire. The guide covers an area that is rich in climbing tradition while also on the cutting edge of sport climbing of the 1990s. Consider the names of some of the first-ascenders of popular climbs at Lover's

Leap, Sugarloaf and Donner Summit: Warren Harding, Royal Robbins, Steve Roper, Jeff Lowe, TM Herbert, Jim Orey, Bob Kamps, Mike Covington and Gordon Webster. And, of course, Tony Yaniro, author of Grand Illusion at Sugarloaf in the late '70s, recorded as the world's first 5.13. And lately, Jay Smith, Paul Crawford, Dan Osman and others at Cave Rock.

This also is a region of amazing diversity in climbing, from the fine hard granite of Donner Summit and Sugarloaf to the amazing dikes at the Leap—making possible such classics as Traveler Buttress and Robbins' Fantasia—the rhyolite of Cave Rock, and the limestone-like rock of the Emeralds on the South Yuba River. You can climb almost literally in the middle of a major highway (at Cave Rock) or in the wilderness (Eagle Lake Buttress). In all, there are routes on 13 distinct climbing areas as well as good sections on bouldering and ice climbing.

BILL STALL

Southern Sierra Rock Climbing, Needles. Sally Moser, Greg Vernon, Patrick Paul. Chockstone Press, Evergreen, CO, 1992. 230 pages, 118 photos, 69 drawings. $18.00.

It was with mixed feelings that I first opened the new guidebook to the Needles. Although the original *Stonemasher Guide to Kern River* has been out of print for several years, the area still hasn't caught on with the majority of California climbers. Certainly, most have heard about this magical place of spires, knobby faces, and steep, difficult cracks; yet, until recently, few have come to climb.

For Needles aficionados, keeping the place at minimum impact and in the same timeless condition has been the most important consideration. Will the new guidebook change that? I hope not. . . . But with Joshua Tree, Tahquitz, Yosemite and Tuolumne becoming rapidly overrun with climbers, the need exists to disperse those climbers who seek solitude and wilderness experience into new areas. The vast area of southwestern Sierra Nevada with its domes, spires and rock walls offers a huge climbing potential, as well as a lifetime of exploring. It was this understanding that led Greg Vernon, Sally Moser and Patrick Paul to compile the region's climbing history. The Needles guidebook is the first of the three guidebooks for Southern California. It covers the rocks in southern Sierra from Trilogy/Jordan Peak and the Needles off Highway 190 on the north, to the town of Kernville on the south.

There are many things to like about this volume. It will guide any first-time visitor very well. The southern Sierra can still be considered backcountry climbing area, with spread-out locations, lack of "scene" and until recently, scant literature on the area. A good, thorough guide is essential for enjoyment here. The Needles guide is not only that, it's comprehensive as well. Its 118 quality photos, 69 maps and drawings will make it almost an effort to get lost (but you will, trust me). The authors also thoroughly researched and documented the sometimes tricky descents off these formations. Routes in Needles can be extremely satisfying but also bold and lacking in protection. Some creative styles have been employed on routes sporting large knobs, i.e., throwing ropes over them or lassoing them. The authors have given consideration to these varied techniques and each area is prefaced with general information about its routes. An "R" and "X" ratings signifying protection possibilities have been added.

The authors are well qualified to write about Needles. They've spent many years and done numerous first ascents there. Their combined effort, at least in this climber's opinion, can be considered a complete success.

So buy the guide and have fun in Needles. But please treat the place as the gem it really is. Act responsibly, don't litter, climb in the tradition of first-ascent pioneers and be friendly to your fellow climbers. Needles locals, in my experience (especially one of the authors of this guidebook), have not had a possessive attitude and been generous to newcomers. Let's hope that continues.

ALOIS SMRZ

Rock Climbs of Indian Cove, 74 pages, $8.95; *Rock Climbs of Lost Horse Valley,* 92 pages, $8.95; *Rock Climbs of Hidden Valley,* 108 pages, $9.95. All by Alan Bartlett, 1992. Topos. Quail Springs Publishing, PO Box 240, Joshua Tree, CA 92252.

Joshua Tree Rock Climbing Guide, 2nd edition, 624 pages, photos and maps, $40.00; *Joshua Tree Sport Climbs,* 100 pages, $12.95. Both by Randy Vogel, 1992, Chockstone Press, Evergreen, CO.

Randy Vogel's first (1986) edition included over 1300 routes, enough to keep one from Yucca Valley's fleshpots; then a 1989 Supplement, co-authored by Vogel and Alan Bartlett, described an additional 1200 routes. Now Vogel has a 1992 edition, with an overwhelming 3854 routes, and Bartlett has published the first three of a projected series of *eight* guides that will cover subdivisions of the monument. And, though not adding to our information overload, Vogel's *Joshua Tree Sport Climbing* recently hit the newsstands.

The first thing you may notice about Vogel's complete guide is a sticker price of $40.00. That's only a penny a route, though, and Vogel masterfully meets the challenge of presenting thousands of rock climbs—by marking most of the typically short, densely-packed routes on photos, recommending them with 1 to 5 stars, and striving for accuracy. In an era when guidebooks get away with a misspelled title on the cover, and blatant errors in the first edition can persist even unto the fifth edition, it's reassuring to suspect only one mislocated route in *Joshua Tree Rock Climbing Guide* and expect it to be in place in an update. (The book even comes with a few loose pages of errata.)

If you have the first edition, perhaps the supplement, and are wondering about the new edition, you may be tempted by subtly improved maps, more plentiful warnings about sparse protection, photos and recommendations for the supplement's routes (it had few photos and no stars), and more accurate ratings. Not much is new around Hidden Valley Campground (except for the Pinched Rib's ever-increasing rating). So Vogel offers mostly new, obscure areas. Whether Oz, Planet X, the Oyster Bar, Human Sacrifice Boulder, and the Galapagos are worth the new book depends on the quality of the climbs.

Vogel lured me to Oz, undiscovered at the time of the first edition, the site of only six routes in the supplement, but now subdivided into Munchkinland and the Emerald City. The maps led me uneventfully over the desert into the intended canyon, and from one canyon to another, but the quality of some of Oz's rock implied I was doing a second ascent. Such present-day classics as *Loose Lady* no doubt had similarly friable origins, but it's hard to imagine *If I Only Had a Brain* and *Oil My Joints* with weekend queues.

In earlier editions, Vogel often perplexed climbers with his inconsistent ratings. So I checked my grievances in the new opus: they're rectified. The most memorable, of course, were underrated climbs at my limit. Their upgrading makes the new guide valuable for self-esteem alone.

The main differences between Vogel's and Bartlett's endeavors are pictorial and financial. Bartlett relies on topos, rather than photos, and you can acquire Bartlett for $8.95 or $9.95 per installment. Like all such plans, you pay more in the end for the whole set. But if you're in Hidden Valley Campground without a car, or climb only in winterized Indian Cove, or lack interest in the Zebra Cliffs, you won't need the whole set.

In Joshua Tree's climbing store (managed by Bartlett), there's a loose-leaf "notebook" that could well be the dream of a guidebook writer who ate anchovy pizza too near bedtime. On motel stationery or paper bags cut into 8½ x 11 scraps, first ascentionists proclaim their creations. They all seem to be located on "the aesthetic arête" on the "most prominent" 30-foot tower among the "obvious" jumble of boulders seen from "the" sandy turnout along one road or another. Vogel and Bartlett both have pored over this notebook's mystifying entries, but also perhaps because of their earlier collaboration, or perhaps because they can interest only each other in doing the odder routes, their information agrees better than either may have intended. Both, let me emphasize, have done a first-rate job.

For routes I've done in Bartlett's Lost Horse area, I subjected his and Vogel's ratings to a comparison more scientific than the fuzzy decimal system warrants. Their ratings agree for 48 routes. Of those that disagree, I agree with Vogel on 3 and Bartlett on 4, and the disagreements are petty: 5.7 vs. 5.7/5.8, or 5.9+ vs. 5.10a, which indicates that both writers listen to dialogue and consensus and that by using one book rather than the other, you're not necessarily setting yourself up for the fire department.

While Vogel's photos are more reassuring, Bartlett's simple topos are as effective as need be. He's good at using one-liner text to characterize one-pitch routes—for instance, "This route is harder and better than it looks." The books' difference may be no more than ambiance—Vogel's has a polish that would fit better on the proverbial coffee table. Bartlett's hints at days spent clamboring through prickly pear to see if a 30-foot psoriatic lump could be the classic the notebook asserts. Bartlett includes a few more routes (and upcoming volumes presumably even more), though they tend toward the unprotectable 5.4.

Finally, there's Vogel's *Jushua Tree Sport Climbing*. The routes are a subset of the 3854—same ratings, same stars, though topos instead of photos. I was anxious to see if Vogel would offer a more rigorous definition of this activity than the only precise one I've seen—John Sherman's bumper sticker, which reads "SPORT CLIMBING IS NEITHER." However, the introductory section "What Is a Sport Climb?" gives three criteria—"mostly all fixed protection," "usually fixed anchors," and "reasonably good protection"—with a vagueness that may allow a climb more *sport* than a sport climber seeks. The routes span the range from low-angle, sparsely bolded, 5.7 *Stichter Quits* to a few 5.13ds.

The *Sport Climbing* guide seems more for those who can't afford 4000 routes, nor much gear beyond a loopful of quick-draws, than for prototypical sport climbers. Some routes require plodding a few miles across desert, searching, and impaling lycra on yucca.

This book doesn't violate the Joshua Tree tradition of undocumented, convoluted descents. Someone who expects to slap a chain and shout "Sport lower!" at a ground belayer will broaden his/her perspective seeking the way down from *Run for Your Life*—which Vogel does qualify as "Not quite a sport route, but very good" (both true).

JOE KELSEY

Red Rocks Select. 500 Selected Routes in the Red Rocks of Nevada. Todd Swain. Chockstone Press, Evergreen, Colorado, 1993. 186 pages, 42 black-and-white photographs, 20 sketch maps, numerous topos. $18.00.

The desert is a land of contrasts and Red Rock is a shining example. The extremes of sun and shadow, of searing heat and bitter cold are reflected in the climbs of the area. Classic thousand-foot climbs and remote committing wall routes neighbor convenient user-friendly sport climbs. In the north, the Calico Hills harbor the densest concentration of modern bolted sport routes in the area. On numerous accessible, well-equipped cliffs are found routes of every grade.

Easy-to-moderate, hard-to-extreme, there are tendon-wrenching test pieces to rival any area. In the southern canyons, many long adventure routes ply the steep varnished walls. On many of these climbs, arduous approaches and long convoluted descents become part of the whole experience of canyoneering. Although modern styles and technology have been embraced by many local climbers, a strong ethic of bold ground-up ascent still thrives here and, surprisingly, there exists a climate of understanding and mutual respect of these diverse styles. These contrasts were not lost on the author of *Red Rocks Select,* who approaches this project with experience and objectivity.

The presentation of this guide is in the usual high quality typical of Chockstone Press. The text and photos are crisp and correctly aligned. The layout is simple and logical with an attractive typeface. The book is of a manageable size and well bound so it shouldn't explode in your pack. The guide is organized by canyons from north to south. Approaches into canyons and descriptions of individual features are supplemented with excellent sketch maps and photos. The verbal route descriptions are generally accurate and understandable, and they note any special gear requirements or peculiarities of the route. These written descriptions often contain interesting notes of humor or history that add to the character of the climb. A generous selection of well-done topos and photos accompany these descriptions. Instead of a separate list of multiple stars, a "thumbs-up" symbol denotes recommended routes. Where known or appropriate, the author has utilized the PG, R and X protection rating system. This might not only save someone's life, but it also recognizes the risk/danger/boldness factor in climbing.

There are many positives to this guide. Swain did much research and contacted many first ascentionists to obtain a broad base of information from which to write descriptions. The numerous maps are well drawn and will be an invaluable aid to someone unfamiliar with this complex area. The author has struck an equitable balance of sport climbs and traditional adventure routes. The introduction contains some useful information about getting to Las Vegas as well as the usual ecology, weather, ratings, etc. There are also notes about some neighboring areas and a few maps on how to get there.

The principal shortcoming of this guide is that it only touches the surface of the southern canyons. Although many of the true classics there are listed, this represents only a fraction of the routes done. Remember that this guide is a compilation of *selected* routes and is not intended as a comprehensive historical tome. Invariably, there are a few misspelled names and incorrect credits, but these are minor points and detract little from the overall quality of this excellent guide. Buy it and enjoy Red Rocks, but please respect the area. Climbing here is a privilege and the rewards are great.

NICK NORDBLOM

Illustrated Guidebooks. Jan Kielkowski. Potsdamer Strasse 45, 4000 Düsseldorf 13, Germany. Paperback booklets.

Jan Kielkowski continues to put out guidebooks to some of the high-mountain areas of the world. The mountains in various regions are given with a description of each peak, the different routes with the first ascensionists, sketch maps and line drawings of the peaks with ascent lines marked. The series keeps being added to. At this writing, there are 12 booklets on the Himalaya, 9 on the Karakoram and 6 on the Cordillera Huayhuash in the Peruvian Andes. Some of the volumes are in English or German, but unfortunately for many of our readers most of the recent ones are in Polish. With the maps and drawings, this makes little difference and where the text is dealing in proper names and dates, a little guessing helps the reader who has no knowledge of Polish. A person planning an expedition or a serious student of mountain history will be well advised to get into contact with Pan Kielkowski.

H. ADAMS CARTER

In Memoriam

TERRANCE MANBECK "MUGS" STUMP
1949-1992

Snow swirls softly in the gray sky and settles deeply over the fractured ice, muting its soft edges. Higher, the bitter wind hurls itself against the ridges and buttresses of Denali, the Great One, the soul of the Alaska Range. Here it is calm, even peaceful. For the party of three climbers, the tension of the struggle with the storm above has given way to the lesser anxiety of being out of the maelstrom but still miles from home. Suddenly the edge of the crevasse collapses—that happens often in places like this—and a climber is sucked into the abyss. The rope comes tight on his companions, drags them toward the void, then stops, disappearing into a jumbled mass of ice. All is still.

Mugs is gone—even months afterward it's difficult to say the words, let alone grasp their meaning. When I heard of his death on the South Buttress of Denali, it was as if a piece of the earth or the sky had suddenly disappeared. He was one of the constants of my universe, sharing tales of his most recent grand adventure in Zion, Yosemite, Alaska or the Antarctic, or trying to tempt me into joining him on one of his upcoming projects.

A true "climber's climber," Mugs was always psyched—long free routes, big walls, frozen waterfalls, alpine faces, sport routes, as long as it was climbing. His dedication was complete, and he never strayed far from his own demanding set of standards; above all, he wanted to be out on the edge, pushing the envelope of what was possible in the mountains. He was a survivor, but more than that he had an intuitive sense of how closely to tread the fine line between the reasonable and the risky, something he did far longer and more skillfully than most climbers of his caliber. He also had an intuitive sense of his partners' limits—and he respected them. Mugs helped me to push myself. Yet, when I wasn't up to the task, he would harness his own incredible strength and drive, take over, and get us up that pitch or to the next bivouac.

Born and raised in Mifflintown, Pennsylvania, where his parents still live, Terrance Manbeck ("Mugs") Stump started fishing, hunting and camping with his three brothers at an early age. Although he never took well to authority, he excelled in sports, finishing high school as an all-state quarterback. He attended Pennsylvania State University on a football scholarship, where his teammates came up with the moniker he's been known by since. He played in two Orange Bowls before graduating in 1971 with a degree in Recreation and Health. After college he played a year of semi-professional football but, disillusioned with that, moved to Snowbird, Utah, in the winter of 1972-3 in hopes of pursuing a career in freestyle skiing.

After two year's of competing in local freestyle events and skiing virtually anything that held snow, Mugs found himself increasingly drawn to the back-

TERRANCE MANBECK "MUGS" STUMP
1949-1992

country. He spent his summers roaming the Wasatch wilderness surrounding Snowbird and by the winter of 1974-5 had given up lift skiing in favor of touring. As he ventured into steeper and wilder terrain, he sought out local climbers and avalanche experts for advice, and in the summer of 1975 made his first roped climbs.

Mugs developed his climbing skills rapidly, and in the spring of 1977 he made the first ascent of Merlin (V, 5.10, A3) in the Black Canyon of the Gunnison, Colorado, with Bob Sullivan. That summer, he spent two months in Chamonix climbing classic ice-and-snow routes. The trip culminated in an epic attempt on the Dru Couloir (then regarded as one of the most difficult ice climbs in the Alps) with Randy Trover, Steve Shea and Jack Roberts. Starting out with no bivy gear, and food and water for a single day, the four got off route, were trapped by a storm for two days and barely made it down alive when their ropes repeatedly froze to the rappel anchors during their descent.

Mugs had plenty of drive and quickly came to know how far he could push himself. The climbs only got harder. In the spring of 1978, Mugs attempted the Hummingbird Ridge on Mount Logan, Canada's highest peak, with Trover, Jim Logan and Barry Sparks. After ten days of climbing, they reached the point where the original party had gained the ridge, but with several thousand feet and many corniced miles still to go, Mugs and his party retreated. Later that summer, Mugs and Logan made the first ascent of the often-tried Emperor Face on Mount Robson in the Canadian Rockies, a landmark mixed climb that has yet to be repeated. In 1979, Mugs and Sullivan climbed the Shield on El Capitan in Yosemite Valley, California. A year later, they made the fifth ascent of the Pacific Ocean Wall, then one of the hardest aid routes in the world. Mugs would climb numerous other big walls in Yosemite and elsewhere. He made the first ascent of the Streaked Wall in Zion National Park, Utah, with Conrad Anker in 1990 and the first winter ascent of the Hallucinogen Wall in the Black Canyon of the Gunnison with John Middendorf in 1992.

In the winter of 1980-1, Mugs made the first of four trips to Antarctica. He developed a special affinity for the pristine and barren continent and did much exploratory mountaineering there while working as a safety consultant for the National Science Foundation. In the Ellsworth Mountains in 1989, he made two of the best climbs ever, the 7000-foot southwest face of Mount Gardner and the 8000-foot west face of Mount Tyree—each done solo, without bivy gear and in a single day.

The Himalaya beckoned. Mugs and I attempted the west face of Gasherbrum IV in Pakistan in 1983. He and Laura O'Brien tried Thalay Sagar in India in 1984 and he returned to India twice to attempt the east face of Meru with various partners. But Mugs didn't like the organizational hassles and expense, or the sheer inefficiency of climbing in Asia. Instead, he turned increasingly toward the Alaska Range, which in many ways became Mugs' spiritual home. In the late 1970s and early 1980s, he earned his living between climbs by salmon fishing off the coast of Alaska; later he guided extensively on Denali and elsewhere in the Alaska Range. He returned again and again to peaks surrounding the Ruth Gorge, attempting Mount Johnson and the Broken Tooth several times and climbing numerous routes on the less well-known peaks in the area.

His greatest climbs in the Alaska Range, however, were on three of the region's most celebrated mountains. In March, 1981, Mugs and Jim Bridwell made the first ascent of the east face of the Moose's Tooth, an exceptionally bold route climbed in frigid conditions with minimum food and equipment. The pair carried no bolts on the climb and the experience tested their well-developed skills to the maximum. A few months later, Mugs climbed the Moonflower Buttress on Mount Hunter with Paul Aubrey, a route that represented a quantum leap in technical difficulty for climbs in the Alaska Range. And in 1991, he made the visionary solo ascent of Denali's Cassin Ridge. Starting at the 14,200-foot camp on the West Buttress with his climbing gear, a liter of water and a pocketfull of energy bars, he descended the West Rib to the base of the Cassin, climbed the route in a storm, reached the summit as the sun set and returned to his West Buttress camp, all in 27½ hours.

Mugs and I shared some incredibly good and some equally bad times in the mountains of Pakistan and India. In 1983, we spent seven long, difficult days on the west face of Gasherbrum IV, including four storm-wracked nights at 22,500 feet, before retreating. When we reached the relative safety of the West Gasherbrum Glacier, Mugs strode out ahead, anxious to rid himself of the intensity of the face, to go the last few miles at his own pace. I trudged on well behind him, lost in my disappointment at not being able to fulfill a longtime dream. A couple of hours later, I crested a little bump in the glacier. There was Mugs, waiting so that we could walk into Base Camp together.

At his very best, Mugs was generous, enthusiastic and supportive. But he could be selfish, insensitive and moody. All of us who had the privilege to climb with him experienced both of these personae—in Mugs and, too often, in ourselves. The good spirit in Mugs, that warm part of his being that inspired me so much, was by far ascendant. In the past few years, it seemed to me that Mugs had really come into his own. He had great adventures in the mountains, but he was more at peace with the world and at home with himself. He had dreams sufficient for several lifetimes, and it's our loss, too, that those dreams won't be fulfilled. I'll remember Mugs for his boundless enthusiasm, for offering me a quick smile and a brief word of encouragement before a hard pitch, for laughing at himself while recounting some grim epic—for just being Mugs.

(This is reprinted with Michael Kennedy's permission from Climbing *of August/September, 1992. Mugs Stump's climbing record was sadly unreported. He would often cheerily promise the Editor reports on his exploits and then be too busy to comply. For that reason, his friends will be happy to read a carefully researched compilation of his climbing career in* Climbing *of February/March, 1993.—Editor.)*

MICHAEL KENNEDY

HAROLD B. BURTON
1908-1992

Harold B. Burton died on March 8, 1992 at the age of 84 after a distinguished career as a newspaper reporter and author as well as a mountaineer who in World War II was involved with the training of thousands of soldiers in assault climbing. He was also a skier whose voluntary efforts led to the creation of the Whiteface and Gore Mountain Ski Centers in the Adirondacks through constitutional amendments.

He was among the first World War II volunteers to join what eventually became the 10th Mountain Division. Assigned to a detachment that camped on the Saskatchewan Glacier north of Lake Louise in Alberta, Canada, to work on military operations in the high mountains, his group tested *Weasels,* army snowmobiles, under alpine conditions and drove them across crevasses on improvised bridges. In charge of training artillery officers at Camp Carson, Colorado, to climb mountains for fire-observation purposes, Hal developed the Cheyenne Canyon climbing area, which has been used by the military ever since to train National Guard and Reserve units in rock climbing. He also persuaded generals to send his climbing school to the Crestone Needles, where climbing classes engaged in some of the finest climbing in the Rockies.

In 1943, Hal was one of the officers in charge of a climbing school at Seneca Rock, West Virginia where units of twelve other divisions were trained by instructors from the 10th Mountain Division. The climax of training was Hal's invention. With the enemy on top of a 300-foot cliff supposedly held down by artillery fire, assault teams would wade the Potomac River and climb the cliff, driving pitons and setting fixed ropes up which reinforcements could climb. Hal's instructors sat at various spots on the cliff throwing fuse-lit dynamite sticks down unclimbed gullies to furnish appropriate atmosphere. Some soldiers conceded later that actual combat was an anticlimax after this operation. Toward the end of 1943, Hal and the late Ed Link led a detachment of climbing instructors to Italy, where they trained British attack troops and especially Gurkhas, who proved to be superb climbers.

Hal spent years working on conservation and recreational projects in the Adirondacks. He is also remembered by *Saturday Evening Post* readers in the 1950s for a graphic account of his traverse of the Matterhorn via the Hörnli and Italian Ridges with the guide Otto Fuhrer. He was a member of the American Alpine Club from 1945 until his death.

Serving in his latter years as a book editor for *Newsday,* Hal lived in Glen Cove on Long Island but had a second home in Keene Valley, New York, where he was a popular participant in community affairs. Pre-deceased by his wife, Henrietta Ward Burton, he leaves his son Frederick, his daughter, Mary Burton Mulligan, and two granddaughters.

JAMES A. GOODWIN

PETER RITTENHOUSE KELLOGG
1966-1992

Peter Rittenhouse Kellogg was killed on June 18, 1992 after completing the major difficulties of the Pink Panther route on Mount Foraker. He and two companions were struck by an avalanche, which they had no way to anticipate, and only one of them survived.

Ritt was born in Summit, New Jersey and graduated from the Berkshire School in Massachusetts. His early love of outdoor adventure developed during sailing expeditions with his father and uncle and, later, from expeditions with Outward Bound. He began rock climbing at the Berkshire School, where he was also a talented skier and a member of their championship winning team for three years. His passion for mountaineering grew during his years at Colorado College, where he graduated with a Bachelor of Philosophy degree in 1990.

His mountaineering career included difficult rock-and-ice climbs in Colorado and desert rock climbs, including Castelton Tower. Ritt made winter ascents of Pikes Peak and Crestone Needle. For two seasons he worked as a guide on Mount McKinley. During this time, he climbed the Lowe-Kennedy route on Mount Hunter. He joined the American Alpine Club in 1990.

Friends remember Ritt as a considerate and reliable person who always saw the positive side of situations and found humor in adversity. He was respected and liked by his friends and associates and was never critical of the people he met. He found joy in helping others, often when they did not expect it. In 1989, he was an organizer of the Climb for Cancer, which raised money for charity through a climbing expedition to Mount Elbrus.

Ritt shared the lessons of his adventurous life willingly with young people, serving as an instructor for Outward Bound for three years. At Outward Bound, Ritt was known for his quiet competence, ready smile and ability to get on with people of all ages. A memorial to Ritt was placed by his friends on top of the climbing cliff on Hurricane Island, Maine in a location that blends Ritt's love of rock climbing, the ocean and helping others.

IAN WADE

THOMAS WALTER
1958-1992

Tom Walter was climbing toward the southeast ridge of Mount Foraker after two days on the Pink Panther route. Tom, Colby Coombs and Ritt Kellogg were climbing quickly, anxious to finish the route in worsening weather when from out of the mist above an avalanche struck. It ripped the team off the face, hurling them down 1000 feet, where they were stopped by a snag of the rope. Tom and Ritt died in the fall. Colby was lucky enough to survive, seriously injured, and incredibly he rescued himself from the face.

Tom Walter was a natural. He was a student and an educator of mountaineering. He learned and developed his trade over 17 years, beginning in the mountains and valleys near his family's home in California. He was drawn to the remote ranges all over the world. A natural climber, he moved over rock, ice and snow with equal speed and skill. His intellect and experience not only led him to beautiful mountains and unclimbed faces but also to explore the fine line between safe and unsafe, an art at which he became excellent.

In Pakistan in 1987, Tom made the first ascent of the Ogre Stump and the second ascent of Gama Sokha Lumbu with longtime friend, Tony Jewell. On the same trip, he and I got close to the summit of Latok I. In Nepal in 1988, Tom teamed up with Andy Selters, climbing two new routes on Cholatse. He also climbed in India and South America, but for many years he called Alaska home. In Alaska, I was lucky to make the first ascent of Alaska Angel and the Four Horsemen in the Revelation Mountains with Tom. He did a new route with John Bauman on Mount Hayes and more recently he, Phil Powers and I did the first ascent of McKinley's "Washburn Face."

Winter ascents, waterfall ice, skiing. Tom took to the wilderness as the preservation of the human spirit. He was active in conservation, but it was through education that he made his impact. As an educator in the National Outdoor Leadership School and the University of Alaska Pacific, Tom brought people to the mountains, to the summits of Aconcagua, McKinley, Marcus Baker and many others. Tom's students saw a brilliant, strong, honest and comfortable man. Whether in violent mountain storm or peaceful arctic sun, Tom was a level human being, free of preduduce, bent on progress. He will be missed by his family, his wife Lisa and all who knew him.

GREG COLLINS

HENRY IVES BALDWIN
1896-1992

Henry Baldwin was born in Saranac Lake, N.Y. and brought up in the Adirondacks, where he was one of the founders of the Adirondack Mountain Club. He was one of the early enthusiastic skiers, learning and perfecting the telemark technique, which he and his wife Birgit practiced until shortly before her death in 1987.

He studied forestry in Germany and Scandinavia and at Yale University, graduating from the School of Forestry in 1920. He also received from Yale a Ph.D in botany.

He was a flying officer in World War I and an intelligence officer in World War II, leaving the Air Force as a lieutenant colonel.

He was one of the first professional foresters hired by the forest industry, working as a research forester for the Brown Company in northern New Hampshire and Maine in promoting the growing of softwoods for their paper mills in New Hampshire and Quebec. He then was a professor of forestry at Penn State University.

In 1933, he became the research forester for the New Hampshire Forestry Department, a post he held until his retirement in 1965. For the next ten years, he returned to teaching as professor of botany and ecology at Franklin Pierce College in Rindge, New Hampshire.

His interest in mountaineering started in 1939 when he helped pioneer one of the new routes at the south end of Cannon Mountain. He joined the American Alpine Club in 1943 and made a number of climbing trips in the Wind River Range of Wyoming and in British Columbia.

He remained an avid skier and outdoorsman until shortly before his death on December 10, 1992.

WILLIAM P. HOUSE

JAMES HUNTER HOLLOWAY
1934-1992

J. Hunter Holloway was killed on April 30, 1992 in a car crash near Donnellson, Iowa.

Hunter was many things to many people and organizations. He was a veteran wire-service journalist and government communicator, most recently holding the position of Director, Office of Public Affairs, Region 5, Department of Veterans Affairs. He was vice-president of Fulcrum, Inc., a book publisher, for three years and president of the Fulcrum Group, a communications firm. After twelve years with the Associated Press, he served for thirteen years as a public-relations officer for the Department of the Interior. He was in the U.S. Marine Corps from 1953 to 1956. An inspiration to the mountain rescue community, he was elected to the American Alpine Club in 1987.

During more than 40 years in mountain and wilderness search and rescue, Hunter was directly involved in over 1400 missions. His first occurred at the age of 14 in July 1948 when he was called upon by the Ontario Department of Lands and Forests to ascend a cliff and assist a climber who had fractured a leg in a fall. After that, he hiked, backpacked, climbed, canoed and kayaked throughout eastern Canada, the Canadian Rockies, Northern New England, the Adirondacks, the Appalachians as well as the U.S. Rockies.

He served as instructor in outdoor skills, leadership and emergency medical care for many outdoor organizations including the Adirondack Mountain Club, Appalachian Mountain Club, Colorado Mountain Club, Boy Scouts of America, American Canoe Association, Colorado Whitewater Association, Colorado's hunter-safety program, U.S. Marine Corps, American Red Cross and others.

Although his climbing accomplishments were modest, he did record some first ascents in the Shawangunks in the 1950s. Of significant importance was his dedication to mountain rescue operations.

Hunter was past-president of the International Mountain Rescue Association, an original Colorado State Search and Rescue Coordinator, a director and life member of the National Association for Search and Rescue. For more than 15 years, he was a senior mission leader of the Alpine Rescue Team of the Mountain Rescue Association, past-president and 9-year board member of the Colorado Search and Rescue Board. Although Hunter never climbed the world's highest peaks, his dedication to mountain rescue earned him the respect of the entire rescue community. Hunter will remain a true inspiration to those who follow!

He is survived by his wife Pat, a son Jamie and a stepson James.

For myself and countless others, Hunter will always be remembered as a friend who was "Semper Fi."

TIMOTHY COCHRANE, *Mountain Rescue Association*

LOUIS L. BERGMANN
1907-1992

Louis M. Bergmann, M.D., a member of the American Alpine Club since 1949, passed away after a long illness on January 4, 1992 in his 84th year. Born in Austria, he received his medical degree from the University of Vienna in 1932. In 1934, he spent a year in China, helping to develop a medical program for Chiang Kai-Shek's government. Emigrating to the United States in 1938, he joined the faculty of the New York University Medical School and New York Medical College, where he became a Professor of Anatomy and Neuroanatomy. An inspiring instructor and mentor, he won numerous teaching awards. He left a profound impact on many lives and careers, a fact that became very evident when at his memorial service scores of his former colleagues and students came forth to remember him fondly.

There was another important dimension to this scholar and teacher. Beginning at an early age, Lou was a skilled alpinist and skier. He was one of the very first Austrian ski instructors, learning his craft from the great Hannes Schneider, founder of the Arlberg technique. In 1949, he applied for membership in the American Alpine Club and was quickly accepted. In reviewing his record, the Board said, "Dr. Bergmann's outstanding record of 103 ascents includes climbs from every year from 1921 to 1937. Many trips were guideless and under winter conditions." A photograph of Lou on the Biancograt, that great stairway in the sky, is one of the great classics of Alpine photography and hangs in the American Alpine Club museum. After his first wife Herta died, he lost no time in making his second wife Marianne a willing accomplice to his climbing passions. Together, they made numerous ascents in the Alps and Canadian Rockies during their summer holidays.

Lou had a great gift of communicating the joy of mountain experiences—as a writer, artist and illustrator—always with style and a gentle, self-effacing humor. For Lou loved being among the mountains more than conquering them. They were his friends and life-long companions. Lou loved to share and to give. Six years ago at the New York Section Annual Dinner, Lou contributed ten of his finest oils and watercolors, the lion's share of his personal collection to be sold for the benefit of the American Alpine Journal Publishing Fund. The works weren't on exhibit very long when a well-known Texan and ski-resort owner bought the entire collection, at list price. I thought Lou would have second thoughts about parting with his "babies," but this wasn't the case. He was happy because others would now get pleasure from his efforts.

So the Lou Bergmann many of us knew—pioneer skier, climber, writer, artist and illustrator—has gone on ahead. He leaves a legacy more important than his many accomplishments: an enthusiasm for life and people and the sharing of life's experiences and accomplishments. The last paragraph of *Mountain Memories*, a beautifully illustrated autobiographical sketch, written just before his health began to fail, reads, "Looking back to all the years spent in the mountains, I cherish the most glorious recollections as well as I recall the hours of toil and fear. I have only one regret: It's over."

We will miss the Berg-mann, this man of the mountains.

PHILIP ERARD

HORST von HENNIG
1902-1992

On November 30, Horst von Hennig passed away at this home of over 50 years in Greenwich, Connecticut. The day before, he had celebrated his 90th birthday. He had been a member of the American Alpine Club since 1952. He was also a member of the Alpine Club of Canada and the Swiss Alpine Club. He was an enthusiastic mountaineer and skier throughout his life until ill health during the last few years curtailed such activities.

Dad loved the literature of climbing as much as he loved the mountains. He served as head of the Library committee for over 20 years. During this time, the Library grew tremendously and became a smoothly functioning operation. In 1981, he was awarded the Angelo Heilprin Citation in recognition of his many years of devoted service to the Club and its Library.

My father was born in Rathenow, Germany on November 29, 1902. His introduction to the mountains came when, as a young boy, he accompanied his mother to the Alps. In his late teens, a cousin introduced him to hiking and climbing.

From 1919 to 1937, he climbed actively in the northern and western Alps, Dolomites, Apennines and in Sicily. In 1929, in Stuttgart, he married Elisabeth Doertenbach.

He made many winter ascents. I recall spending the winter of 1936-37 in Zermatt. While I was struggling daily to herringbone and sidestep up and snowplow down, Mom and Dad would be off on trips to the Breithorn, Oberrothorn and Tête Blanche. Mom said she always stayed behind at the huts to melt snow and tidy up.

Late in 1937, we moved to the United States. After living in New York City for several years, we moved to Greenwich, Connecticut in 1942. In the summer of 1951, while vacationing in Canada with my mother and sisters Tilda and Margaret, Dad met Henry Hall at Amethyst Lake in the Tonquin Valley. It was this chance meeting that led to Dad's joining the American Alpine Club. He always considered his membership to be a particular honor and took special joy and pride in participating at meetings.

Dad passed his love for the mountains on to his children and grandchildren. I still vividly remember climbing the Allalinhorn, Alphubel, Zinalrothorn and Matterhorn during a spell of spectacular summer weather in 1949. The following summer, we visited the Dolomites and climbed the Torri Grande and Inglese, and Punta Fiammes. He climbed Mount Rainier with his son-in-law Eckart Colsman. In winters, we skied in Vermont or St. Moritz. He attended many Alpine Club of Canada summer camps. Hans Gmosser remembers climbing Mount Edith and the south face of Yamanuska with him in the mid 1950s.

A man of values, with a true sense of integrity and right and wrong, a member of the old guard, a gentleman, the last of his generation—this is how his grandchildren eulogized him. And it is the way many of us remember him. He was gentle and kind, thoughtful, considerate and generous. Above all, he inspired us and taught us to love the mountains, a gift for which we are grateful. And it is in this spirit that his memory lives on.

DIETER VON HENNIG

PIERRE BEGHIN
1951-1992

Another of the world's foremost mountaineers has lost his life in the Himalaya. Pierre Beghin, the Frenchman who during the last decade broke the barriers of the impossible, was killed on October 11 on the south face of Annapurna when a rappel anchor pulled out. Engineer by profession, he worked in the Division de Nivologie of the CEMAGREF in Grenoble as an expert on snow problems and avalanche protection.

Born in 1951, Pierre excelled in rock and ice climbing, extreme skiing and high-altitude mountaineering. In the Alps, he made many bold climbs, solo and in winter, including the first winter ascent of the Bonatti route on the Grandes Jorasses from December 25 to 29. In the Andes, from July 20 to 24, 1978, he climbed the 1966 Paragot route on the north face of Huascarán Norte—with a broken shoulder and alpine-style.

His high-altitude experiences in Asia started in 1974 with an attempt on the Uli Biaho Tower in Pakistan. His outstanding stamina and determination at high altitude were well recognized. The list of his accomplishments is long and distinguished. We mention only a few. On October 7, 1981, he completed the ascent of the virgin, rocky west face of Makalu. On October 17, 1983, he became the first Frenchman and the first solo climber to ascend Kangchenjunga. Doubtless his two most exceptional feats were the 1989 five-day traverse of Makalu via the south face and west ridge, three-fourths of which he did solo, and his 1991 ascent with Christophe Profit of K2, via the northwest ridge and the north face, linking the Polish and Japanese routes.

Pierre wrote dozens of interesting articles. Recently, he had a regular monthly page in *Montagnes Magazine*. He faithfully reported all his expeditions in full articles or notes in the *American Alpine Journal,* which he stated "stood in the key position of all overseas mountaineering literature." He published a number of mountain books, often illustrated with his own excellent photographs. The most outstanding was perhaps his last: *Hautes altitudes: Voyage dans l'oxygène rare.* He leaves his wife Annie, who has received much sympathy from all corners of the world.

JÓZEF NYKA, *Editor, Taternik, Poland*

It is unusual to have obituaries in the *American Alpine Journal* for other than members of the American Alpine Club. However, the mountaineering community is poorer because of the loss of both Pierre Beghin and Wanda Rutkiewicz in 1992. (See also below.) The Editor remembers vividly walking into the French camp below the Uli Biaho Tower in the Karakoram in 1974 with Bob and Gail Bates and my wife Ann and the warm welcome given to us four ancient American sextegenarians by Pierre Beghin and his companions. Pierre and I kept close in contact over the years and the *American Alpine Journal* and I have benefited enormously from his warm friendship. —*Editor.*

WANDA RUTKIEWICZ
1943-1992

The mountaineering world suffered in 1992 the loss of the greatest woman climber of all time. Wanda Rutkiewicz was last seen when she chose to bivouac alone several hours below the summit of K2 during the attempt to climb her ninth 8000-meter peak. She was preëminent not only for her own accomplishments but equally for her championing of women climbers in the high mountains of the world. More than anyone else, she accomplished ending the male monopoly on climbing on the highest peaks.

Born as Wanda Blaskiewicz on February 9, 1943 in Lithuania, she moved with her family in 1947 to Wrocław, Poland. She began climbing in the Tatras in 1961 and rapidly sharpened her outstanding skills. In 1970, she married and thereby acquired the name of Rutkiewicz, by which we have known her. Both this marriage and her second ended in divorce.

I shall not attempt to give a complete list of her mountain successes. Her first ascents of 7000-meter peaks took place in 1970: Pik Lenina and Noshaq. In 1975, Wanda organized and led the Polish Women's Gasherbrum Expedition, to which she did add several men. Since 1964 Gasherbrum III (7952 meters, 26,089 feet) had been the highest unclimbed summit. With Alison Chadwick

Onyszkiewicz, Janusz Onyszkiewicz and Krzysztof Zdzitowiecki, she made its first ascent. The next day, she sent Halina Krüger and Anna Okopińska to the summit of Gasherbrum II, making them the first European women to climb an 8000er. In 1978, she was the first woman to climb the north face of the Matterhorn in winter. On October 16, 1978, she became the third woman and the first Western woman to climb Mount Everest. She broke her leg seriously on Mount Elbrus in 1980. This hampered her and would have ended the career of a less determined person. She even led an expedition to K2 while convalescing, walking the many miles to Base Camp despite not being able really to climb. Her eight 8000-meter peaks were Everest 1978, Nanga Parbat 1985, K2 1986, Shisha Pangma 1987, Gasherbrum II 1989, Gasherbrum I 1990, Cho Oyu 1991, Annapurna 1991. This doubles the number of the next most successful woman.

Wanda was a most forceful, determined person. She would not be stopped by her badly broken leg, which at first received extremely bad medical care. In 1983, when she, I and others accompanied Chris Bonington and Jim Fothering-ham to their Base Camp below Shivling, it was still very painful, three years after the accident. But she never complained. She willed herself to get better and did seven of her highest climbs after her recovery. Hers was a pioneering spirit in fighting for female mountaineering. I always found her warmly friendly and thoughtful and she went out of her way to welcome me to Poland and elsewhere. We have all lost a good friend. Wanda has earned a permanent place in mountaineering history.

H. Adams Carter

Club Activities

EDITED BY FREDERICK O. JOHNSON

A.A.C., Cascade Section. Several members were very active on climbing trips to Pakistan. Scott Fischer succeeded in reaching the summit of K2 along with Seattleite Ed Viesturs. Steve Swenson led an expedition attempt on Gasherbrum IV. Greg Child climbed Trango Tower. Howard Weaver will attempt Mount Everest in the spring of 1993.

The 1991 annual banquet, held last December in Seattle, included a presentation by Joe Simpson, author of *Touching the Void*.

James Frush is the Chairman-elect of the Section.

JOHN PETROSKE, *Chairman*

A.A.C., New York Section. Why do people join organizations like the American Alpine Club? Certainly one of the main motives is to expand one's circle of climbing friends and partners and to share the fellowship of like-minded people. Facilitating this objective is a primary goal of the New York Section, which it attempts to achieve with a variety of social and other events: illustrated lectures followed by a social hour; an Annual Black Tie Dinner featuring a celebrity speaker and where new members are individually introduced and presented with their membership pins; weekend outings—both spring and now winter—in the Adirondacks; and finally our very own film festival—*Alpinfilm*—which, in only its third year, now attracts leading filmmakers from all over the world competing for cash prizes and important exposure in the world's media capital. The Section also attempts to do some good: contributing the net proceeds from the programs and dinners to various climbing-related causes.

The 1992 Annual Dinner featured Rick Ridgeway as special guest speaker discussing "Adventure Capitalism," or the art of adventuring all over the world on someone else's money. Rick, ever the consummate after-dinner speaker, was introduced by new member, Tom Brokaw, who had the audience in stitches describing various misadventures in the Tetons with Rick and Yvon Chouinard.

A progress report on an unprecedented attempt to solo the Seven Summits was also presented by Robert Anderson. At the time of the Dinner, "only" Vinson and Everest remained on Bob's list. Finally, Fred Selby gave a short presentation on a recent attempt by a group of New Yorkers on an unclimbed 9000-foot peak in Bhutan, thus rounding out the evening's program. Proceeds from the year's Dinner were once again earmarked for the American Alpine Journal Publishing Fund.

Alpinfilm '92, held in March, attracted a sell-out audience of knowledgeable and opinionated film buffs. A jury consisting of representatives from *Outside*

Magazine, Rolex and Paragon Sporting Goods, as well as the American Alpine Club, awarded the Grand Prize to "Shadow Hunters," a French documentary by Alain Majani on swallow's nest hunters in Thailand. To no one's surprise, this film was later nominated for an Academy Award. A close second was "Sheer Courage," an inspiring National Geographic documentary on the physical and spiritual comeback of Hugh Herr following a devastating accident on Mount Washington. Hugh's simple yet eloquent comments on the experience drew a standing ovation. The Award for Outstanding Cinematography went to "Pacha-mama," a snow-boarding adventure in the Andes by Patrice Aubertel. Proceeds from the festival were contributed to help fund the equipment needs of the Adirondack Volunteer Technical Rescue Team of Lake Placid.

The New York Section now numbers over 300 active members, an increase of over 15% from a year ago. Members from other Sections desiring to be on our mailing list or filmmakers interested in submitting their work to *Alpinfilm,* should write to us at: P.O. Box 5475, Rockefeller Station, New York, N.Y. 10185.

PHILIP ERARD, *Chairman*

A.A.C., Sierra Nevada Section. The continued high level of member involvement made 1992 an important year for the Sierra Nevada Section. Section members have made ascents of mountains from South American traditional summits, i.e. Aconcagua, to new routes on the Central Tower of Paine in Patagonia. In Central Asia, Al Steck completed a three-week Silk Route odyssey from Beijing to Rawalpindi, and R.D. Caughron on a Polish expedition just missed the summit of Nanga Parbat. On a local level, many classic routes have been revisited and impressive new routes of 5.11 through 5.13 have been put up throughout the Sierra Nevada.

Section access issues have included Paul Minault of the Section and the Access Fund representatives working together with the Forest Service to solve the problem of overuse of the Lover's Leap campground. The Section has long been involved in issues of the Leap, and in 1983 built the first out-house for Leap climbers.

Russ Faure-Brac has been involved in minimizing the impact of the Mount Shasta wilderness management plan that would open a large area of the mountain for ski development, while restricting the number of climbers that could be on the mountain at any one time. David Chick has been representing the AAC and the Section on the Yosemite Climbing Management Plan Committee. This committee has been meeting for a year and is charged with developing a resource management plan for all climbing activities. Our stated goal is to try to minimize resource impacts by climbing, while minimizing the National Park Service impact upon climbers.

During this year the Section activities included the annual Sierra ski weekend at Grover Hot Springs, climbing weekends at Lover's Leap, Tuolumne Meadows, and Yosemite Valley. Section Socials were held in the Bay Area both in the spring and the fall. The annual Section fund-raising dinner to provide funds to publish the quarterly section newsletter was held in May. The dinner, attended by 95 members and guests, was a gala affair featuring George Lowe. George dazzled the audience with his trilogy slide show of extreme exposure on the Nose of El Capitan, accomplishment tempered with survival on K2, and his solo of Dhaulagiri.

DAVID N. CHICK, *Section Chairman*

A.A.C., Southern California Section. The major event of 1992 was a meeting at Mammoth Lakes on April 25 featuring a slide show by Don Lauria on his second ascent of the North American Wall on El Capitan in 1968 with Dennis Hennek. More than 80 members and guests, including Eastern Sierra residents and a contingent of members from the Los Angeles area, attended. Lauria's presentation was preceded by a talk and slides by Marty Lewis of Mammoth Lakes on sport climbing in the nearby Owens River Gorge. Lewis is the author of the gorge guidebook. Jim Thomsen of Mammoth Lakes and Allan Pietrasanta of Bishop ably handled logistics for the meeting. The following week, Ted Vaill arranged for section members to be special guests at a preview showing of the movie *K2*.

Member notes: Peter Green of Palmdale and his brother Robert climbed to Camp IV at 26,500 feet on K2 before being forced to retreat in the face of incoming weather. They were part of an 18-member international expedition climbing on a Russian permit. Six made the summit.

Doug Mantle was among the 32 who summited Mount Everest on May 12 as a member of an Adventure Consultants (New Zealand) expedition that also included Ned Gillette. Mantle later went to Antarctica while closing in on his pursuit of the Seven Summits.

R.J. Secor helped celebrate publication of his High Sierra guidebook by joining a commercial expedition to Broad Peak. The group was thwarted by deep, unstable snow after establishing Camp III at 24,000 feet and subsequently having the camp obliterated, presumably by avalanche. R.J. reported, however, that the only expedition injury was his being struck by a polo ball while watching a match in Skardu. The team returned via the little-used Ghondophoro La, as did Robert and Peter Green on their return from K2. In the fall, Secor went to the Khumbu region of Nepal with a Southern California group to climb Mera Peak and Imja Tse (Island Peak).

Kurt Wedberg traveled to Alaska as a member of Rainier Mountain Guides and was on Mount Foraker when the severe weather struck Mount McKinley, resulting in the deaths of a number of climbers. Wedberg and his group were forced to hole up for some time on Foraker and failed to reach the summit, but were not in danger. Wedberg returned later to help lead an expedition to McKinley's summit. On September 26, Wedberg, who is 26 years old, made his 31st ascent of Mount Rainier. His father, John Wedberg, is section treasurer.

Gordon Wiltsie, Allan Petrasanta and Jay Jensen skied the Haute Route of the Alps during the spring. Wiltsie's account of the trip, and photos, appeared in the December issue of *Ski Magazine*. Gordon's article on a unique ski trip to Spitsbergen also was published during the year. Paul Pfau of Shadow Hills spent the year working on organization of his American Sagarmatha Expedition, a 30th anniversary climb of Mount Everest.

BILL STALL, *Chairman*

A.A.C., Oregon Section. Four Section members, Arthur, Cramer, Pooley and McGown together with others, completed the final building requirements for occupancy of Mount Hood's premier climbing-and-ski hut. Silcox Hut is now open for reservations. A phase-two project for the hut has been proposed. This consists of two snow tunnels and a wood storage area. Presently I am organizing an astronomy fund-raiser for phase two. This will be a telescope star party at Timberline Lodge October 15-17, 1993. It will include a lecture series, "Cosmos 1993."

The hut is well situated for high-altitude telescope observations, ski traverses of Mount Hood and southwest face ascents. It sleeps 24 and has three restrooms plus a kitchen. Timberline Lodge will operate Silcox Hut starting in October 1993. Before then bookings may be made through Steven Moskowitz, 2815 N.E. 50th, Portland, OR 97213.

The summer of 1992 saw increased activity at Lamberson Butte on Mount Hood's east side. In the past, logistical problems have kept the area unexplored except for an occasional visitor to Newton Pinnacles. The two-hour approach and Newton Clark Creek's daily periodic flooding from the melting glaciers have hindered activity. Bush Pilot, Weekend Ivory Hunters, Bag of Tricks, Crash of the Titans, Pushover, Quantum Gravity and Pig Iron Dihedral provided 5.9-5.10 routes for Bob McGown, Tim and Cindy Olson and Wayne Wallace.

New routes of up to 220 feet were also placed on French's Dome, the basaltic pillow lava dome on Mount Hood's south side: Alpha Centuri by Bob McGown and Tim Olson; and Darwin Gitti and Static Cling by McGown and Jacob Clayton.

BOB McGOWN, *Chairman*

The Alpine Club of Canada. The A.C.C. continued to meet the challenge of change in 1992 with the election of a new Executive Committee. Ken Hewitt passed the reins of President to Doug Fox, previously Treasurer, at the Annual General Meeting in October. Some of the year's highlights were as follows:

The club's national office moved from Banff to Canmore, Alberta in February. This permitted the club to expand its staff base and to enhance member services. The mailing address is Box 2040, Canmore, Alberta, TOL OMO; phone (403) 678-3200.

The Annual General Mountaineering Camp was held at Fairy Meadow amid the Adamant Ranges of British Columbia and enjoyed four successful weeks.

The 1993 camp has been set for the Scott/Hooker Icefield area, southwest of Jasper, Alberta.

The environment portfolio was expanded to include Access. The year's highlight was the successful intervention by the A.C.C. in cooperation with the Sierra Club and the Canadian Parks and Wilderness Society before the Natural Resources Conservation Board in the proposed Three Sisters Golf Resorts development in the Bow Corridor. While much of the development was approved, Wind Valley was excepted as a unique wilderness area essential to the wildlife found there.

Proceedings from the Energy and Waste Management Symposium, held in October 1991, have been published, and a number of Symposium recommendations have been implemented in both the federal and provincial parks of Alberta and British Columbia.

The new Facilities Directory was completed with a listing of all A.C.C. backcountry huts as well as our clubhouse and the Canadian Alpine Centre and International Hostel at Lake Louise. Major renovations were made to the Fairy Meadow Hut and include the creation of a large kitchen in the east end of the main floor and new tables and padded benches in the old kitchen area. A number of new windows were installed, and the hut now sports two wood stoves. The hut continues to be extremely popular for winter ski camps. The Canadian Alpine Centre at Lake Louise completed its first year. It was booked almost 100% during the summer season and enjoyed over 17,500 overnights in 1992.

The National Sport Climbing Committee continues to encourage and support sport climbing competitions. The N.S.C.C. now sanctions local and city competitions held at climbing clubs and gyms as well as the Canadian National Championships. The Committee continues to publish *The Flash*, a newsletter with information on sport climbing in Canada. The A.C.C. was granted a seat on the C.E.C. of the U.I.A.A.

The 1992 Mountain Guides' Ball on October 31 was co-hosted with the Association of Canadian Mountain Guides. Over 200 members of both associations attended the ball and auction. Patron of the 1992 Ball was Mr. William Lowell Putnam. Also honoured was Mr. Ken Jones, the first Canadian mountain guide, who celebrated his 80th birthday at the ball. The A.C.M.G. honoured Ms. Diana Harrison, the first Canadian woman to achieve full mountain-guide status.

A proposal to restructure the club's membership received approval in principle from the Board of Directors. The proposal would eliminate the Section-only class of membership and provide members with a lower basic membership fee and the ability to add on various options such as the *Canadian Alpine Journal* and facilities benefits.

The Board of Directors approved the formation of a new club section in the Jasper/Hinton area of Alberta. The section has approximately 55 members.

Past president Ken Hewitt and Dave Dornian, Chairman of the Sport Climbing Committee both received the 1992 Distinguished Service Award.

BEVERLY BENDELL, *Activities Manager*

Dartmouth Mountaineering Club. 1992 was an excellent year for the education and incorporation of new members into the Dartmouth Mountaineering Club. The winter was not spent entirely by the fireside: the club sponsored two educational trips, acclimatizing freshmen to the New England ice and snow and teaching the basics of ice climbing and winter mountaineering.

As the snow began to give way to warmer weather, eyes turned to rock again. Led by Keith Rainville, ten members made the long drive West to enjoy a spring-break filled with sunny skies, unfamiliar sandstone and crack climbing that made even the most experienced granite face climber beg for positive holds. Included were climbs at Colorado National Monument, the Canyonlands area and Castleton Tower.

With the return of the Southwest pilgrims came the start of spring term and the return of Dartmouth Climbing School. Thanks to the many members who donated time every week, 20 people took part in the eight-week course for beginners. A more advanced seminar was also offered on anchors, teaching and basic rescue techniques.

Throughout spring, summer and fall, day and weekend trips were made to the climbing areas of New England, and beginners were offered one-day introductions to climbing. The D.M.C. continued its support of the freshman trips program and offered trips which took first-year students backpacking and climbing in the Franconia Notch area prior to the start of their education at Dartmouth College. Many people took advantage of the classes and seminars given througout the year by Dartmouth's Office of Outdoor Programs on rock climbing, winter mountaineering and back-country medicine.

CHRIS CARSON, *Co-President*

Iowa Mountaineers. The Iowa Mountaineers, as usual, had an active year in 1992. Membership has grown to 5100 members from 38 states. Over 4200 people participated in the many instructional courses, mountaineering camps or foreign expeditions.

The club taught over 400 members cross-country skiing at Devils Lake State Park, Wisconsin, during weekends in January and February. Winter survival skills, emergency shelters, proper dress, measures against hypothermia and frostbite, and avalanche awareness and precautions were taught. Jim Ebert was in charge of instruction.

Fifty-eight members spent five days hiking in Arizona's Havasu Canyon. The flash flood that went down the canyon in September 1990 did most of its visual damage from below Mooney Falls to the Colorado River. Mooney and Havasu Falls have never looked better. Jim Ebert served as outing leader.

A small but enthusiastic group took part in our first organized trip to Colorado National Monument near Grand Junction and the Canyonlands area around Moab, Utah, in May. The area offered exceptional climbing from classic crack climbs to multi-pitch routes up desert spires. These included Independence Monument, Sentinel Spire, Six Shooter peaks and Castleton Tower via the 5.9 Kor-Ingalls route.

Over 62 members from 10 states took one-week basic-rock-climbing courses at Devils Lake State Park. Four courses were offered in May, June and August. Thirty-two members took a four-day intermediate rock-climbing course at Devils Tower, Wyoming, over Memorial Day weekend and the following weekend.

The annual summer mountaineering camp was held in the Sawtooths of Idaho from July 26 to August 5. Twenty-two members attended, doing climbs of the classic peaks of the area: Finger of Fate, the Mountaineers Route on Elephant Perch, Mount Heyburn and Goat Perch.

The club taught 32 three-day weekend courses with 822 members participating in the basic rock-climbing course, and 2809 members in the instructional hiking course. The weekend courses were taught at Devils Lake State Park with Jim Ebert in charge of instruction.

The Iowa Mountaineers held their 32nd annual banquet in May, with 75 members in attendance. Dr. Geoffrey Tabin presented a slide show on his climbing the highest peaks on seven continents.

The club's travel adventure film series presented seven programs at Mac-Bride Auditorium in Iowa City with 2500 members attending.

For further information about membership in the Iowa Mountaineers and its 1993 trips and courses, write to the club at P.O. Box 163, Iowa City, IA 52244.

JIM EBERT, *President*

The Mazamas. Club climbing activity in 1992 under the chairmanship of Jan Schmidt included 253 scheduled summer and 14 winter climbs. However, the usual unfavorable Northwest weather allowed only one winter climb to succeed. The Basic Climbing School enrolled 216 students, Intermediate School 50, Advanced Rock School 22 and Advanced Snow/Ice School 12. Trail Trips, the second most important Mazama activity, involved 326 scheduled hikes, which included some camps, snowshoe trips and backpacks as well as trail maintenance. These varied events resulted in 4488 hiker-days.

Mazama outings included a Yellowstone cross-country trip; skiing at Innsbruck, Austria; a hiking-climbing outing in Czechoslovakia's Tatra Mountains; a trip to Indonesia; and in the West summer trips to the Wind Rivers in Wyoming, Stehekin Ranch, the Wallowa Mountains and Oregon Beach.

The Expedition Committee, chaired by Carol Sturdivant, staged its annual fund-raising biathlon. Participation by 462 runners and cyclists raised $5,934. The Program Committee continued the century-old tradition of hosting outstanding films and lectures at the Mazama clubrooms Wednesday evenings.

Looking forward to the completion of 100 years of climbing and hiking, the club began planning its centennial. Paula Beers heads the committee which will stage special events during 1993-1994 with a centennial party on the summit of Mount Hood to recall the initiation of the club on July 19, 1894.

President Ray Sheldon finished his term of office October 1 and was succeeded by Dennis Olmstead.

JACK GRAUER

Memphis Mountaineers, Inc. The Memphis Mountaineers had a productive year despite what seems to be a slow but steady reduction of available climbing spots. The 1992 membership consists of 63 members not only in Memphis, Tennessee, but throughout the United States.

In addition to the many rock-climbing trips to the local crags of the Mid-South, individual members were active afield in areas such as Oklahoma (Quartz Mountain), Texas (Enchanted Rocks), New York (Shawangunks), Nevada (Lake Tahoe area), and New England for rock-and-ice climbing. The Memphis Mountaineers were represented internationally in the Swiss Alps (Matterhorn, Breithorn, and Pollux), and France (Mont Blanc). The club assisted Memphis State University in training student park rangers in climbing and rescue techniques. A group of Eagle Scouts from the greater Memphis area were also given a course in basic-rock-climbing skills.

The Memphis Mountaineers continue to feel the constriction of access denial, as previously mentioned. We have been working to regain access to Tishomingo State Park in Mississippi. A permit system approved for use by the park has been delayed until the passage of new state legislation on "sovereign immunity." Additionally, the Stoneface climbing area in Southern Illinois has been reclassified by the state as an area off-limits to such activities as climbing and rappelling.

The Memphis Mountaineers met on the second Monday of each month at 6:30pm in the Highland Branch of the Memphis Public Library system. Programs presented during 1992 included slide shows of rock climbing in various areas, alpine mountaineering in Europe, and mountain biking in the Pacific Northwest. Members are notified of club activities through the monthly newsletter—*The Memphis Mountain News*. Anyone interested in climbing in the Mid-South is encouraged to join our club. For more information write: Memphis Mountaineers, Inc., PO Box 11124, Memphis, TN 38111. Club officers for 1992 were: Robin Daniels, *President*; Barbara Knowles, *Vice President*; Charlie Ryon, *Secretary*; and Ted Burkey, *Treasurer*.

The Mountaineers. Early in 1992, The Mountaineers published the fifth edition of *Mountaineering: The Freedom of the Hills*, which for more than 30 years has been the definitive, comprehensive textbook for beginning and intermediate mountaineers throughout the United States. A volunteer group of some two-dozen veteran Mountaineers worked meticulously to fully revise and update the entire book. *The Freedom of the Hills* has new or expanded descriptions and illustrations on dozens of topics, such as avalanche and crevasse rescue, double-rope technique, seconding traverses and pendulums, equalizing protection placements, plastic boots, rock shoes, step-in/clamp-on crampons, ice-climbing tools, belay and rappel devices and more. The fifth edition also includes an entirely new chapter on winter and expedition climbing, prepared by expedition climbers Nancy Jackson and Kurt Hanson. In the spring of 1990, shortly after completing her work on *The Freedom of the Hills*, Nancy Jackson was killed in an avalanche on Nepal's 26,760-foot Manaslu.

The Basic Climbing Course offered by The Mountaineers is a year-long course consisting of six field trips (Knots, Belay Setup, Rock I & II, Snow I & II and Crevasse Rescue), and several lectures, including one which covers basic navigational skills using map and compass. Students must complete all field trips, attend all lectures and pass the quizzes, then successfully summit one rock climb, one glacier climb and one climb of their choice from a list. Graduates may participate in any of the nearly 200 Basic Experience Climbs offered from May through September. Basic Climbs vary in difficulty from one-day alpine climbs involving little more than setting up a handline over a slightly exposed area to two- or three-day climbs of the heavily glaciated peaks of Mounts Rainier (14,410 feet), Baker (10,778 feet) or Olympus (7956 feet, with a 22-mile approach). Students receive training necessary for travelling safely over glaciers and rock, and general skills necessary for survival in the mountains, including ice-axe arrest, setting up a Z-Pulley system for crevasse rescue, cleaning a pitch, and tying off an injured climber. In addition, students acquire the skills necessary to move safely over low fifth-class rock. In 1992, over 200 students enrolled in the course and close to 120 graduated.

Under the auspices of The Mountaineers International Exchange Committee, five climbers traveled to New Zealand where they were hosted by Ben Winnubst and Richard Pearson, Past President, of the New Zealand Alpine Club (NZAC). Ken Bryan, Joe Chaffee, Steve Cox, Max Junejo and team leader Donna Rigas were welcomed by NZAC officers at a giant barbecue. Richard and Ben guided the group to many of the best climbing areas on New Zealand's South Island. A week was spent in Mount Cook National Park, where the climbers were successful on several summits. They utilized NZAC huts at the top of the Tasman Glacier and high in the Beetham Valley as base camps. Plainly visible was the scar from the recent collapse of Mount Cook's east face. One-day climbs were enjoyed on Rapaki Rock at Christchurch, Arthur Pass National Park and the Sea Cliffs at Sea Dreamer Wall and Wonder Wall at Charleston. The team also enjoyed a day at one of New Zealand's finest areas, climbing on the sandstone sculptures of the Castle Hill Conservation Area. Precious rock drawings are reminders that ancient Maori tribal groups often visited the area seasonally to gather food. The area also shelters some of New Zealand's most rare and endangered plants. The Mountaineers is deeply grateful for the kindness and hospitality that was extended to the team while in New Zealand, and was privileged to host a NZAC climber during her visit to the Northwest.

In 1992, as part of our ongoing concern for the safe, responsible and enjoyable use of the mountains and wilderness, The Mountaineers adopted a formal policy on wilderness ethics and backcountry use, aimed toward minimizing the impact of our 13,500 members on these beautiful and often fragile areas. As a club which sponsors nearly 2000 wilderness activities for our members every year, we recognize our responsibility to keep our impact as low as possible. In addition to promoting wilderness ethics and minimum impact education in all club courses and activities, the new policy also sets a maximum limit of twelve people on Mountaineer outings. Smaller limits may be imposed as warranted by the sensitivity of the environment or safety considerations. The heart of the policy is the following eight principles: 1) Stay on established trails; do not cut switchbacks. 2) Camp in established campsites whenever available. Do not camp in fragile meadows. Camp on snow or rocks when away from established campsites. 3) Properly dispose of human waste away from water, trails and campsites. 4) Use a camp stove instead of building a fire. 5) Wash well away from camps and water sources. 6) Leave flowers, rocks and other natural features undisturbed. 7) Keep wildlife healthy and self-reliant by not feeding them. Pack out all uneaten food. Leave pets at home. 8) Pack out all party litter plus a share of that left by other parties. In addition to this work, we began an outreach program in September to bring our conservation message into K-12 classrooms in Seattle schools.

The Mountaineers worked with Volunteers for Outdoor Washington and the USDA Forest Service to transform an abandoned stretch of the Great Northern Railway near Stevens Pass in the Cascade Mountains into a day hiking trail called the Iron Goat. The goal is to convert 12 miles of Great Northern Railway constructed in the early 1890s and abandoned in 1929 when the New Cascade Tunnel was built. The first four miles of the Iron Goat Trail will be dedicated October 2, 1993, on the 25th anniversary of the signing of the National Recreational Trail Act. This event will also commemorate the centennial year of the Great Northern Railway, which, crossing the Cascade Mountains, opened the Pacific Northwest to trade and settlement. In 1992, 281 volunteers participated in 45 work parties. Our work on this rail-trail conversion will continue into 1993 and beyond.

DONNA PRICE, *Activities Division Chairwoman*

THE AAC PRESS

THE AMERICAN ALPINE JOURNAL, Current Edition. $25.00
(Inquire about prices for past editions.)

ACCIDENTS IN NORTH AMERICAN MOUNTAINEERING,
Current Edition. 7.00
(Inquire about prices for past editions.)

THE AMERICAN ALPINE JOURNAL INDEX.
1929-1976, Edited by Earlyn Church. 8.50
1977-1986, Edited by Patricia A. Fletcher. 8.50

THE COLUMBIA MOUNTAINS OF CANADA—CENTRAL. . 28.50
(The Interior Ranges of British Columbia: Southern Selkirks.)
Editors: John Kevin Fox, Roger Laurilla, William Lowell Putnam.

**THE COLUMBIA MOUNTAINS OF CANADA—
WEST & SOUTH.** 25.00
(The Interior Ranges of British Columbia: Cariboo, Monashee,
Northern Selkirks.) Editors: Earle R. Whipple, Roger Laurilla,
William Lowell Putnam.

CONNECTICUT ROCK CLIMBS: TRAPROCK. 20.00
Ken Nichols.

THE GRAND CONTROVERSY: The Pioneer Climbs in the
Tetons and the Controversial First Ascent of the Grand. 28.50
Orrin H. Bonney & Lorraine G. Bonney.

THE GREAT GLACIER AND ITS HOUSE. 35.00
William Lowell Putnam.

GREEN COGNAC: The Education of a Mountain Fighter. 35.00
The 10th Mountain Division in the Italian Campaign of
World War II. William Lowell Putnam.

HIGH ALASKA. 29.50
Denali, Mount Foraker & Mount Hunter: An Illustrated History &
Guide. Jonathan Waterman.

MOUNTAIN SICKNESS: Prevention, Recognition & Treatment. .. 6.50
Peter H. Hackett.

MOUNTAINS OF NORTH AMERICA. Fred Beckey. 35.00

THE NEEDLES IN THE BLACK HILLS OF SOUTH
DAKOTA: TOUCH THE SKY. $14.50
Paul Piana. Includes set of maps of the area.

THE RED ROCKS OF SOUTHERN NEVADA. 14.50
Joanne Urioste. 2nd Printing.

THE ROCKY MOUNTAINS OF CANADA—NORTH. 14.50
Robert Kruszyna, William Lowell Putnam.

THE ROCKY MOUNTAINS OF CANADA—SOUTH. 14.50
Glen Boles, Robert Kruszyna, William Lowell Putnam.

SHAWANGUNK ROCK CLIMBS. Dick Williams.
Third Edition; completely revised, published in three volumes.
THE TRAPPS. 25.00
THE NEAR TRAPPS & MILLBROOK. 20.00
SKY TOP. 20.00

SURVIVING DENALI: A Study of Accidents on Mount
McKinley 1903-1900. .... 20.00
Second Edition, completely revised. Jonathan Waterman.

TAHQUITZ & SUICIDE ROCKS. Chuck Wilts. 5.00

A WALK IN THE SKY: The First Ascent of Hidden Peak. 18.00
Nicholas Clinch.

WASATCH ROCK CLIMBS. 14.50
Les Ellison & Brian Smoot.

WHERE THE CLOUDS CAN GO: An Autobiography.
Conrad Kain. 17.50
The 1935 Classic edited by J. Monroe Thorington. Third Edition.

THE WORST WEATHER ON EARTH: A History of the
Mount Washington Observatory. 30.00
William Lowell Putnam.

YURAQ JANKA: A Guide to Cordilleras Blanca and
Rosco. John F. Ricker. 15.00

Maps

ACONCAGUA. .... $ 6.50
>   Reprinted from the 1987 *AAJ,* the map is 11"x16" on a sheet
>   16"x21" and includes 14 routes. Scale 1:50,000. 2nd printing.

ANTARCTICA: McMurdo Sound Area, by Dee Molenaar. 7.00
>   Four-color, 24"x36", folded; the reverse includes 22,000-word
>   text illustrated with sketch art.

*   *   *

When ordering books, please include money for postage in a check or money
order in U.S. funds or pay by Mastercard or Visa. *Foreign Postage is more
expensive than the scale given below, which is for domestic postage only.*

Amount of Order to:	Add	Amount of Order to:	Add	Amount of Order to:	Add	Amount of Order to:	Add
$15.00	$1.50	$40.00	$3.20	$65.00	$5.00	$ 90.00	$ 7.20
20.00	2.00	45.00	3.60	70.00	5.60	95.00	7.60
25.00	2.50	50.00	4.00	75.00	6.00	100.00	8.00
30.00	2.75	55.00	4.40	80.00	6.40	over	
35.00	3.00	60.00	4.80	85.00	6.80	100.00	10.00

THE AAC PRESS, American Alpine Club, 10th and Washington Avenue,
Golden, Colorado 80401.

INDEX

Volume 35 ● Issue 67 ● 1993

Compiled by Earlyn Church

This issue comprises all of Volume 35

Mountains are listed by their official names and ranges; quotation marks indicate unofficial names. Ranges and geographical locations are also indexed. Unnamed peaks (e.g., P 2037) are listed following the range or country in which they are located.

Most expedition members cited in major articles are included, whereas mainly the leaders and persons supplying information in the **Climbs and Expeditions** section are listed.

Titles of books reviewed in this issue are grouped as a single entry under **Book Reviews**. Abbreviations used: Article: *art.*; Bibliography: *bibl.*; Obituary: *obit.*

B

INDEX